Free
Spirit
in a
Troubled
World

John Phillips

Free Spirit in a Troubled World

With an Editor's Note by Walter Keller

Scalo Zurich – Berlin – New York

Special thanks to the John and Anna Maria Phillips Foundation

John Phillips—Free Spirit in a Troubled World
Edited by Walter Keller
Picture editor: Axel Schmidt
Co-editor: Liz Jobey
Typescript: Mary Chapman

Design: Hans Werner Holzwarth, Berlin
Typesetting: Rupert Hertling, Berlin
Production co-ordinator: Roland Läuchli
Production: Steidl, Göttingen

© 1996 for the texts and photographs:
John and Anna Maria Phillips Foundation
© 1996 for this edition: Scalo Zurich – Berlin – New York
Head Office: Weinbergstrasse 22a, CH-8001 Zurich / Switzerland,
phone 41 1 261 0910, fax 41 1 261 9262
Distributed in North America by D.A.P., New York City;
in Europe and Asia by Thames and Hudson, London;
in Germany, Austria and Switzerland by Scalo

Contents

Editor's Note

In late 1994 John and I started talking about doing a new book of his photographs and writings that would encompass his vision at the close of this century. From various conversations with John since the publication of his first Scalo book, *Poet and Pilot Antoine de Saint-Exupéry*, I became aware what a unique witness John would be. I wanted to have his voice and eye illustrate the tumultuous changes of recent history — the breaking-down of mentalities, classes, political systems and styles, catalyzed by the outbreak of World War II, and the emerging new world order in the years after. For me he was a living legend of three decades — the Thirties, Forties and Fifties — which I perceive to be the formative times of our era.

We agreed to follow the basic idea that he, an 80-year-old photo-reporter, would write a book for me, a publisher half his age and of an entirely different generation. John showed me his archive and his files. I was immediately stunned by their quality and perfectly systematized order; contact sheets and respective captions were stored in yellow envelopes, precisely dated from the time when John took the photos and wrote the accompanying texts. It was all there.

Whenever I was visiting New York we would have early morning break-fast meetings, slowly deciding on the future table of contents, and then, chapter by chapter, we would talk about what he would write. I suggested leaving out certain elements, perhaps because they were too anecdotal or no longer relevant, or I encouraged him to reveal more when he seemed reluctant to give his personal point of view. John would write the first version, I would read it, give my comments. Sometimes we would agree immediately, and at other times we had long conversations, and he would get a slightly impatient about my short-sighted view. He looked at the world from a distance, recognizing a lot of its larger, often cyclic movements, while I came from a news-oriented, actuality-driven point of view. It was fascinating for me to see how his knowledge would be transferred to us, the younger ones, in the book that took shape with every chapter we slowly added.

At the time we started talking about the pictures I distinctly remember how astonished John was when I told him that I wanted to go back to the negatives and make new prints which would show the full frame and not follow the cropping that many of his older prints show; a cropping that often dated from the way his photographs were published in *Life*. When my picture editor Axel Schmidt showed me the first selection of the photographs, we immediately knew that we had made the right decision by staying faithful to the negatives. John usually only took very few shots, often creating amazingly well-composed photographs, especially in his treatment of space. There was a great photographer to be rediscovered whose pictures were of important value for future generations.

When we started talking about the book as an object, we soon agreed on the size of the book, the paper, the typography, how to position the pictures on the pages, etc. I brought proof printings of the first images and showed him the first layout sequences. In our minds we were both already turning the pages of the finished book. The book remained simple in its structure — chronological — one of the main goals we had agreed on from the very first moment.

During all this time I realized what a generous, cultivated, and at the same time humorous, wide-awake mind John possessed. He was a great old man in the purest sense. He was international in his birth and his mind. He incorporated the skepticism of someone who had seen a lot — maybe too much — and he represented a past that he had recorded long before my generation was even born. Do you remember when your grandparents or your parents told you all the stories about how it was when they were young? That's how it was to talk with John, only he was well trained to tell many people a story, so it became more than a subjective tale of a single youth.

The river of life flows where it wants to flow. In early 1996, John's wife Anna Maria passed away without seeing the book she had been such integral part of. John kept on working as hard as he could, although it sometimes broke my heart to see how sad he was. Then, on August 22, 1996, just before he had finished the final versions of the last chapters, John died in his sleep. There was no doubt I would continue, unfortunately without his warm voice, his humor and his sadness, and publish this book. *Free Spirit in a Troubled World* has become a memorial for John Phillips, a great photographer, a great human being and a grandpa one will never forget.

Walter Keller

John Phillips, Algeria, c. 1915

Young and Innocent

My father was an enthusiastic amateur photographer. Although I never knew when he started taking pictures, my mother recalled that on his arrival in the United States to marry her in 1904, he was carrying a camera. He did not give up this hobby when he and my mother moved to Algeria, where they took up farming. After I was born on the farm in 1914, my father often used me as a model to try out the various printing processes he loved to experiment with.

During World War I my father sold the farm and moved my mother and me to Algiers before he enlisted in the French army. I must have been three when I first had my picture taken in a photographer's studio, wearing a small garrison cap my father had sent me from France. After propping my right elbow on a *papier mâché* Grecian column, the photographer then had me sling my left leg in front of my right. Thus precariously posed in front of a painted backdrop with an Alpine lake, I swayed and tumbled backwards, bringing the lake down on my head.

My father took his hobby far more seriously, required far more equipment and far more space than any of the professionals I got to know in later years. Between meals our dining-room table was cluttered with paraphernalia. Wet prints were strung out to dry across my father's bedroom. The bathroom was converted into a darkroom and the tub was used to wash the prints. I was scrubbed clean in the laundry bin. I spent so much time watching him print that darkness did not disturb me the way it did most children of my age. To me it spelled anticipation as I stood beneath a pale yellow light and watched my father slowly coax images out of blank sheets of paper in the rippling developer.

I was growing up in an Arab world, where the Moslem population was guided by *mektoub*—the belief that whatever happens is decreed by the heavens. I must have inherited some of this fatalism, because whenever I look back at all the extraordinary coincidences that made me a *Life* photographer, I sense Fate's indulgence.

As I was learning the rudiments of photography, I was also gaining a reputation for being rowdy at school. The reason for this, or perhaps the excuse, was my nationality. Although I had the option of three different passports—French by birth in Algeria, British through my father (who was born in Wales) and American through my mother (who was born in Troy, New York)—I was known as *l'Anglais* at school. Since I was the only example of that species, I drew the wrath of my French, Algerian, Italian, Spanish, Portuguese and Maltese classmates, who all reflected their parents' resentment over "perfidious Albion". By the age of 11 my nose had been broken in tardy retaliation for Joan of Arc being burnt at the stake. I escaped more of this when, without warning, my father decided we should move to Paris where he would find clients for his color portraits.

We reached Montparnasse in the summer of 1925 and put up at the Studio Hotel across the street from the Dingo bar and around the corner from the Café du Dôme. It was a time when a dollar bought 20 Pernods, enough to keep anyone incoherent for days. When I wasn't attending classes at L'Ecole Alsacienne, I would fidget at the Dôme, at Le Select, or La Coupole, while my father, carried away by expatriate life, forgot the original purpose of our move to Paris.

For almost two years I mingled with the most talented drunks of the time. Had I been older, or owned a camera, I would have recorded these great artists the way they really were, and we would not have been left with those solemn chin-in-hand portraits so untypical of them. In reality they were bursting with life and even had time for a 12-year-old like me.

There was, for instance, Lady Duff, the Lady Brett of *The Sun Also Rises,* who referred to Hemingway as "the beastie"; there was the magical Foujita, who could pluck yards and yards of glove from his sleeve. Kiki, Man Ray's model and mistress, gave me my first dancing lessons at Le Jockey. Florian, the lovely nude dancer in the lion's cage at Luna Park, kissed me in a way I was not accustomed to. The surrealist poet, Robert Desnos, who did not survive a Nazi concentration camp, left me with a feeling he had been my own age.

I can still recall the night Isadora Duncan—unkindly nick-named "Stinkadora Drunken"—triumphantly marched into the Dôme after tossing a rock through the American consulate's window the day the Italian immigrants Sacco and Vanzetti were executed in America for a murder they almost certainly didn't commit. And I shall never forget being introduced to Gertrude Stein, in her severe double-breasted jacket, saying to her with my best manners, "Good evening, sir."

My father's great friend was Man Ray. They would spend hours talking together. At one of these *kaffee klatsches,* Man Ray described scenes from the new Russian movie, *The Battleship Potemkin.* The next day in school our teacher asked us to write an essay on our favourite film. While my class-mates got tangled up in the exploits of Rin-Tin-Tin, I wrote about *The Battleship Potemkin.* As I obviously hadn't seen the movie, I repeated what I had picked up from Man Ray, using film-makers' jargon. Even for a school like L'Alsacienne, where brilliance was the norm (I was there through patronage), I managed to impress my teacher until, late one Saturday night, he dropped by the Café du Dôme to buy some cigarettes. There he found me leaning against a bar munching a chocolate wafer while my father and Leo Stein argued whether good art was better than bad, and if so, prove it. Realizing he had been taken in by a 12-year-old, my teacher ex-ploded, "You're nothing but a charlatan!"

During our stay in Paris we ate twice a day at restaurants and moved every few months from hotel to hotel, their degree of elegance dependent upon whether or not my father had recently sold some property. A class-mate first made me conscious of this. "You always change addresses," he said. "Why?" I had no answer to this question, although it did make me feel uneasy for reasons I could not explain.

During the Easter holidays of 1927, my father decided that the Riviera was now the place to be. As Fate would have it, we moved into an apartment over a small photographic shop named Paris Photo, owned by a cheerful middle-aged Frenchman called M. Pansier. My father soon became close friends with M. Pansier, and in the school holidays and weekends, I became his assistant.

It was M. Pansier who would give me my first camera, a Pfaff equipped as a reflex, and who would take me on commercial jobs with him, especially during the summer, when we were in constant demand by an English real estate company which rented apartments on the Riviera by displaying photographs in their London offices (our talent was for shooting cramped balconies with a wide-angle lens, thus creating the impression they were big enough to have breakfast on). It was M. Pansier who taught me how to use magnesium powder when we photographed banquets (another of our specialities), and it was M. Pansier who would share his enormous ent-husiasm for the new miniature Leicas with me, and who would give me the idea of (and the rudimentary knowledge for) becoming a photo-reporter.

When I was 19, my father finally decided we should return to England. My colorful but erratic upbringing had been of great concern to a friend of my father's in Nice, Eugene Paul Ullman. Years later, he told me he had done all he could to convince my father that it was not in my best interests. I was, after all, a British subject, and I should be educated in England. Eventually I would have to earn a living there. A French education made little sense as attending a British public school was the prerequisite for a successful career in England at the time.

Mr Ullman was right. When I finally did reach England, I felt like a foreigner in spite of my passport.

Cecil Beaton as a scarecrow at his *fête champêtre*, Ashcombe, 1937

Young woman at Cecil Beaton's *fête champêtre*, Ashcombe, 1937

The
Frivolous
Thirties

Dog show, London, 1937

London

"Be original," the editor said. "That's what *Life* expects."

I had first heard about this magazine two days before. That morning the postman greeted me with a cheerful, "Mail from America!" The letter was from *Time*. I had despaired of ever receiving a reply. It started with an apology for not answering sooner—a refreshing change from the way Fleet Street treated freelance photographers. Then I was thanked for the picture of Walter S. Allward, the Canadian sculptor, I had sent in. Although *Time* had no present plans to publish it, the magazine wished to acquire it. The check told me that I earned more from rejection in the States than for publication in Britain. Finally I was given the address of *Time*'s London Bureau along with the suggestion that I keep in touch as Time Inc. was about to launch a new illustrated magazine to be called *Life*. *Life*, it was felt, might have use for my work. The letter was signed "Mary Frazier". Without a clue whether she was a Miss or a Mrs, I simply referred to her as "Mary Frazier" over the phone, which in those more formal times suggested an intimacy that did not exist.

That afternoon I sat in *Life*'s outer office prepared to be kept waiting. To my surprise, I was shown straight in. Within a quarter of an hour I was shown the magazine dummy with its innumerable pages of spectacular layouts. I had given my telephone number and was ready to work when the call came. It came two days later.

King Edward VIII was to open Parliament. My assignment was to cover the local color and pageantry surrounding the event. As I hurried down the hall, the editor called out, "Remember. I expect original pictures."

This was my great opportunity, but I knew that with my numbing shyness I couldn't bring myself to photograph people face-on. So I simply shot people's backs. By the end of the ceremony I had run the full gamut, from squealing youth to painful old age, a total of 44 backs.

A peculiar look came over the editor's face as he flicked through my pictures. Putting down the last print, he said, "It's either of two things and I don't think you're a half-wit. I asked for pictures that were different and I sure got them."

My backs ran in the first issue of *Life*. By chance I had hit upon the *Life* style. At 21 I went to work for the magazine. Starting at the top, I had nowhere to go but grow old.

I had never heard of Mrs Simpson and had no idea that the King of England was infatuated with an American until I went to work for *Life*. This was equally true of the general public. In the 1930s, the British press exhibited a restraint regarding "the Royals" it no longer observes today. British magazine distributors systematically censored all foreign publications entering the country, and in those pre-television times, that was all it took to keep the public in ignorance. Even the scandal-loving *News of the World*, affectionately called "the barmaid's bible", kept mum.

This, however, was not the case with the foreign press, which was having a field day. The romance of "Prince Charming" and "his American divorcee" was regarded as a 20th-century fairytale to be thoroughly exploited for an avid public. *Time* had a "mole" in Buckingham Palace who closely observed the romance and allowed the magazine to carry a weekly story regarding the latest sentimental developments. *Life* was no less eager to cover the goings-on. I was assigned to get pictures. This was much more complex than filing a regular picture story. For days I followed up the mole's leads, chasing after the inaccessible Mrs Simpson. I never did get to see her. But I did manage to take a picture of Edward VIII when he toured South Wales' distressed areas 23 days before he gave up his throne for "the woman I love".

The Welsh population, unaware of the impending constitutional crisis, gave the King a rousing reception. Recalling those times many years later, Edward—by then the Duke of Windsor—said, "One thing I did well was make inspection tours."

Possibly on account of my Welsh origins I admired these unfortunate people. Many of them had never found a job and never would, with unemployment fluctuating between 40 and 70 per cent. Yet they all had faith in "Teddy" when he promised that, "something must be done". I got a more realistic view from a Pontypridd barmaid. "They're so damn miserable," she told me. "They have no idea how awful their plight is. In the good old pre-war days the fines for being drunk and disorderly were over a thousand quid a year. Now it's not even ten bob."

I never got another chance to photograph the monarch. While waiting for him to pass through Merthyr Tidfil, a burly constable knocked me across the street. "If you bloody Yanks try and follow the royal procession, I'll run you in," he said. Until then I had no idea of the authorities' outrage over *Time.* My Welsh experiences did nothing to reassure me when New York cabled: "What about a fast act on Eddie's servants at Buck House?" Translated this meant: the King's servants — an assignment for yours truly. A pretty formidable order, I thought, feeling like the ham in the sandwich, wedged between the British upper-crust and the buttered American side. The Royal family's traditional reserve and desire for privacy had never been greater than now.

The only way I could hope to get into Buckingham Palace would be through the tradesmen's entrance. But who would let me in? Certainly no Englishman. Only a foreigner might be willing to help. A friendly Frenchman was what I needed, and that could mean no other than the master of the royal kitchens: the King's chef.

As fate would have it, M. Avignon, the chef at the Ritz, lived three floors above me. A staircase acquaintance, I was able to tell him about my ambition to meet the King's cook, whose name I didn't even know. "Don't know him myself," M. Avignon admitted, but in a very French way he wanted to oblige someone with the good taste to speak his language. He gave the matter some thought before adding, "He does belong to our club, the Association of French Chefs. I can therefore invite him for tea."

A week later I met M. René Legros. As his name implied, he was both fat and French and despite a brand-new bowler hat, everything about him was resolutely Gallic. He was small, and wore a loose black jacket which gave him gentle billowing lines. A casual observer would have mistaken him for a member of that long-suffering species, the French teacher, but he was indeed chef to His Majesty the King of England.

This disciple of the formidable Montagné was a most unusual chef — he lacked the terrible temper that generally goes with gastronomic talent. Nevertheless, M. Legros had charmed the most demanding gourmets of his generation, including M. Charles Bedaux, his former employer. M. Bedaux, a Franco-American, had made millions by inventing a system for speeding up assembly-line production. When Edward became King, M. Bedaux, who didn't even know the monarch, sent him his chef as a gift. The new monarch graciously accepted M. Bedaux's present and took M. Legros along when be moved to Buckingham Palace. Among the first acts of his reign, Edward fired his father's chef.

During our tea-party, fearing M. Legros might get upset if I told him why I wanted to meet him, I decided to say nothing. Of his own free will, however, he talked openly about palace life. Apart from the kitchens, the servants' quarters were always cool and quite chilly during the winter. Queen Victoria's superintendent of works had neglected to install any heating during the construction and none of the successive rulers had seen fit to have it put in. In spite of this, M. Legros was a happy man and discussed "*le climat anglais*" without a qualm. Noticing it lurking outside black and wet, he was suddenly reminded of the time. "I must hurry back to the palace," he exclaimed.

In our steps from the living-room to the front door, M. Legros expressed the hope that we would meet again. "Why don't you visit me at Buckingham Palace?" he said. "You can't miss me if you go through the gate in the right wing. It leads straight to my office." I assured him I would do just that.

A few days later, Lloyds of London's odds on Edward's coronation in May lengthened significantly. Soon after that Mrs Simpson entered English history on the front pages of the daily press. This heralded a crisis. The lady left for the Continent, while the King retired to Fort Belvedere, abdicated, and in turn hurriedly departed, leaving much behind, including a French cook. Among the first acts of his reign, George VI had M. Legros sacked and rehired his father's chef.

On M. Legros' last day at the palace I paid him a visit. There was no one at the gate. I found him in his office, a bleak oblong room with a high ceiling which had not been repainted since Victorian times. M. Legros was seated on a swivel chair looking as though the prevailing gloom had penetrated him. When I expressed my regrets, he simply shrugged his shoulders and, looking straight ahead, said, "I'm sailing for France tomorrow."

I felt I was seeing someone cry without tears. The host, however, came out in the Frenchman. Turning to a small table on which a bottle of port and two Burgundy glasses rested, he carefully poured out the drinks. We sipped in silence. "It's a very good port," I remarked, to say something. Absently he answered, "His Majesty only drinks the very best."

Whenever he said "His Majesty" M. Legros meant the Duke of Windsor. He prefaced his next sentence with a heavy sigh. "There was a man who appreciated *la bonne cuisine*." His face lit up. "It was a pleasure to cook for His Majesty. How often we discussed the menus together. We used to make them up from day to day. Now…" His voice trailed off, forlorn. "Now menus go up to Queen Elizabeth for approval two weeks in advance. Two weeks in advance!" He sighed, and once again his eyes expressed eloquently what words failed to say. We had another glass of port and M. Legros smiled at a recollection. His mood changed. "I remember preparing *moules marinières* for His Majesty. We were at Balmoral castle in Scotland. His Majesty enjoyed them so, he had a second helping." It was as if he was recounting happy memories of the deceased in the next room.

At our third glass of port he said suddenly, "I was very much displeased with the quality of the food purchased." He raised his eyebrows in disapproval. "And although that was not my department, it was up to me to see that the meals were perfect. I pointed this out to His Majesty. "Don't worry, M. Legros," he said to me. "We will work together. You will straighten out the kitchen problems and I will do the same for the country."

"He said it, but just like that," M. Legros added, nodding to give greater emphasis to his words. "I can assure you that I did my utmost to satisfy King George and Queen Elizabeth." He looked miserable at the thought that his efforts had been in vain.

"Let me give you an idea." He picked up an agenda on which the daily menus were transcribed. He pointed to terse notes written in the margin. "The Queen's handwriting," he said. "She made all the changes on my menus herself—in French." He paused and looked up. "But there was no personal contact, *vous savez*." Finding the page he had been seeking, M. Legros stared in wonder at an order written in sharp angular letters with a pointed pencil. "I have here," he said very deliberately, "instructions from the Queen to serve potatoes with every meal." M. Legros closed the book. He sounded discouraged. "I understand the King likes them boiled," he said sadly. "Potatoes with every meal," he repeated. "Who would have expected that from a Queen who speaks perfect French?"

French voices were heard as the chefs from London's most fashionable restaurants arrived to say goodbye. Most stayed on for lunch. "Of course you'll join us," M. Legros told me. We followed him into a large dining-room, painted a creamy white, which adjoined the pastry cooks' trophies. We sat on benches placed either side of a large table presided over by M. Legros. He faced the windows looking out on the driveway which led to the main gates, where expressionless guardsmen paced slowly up and down. Unconcerned by their surroundings, the chefs made themselves comfortable. Some shed their jackets, others unbuttoned their waistcoats or loosened their belts. One actually removed his celluloid collar. They tucked napkins under their chins. There was an expectant silence, while the *commis* hovered around respectfully whispering in French.

Just as avarice is frowned upon in France when it affects the meals, calamities are not allowed to ruin the appetite. During the soup course, the silence was broken only by sighs of satisfaction. The chef who had removed his collar flattened his moustaches against his lips and drained remnants of soup out of his whiskers, making sharp sucking sounds. Conversation between courses remained general and dealt with the merits of what we had eaten. Animation appeared with the Dover sole, while the roast beef *à l'anglaise* was consumed *à la française,* chunks of bread soaking up the gravy. The bottles of wine were emptied, the tone of the voices rose, while outside in the distance, sentries stood guard like small figures in another world.

Our faces glowed by the time we dropped our crumpled napkins beside the coffee cups and liqueur glasses. The time had come to bid our host goodbye. M. Legros rose from his armchair as we lined up alongside the table, looking grim. It was like a scene outside the cemetery after a funeral before the mourners scatter.

When the time came for Edward—by then the Duke of Windsor—to consider where he should marry Mrs Simpson, M. Legros' old employer M. Bedaux solved his dilemma. He loaned his French château to the Duke. At the time, the Franco-American entrepreneur had maintained excellent relations with Nazi leaders. He proposed to the couple that they tour Germany (tea with Hitler was included in the program). The tour caused a furore. Hastily, the Duke canceled his forthcoming visit to the USA. For purely selfish reasons, I was sorry the Windsors did not sail for New York aboard the German liner *Bremen* as planned. I was to cover the ocean crossing

During World War II, M. Bedaux collaborated with the Nazis. Arrested for treason in 1945, he committed suicide while awaiting trial. The Duke of Windsor never rehired M. Legros.

Young students, Eton, 1937

Etonian group in front of Spottiswode's book shop, 1937

Handicapped World War I veterans, London, 1937

War veterans, London, 1937

Ballet Russe de Monaco at Covent Garden, London, 1937

The Carlton Hotel, Cannes, 1937

Nice

My first foreign assignment was to cover a Rotary International convention in Nice — a town I had lived in until only three years before. This would prove to be more than a break from preparations for the coronation.

To be returning to Nice, where I had been a poor student, and now finding myself enjoying the luxuries of the Riviera, was very pleasant, though tinged with nostalgia. I had a suite at the Ruhl, the hotel whose ornate façade on the Promenade des Anglais was all I had known of it before. And I enjoyed entertaining my old classmates, plying them with stingers, a drink they didn't know and couldn't handle too well, as I observed their stupefaction over my good fortune. But the nostalgia caught up with me when I returned to the neighborhood where I had lived for seven years, and discovered that M. Pansier's camera shop no longer existed. From a waiter at the local café we once patronized, I learned that M. Pansier had moved to San Remo, across the border in Italy.

Although I had grown up in the midst of cameras and chemicals, and the acrid smell of hypo was more familiar than the pungent scent of the jasmine the Arabs peddled in my native Algeria, it was not my father, the enthusiastic amateur, who made me a photographer, but M. Pansier, the calm professional. Mr. Pansier had taught me just about everything I knew when I was hired by *Life*.

I was 13 when we moved to Nice in 1927. As luck would have it, our apartment was two floors above Paris Photo, M. Pansier's shop where, for the next five years, I would be his holiday apprentice. On Sunday mornings, when he took the day off, I was left in charge and loaded films into box Brownie cameras for clients who brought them back on Monday mornings. I followed these films through tank development and printing. I dried the prints, trimmed them and sorted them. This way I got to know more about the private lives of our clients than the parish priest. I was not at all surprised when the baker's daughter hurriedly married our local plumber. Photography has a way of bringing out the erotic in people. (Stupidly, I did not take advantage of this knowledge to buy stock when the Polaroid camera first came on the market.)

We marked the erotica with a discreet "X" in one corner of the folder to avoid possible embarrassment before a shop full of customers. Because of my youth, I did not serve the X-rated clients. Once, however, I was alone in the shop when one walked in. She was a very attractive young woman who, week in and week out, brought us a roll of film of herself posing nude in a garden. Without the slightest concern, she looked over the prints showing me, as though I had not seen them, the ones she liked best, remarking, "They're to bolster the morale of my husband who is an officer in Madagascar."

In 1931, M. Pansier had been appointed the official photographer for Nice. I helped him cover the important events promoting the city. We photographed shivering young women in light frocks tossing bouquets during the "Battle of the Flowers", which was staged in mid-February to create the illusion abroad that the Riviera was warm in winter. We shot beauty contests, learning to cope with the girls' aggressive mothers, and took pictures of automobile shows where glamorous women in the latest fashions competed for first prize with custom-built cars driven by chauffeurs in pastel livery.

In this way I followed the life of the city, even to the bedsides of Nice's distinguished dead. On such occasions, M. Pansier and I would appear at the home of the deceased in dark clothes walking on tiptoe. Eyes downcast, we expressed our condolences and insisted on being alone with "the departed" while we were taking our pictures. "It would be too painful for you," M. Pansier soothingly convinced the bereaved. No sooner had we closed the door behind us than we removed our coats and stopped whispering. While M. Pansier eyed the corpse professionally, readjusting rows of medals or rearranging a rosary and olive branch in clasped hands, I flung back the curtains to catch the light. We could not use the magnesium powder we normally used for flash, as it would have cast a film of black dust upon the funereal bed.

By this time I had outgrown the box camera M. Pansier had first given me. It had belonged to a failed Polish painter who, unable to get good results, had traded it in shortly before hanging himself. I sold it in turn for 100 francs to Edwin Rosskam, another failed painter, who went on to be a successful photographer in America

The Leica burst upon the photographic world to shattering effect. It left the old-timers with their large press cameras apprehensive about this revolutionary technique, while M. Pansier and I were swept away. The Leica allowed photographers to take pictures for the first time unobserved and under minimum lighting conditions. To achieve this we trained ourselves to shoot at very slow speeds, which meant anticipating the moment our subject, unaware he was being photographed, would remain motionless for the necessary length of time. This gave birth to a style called "candid photography", which, while not always flattering, did reveal aspects of people's character never before photographed.

We got so proficient that a salesman from Zeiss Ikon, the famed German lens manufacturer, asked us to test his company's latest camera: the 35-mm Contax. When the salesman saw the results, which included a shot of M. Pansier's German shepherd dog, he asked us if we could produce a life-size print of the dog for an exhibition. Could we? You bet we could, and did. The Zeiss salesman was enchanted. The picture was the sensation of the photographic show and a triumph for Contax. It was only later that M. Pansier discovered we had inadvertently used a Leica negative.

Thanks to the Leica, I learned the basic axiom of photography: everybody loves to have their picture taken. I was sneaking a shot in class when my chemistry professor caught me in mid-exposure. He did not punish me. Instead he combed his hair, gathered the class around his desk and asked me to take a group picture.

Memories like this came back to me as I wandered around my old haunts, waiting to shoot the Rotarians. The convention's main event was a luncheon attended by the President of the French Republic. I was seated at the table of past Rotary presidents as "Albert D. Albert", a past president who had been unable to attend the lunch. From the banqueting hall, which looked out on the Promenade des Anglais, I had watched the cars drive up. It took me back to an earlier presidential visit to Nice for a similar type of banquet in 1932. On that occasion M. Pansier taught me one of the most important tricks of the trade: how to get into places where you and your camera are unwelcome. His ploy was to convey the impression that you had every right to be present. He demonstrated this by hopping over the police barrier with me in his wake. We walked right up to the cop on duty to protest about the delays. "It's way past my deadline," M. Pansier complained.

"I haven't heard of any delays," the cop said.

"Well, I have, and it's way past my deadline," M. Pansier repeated.

This led to an exchange between the two which carrried on until a ranking police official standing in the lead car of the presidential motorcade drove up and called out, "Do these two have the proper credentials?"

"Yes, they do," our new-found friend responded as we stepped back to photograph the smiling President Doumergue, driving past, top hat in hand.

The Rotarians' lunch was over. I was making my way out of the diningroom when I suddenly saw him.

"M. Pansier!" I called out, "You! Here!" as I hugged him.

French Riviera, 1937

Londoners waiting for George VI, 1937

Lyon's waitresses waiting for George VI, London, 1937

Coronation Day

The evening Edward abdicated I roamed London's streets in search of the "meaningful picture" that would express the nation's mood to the readers of *Life*. There was nothing to photograph. Whatever the Londoners felt that night they were keeping to themselves. Even at the Cheshire Cheese, Fleet Street's favorite pub, the atmosphere was subdued. The reporters drank silently as they considered the overblown stories they were expected to produce about every aspect of the new Royal family's public life by May 12, Coronation Day. During the crisis, a jovial mood had prevailed, producing wisecracks such as, "It would never do for our monarch to be the third mate on an American tramp." Now, as Coronation Day neared, that mood gave way to weariness and doggerel, Britain's favorite way of expressing serious thoughts. One of the most apt rhymes went:

> A George is on the throne again.
> And dullness now resumes her reign.
> And in fresh guise of favor bids,
> As Daddy, Mummy and the kids.

While Fleet Street was busy remaking the retiring Duke of York into a regal presence, the new monarch's increasing popularity was in evidence when he received King Leopold of Belgium and drove to Buckingham Palace with his guest. The public lined the streets, while the waitresses at *la maison* Lyons peered out from behind the restaurant window lost in wonder. Meanwhile, scaffolding went up along the Royal route. Even the grandest English families were not averse to erecting stands for Americans to rent.

There were the inevitable letters to *The Times*. My favorite came from an irate curate who bemoaned the fact that Hyde Park's spring crocuses were being trampled to death by the stands erected for purely commercial purposes. Edward's old coronation souvenirs were disposed of at cut rates, making way for George's new line of knick-knacks. Selfridge's, the store whose boast was selling everything from a pin to an elephant, was stocked with "kidney pads" for the relief of those ladies and gentlemen trapped in the Abbey and unable to reach any facilities for approximately ten hours.

Commercialism now made way for royal fervor. At around 7pm on Coronation Eve, groups began to line up along the route to assure themselves of a front row view the next day. I can't forget the sight of an elderly lady clutching a chocolate bar stoically settling down for the night. Families equipped with food and drink, blankets and flimsy Union Jacks made in Japan, camped cheerfully along the route. By nightfall, the streets had grown a human hedge.

At dawn on Coronation Day there was a threat of rain.

By 4am, the hour when all traffic came to a stop, everybody, including the distinguished guests inside Westminster Abbey, was in place. My station was the statue of Eros in Picadilly Circus. To my great relief it was boarded up with a platform on top of the scaffolding. The authorities I felt were being very considerate of the photographers. Unfortunately the two plain-clothes men occupying the platform set me right. Exhibiting a total disregard for the crowds hanging out of every window around Picadilly, they informed me that the Coronation was a family festivity on which the "bloody press" was not to intrude, "So bugger off!"

By 5am, the police assigned to keep a clear space for the photographers had been swept away by the crowd. By 6:30am, I found myself jammed up against Eros's boarding. At times my feet did not reach the steps. At 9am it started to drizzle.

By 9:30, the guests in the rooms overlooking the Circus held cocktail parties. By 11:30, oranges, bananas, and buns rained on us from their windows. "My God, they're as tight as ticks," a colleague remarked. By 1:30pm, people started to faint. For the next two and a half hours, more fainted and feebly protested to the first-aid teams taking them away.

It was 4pm when a shout heralded the appearance of the Royal procession. I braced myself to shoot over the crowd's heads. At that very moment the men raised their hats while the women and children frantically waved their flags. When the cheering finally stopped, the procession was out of sight. I did not get a picture.

George VI, Queen Elizabeth, Princess Elizabeth and Princess Margaret Rose,
Braemar, 1937

Spectators at Scottish games, Braemar, 1937

Scottish games, Braemar, 1937

Grouse shooting, Scotland, 1937

Grouse shooting, Scotland, 1937

Coco Chanel and Cecil Beaton at the *Bal du Directoire*, Paris, 1937

Bal du Directoire, Paris, 1937

Le Directoire

"Coronation Year", as 1937 came to be called, provided an escape from reality. The festivities spread from London to Paris, to the French Riviera, and all the way to Salzburg as Café Society, the Mayfair Set, and *le tout Paris* joined in what would be remembered as one last glorious fling before the deluge. I was assigned to many of these events and as a result got over being a shy young man. Parties were hard work. It demanded considerable diplomacy for a classless person like myself to perform in a highly class-conscious society. Since this world was both small and exclusive, I was soon recognized and accepted as its photographer. I had forged links with a group of people with which I had nothing in common save knowing how to knot my black tie. On occasion, however, I would be sharply reminded that my presence was tolerated simply because I was useful.

The theme for the grandest Parisian costume ball that Spring was *"Le Directoire"*. The organizing committee did not consider the similarities between conditions in present-day France and the 18th-century *Directoire*, frivolously drifting toward disaster. Aesthetics alone guided their choice. The ball was to take place in the Tuileries. Women in flowing chemise dresses and white bonnets worn at a saucy angle, men in smart tail-coats, skin-tight white breeches, high boots and top hats with cockades would provide the perfect ensemble in the lavishly illuminated gardens.

The public, however, did not miss the parallel and made much of the fact that France was being torn apart by political dissent. This was best illustrated by the fiasco of the World's Fair: inaugurated before completion, only the massive German and Soviet pavilions emerged as symbols of power in the midst of scaffolding.

In view of the fact that I was a newcomer to French society, *Life*'s Paris bureau arranged for a young Philadelphian, Braddish Johnson, to show me around. Braddish was enjoying his youth and family fortune keeping up with the smart set with whom he was more often than not on first-name terms. Nonchalantly the amiable Braddish guided me, pointing out those I should photograph. At one point he said, "I'll introduce you to Momo." That is how I met the Baron Maurice de Rothschild. The Baron was cordial and even directed me towards Coco Chanel, who was deep in conversation with Cecil Beaton. He made it very clear, however, that he didn't want to be photographed.

"Pay no attention to what he says," Braddish whispered. "Momo loves to have his picture taken."

"Are you sure?" I asked, dubious about defying a Rothschild.

"Trust me," Braddish promised. As I still hesitated, he nudged me several times.

The flash from my camera was nothing compared to the Baron's fury. He called me "a shit" with such conviction that he convinced me I must be one. "Momo was a bit touchy tonight," Braddish sighed as we left the ball.

Apart from this *faux pas*, Braddish was very much with it as he enjoyed his delightfully idle life which suited him so well. Nevertheless, his mother decided that Braddish should do something "meaningful"—something Braddish was not cut out for. To that end, she arranged for him to be sent, on a freelance basis, to cover the Spanish Civil War on the side of Franco's forces—which she considered more respectable than the Republican side. Soon after his arrival in Spain, Braddish was driven up to the front with several colleagues. A Republican shell hit the car, and brought poor Braddish's short and happy life to an end.

"You're not a Frenchman"

A New York editor's interest in the beards of France had landed me in Paris. What began as an uneventful assignment turned out to be anything but. At the small hotel where I usually stayed, the manager greeted me with: "The *gardes mobiles* were here shortly after you left to arrest you for desertion from the French Army." Observing my consternation, he added consolingly, "Well, don't worry. *Ça s'arrangera* one way or another."

Aware that I would be in a stronger position debating my case at the French consulate in London than attempting to cope with the *gardes mobiles* I had seen in action during the riots in Paris in 1934, I nevertheless decided to stay and shoot the story. I didn't fancy having to explain why *Life*'s newly hired photographer was wanted for desertion.

I shot the beards in record time and got out of town. Safely back in London, I visited the French consulate and walked into a legalistic maze.

"All you require," an official said, "is a declaration from this consulate certifying you are British," adding, "It's free of charge." This sounded reassuring, so I applied on the spot.

"Your birth certificate, please," a second official said.

"Why, you're French," a third exclaimed, peering over the shoulder of the second. "The commune of Bouira belongs to the Department of Algiers, and the Department of Algiers is French territory."

"My father is British, even if he did own a farm in Bouira when I was born. So is my passport, and so am I."

"That remains to be seen," said the first, reaching for a heavy book and frowning through the pages.

"He was born on a Friday the 13th in 1914," said the third.

"Leaving all superstitious considerations aside, he's French then," said the first looking up from his book.

"Until he's twenty-one," the second remarked.

"Then he has the choice of becoming *Anglais* if he likes," the third said with a shrug.

"That was amended," the first official pointed out, rifling back through the pages.

"By a law passed when the franc dropped and we were flooded by tourists taking advantage of the exchange rate," the second reminded him.

"But he still could become a French citizen," the first insisted.

"Only by residing in France on his twenty-first birthday," added the third.

"I celebrated my twenty-first birthday in London," I said.

"He must be English then," the third decided.

"Well why didn't he notify the competent authorities," the first complained, "and save us the bother of tracking him down all the way from Bouira to Metropolitan France?"

"My mother asked a friend to tell the Mayor of Bouira that the British consulate in Nice had issued me a passport," I explained.

"Registered mail?" he inquired.

"No, postcard."

The three sighed in unison.

The third was about to fill out the declaration when the first, who had not given up hope, slapped his book triumphantly, exclaiming: "*Un moment!* I regret but I must ask you a most embarrassing question, but you'll appreciate it's my duty." He had just hit upon a law which charitably offered protection to foreign children born out of wedlock on French soil by making them citizens automatically.

"Were your parents married?" he inquired.

"I'm no bastard, sir," I said.

"Then *monsieur,* you're not a Frenchman."

Elsa Schiaparelli's *maison de couture,* Place Vendôme, Paris, 1937

Elsa Schiaparelli, Paris, 1937

La Maison Schiaparelli

I was soon back in Paris to photograph Elsa Schiaparelli and her *maison de haute couture*. Schiaparelli's success was due to her daughter, Gogo, who had contracted polio. Until then Schiaparelli had simply knitted chic sweaters for wealthy clients, but the expenses of her daughter's illness inspired her to seek the backing of a large department store so that she could open her own *maison de couture*.

At first unable to afford professional mannequins to model her sportswear, she got her wealthy clients to do it for her. "Schiap" was an instant success. By the time I was to photograph her, she was not only well established, but had only one rival: Coco Chanel. The rivalry between the two was intense. Chanel only referred to Schiap as "the Italian." Schiaparelli merely shrugged.

Without the slightest regard for the Depression, Schiaparelli had moved into the Place Vendôme, the most expensive address in Paris. This rectangular *place* had been laid out during the reign of Louis XIV as a setting for the monarch's equestrian statue. Through the passage of history, the statues and the names of the *place* came and went. However, the magnificent 17th-century façades remained, protected by a strictly enforced building ordinance. There, at 21 Place Vendôme, was Schiaparelli.

Luxury greeted me in the person of Georges, the doorman, resplendent in midnight-blue livery with twin rows of golden buttons, a golden "S" on his cap, and white gloves. He ushered me into the ground-floor boutique, where a stylized gilt bamboo birdcage displayed bottles of Schiaparelli's famous perfume, "Shocking". The salons where the mannequins modeled the latest creations were on the first floor. Their high ceilings, large mirrors, heavy carpets, expensively fragile bamboo chairs and comfortable cream sofas created a feeling of understated elegance as the mannequins glided through in groups of twos and three, the scent of Shocking trailing in their wake.

The mannequins themselves were less understated. Schiaparelli's group of beauties included an extremely distinguished Russian Princess. Her husband, once an officer in the Imperial Guard, was now a cabby. He would drive her to work and back home. She always sat next to him in the front seat so that he could still pick up fares.

On the same floor was the studio where Schiap conjured up her designs. The muscle and sinews of fashion were on the second floor and under the mansard. There were warrens of small offices and a cluster of seamstresses, cheerfully chatting about love. The mood in the accounting department was more subdued, under the supervision of a bearded chief accountant. By accident I learned about the working relationship between the accountant and the doorman. Georges was president of the Place Vendôme Chauffeurs' Association, and as such was party to the chauffeurs' gossip. "Did you know that Mlle. Y has just broken with M. Z, the one with the Hispano Suiza?" Immediately Georges reported this to the chief accountant, who just as promptly put a stop on any further purchases by Mlle. Y. No sooner had Georges learned that the same Mlle. Y was now seen in the Baron X's Bentley, her credit line was restored.

Except when collections were being prepared, the pace was leisurely. This easy-going impression was deceptive. Schiaparelli's iron will might not be noticable but it was always present. Once I asked for a photograph of a very smart society woman alighting from her car and being greeted by Georges at the door. Without hesitation the order went out. "Tell Daisy Fellowes we need her and her Rolls Cabriolet for a picture." Daisy Fellowes, one of the wealthiest women in Paris, soon arrived, and was kept waiting.

Although I had been given complete freedom to photograph what I wanted — except for the gowns for next season, I got nowhere when it came to Schiaparelli herself. My daily requests became more urgent and eloquent, to no avail. Finally, around noon one day, Schiaparelli suddenly emerged from her studio. She wore a wide-brimmed hat of her own design, almost certainly inspired by Bonaparte's famous bicorne. "The shadow of Napoleon has just passed," I exclaimed as she swept by.

Schiaparelli wheeled around. "I understand, M. Phillips, that you go out with my mannequin, Christiane."

"Aren't you fortunate, Madame Schiaparelli," I replied.

"Fortunate, M. Phillips?"

"Why yes. What would people say if a *Life* photographer doing a story on *la maison* Schiaparelli went out with a mannequin from Chanel?"

"You may take my picture after lunch," Schiap said, and swept on.

Elsa Schiaparelli sketching a new creation, Paris, 1937

Maud Gonne MacBride addressing Dubliners, 1937

Dublin

Back in London, my editor greeted me with, "Any idea where you're spending the weekend?"

"In Dieppe with my French girlfriend."

"Wrong. In Dublin with Maud Gonne."

On landing in Dun Laoghaire, a beggar came up to me and in an irresistible Irish brogue, asked me, "Can ye spare a copper, your honor?" I gave him one. By the time I'd obliged the fifth beggar, "his honor" had run out of coppers. When I tried to explain, he eyed me coldly and said, "may ye roast in hell you Protestant bastaad!"

Life didn't have a bureau in Dublin, but relied upon a stringer, Geoffrey Coulter. Coulter took me to a pub in the basement of a Dublin police station where reporters could drink after hours—a spirit of openness that did not extend to contraception. In this smoky atmosphere, Coulter filled me in on Maud Gonne MacBride: the woman James Joyce had called "the Irish Joan of Arc".

Maud Gonne was born in England in 1866. She was two months old when her father, an Irish officer, was assigned to the Curragh, England's largest military base in Ireland. By the time she was 16 she had been described by George Bernard Shaw as "outrageously beautiful". Her political views on Irish independence were thought equally outrageous. The great Irish poet William Butler Yeats fell madly in love with her and together they created the Abbey Theater in Dublin. "Willie believed in art for art's sake, Maud Gonne told me when we met. "He was a sissy. For me, it was art for propaganda's sake." When Yeats wrote the play *Cathleen ni Houlihan* for her, the press dismissed Maud Gonne's performance as merely "acting herself", but the play was never forgotten and became the symbol of Irish nationalism.

Maud, the Irish revolutionary, traveled to France, where she became the mistress of a French reactionary who was violently anti-Semitic and virulently anti-Dreyfus. When she came back to Dublin, she married a swashbuckling Irishman, Major John MacBride, with whom she had nothing in common except a shared passion for Irish independence. They had one son, Sean. The couple no longer lived together by the time MacBride participated in the 1916 Easter Uprising, for which he was executed by the British. From that day on, tall, gaunt Maud Gonne wore widow's weeds.

The Uprising had taken place 21 years before I landed at Dun Laoghaire, but the "troubles" still rumbled on like the thunderclouds overhead that gave Yeats's city its "terrible beauty". By the time Coulter had updated me, I had consumed more Guinness than I had ever drunk before, and ever would again. Seeing me back to my hotel, he warned me not to go out alone that evening. Sean MacBride, Maud's son, was "on the run" and reported to be in town. As, according to Coulter, I was supposed to bear some resemblance to him, he did not want me to be the victim of mistaken identity. (At that time, Sean MacBride was a member of the outlawed IRA. Shortly after I photographed his mother, he started to practice law and represented defendants who might once have been himself. From 1948 to 1951, he served as Minister of External Affairs in a coalition government. In 1974, he was awarded the Nobel Peace prize as the Chairman of Amnesty International.)

The next morning I visited Maud Gonne at her home. The livingroom chairs were overturned and several window panes were smashed.

"What happened?" I asked, surveying the damage. "It was O'Duffy's men," she said, scornful of Ireland's blue-shirted fascists.

"This morning?"

"No, seven years ago," she replied. She was now opposing the de Valera government with the same fervor with which she had fought the British years before. I photographed her addressing groups on street corners, demanding the release of political prisoners, always under the watchful eyes of two policemen.

Maud Gonne gave me a glimpse of how very different 19th-century rebels were from 20th-century revolutionaries. Reminiscing about her many trips between Dublin and Paris to visit exiled Irishmen, she recalled smuggling in their favorite brand of tea, unavailable in Paris. A customs inspector said to her gallantly, "Mademoiselle Gonne, I don't like searching your luggage. Tell me you have nothing to declare and I'll take your word for it."

"It was very naughty of him," Maud Gonne complained. "How could I smuggle anything after I gave my word?"

Back in Ireland some months later, I ran into Maud at the Dublin Horse Show. She had seen my story in *Life*. "You were very naughty," she scolded. "You made me look old."

Dublin Horse Show, 1937

Cecil Beaton's *fête champêtre*, Ashcombe, 1937

Cecil Beaton's *fête champêtre*, Ashcombe, 1937

Beaton

I first met Cecil Beaton in July 1937 when I photographed his famous *fête champêtre*. By the time of this ball, nobody remembered that Beaton had invented a persona for himself by transforming his middle-class mother, the wife of a timber merchant, into a society hostess via misleading letters to *The Times*, the *Telegraph*, and *Tatler*, while propelling his sister Baba into society as "Lady Mary Beaton", thereby enraging the legitimate descendant of the famous lady-in-waiting to Mary, Queen of Scots. In those days Beaton was frequently snubbed more often than not by members of the only class he admired. In 1926, back from Venice, he noted angrily in his diary, "I like publicity. It's necessary to me. No one has taken any notice of me — treated as dirt. Wait until I am a success."

Success came to Beaton in 1928. He did fashion pictures for *Vogue*, flitted from London to Hollywood via Paris, Salzburg and New York, photographing and sketching the smart set along the way. By the time we met, he was making news by being photographed himself. Beaton was in such demand that no party could be a social success without him.

This *fête champêtre*, which he organized at his home in Ashcombe, in Wiltshire, was to be his entertainment masterpiece. Weeks before it took place, Beaton and his friends went to work. Enormous paper *cotillon* flowers to decorate the house and garden were flown in from Paris. Drawings were made of the costumes various groups of friends must wear. The guests of neighboring house parties were to appear as a unit: one group represented characters from Greek mythology; another oriental peasants, a third, characters from *The Beggar's Opera*. Salvador Dali suggested the disguise for the servants: animal and bird masks. A member of the party with a gift for spontaneously composing couplets of mock-Shakespearean verse produced within an hour's notice a Restoration play, *Chastity Rewarded*.

On the morning of the *fête* there were showers. Guests who arrived early were given last-minute jobs to do and the *al fresco* preparations carried on optimistically. The marquee was erected. The catering vans turned up. The fancy dress, however, did not. Karinska, a Russian genius at theatrical costumes, had missed the last train from London. The Embassy Club Band got lost. Fortunately the rain stopped, the band and the dresses showed up in time. Cars arrived from all over the countryside, filled with costumed guests, guided by *papier mâche* figures and floating draperies. Dancers from neighborhood villages performed a rustic maypole dance. There was a bonfire. The band played in the converted stables. The *divertissement* was performed with the brightly lit house as a backdrop, lit by glass candelabras on balustrades decorated with paper roses.

There was a buffet and dancing after the *divertissement*. The waiters in their sheep, goat, horse, and bird masks circulated bearing food and drink. Among the costumed guests, Beaton's co-host Michael Duff came as Apollo and his mother Julia as a Winterhalter shepherdess. Mona Williams was in pink tulle, while Rex Whistler and Caroline Paget made a pair of extremely romantic Victorians. Beaton himself made four costume changes. Twice he appeared in white satin knee-breeches and a richly colored brocade Regency *justaucorps*. He wore a brown Restoration costume for his part in the *divertissement*, and ended the evening as a scarecrow. At 7am we ate breakfast in the light of the early morning sun.

In 1978 I visited Beaton at his home in Salisbury. By then he was Sir Cecil Beaton, a distinguished figure knighted for his achievements, which included two Oscars for his costumes for *My Fair Lady* and *Gigi*. He was recovering from a stroke, which had left his right hand crippled. With his usual tenacity he had trained himself to draw with his left hand and continued to take fashion photographs. At the mention of his *fête champêtre*, Beaton's face lit up. He settled back to recall every detail of the memorable night.

Cecil Beaton in Regency costume photographs his party, Ashcombe, 1937

The restaurant "Chez Pascal", Marseilles, 1937

Man selling *langoustes*, Marseilles, 1937

Antibes

Another of my assignments that summer of 1937 was to photograph Lady Mendl's Sunday lunch at her villa in Antibes. Born Elsie de Wolfe, Lady Mendl had been the most successful American decorator at the end of the 19th and beginning of the 20th century. Late in life she had married Sir Charles Mendl, the British Press Attaché in Paris.

By then, she was a major figure in international society She knew everyone worth knowing and was on intimate terms with the Windsors. An invitation to lunch at her villa during the summer was tantamount to a royal command.

In typical Riviera style, the setting was simple but luxurious. The tables were laid out around a magnificent tree in the center of the garden. I was greeted by a fey character, Lady Mendl's adopted son, who told me there was no space for me at any of the tables. I would be fed in the kitchen.

"I never eat when I work," I told him. This settled, he led me out to Lady Mendl.

She was sitting at one of the tables and wore a white striped dress, a nun's wimple, and a pair of white cotton gloves. She was lost in thought and seemed totally unaware of me as I took her picture. Sir Charles, who was mixing himself a drink, stopped me. "I'd rather you not take my picture with all of these... Well, you know what I mean," he told me.

The meal was buffet-style, very much in vogue since the Hôtel du Cap at Eden Roc had given the Swedish *smörgasbord* a French look. After photographing the guests helping themselves, I perched on a branch of the tree and proceeded to shoot pictures throughout the meal, to the consternation of Lady Mendl's adopted son, who suddenly discovered an empty place for me and begged me in vain to join the party.

"You were horrible up that tree photographing every mouthful we ate," said one of the ladies as the party broke up. "I hope you realize you bitched up the whole luncheon."

Bruno Walter conducting at Salzburg Festival, 1937

Max Reinhardt (centre), Salzburg Festival, 1937

Salzburg, 1937

Bruno Walter, Salzburg, 1937

Arturo Toscanini, Salzburg, 1937

Max Reinhardt and his wife, Helene Thimig, at their home in Leopoldskron, 1937

Salzburg

The 1937 Salzburg Music Festival came to an end with the Austrian director Max Reinhardt's production of *Faust*. In his usual grand manner, he had converted the famous *Felsenreitschule* — the riding school built against a rocky cliff — into an open-air stage facing a covered grandstand.

Faust would be Reinhardt's last production in Salzburg, a festival he more that anyone had helped bring about after World War I. At the performance I attended, the Austrian Chancellor, Kurt von Schuschnigg, had dropped by unannounced and was given the seat reserved for the house doctor.

The evening performance opened with a dramatic prologue: floodlights revealed a row of angels standing on the high rocky cliff. Scene I followed as the lights swept down to Faust's room on the stage. Well into the play, a violent storm that had been threatening all afternoon brought the performance to a halt. Rain lashed the rocks as flashes of lightning threw into harsh relief the line of the Chancellor's security troops, who had replaced the angels on the cliff. The storm grew in intensity — it seemed as if the elements were out to destroy Austria, a portent of things to come in under six months. I often wondered what must have gone through the Chancellor's mind during that storm.

In 1974 I found out. I had sent the ex-Chancellor a portrait taken of him during that performance. In my letter I had referred to the dreadful storm. A courtly Austrian with old-world manners, von Schuschnigg took the trouble to reply in great detail.

"How strange to remember days when one looked considerably younger enjoying life, though it was not always very enjoyable.

"I remember very well the *Faust* performance in the *Felsenreitschule*, partly because it was an extremely well done production by Max Reinhardt, with stage arrangements by Clemens Holzmeister, with Paula Wessely, an excellent Gretchen, partly because in the days before we had quite some trouble to get a reliable hold on our Mephisto (Werner Krauss) who lived in Germany and needed a special exit permit from Mr Goebbels, partly also — an entirely unpolitical sideline — because Werner Krauss was not only an extraordinary actor, dedicated to Melpomene, but also in an unpredict-able way dedicated to Bacchus. However, as I remember, everything went well. I would guess the streaks of lightning revealed silhouettes of soldiers who could have come from the fire brigade or just 'cops' in festival outfit."

To my stupefaction, the ex-Chancellor, who longingly and in great detail remembered everything about that fateful evening, did not recall the soldiers who were guarding him against the kind of Nazi machinations that had led to his predecessor's murder and would bring about his own resigna-tion followed by years of imprisonment.

W. Somerset Maugham, Salzburg, 1937

Fedor Chaliapin, Salzburg, 1937

Eugene, Archduke of Austria, Salzburg, 1937

Lillian Gish leaving Czechoslovakia, 1938

Then came
the Nazis

Young Nazis, Vienna, 1938

The arrival of German troops in Vienna, 1938

Two members of the SS patrolling Vienna's streets, 1938

Units of the German army driving down the Ring at night, Vienna, 1938

Two women cheering the arrival of German troops, Vienna, 1938

Window of a Jewish-owned store, Vienna, 1938

Woman selling portraits of Hitler, Vienna, 1938

Vienna

"We feel something's happening in Austria," the cable read from New York. "Find out." I set off to do just that on Friday, March 11, 1938. Packing my dinner-jacket as a matter of course, I caught the Paris flight which made a connection with the Arlberg Express that got into Vienna on Saturday afternoon. At Le Bourget, I ran into Lady Brownlow, a friend of the Windsors whom I had photographed in Salzburg. "I'm off to London, what about you?" she called out.

"Vienna," I said and waved back, unaware that I had just bade farewell to my life as a society photographer.

The express was in the station when I joined Gilbert Comte and Marcel Rebière, the director and cameraman of *The March of Time,* who were on their way to shoot another in the documentary series for Time Inc.'s film company. Comte said he hoped he'd have time for the Brueghels, and remarked casually that he relied upon me to get him back to his wife should he be wounded in Vienna. Rebière was more down to earth. He had lost a finger on his right hand to an Austrian shell during World War I and lumped Austrians and Germans together as one distasteful bunch. For my part, I felt trapped and promised myself never to let this happen to me again.

A loud banging woke me up with a start. Groping for a light, I slowly realized where I was. The train had stopped. Funny this banging. Conductors on sleepers were usually courteous. I answered, "Yes, yes," before opening the door.

"We're in Innsbruck, Germany."

The Austrian conductor, so servile in Paris, now behaved with the truculence of a man whose homeland had grown from a population of six to 65 million overnight. "We Germans," he announced imperiously, "now want the return of Czechoslovakia's Sudetenland."

Innsbruck station was dripping with Nazi flags. "Austria is now a German province," M. Fernand de Brinon, a traveler on the express, told me. "The Wehrmacht crossed the Austrian border a few hours ago." M. de Brinon, the president of the Franco-German Association, appeared elated.

A plain-clothes man and two stormtroopers marched through the train making arrests as they went. In haste, I destroyed letters of introduction to Austrian government officials, most probably arrested by now. At a level-crossing outside Linz, our train held up a mechanized column, the first obstruction the Wehrmacht had encountered on its march across Austria.

When we got into the station at Vienna calm prevailed. Betrayed and abandoned, Austria had slumped into submission without a fight.

At the New Bristol Hotel, old-world Austria reappeared in the person of an elderly receptionist with sideburns. He greeted me in perfect English and regretted being unable to provide me with a room overlooking the Ring. They were all already booked, he said, and coughed. (Hitler's route into Vienna had already been mapped out, and every window on these streets was to be guarded.) He managed to give me a suite which faced the Opera House and offered an oblique view of the Ring.

Bob Best, The United Press's Vienna correspondent, dropped by to brief me. "Photographers now require a special permit to take pictures, and if I were you, I wouldn't apply for one. The Nazis hate *Life*, and if they catch you taking pictures without a permit, you'll be in serious trouble." So much for my choice.

We were both leaning over the balcony watching the dimly lit crowd below. The persistent chant, "*Deutschland Sieg Heil!*" was like the shrieking wind in a storm, and the thousands of outstretched arms in the Nazi salute the rolling foam of the waves. What made it all the more dramatic was that I had to go down into that seething mob and take pictures. "You'll need a guide who speaks English," Best said. "I've got just the person you need. He's a Jewish journalist."

"Under the circumstances," I said, "a Jewish interpreter is not ideal."

"At least he's someone you can trust," Best replied.

Loudspeakers hooked up to trees blared out, "*Achtung! Achtung!* Here is your Führer, Adolf Hitler." For the fifth or sixth time that day Hitler's voice came over the radio. When he was through, the Horst Wessel song was performed. Every arm in the crowd shot up in salute to the battle cry, "*Deutschland Sieg Heil!*"

"Well," I said to Rebière. "Let's go down and see what we can do."

General intoxication swept the public lining the sidewalks, standing on cars or perching on trees, as they waved small Nazi flags and cheered themselves hoarse watching the Austrian brown battalions march past. It was hard to believe that days before, when the Austrian Chancellor had defied Hitler and announced a plebiscite, the same throng had applauded the clenched fists of the parading socialists.

From among the crowd, a well-dressed elderly gentleman, his eyes red from crying, stopped me to ask what to expect from Anthony Eden, the British Foreign Secretary.

"Haven't you heard? Eden has resigned and France is without a government," I said. The old man raised his shoulders in helpless despair and hurried away.

By midnight the exhausted Viennese had fallen into bed. The city was deserted. Only the dutiful Hitler Youth drilled and a few solitary figures patrolled the streets. The German army units would not be in Vienna before morning.

It had been easy so far to remain inconspicuous among the ecstatic Austrians. No one had paid any attention to me when I took pictures. But the methodical Nazis would be another matter. I had to figure out how to take pictures without getting caught. My plan, if it worked, would allow me to get the pictures I wanted.

At seven the next morning, the first units of the Wehrmacht drove into Vienna and took over the military barracks evacuated by the Austrian army. Bob Best appeared with Ernst Klein, a surly character lugging a large press camera. There and then I made it clear: "I'll pay you what you normally earn, but I won't have you taking pictures and attracting attention to us." By then I had hired an aristocratic black Daimler limousine—the same one the Duke of Windsor had used. Two swastikas gave the car an official appearance as they fluttered from the mudguards. My chauffeur was in black livery. I was so conspicuous, I hoped to be mistaken for someone of sufficient importance that I'd have time to take my pictures—and get out before anyone asked me for credentials I did not have.

Feeling that the best strategy was to find out right away if this would work, I ordered the driver to honk the horn and drive to the palace where Kurt von Schuschnigg was held prisoner. On reaching the palace, I got out of the car, photographed the Austrian youths on duty at the gate, and the SS leaning from the first floor windows. The moment I felt that their curiosity was turning into interest, I sauntered back to the limousine and told the chauffeur to step on it. We drove around the city as I took pictures of the German army in Viennese settings, frequently shooting from the car. In this way, I got a picture of three senior Austrian officers as they left the Ministry of War, totally ignoring the German officers who had just pulled up and were about to enter the building. It looked to me like the changing of the guard.

By late morning, I had made the decision to air-express my films to London for safety's sake. I wouldn't mail them via friendly Czechoslovakia, which I expected the Nazis would watch, but via Berlin. No one, I thought, would check my packet when it left Vienna for Berlin. No one in Berlin would be suspicious of it going to London. (All my negatives arrived safely.)

Hitler entered Vienna on the afternoon of March 14. He stood next to the driver in his six-wheel Mercedes, head high, arm outstretched. I got pictures of him from my hotel balcony. The next day there was to be a military parade. That's when I got nabbed.

I had spent the morning on the roof of a building I recall as the Museum of Natural History. From there I got a general view of the city sweeping down from the war memorial to St Stephen's Cathedral in the distance and, more interesting, the German armor lined up for that afternoon's parade seven floors below.

On my return I found some changes had taken place at the New Bristol. A sentry stood at the revolving door. The reception staff had been replaced by SS, who had also taken over the switchboard. A stormtrooper stood at the foot of the stairs, while another rode up in the elevator with me. On each landing two more SS sat in armchairs, their pistols resting on a table. On my way to my room I ran into yet another stormtrooper patrolling the floor, throwing doors open and peering in.

I went straight to my exposed films. This was obviously no place to leave negatives lying around. As soon as I could manage to leave the hotel again without raising suspicion, as planned, I air-expressed them to London. Then, unthinkingly, I slipped the waybill into my pocket and returned to the New Bristol in time to greet the correspondents who had come to watch Hitler's parade from my balcony.

The Viennese, ordered into the streets to provide huge crowds for the German newsreels, had been there for hours, jammed against trucks full of the party faithful which served as dikes to keep the mass of people under

Austrian officers leaving the Ministry of War, Vienna, 1938

control. Hitler drove by so fast that only those in the front rows caught sight of him. I was eating a sandwich and idly watching a solitary photographer taking pictures from atop a limousine. He won't get anything from where he's standing, I thought until, horrified, I recognized the photographer. It was Klein, and the limousine was mine. Angrily, I shouted at him, rushed downstairs, but arrived too late. Three stormtroopers were hauling him down while he frantically pointed up to my window. I ran back to warn everybody we could expect visitors. A few minutes later, the door flew open and Klein was tossed into the room as he pointed to me and screamed, "I work for him!" Everyone was asked for his credentials. "Don't worry," Best told me before leaving. "I'll notify the American consulate."

Comte, Rebière and I remained behind, with Klein huddled in a corner. I simply could not figure out his behavior. Why did he get us all arrested? He surely knew that would attract their attention. So, why did he do it?

Hoping to get rid of our guards before they got on the phone and set the legal machinery in motion, I asked why we were being detained. A volley of abuse about the *Schweinerei* of the foreign press greeted my question. In an attempt to pacify them, I produced my cable from New York which read, "Get scenes of wild joy in Vienna." This was having some effect when Klein started to insult them. That settled it. One of the troopers got on the phone and described us as "four Jews". Rebière, on hearing this, unzipped his pants, whipped out his uncircumcised penis and demanded, "Call this kosher?" It took the stormtroopers by surprise and almost gave him time to reach the bathroom and flush his trade union card down the toilet, before a stormtrooper flung open the door to watch him.

"Why?" I demanded.

"He might try to dispose of some documents."

"Why don't you search us then?"

"Because you're not under arrest."

"Then we are free."

"No. Because you are under observation."

I knew I was in trouble. The question was, how much? All the Nazis would have on me were a couple of shots of Hitler driving past, unless they found the waybill for the films I had sent. And there was the map I had bought at a bookshop shortly before it went out of circulation. It showed the German aspirations: two thirds of Switzerland, most of French Alsace Lorraine, the Czech Sudetenland, the Polish Corridor, parts of Italy along with dribs and drabs of the Soviet Union, thus adding 15 million more Germans to the Third Reich. Convinced that *Life* would be interested in this, I had tucked it away inside the dress shirt of my dinner-jacket, which I had brought along out of old-fashioned ideas about an Austria which no longer existed.

To my great surprise, having been terrified something like this might happen, I now found myself angry, as I reasoned that I was not worth the row it would create in the international press should anything happen to me. I looked at my watch. In half an hour my films would be leaving Vienna. With a bit of luck, they would be out of harm's way if the Nazis did not find my receipt.

Rebière returned to the bathroom, and again the trooper jumped up to watch him. Time dragged on. Rebière kept going to the bathroom and the stormtrooper, finally weary of jumping up, let Rebière out of his sight once. When he reappeared he told me he felt "much better", having finally flushed away his trade-union card. This made me regret I had not thought of this to dispose of my waybill.

Finally, at about the time the films should be reaching Berlin, two SS appeared and took over from the stormtroopers.

"How many pictures have you taken?" one SS asked me.

"Several of the Führer, but your friends came after that."

"Anything else?"

"Nothing else," I said, praying I would not be searched.

"Good thing. You have no authorization to take pictures."

At this point, two American consular officials arrived dressed like seconds for a duel. They demanded to know why we were being detained, and announced they would take this up with the authorities. I thought this extremely generous on their part considering that my only link with the United States at the time was an uncle, an aunt, some cousins, and an employer.

In a quandry over what to do with us, the SS called the Gestapo. That was when Klein screamed, "Admit you're wrong and let me go!" We were ordered to gather up our films and follow them.

"Where are you taking us?" I asked.

The SS shrugged. Under the curious stares of the hotel guests, we were marched across the lobby. A bellhop handed me a wire from my office: ADVISE IMMEDIATELY IF ANY MORE MATERIAL DUE PICKUP CROYDON AIRPORT AS QUEEN MARY SAILING DEADLINE SEVEN AYEM TO-MORROW. As the SS paid no attention to my cable, I asked if they minded my sending one. They most certainly did. The films would be at Croydon in time, but there would be no one to pick them up; they would miss the ship and the issue.

Our police car was held up by a human barrier. One SS stood on the running-board bellowing "*Platzmachen!*" as we slowly drove through the throng. The car might easily have been crushed like an eggshell. We reached a large, very old building and were marched through moldy halls and chilly corridors. Passing an open door, I saw several hundred naked men lined up with their arms raised while stormtroopers searched their clothes. "Think we'll catch cold?" I asked Rebière, who glared at me.

We were left in a crowded anteroom before being led into an office where an official in uniform studied our passports, kept our films, and told us we could leave. This struck me as much ado about nothing and I asked, "What about my interpreter?"

The official shrugged. "He's a German now. Why worry about him?"

In spite of what he had done, I could not help worrying, at the thought of the long line of naked men. In the street, I gave a sigh of relief and hurried off to cable London that my films were on their way.

During the next two days, I photographed Vienna's steady Nazification. Then, no longer trusting the air service, I knew the time had come for me to get out, and take my films with me.

I booked a reservation aboard the *Mitropa*, which crossed the border during the night when customs officials were usually less vigilant. Leaving my unexposed films behind, I slipped the three rolls I had shot in an envelope and boarded the train. My bunk was the upper one in the compartment. In the lower was a heavy-set man who had been hailed by a large gathering at the station. I was traveling with a Nazi of some importance.

Getting into bed, I slipped the films into my pajama pocket and lay back wondering what to do with them, until I realized I had been gazing at my traveling companion's heavy overcoat. "Why not?" I thought to myself. "He's far less likely to be frisked than I am." I turned my light out and settled back, listening to the man below rumple through newspapers until he finally switched off his light. Now I waited until his heavy breathing turned into a snore. Leaning over, I fished around for his overcoat, found the pocket, and dropped my films into it.

We were awakened by the customs officials. They diffidently saluted my traveling companion and made a thorough search of my suitcase. As they respected the seal I had stuck back on the wrapper of my dress shirt, they did not find the map. They examined my cameras carefully but, as I had no film, said nothing. Finally they moved into the next compartment and we returned to our beds. Now I had to make sure not to fall asleep and wake up to find my traveling companion wearing his overcoat. He took a long time to go back to sleep. Finally he did. I leaned way out of my bunk, my fingers searching for his overcoat. When they found it they patted their way to the pocket and slowly sank into it. This was more delicate than dropping the films in. Down went my hand. I grabbed a handkerchief, let it go. I found my films and started pulling them out. The train was rocking violently and my arm was swaying in the overcoat pocket. I felt nervous and my hand was clammy. Suddenly the compartment was flooded with light. Instinctively I threw myself back and whacked my head against the partition. Just as suddenly, it was dark again. We had just passed a lit-up wayside station. As our window shades were up, it had cast a glare into our compartment. In the berth below, my companion gave a groan and turned over.

Several months later I learned that through Bob Best's efforts, the Governor of Pennsylvania, George Howard Earle, on a visit to Vienna, had been informed about Klein's case and miraculously obtained his release from a concentration camp. The next news about Klein was that he was in the States—a victim of Nazis oppression. After failing to hold *Life* responsible for his arrest, he made demands upon Justice Felix Frankfurter, on the strength of having been in the same camp as relatives of a member of the Supreme Court.

After Germany declared war on the US an exchange of journalists took place. To the stupefaction of those who knew him, Bob Best decided to remain in Vienna. He became an American traitor, broadcasting scurrilous attacks on his own country and vilifying American Jewry. (Captured after the war, Best joined the poet Ezra Pound, his more talented Italian counterpart, in an asylum.)

Best's defection left me even more puzzled about Klein. Why had Best, the anti-Semite, helped an Austrian Jew reach the United States? Back in New York, a friend of mine in Time Inc. told me that the FBI had expressed interest in Klein's activities during the war. An agent had produced pictures taken by Klein and asked for an expert opinion of his work. Alfred Eisenstaedt, the *Life* photographer, examined the prints. He felt that the pictures had been taken by someone who had no interest in what he photographed. This apparently satisfied the agent.

I never heard of Ernst Klein again. To this day I'm of two minds. Was Bob Best acting in good faith when he produced Klein as an interpreter? Was he genuinely trying to help this inept character with a genius for getting himself and others into serious trouble? If so, it required the most extraordinary series of coincidences for everything to turn out the way it did. Or, was Bob Best already a traitor who had set us up to get a Nazi agent into the States? If so, Klein's successful cover had been presenting himself as a Jewish victim of the Nazis. I had taken it for granted that he was Jewish on Best's say so—a pretty unreliable source as it turned out.

Window of a coffee house, Vienna, 1938

Warsaw Ghetto, 1938

Two men in the Ghetto, Warsaw, 1938

Three sisters in the Ghetto, Warsaw, 1938

Warsaw Ghetto, 1938

Poland

"You'll never get a visa," Gilbert Redfern, *Life*'s Warsaw stringer, said over the phone. "The Polish government hates the press, and if you manage to get a visa, you won't be allowed to photograph the subjects *Life* expects."

"Your friends are pretty snotty," I said.

"Right," Redfern agreed.

"I'd better out-snot them," I decided, "if I want to get my visa."

Before setting off for the Polish consulate in Prague, I exchanged ten 100 Czech *kronen* bills for the unwieldy 1,000 *kronen* bill usually reserved for major transactions. Jauntily, I demanded to see the consul, ignoring the line patiently waiting. Ushered right in, I tossed my British passport on the consul's desk announcing, "I'm a gentleman of leisure. I plan to visit Poland as I'm told you're a horse-loving country." On this I produced my 1,000 *kronen* bill. Although it caused some trouble getting the proper change, it established the persona I claimed to be. I got my visa.

As matters turned out, I could not have landed in Warsaw at a better time. The Polish government only maintained itself through a formidable police force—with over 50 per cent of the population favoring the exiled opposition—and was eager to improve its image. Its reputation, unfortunately, could hardly have been at a lower ebb. France, historically Poland's ally, suspected the Polish Foreign Minister, Colonel Beck, of having sold French military secrets to Germany while he was the Polish Military Attaché in Paris. Although Beck represented a very Catholic country, the Pope had not granted him a private audience during Beck's state visit to Italy. Contributions from Polish Americans, once an important factor in the economy, had dwindled to a trickle because of the treatment of the Jews.

What made me so appealing to Polish officialdom was *Life,* with its huge circulation and very considerable influence. Besides, I was very young and appeared harmless enough. This might not have been sufficient, however, had not fate intervened in the person of Ambassador Anthony J. Drexel Biddle Jr. The American Ambassador was extremely popular in Warsaw. Whenever he drove around the city, people recognized his car, which, because of its color, they called "the Cream Puff". They also knew that his ancient Great Dane, "Okay", suffered from rheumatism and was carried up the two flights of stairs to his couch by the Ambassador himself. Biddle entertained a great deal, which appealed to the Poles. Whenever a foreign correspondent came through Warsaw, the Ambassador arranged a lunch to acquaint them with Polish officials. As the only *Life* representative around, I got invited, and met a member of the Foreign Office. Lunching with him made things considerably more cosy than a more formal meeting at his office. He was very suspicious about the press, and you could hardly blame him, since his boss was routinely referred to in the foreign papers as "Josef Beck and his fascist clique".

To reassure my diplomat that I really was the naive person he hoped I was, I had to overcome his dislike and convince him to allow me to photograph the three leading cabinet members. (I never mentioned that *Life* also wanted me to photograph the Opposition leaders, the Warsaw Ghetto, the German minority, and the Soviet border, since that would have got me expelled at once.) I demonstrated to him that I was not one of those hated press photographers by proposing "camera interviews", a term I coined on the spot, and explained as "symbolic portraiture". That went down well. I nevertheless was expected to submit to the Foreign Office's censorship program. I must not photograph anything the government deemed prejudicial. This meant no contact with the Opposition, especially Paderewski, the aged patriot and world-famous pianist living in exile, on the grounds it "would offend Colonel Beck".

With no intention of observing these demands, I consulted with Redfern about getting the pictures *Life* expected. He told me he had contacts more than willing to help me get the story out.

The general air of secrecy affected everybody, even foreigners. At a reception, the British Military Attaché's wife sidled up to me and half-whispered, "Good show". When I looked blank, she hissed, *"We know all about you and the map."* She was talking about the map I had smuggled out of Austria which *Life* had run as a double-page spread.

My first "camera interview", according to protocol, was with the President, Móscicki. He granted me 15 minutes. As an added favor I was given a tour of the royal palace: the Zamek. Being a presidential guest, I was not required to wear the usual protective overshoes and left a hideous trail of footprints along the highly polished parquet floors.

Before I could get around to my next portrait, the Marshal of Poland, a new name was added to my list: General Slawoj Skladkowski.

"Who's Skladkowski?" I asked.

"The Prime Minister," the press chief said. "Protocol demands that you take his picture."

"Don't waste time on him. He's a figure-head," Redfern said.

The Prime Minister, however, was insistent. In the five minutes allocated to me, he also demanded a full-length portrait.

At first sight, Skladkowski could have been mistaken for his mentor, Joseph Pilsudski, who had regained Poland's independence in 1918, but the resemblance went no further than his bushy eyebrows. Pilsudski had been both head of state and head of the army. In 1926 he had overthrown the legitimate government, declared himself Minister of Defence, and virtually ruled Poland until his death in 1935. Skladkowski was one of a bunch of generals Pilsudski brought with him after the coup, who had taken up the running of the country after his death.

When I got round to the Marshal, Smigly-Ridz, I was told, "Marshal is very busy". I would be allowed only two pictures. I found a mild-mannered man with a pleasant smile, immaculate in uniform with the fragrance of after-shave lotion lingering about him. Painting was his hobby—a fact which irked many Poles who preferred their Marshals tough like Pilsudkski.

But Josef Beck was the *pièce de résistance*. I was escorted to his home behind the Foreign Office by an obsequious secretary in a cut-away jacket. I was less formally dressed, having declined Ambassador Biddle's friendly loan of his morning-suit for the occasion. Beck was gaunt and smoothly dia-bolical, with his oblong head, receding hair, bushy eyebrows, a monocle in his right eye, and a crooked smile. After a *demi-tasse* and small talk, he led me into his modernistic study. There, prominently displayed, was an auto-graphed portrait of Adolf Hitler.

Beck, aware that I was trying to photograph him next to Hitler's por-trait, deftly stepped away. Before I left, he fingered my lapel as he chatted, and without changing his tone told me that I'd be very sorry if I did not make "proper use" of his pictures.

My anxiety was not dispelled when I got an urgent call from Gilbert Redfern. He had received the latest issue of *Life*, which featured a story on the history of the Jews. Poland's contribution was a gruesome pogrom.

"You're lucky that *Life* isn't on sale in Warsaw," Redfern said. "If Beck sees this issue, you'll be in trouble."

"The Foreign Office expects to send my negatives of the cabinet members to London by diplomatic pouch. If I don't produce them, they'll be suspicious," I sighed.

"If you do and they see *Life*, you can kiss goodbye to your work," Redfern concluded. The next morning I turned over four rolls of film to be sent via diplomatic pouch. There were no repercussions except from my lab, which notified me to have my camera checked as all the films were blank. I had sent four unexposed films via the Foreign Office, and kept the material I had shot with me.

A few days after my picture session with Colonel Beck, Ambassador Biddle went to the Foreign Office to lodge a complaint from the State Department. He had only requested a 15-minute slot, which in diplomatic tradition meant that the content of the interview would be brief and unpleasant. After greeting the Ambassador, Beck raved about my work for the full time allotted. Biddle never got a word in, apparently unaware that Beck had used me as an excuse to dodge whatever complaint was on its way. He generously wrote to Henry Luce, *Life*'s founder, to report how I'd impressed Colonel Beck. This came in very useful after the Polish Ambassador in Washington, on instructions from the Foreign Office, traveled to New York to complain about me to Henry Luce personally when *Life* ran the Polish story.

I now set out to get pictures of the Polish-Soviet border. I obtained permission by promising to illustrate how this tangle of barbed wire that stretched the entire length of the border contained the Soviets in the East and would gain the Poles popularity in the West.

I was taken to Kolosovo by a lieutenant in the KOP, the special border force. This was where the Nord Express, which linked Moscow to Paris via Warsaw, entered Poland. "From our observation tower," the lieutenant said, "you can see the Russians. Since we have an agreement that no photographs can be taken of the border, please hide your camera until you're out of their sight. Though as far as we're concerned, you can take all the pictures you like from here."

The border ran between the Russian barracks made of wood and painted green and the Polish observation tower. The Nord Express entered

Poland through an archway inscribed "Hail to the workers of the West." On either side of the border posts, the sentries ignored each other.

"Do they ever exchange good morning greetings?" I asked. The Polish officer stared at me as if I'd gone mad. "Certainly not. Some years ago the Russians smoked on duty and offered our men cigarettes. They naturally refused. The Russians simply did that to annoy us." Just to make sure no communication was possible, both sides set up outposts manned by troops which patrolled the zone night and day.

While we waited for the Nord Express to arrive, a forest fire broke out on the Soviet side. The Russian garrison dashed into the forest with spades and shovels to dig trenches. This struck the Poles as screamingly funny. "Aren't you amused?" the lieutenant asked. "Why no," I replied. "The wind's blowing our way." Leaving a trail of white smoke, the Nord Express thundered across the forest. After stopping on the Russian side, the locomotive let out a belch of smoke and entered Poland. I then took the picture I had been waiting for.

At lunchtime, the lieutenant took me to a block post where a sumptuous meal had been prepared by the commandant's sister. "We enjoy having guests," the commandant said. "It's an excuse for a party. It breaks the monotony of life here."

It was indeed a party. We not only freely sampled the vodka, but indulged in bottles of Tokay wine the commandant had brought back from his holiday in Hungary. Feeling exhilarated and somewhat unsteady on my feet, I set off with the border patrol, made up of three soldiers and a German shepherd dog. Standing alongside the Polish side of the barbed-wire fence, I decided to shoot the Polish border patrol from Russia. "Why not?" the commandant said. Laughing, we crawled through the tangled wire and stood in front of the Soviet signpost with the hammer and sickle. Noticing that the commandant had drawn his pistol, I said, "Trying to make it look exciting?"

"There might have been a Russian patrol around."

"And had there been?" I asked foolishly.

"Border incident," he said laconically. "The Russians shoot without warning." My head cleared and I dived through the barbed wire back into Poland.

On our way back, the commandant confided that he was expecting another visitor the following day. The Nazi Gauleiter for Danzig had asked to see "the Bolshevik swine in his pigsty". That Poles played host to a Nazi did not imply they either liked or toadied to the Germans. Poles don't toady.

In Poznan, I was to find out how the Poles really felt about the Germans. I managed to reach this city in the Polish Corridor through subterfuge. Two embassy officials and their wives were making an inspection tour and I asked for a ride. I then shook off my official guides with the explanation I was interested in the scenic beauty of Poland. This enabled me to stop off and photograph an Opposition general on his farm.

As luck would have it, we drove into Poznan on the eve of a German rally. We were having a drink before dinner when one of my embassy friends offered me a cigarette. (At that time I hadn't smoked for five months and had got out of the habit.) Without thinking, I took a Camel and smoked it. Of all the things that could possibly happen to me at that time, smoking seemed the least harmful to my health. (That one cigarette led me to smoke for 30 years.)

The next day, when I asked the hotel doorman how to get to the German rally, he looked blank.

"What rally?" he asked.

"The one at the circus."

"What circus?"

I got the same reply from every Pole I met. Fortunately, I ran into a German only too happy to direct me. The area around the circus was cordoned off by a grim-looking police force. Inside I found a group of Germans—dressed in the same uniform as their counterparts in Czechoslovakia: white shirts, black breeches, and jackboots—seated around the circus ring. The band's shiny brass instruments were neatly stacked up in the center. "Can you imagine?" my guide complained. "The police have forbidden us to play the German national anthem."

The speakers' platform was across the ring from where I stood. As a backdrop, there was an insignia that came as close to a swastika as was legal. Above it hung a streamer: "Make Way For German Labor". Speaker after speaker incited the audience to sedition while warning them to be orderly on leaving the circus. They suspected the police would gladly contribute a few more martyrs to the Nazi cause. Back at the hotel, I called Redfern to fill him in on the rally. Leaving the phone booth, I ran into a smiling hotel porter. "Why didn't you tell me you were a journalist. I could have been very helpful."

"How did you know I'm with the press?" I asked.

"I listened in to your call, and liked what you said."

Spying on people, Redfern told me, was a local custom.

I was not to escape it. The official guides provided by the Foreign Office to make sure I did not get wrong impressions pretended to be journalists, while in fact they were government functionaries. One in particular had an unorthodox approach to his work. Early one Sunday morning he picked me up in his small Italian car to drive me and his wife to a town where the peasants went to church in national costume. We had just driven past a village when we caught sight of an elderly Jew in his flowing black coat. He was walking on the left-hand side of the road. As we approached him, I felt the car lurch clear across the road. We sideswiped the old man with the bumper and sent him into the ditch head first.

"Did you skid?" I asked, and before he could answer I realized we were driving on. "You aren't stopping?" I asked.

"To be stoned by those lousy Jews?" he replied. It was only then I realized that he had done it on purpose. I stared at his wife who was casually smoking her cigarette, then back at him. My lips were trembling, I was so angry. The only thing that saved him was that I had more pictures to take before I was willing to risk expulsion.

Guided by a Jewish contact in Warsaw, I sneaked into the Ghetto. At first, no one paid any attention to me as I photographed street scenes and the small booths with their gaudy painted signs advertising their wares. As I moved around, I eventually became aware that I was being followed by a crowd which steadily increased in both size and hostility. For a moment it looked as though there might be a reversal of roles, with a gentile getting beaten up by Jews in the Ghetto. The problem was that a few weeks previously, a German photographer had been there taking pictures for a Nazi paper. What got me out of trouble was my Jewish contact, who shouted in Yiddish, "He's an American!"

I nearly got into much more serious trouble at Marki. I had gone there with a reporter who worked for a pro-government paper, while he himself belonged to the Opposition. Marki was a spectacular example of the hovels many Poles lived in. I was photographing a particularly dreary shack made from gasoline cans, loose bricks, sacking and wood when the local police chief descended on us. His superiority crumbled on learning that the reporter worked for a government paper. Under the impression that he was being investigated, he went to great lengths to assure us that he had not misappropriated any of the relief funds. Although his conscience was clear, he pleaded that my pictures not be published in Warsaw. He sighed with relief as we left. "Thank God you didn't open your mouth," the reporter also sighed. "He mistook you for a Polish photographer. Otherwise we'd have been in a nice fix."

I made contact with General Wladyslav Sikorski through a friend of his. Sikorski had been a prime mover in the Soviets' defeat at the 1920 Battle of Warsaw, which brought Russia's Western expansion to a halt. Too good a soldier for Pilsudski's ego, and too democratic for his taste, Sikorski was sidelined after the coup that brought Pilsudski to power. The method was both ingenious and economical. Sikorski was put on the semi-retired army list. He only received half-pay, and was prohibited from making political statements.

"You'll find Sikorski very European," I'd been told. He certainly was not the martial type, and might well have been a Frenchman in civilian clothes. The walls of his study were covered with autographed pictures of the leading generals of the last war. "Aren't you bored to tears?" I asked him when he told me he had nothing to do. "Your question is impertinent," he replied, "but the answer is yes." After taking his picture, he promised to send me an address where I could reach Witos and Korfanty, the other two Opposition leaders, exiled in Czechoslovakia.

Having met Poland's most distinguished soldier, I now had the opportunity to get an idea of its army since he had been retired. Warsaw's annual military parade attracted huge crowds. Only a loosely drawn rope kept the spectators from overflowing on to the parade grounds. I had been warned that I might get beaten up. "Nothing personal, really, but the crowd does get out of hand and must be kept in line." Taking heed of this advice, I retired to the top of a newsreel truck. The moment the parade started, the crowd surged forward and the police, having taken no preventitive measures, merely drew their truncheons and clubbed people back into line.

I was even more startled by the military equipment. It was so old-fashioned, with its cavalrymen armed with lances, infantry on bicycles and obsolete planes, that two of my pictures accidentally wound up in a World War I exhibition. (Whenever conversation turned to the possibility of war, nothing would convince a Pole that their famous cavalry could not destroy Germany's tanks on their triumphal march to Berlin.)

Several days after the parade, I was hurrying to the Europeski restaurant to keep a dinner date with a Foreign Office official and ran into General Sikorski. To my great embarrassment, he stopped me.

"I'm very sorry," I stammered, "but I have an appointment with a member of the Foreign Office."

"I understand, I won't detain you," Sikorski said, handing me the Prague address he had promised before walking away smiling.

It led me to Wojciech Korfanty. Through Korfanty, I would meet Wincenty Witos, the Prime Minister of the Peasant Government Pilsudski overthrew in 1926. Twelve years later, Witos was still regarded as the country's legitimate leader with the 20 million peasants he controlled (roughly 57 per cent of the population with the addition of two million socialists).

Korfanty, whose political career went back to the Versailles Peace Treaty after World War I, had a talent for innuendo. "Mr Witos lives near the Polish border," Korfanty told me. "I plan to visit him on the 20th. You can come with me if you wish."

We agreed to meet at Prague station on May 20. There I found Korfanty extremely agitated, which was not in character. He led me to the coach we were to travel in and somewhat dramatically flung open the carriage door. A man was sitting in the compartment. He was looking out of the window and was dressed like a peasant with his trousers tucked into a pair of high black boots. He looked around. A prominent nose protruding from under a felt hat pulled down over the eyes first attracted my attention. Then the shaggy moustache. I didn't need Korfanty's introduction to recognize Wincenty Witos. "Mr Witos came to Prague unexpectedly," Korfanty explained acting as an interpreter, "at the urgent request of Mr Milan Hodza."

If the Czech Prime Minister finds time for a Polish exile at a time like this, something pretty serious must be up, I thought.

"Mr Hodza," Korfanty went on, "was anxious to find out what were the chances of a Polish uprising led by Mr Witos if Germany invades Czechoslovakia tomorrow."

"Tomorrow?" I exclaimed. The arrival of the conductor interrupted Korfanty. All three of us, I noticed, had government passes. "It's as bad as that?" I said, after the conductor had left. "The Czech government suspects Hitler is massing additional troops on the border in readiness for the invasion," Korfanty concluded.

We traveled in silence, lost in our own thoughts. I wondered whether I'd be returning to Poland in the next few days under totally different circumstances. Looking at Witos, who had the peasants' solidarity and 20 million followers, I wondered where this down-to-earth Don Quixote might lead me.

On arrival, we went straight to Witos's small house which was surrounded by a field. There he and Korfanty closeted themselves for hours. With nothing to do, I sat in the field and waited—an important feature of a photographer's life. Finally, Korfanty joined me. He said that the French government was ready to mobilize if Germany invaded the Sudetenland. The British, for their part, had been less evasive than usual regarding their neutrality. Sitting in the field Korfanty went over Hitler's interest in the Sudetenland: control of the Bohemian basin with its strategic value, its industrial wealth and source of raw materials, with an additional three million Germans. This reminded Korfanty of a passing remark the British Prime Minister David Lloyd George had made to him at Versailles in connection with an act of injustice inflicted upon a small country.

"You must remember this Korfanty," Lloyd George had said. "It's a sad fate to be a small fish in the Mediterranean and a small country in Eastern Europe."

The government had decreed partial mobilization, and we watched units of the Czech army drive past that evening. But there was no German invasion. I returned to London.

To this day, no one knows who started the rumor of the German invasion on May 20. It is now known that Germany's final military plans for the invasion of the Sudetenland had been submitted to Hitler that week. Enraged at being falsely accused of invading Czechoslovakia, and humiliated by Benes, the Czech President, Hitler summoned his generals on the 28th and announced his decision to settle the Sudeten question once and for all by October 1.

Polish cavalry, Warsaw, 1938

Polish tank, Warsaw, 1938

Maneuvers, Warsaw, 1938

Chamberlain leaving for Munich, London, 1938

Destination Munich

I was in London, strolling along the Strand shortly before midnight, the time when it's still today and yet already tomorrow and the early-morning editions are out, when I came upon the headline: "CHAMBERLAIN FLYING TO HITLER."

I stood and gaped. Until then, the flying visit had been confined to dictators. Now the habit had spread to Prime Minister Neville Chamberlain, a man who, in the caustic words of Lord Birkenhead, "would have made a good Lord Mayor of Birmingham in a lean year".

This momentous announcement had been withheld until after the evening news. By the time the public heard about the trip, Chamberlain would be well on his way. The reason given was the belief that Hitler's evil entourage was preventing the German Chancellor from appreciating the gravity of the situation. Mr Chamberlain was going to set him straight.

I drove to the airport with a sense of foreboding. There I found about 30 reporters along with a few onlookers and a handful of policemen.

For his historic journey, Chamberlain chose to fly in an American-built twin-engine DC-2 that belonged to British Airways, an independent airline. This may have been because the state-subsidized Imperial Airways had already been lampooned by the Nazis, who had fastened a birdcage to the tail of one of their unwieldy planes.

British Airways took full advantage of the photo-opportunity. Their plane was carefully placed so that "British Airways" above the cabin door stood out clearly in the morning rays when the press photographed the PM's departure.

Chamberlain arrived in an open car, from which he scrambled to greet the German Chargé d'Affaires. I had the dubious privilege of hearing the German diplomat tell the British Prime Minister of his delight that Mr Chamberlain would now finally realize just how much the German people adored him.

Unfortunately, the plane door was low and the Prime Minister was forced to duck inside. Chamberlain turned and blinked out at us. A voice shouted, "Don't appease Hitler!" Its owner was promptly led off the field.

Chamberlain worked his way further out of the plane. Drawing himself up, he cleared his throat and his Adam's apple bobbed between the wings of his butterfly collar.

"I am flying to see the German Chancellor," he announced.

"Fly to Prague and see Benes!" another heckler shouted, as he too was led away. Chamberlain ignored the interruption and completed his brief homily. He waved his hat before struggling back into the plane. Although he had brought Lord Halifax with him, he left his Foreign Secretary behind at the airport. He intended to tackle Herr Hitler single-handed.

The plane slowly wheeled around and trundled down the field as the Prime Minister waved. Gathering speed, it rose slowly as it swept past us. Everybody removed his hat.

Chamberlain entering the plane for Munich, London, 1938

Nazi propaganda in a Sudeten German shop window, Czechoslovakia, 1938

Czech army leaders, 1938

Nazi decoration at a Sudeten German house, Czechoslovakia, 1938

Czechoslovakia

I met George, the son of Alphonse Mucha, the famous Art Nouveau painter and illustrator, at the time he became a censor. At Munich, Hitler's claims to Czech Sudetenland had been recognised. President Benes had resigned and left Czechoslovakia, and German armies were ready to move in. An unsuspecting population, still unaware of the outcome of this four-power meeting (between France, Britain, Germany and Italy), waited to learn its fate; security measures, such as censorship, were put into effect. I paid the censor a visit—and met George.

Photographic censorship, created overnight, operated from an abandoned wing of the Wallenstein Palace in Prague. In a grand room of 17th-century proportions, sparsely furnished with a large table, a chair and an ink pad, a young man in well-worn tweeds lolled in the chair, twiddling what turned out to be a censor's stamp. "Welcome," he said in a better English accent than mine. "I'm George, the censor. You're the first person who's bothered to call on me."

Amiably he offered me his chair. "I must tell you at once that, as a poet, I disapprove of censorship. But as a Czech, I wanted to help my country and wound up with this job. You can see I was an optimist; I believed there would be war. Now we've got peace—and censorship. Don't you think this lends ridicule to our tragedy?"

"It's amazing," I told him. "You could pass easily for an Englishman, if you don't mind my saying so today."

George shrugged. "We Czechs are linguists. We have to be, since so few speak our language. Now what can I do for you?"

"I want to hire a car and drive to the Sudetenland and photograph it becoming German."

"Good. I'll come with you," George proposed, brightening up. "I can be very helpful," he added, juggling his stamp. "I know a castle where we can spend the night, I have plenty of gas coupons, and I'm a government official, which can be useful, too."

Normally no journalist would chose a censor as a traveling companion, but George seemed different. A friendly government official could come in handy for an Englishman like myself, who would not be popular when the Czechs found out what had happened at Munich. There was only one drawback. "Won't you be in trouble in the Sudetenland if the Germans catch on you're a Czech?" I asked.

"I can pass for English, you said so yourself." Unlike most of his compatriots who were short, stocky and moonfaced, George could well have been the arrogant Englishman he impersonated a few days later to get us out of trouble.

"Who is going to censor the pictures while you're away?" I asked.

George produced a key, made the gesture of turning it in the lock and winked.

That settled it. I was going to scoop everybody and accepted the invitation to the castle, the gas coupons, and George's unexpected company, as providential.

"Won't that create complications?" I asked, afraid the set-up was too good to be true.

"Complications!" George shrugged. "Don't you realize it's all over with Czechoslovakia? I'll be ready as soon as I've hidden this censor's stamp I'm responsible for."

We had trouble hiring a car. Finally George located a slow-witted chauffeur willing to drive us. There was, however, a slight problem he wanted to discuss first. Aware that he was our only chance, George never gave the driver an opportunity to explain. We drove down Prague's main thoroughfare as the loudspeakers announced to the stunned people the terms of the Czech capitulation. Men and women lined the sidewalks, tears rolling down their cheeks.

"We wanted to sing with the angels, but we must howl with the wolves," George said. "That's tomorrow's headline."

At the first bridge we discovered the problem which had troubled our driver—the water pump on his car leaked. "It's just as well that we found this simpleton," George said. "No Czech in his right mind would dream of making a trip to the Sudetenland."

Road blocks interrupted our route. The guards eagerly told us they were ready to fight. When they heard about the capitulation they were incredulous. Some cried, others said they had been betrayed. We drove in silence until George remarked quietly, "We always believed we belonged to the West. Now the West doesn't want us. I guess we will turn to the East—to Russia. What else is left for us?"

I didn't answer and sullenly stared at the road. The sun had set by the time we reached the Sudetenland, and immediately we ran into blackout difficulties. An irate Sudeten German drafted into the Czech home guard threatened to shoot out our bright headlights. "My orders," he growled.

"Save your loyalty for your new masters," George told him. The Sudeten was adamant. "Nobody's rescinded the orders!" So we doused our lights until we were out of his sight.

The high walls of George's castle looked eerie when we finally located them. When we banged on the gate, a soldier switched his flashlight on us. Most of the castle had been requisitioned by the Czech army. A sergeant led us through long hallways filled with sleeping men and up winding wooden stairs which creaked. Eventually he knocked on a door which was opened by a very stout woman in a dressing-gown and curlers. "Come in," she said, recognising George. The mistress of the castle was Swedish and also happened to be hysterical. "They won't stop until they reach Prague," she announced. "I'll have to seek refuge at the Swedish consulate,"

"Let's go," I whispered to George as her Czech husband limped in. He sank into an armchair and looked around the room which had belonged to his forefathers. "They will be here in a day or two," he said. "But they will not find me. They will turn this old house into a pigsty by their presence. Czechoslovakia will get this land back but not, unfortunately, in my life-time."

"Let's go," George agreed.

"When we got out he told me, "I'm hungry. I want to eat with Czechs. I simply couldn't stand to see Germans gloating tonight."

We found a small restaurant where a few customers were silently drinking beer. Our driver joined us. "I'm going to eat a great number of *knedliky*," he announced. A meal without dumplings was no meal at all. When the food arrived the driver peered like a child. There were no *knedliky*. He let out a long, pent-up howl. "First the Germans take our country away. Now we have no *knedliky*. What is happening to Czechoslovakia?"

His car broke down halfway up a hill, several miles from Plana, the nearest town. We waited for help in the night. The driver curled up on the seat and fell asleep, while George and I paced the road. "'In these few contradictions you have the whole of Czechoslovakia,'" George began to recite. "'It is a country old and yet new. Great, yet small. Highly civilized, yet very simple. It is beautiful but there are possibly places more so. It is rich but there are wealthier lands. It has a high level of culture but there are states with higher. Still there is perhaps no country in the world which displays such vital determination and capacity as this small nation which has held its own and will hold its own in Central Europe...' That's by Karel Capek," George concluded. "Let's get in the car, it's chilly."

When we heard the roar of a motorcycle, we ran out into the middle of the road. A Czech voice ordered us to raise our hands and identify ourselves. After a brief exchange, George dropped his hands. "The Germans have been ambushing our soldiers," he explained. "They weren't taking any chances." We stepped forward and I noticed that the soldier seated in the side-car held a hand grenade while several others rolled on his lap.

"They'll give me a lift to Plana, where I can find some help," George told me, as he climbed on the pillion seat.

Hours later George returned with a sullen Sudeten, the only mechanic in town.

"How did you manage it?" I asked.

George chuckled. "I told him I was a stranded English gentleman, and I talked him into picking us up by saying it was the least he could do for an Englishman after all Mr Chamberlain's generosity."

Nothing, however, not even the magic of Chamberlain's name, could induce the mechanic to tow our car back that night. He dropped us off at a hotel and promised to make the repairs the next morning.

He did not show up. We found him with his wife hanging garlands of swastikas. "It's unthinkable," she told George, "that my husband should repair a Czech car on a day such as this."

While George sought help from the Czech military commander, I went around taking pictures. Even before the Gestapo arrived, Nazi flags adorned balconies on the main square and the bookstores displayed copies of *Mein Kampf*. With the exception of the garrison, which was moving that night, no Czechs remained in town.

I was on the main square when the local Nazi found me. On learning I was English, he was extremely cordial. He had just come out of hiding, he informed me. "I was afraid the Czech criminals would shoot me." To illustrate his sentiments he took me to the station and led me to the station master's room. This official had left in a hurry. Most of his belongings lay on the floor. Another Nazi was scattering obscene postcards around. When he was through, a photographer took a picture of the room.

"It's for the German papers," my guide explained.

Back at the hotel he beamed at George, whom he mistook for an Englishman. Our driver got a dirty look. I asked if he could find a car. "Nothing easier," he said.

"What about our driver?" I asked George. "You saw the look the Nazi gave him."

"Poor chap," George agreed. "If we don't help him, he'll be murdered."

We escorted our driver over to the army barracks. There George arranged with the Czech commandant to evacuate him and his car with the troops. While we were there, the phone rang. Hanging up the receiver, the commandant stared at his boots.

"Pilsen has just issued orders to blow up our fortifications," he said.

"Tell him to let me take pictures before," I said to George.

"The commandant says it's impossible," George translated. "These fortifications are very secret."

"They'll soon be reduced to rubble," I protested. "Why not show the world you were prepared?"

George sighed. "Red tape. The country's already going to pot."

The Nazi not only produced a car, but found two elderly German women who wanted a lift part of the way.

"I guess we have to take them," George grumbled.

"We do hope you'll enjoy your visit to *our* country," they purred at him.

"*Don't*," I told him when I saw the look on his face.

We reached Karlsbad to find the Czech withdrawal practically completed. The last army truck was leaving that night. We decided to take it.

A small part of the town remained under Czech control. George and I went to a restaurant. The triumphant Germans were making merry, and we ate quickly. Taking a cab back to our truck, we had the satisfaction of finding one unhappy German. "Nobody came for the cure this year because of the political crisis. Our season was ruined," the cabby complained.

"Too bad," I said.

The last truck leaving Karlsbad before German occupation, Czechoslovakia, 1938

Our truck was loaded with barrels of gasoline which rocked, rolled and leaked. An old woman with her small grandson sat next to the driver. She had carried the child and a small suitcase 12 miles to catch the truck. A nondescript couple with their belongings, a bundle of rugs, and a basket full of glasses, sat huddled at the back—the last Czechs out of Karlsbad.

The driver handed George his automatic and told him to shoot if anybody tried to stop us, warning him also to keep an eye on the windows along our route. Germans had been tossing hand grenades from them when convoys passed. At the city limits we stopped just long enough for a small figure to leap out of the shadows and climb on the truck. I was surprised to find he was a Sudeten German. Immediately he produced his Social Democratic Party membership card. He had been through a rough time. The Nazi rabble-rousers were rounding up the last few anti-Nazi Germans. They had broken into his apartment before he heard about the capitulation. To escape them, he had thrown himself out of the second-storey window, hoping to be killed. Landing safely, he fled up the street. From hiding, he had managed to get a message to the Czechs to arrange the rendezvous he had just kept with our truck.

"When Hitler enters Karlsbad there won't be an anti-Nazi left," he said. "Those who can't escape will be murdered."

"Are there many anti-Nazis?" I asked.

He shook his head sadly. "If you want Sudeten Germans to be anti-Nazi, change Germany. They will always be what Germany is."

We had one alert when three figures sprang from a field. Luckily George realized it was a Czech patrol. Six hours later we drew up in front of a small hotel whose dining-room was brightly lit. The driver climbed out of his cab and stretched, grinning, We were back in Bohemia.

George made arrangements for a car to Prague. We took the German with us and ran into trouble at the first road block.

"No Germans," the guard said. "Nothing doing. We let them into our country once before and look what happened. No!"

"The Nazis want to kill him. We must help him escape," George explained to the guard. "He won't be a burden to the country because I'll put him up in my own house."

"No," said the guard.

"I understand how he feels," the German sadly agreed.

"Poor chap. If we can't sneak him in, he'll never survive," George said.

He finally succeeded in mollifying the guard.

"Thanks," the German said as we drove through the road block, "but I won't stay long and be a bother to you or anybody. I'm going to try and get into Russia. That's the only place left for me now!"

"Remember what I told you," George said.

The next morning George called me up. "Come over to my office," he said. "I can't censor your films at the hotel. It wouldn't look right, especially as I've lost that confounded stamp."

Some years after the war, I ran into George. "Did you ever find the censor's stamp?" I asked.

"No," he said. They planned to run me in for treason, but I sneaked off to London as the impresario of the Prague Philarmonic. When I got back, the treason charge was forgotten and only the bureaucracy remained. They fined me five *kronen* for the loss of government property.

Pro-Nazi women, Mercurea Sibiu, Romania, 1938

Peasant wedding, Transylvania, Romania, 1938

Romania

Mr Eugen Titianu was very upset by my presence in Bucharest. "How could *Life*," the Under-Secretary for Propaganda demanded, "commit such a breach of etiquette as to publish a story on Hungary before one on the kingdom of Romania, which has twice the population?" He glared distastefully at the heavily blue-penciled magazine he held before him, adding, "I'll tell you why. *Life* is in the clutches of the Hungarian nationalists."

The antagonism between the two countries wasn't new. It went back to the end of World War I, when Queen Marie of Romania had seduced the delegates at the peace treaty negotiations into allowing her to snatch up Transylvania from Hungary, Bessarabia from Russia, and Dobruga from Bulgaria, thus doubling the size of her own country. What amazed me was that 20 years later, *Life* would become embroiled in this controversy because of pictures taken by Margaret Bourke-White. New to Romania, I had much to learn.

Mr Titianu considered expelling me, but with such lack of conviction I suspected he was eager for a story in *Life* precisely because there had been one on Hungary. Nevertheless he appeared to have qualms. This was hardly surprising considering his country's reputation for turning corruption into a national vocation. As Tsar Nicholas II had neatly put it: "Romania is a profession not a nationality." It was a profession shared by Queen Marie, her son Carol the present ruler, and his flamboyant Titian-haired mistress, Magda Lupescu, with her genius for manipulation.

I was attempting to ingratiate myself with Mr Titianu when his presence was required at a censorship screening. I tagged along. It was a French picture, starring Danielle Darrieux, based on a novel by Princess Marthe Bibesco. The Princess was not only a member of a very aristocratic Romanian family, she was also a famous French author.

This tribute to Romanian letters had been highly touted in the press. The premiere promised to be the social event of the season. However, the screening ended in consternation. None of the officials had read the book. For Mr Titianu, as censor, the plot—which though set in Russia, dealt with a royal mistress and regicide—was disrespectful to the King. I was no longer his number-one headache. He turned me over to an underling with instructions to sound me out and produce a report.

Mr Dimonescu was heavy-set, furry, with a dark complexion, large hands and square fingers. Over caviar at Capsa, Bucharest's most exclusive restaurant, he made it clear that a favorable report on his part depended upon good will on mine. I easily convinced him by paying for lunch and handing him the receipt.

In the days Dimonescu prepared his report and made arrangements for our trip, I got to see Bucharest. The city was undergoing rapid expansion. Two wings were being added to the royal residence to emulate Buckingham Palace, and as it grew, it began to look like a hippopotamus among chickens. On the streets, great wealth and abject poverty went hand in hand. Barefoot urchins in rags ran along the palace sidewalk, while further along the street, flashy whores solicited wealthy passers-by. Packard taxis tore down one side of an avenue while a pair of oxen slowly hauled a cart up the other. It was also considered an immoral city—but it took its immorality at the leisurely pace, inherited from its ancient masters, the Turks.

The city was riddled with gossip, and nobody was above suspicion. Magda Lupescu was referred to in whispers as "She", and her erotic, political, and financial feats sped around the city. The fact that she was a cousin of the wife of Doctor Voronoff—famous for sexually rejuvenating the elderly with monkey glands—simply added zest to the conversation.

Even the late Orthodox Patriarch Miron Cristea did not escape slander. The Patriarch was lunching with a friend at his palace when the dining-room door flew open and a ravishing young woman bounced in and promptly bounced out on seeing that he was not alone. Smiling calmly, the 70-year old prelate remarked, "my niece from Transylvania".

Bucharest was also a haven for ingenious rackets. Underpaid postal clerks unstuck the postage stamps on outgoing mail and sold them at half price. Employees of small legations in charge of handling the diplomatic pouches destined for Paris would add one filled with caviar which was resold to French restaurants at impressive profits. But dealing in Bucharest required experience. Shortly after the Munich agreement, which left the country jittery, an American gas-mask salesman showed up. The Defense Ministry decided it was imperative that every Romanian citizen own one.

This meant formulating a law to make it compulsory. The amount it would require to pass the law was given to the salesman along with the expected mark-up. A newcomer to the local business methods, the salesman balked at the plan and was promptly expelled from the country.

Mr Dimonescu's report resulted in his electing himself as my guide. We were also provided with a car and chauffeur, along with a sizeable budget to cover our expenses—which in fact I paid for. According to this set up, the greater our travels, the greater the number of pictures I got, the greater our expenses, and the greater Mr Dimonescu's profits. (I could afford to be generous as I was getting a favorable rate of exchange on the black market.) Dimonescu was helpful, so long as I didn't propose anything that might hinder his career. He only cast me aside when he left for London with the members of his department to publicize King Carol's state visit to England.

We covered some 5,000 kilometers of Romanian countryside where Russian, Macedonian, Bulgarian, Turkish, Greek, Ukrainian, Tartar, Jewish and Gypsy minorities lived much as they had for centuries, strung together by a majority of Romanian-speaking people. In the Carpathians, for instance, I photographed hillside villages painted bright blue where the men were clad in heavy white woollen pantaloons and wore soft black bowler hats with narrow brims, similar to those worn by their ancestors, the Dacians, whom the Roman Emperor Trajan crushed in 101AD, leaving them with the name "Romania," and a semi-Latin language.

In the outskirts of one village, I caught up with a group of barefoot youngsters carrying a school desk and a bench along a dirt road. A ten-year old boy was so engaging, with his sheepskin *caciula* worn at a jaunty angle, I took his portrait, unaware I had just shot the cover of my Romanian story.

In Bessarabia, I photographed the Ukrainian village of Braga from across the Dniestr River. The houses were all thatched with only one large white edifice, the Communist Party Headquarters. In Kishinev, the Russian influence was still felt with its wide streets and low buildings. Taking a horse-drawn *drosky* I was driven around town by a castrated fat cabby in velveteen and silver buttons—a member of the Burjars, a Russian religious sect. In Silistra, I came upon a mosque with its needle-sharp minaret and a cemetery with horizontal tombstones inscribed in Arabic script. The men here wore turbans and the veiled women objected to being photographed—the survivors of five centuries of Ottoman rule. In the Saxon village of Turnidor, I took pictures of the Lutheran women in somber black and Mother Hubbard bonnets as they walked home in groups after Sunday service, passing by neat lines of houses as austere as themselves with roofs shaped like their bonnets. In Bucovina, miles from anywhere, I came upon a medieval monastery, its façade covered with vivid religious murals. At Bacic, I squatted with the last Tartars in Europe, whose small cube-shaped houses glittered in the sun. And at Ploiesti, I saw oil wells chugging night and day under the suspicious attention of Germans, British and Americans who all had stakes in the oil production.

In Dobruja, I finally met up with the fierce Macedonians. At Frasari, a group of men in white skirts stood along the dirt road. I had entered an unspoiled world covered with orchards. A burly character rushed up. "Hello boy," he said in an accent which had recognisable traces of American in it. "What would you say to a rastus gin fizz?"

"That sounds like an American drink."

"Chrissakes, you're telling me, boy. I mixed them for ten years. Was a barman in St. Louis until prohibition come along." He then introduced me around. "Meet Bellu. He's the head of our chamber of agriculture."

"Glad to meetcha. Worked for a Buick service station back in the States."

Chris, who had been a barber in Chicago took over. "It's a sweet town we got here, yessir. We built it American-style: wide streets and square blocks. Nothing twisting and winding here." There was no sidewalk, but the dirt roads were wide and evenly laid out. Everything was neat and clean.

I was led into a house where a young woman bowed and kissed my right hand. I looked at Chris inquiringly.

"She's newly married and gotta kiss the hand of every man her husband brings into the house. It's a sign of submission."

"I bet she was never in the America," I remarked with some amusement. "No way. She's a Macedonian from Greece. When we was in the States, we heard the Romanian government was handing out land, so we sailed for Greece. There we changed our dollars, married Greek girls, and come out here." The young wife served us each a pink-colored paste. It was sweet and wrapped around a spoon resting in a glass of water. This was followed by coffee. We ended with cold meat, sausages and wine.

Chris raved about his orchards. He took me to look at them. His eyes softened as he looked at his fruit trees and the tenderness in his manner remained until he spoke about the Bulgarians. "You've gotta do something for us, boy" he said. "I hear you're gonna see the King. You gotta tell him that we needs our guns and we needs 'em bad."

"Looks quiet enough to me," I said.

"We wants no trouble, but the next Bulgar that comes here, he gets shot. No kidding."

A grinning young man, who spoke no English, handed me a picture. It showed himself pointing to a medium-sized man in uniform, with German hand grenades, propped up against a tree. The most startling thing about him was the peculiar expression on his face. People always show pictures to photographers. Experience had taught me to make some comment. "Odd look on his face," I said.

Chris chuckled. "So would you, boy, if you too was killed dead. Now you see what I mean about them Bulgars. They're terrible people. We just gotta protect these orchards of ours."

Back in Bucharest, I applied for an appointment to photograph the King and his son, Michael. (In 1921, Carol had married Princess Helen of Greece, divorcing her seven years later.) As I waited for my appointment, I delved into the monarch's murky reputation which was due in large part to his mother, Queen Marie. Their quarrels had led him to live abroad, and in his absence the insatiable Marie conspired with the Prime Minister—who also happened to be her lover—to discredit her son. He organized the whispering campaign against King Carol and Magda Lupescu which the press fed on for years. On the death of his father in 1927, Queen Marie rejected Carol's claim to the throne, and established Michael as Regent. But by 1930 the country was in such chaos that Carol, supported by Juliu Maniu, leader of the peasant party, became King.

Suspicious of everybody—even of Maniu—constantly in fear of assassination, with no subordinates he could trust, Carol did the next best thing: he gathered around him unscrupulous men whose future depended solely upon his favour. Through them, Carol cracked down on all of his enemies, playing off one faction against another.

In need of loyal troops against his own *Camarilla*, Carol turned to the army. First he purged it, then he raised its pay. The army, Carol's spoiled child, became grateful and saw him through the first five years of his reign. By 1937, the only political force capable of challenging him was the Iron Guard. Led by a fanatic, Zelia Codreanu, who was both inspired and sponsored by Hitler, Iron Guard hooligans beat up Jews, boasted of the long list of people they planned to murder, while Codreanu announced that the day he seized power, the Berlin-Rome axis would pass through Bucharest.

The terrified Romanians waited for Carol to act. The King decided to give the country a taste of Iron Guard brutality by proxy. He dissolved the government and asked the poet Octavian Goga, the leader of the National Christian Party, to form a government. Goga, whose sympathies were similar to the Iron Guard, but who lacked its organizational power, promptly instituted another reign of terror. After 45 days, Carol tossed Goga out of office and established a personal dictatorship, to the country's great relief. One month later to the day, the German Army occupied Austria. By then, Carol was firmly in control and Codreanu was in jail, his party in shambles. At the time of my visit to Romania, Carol was the only absolute monarch in Europe. His portrait was essential to my story.

Here again, I ran into Romanian intrigue. I was informed that I could take pictures of Carol only on condition that I supply a set of prints for release to the British press when the King visited London. Although I found this *quid pro quo* lacking in regal dignity, I fully appreciated Carol's need to upgrade his image, pictorially speaking. His official portraits, in the flamboyant uniforms he had designed himself, and which made him look like a princeling in a Viennese operetta, had served their purpose: to impress his army. The image Carol now wanted to project was of a powerful chief-of-state commanding an army of two million. That's where the *Life* photographer came in.

The omnipresent Titianu announced he would escort me to the palace personally. On our way, the Under-Secretary of Propaganda, mindful of Carol's forthcoming London trip, reminded me that the King was Queen Victoria's grandson, was an Anglophile, had a British valet, drank scotch, read Shakespeare, and wore a handkerchief in his right cuff.

While a policeman held up the traffic and the royal guards snapped to attention we swept through the palace gates. We were escorted to the first floor where a group of officers in dazzling uniforms manned the royal switchboard and acted as receptionists. Leaving Titianu to confer with them, I looked out of a window and noticed an officer in a field uniform leisurely strolling in the palace garden. As I watched, he plucked a cigarette out of his gold case, slipped it into a cigarette holder and wedged it between his teeth. He went through the motions with rapid but graceful precision. "His Majesty's a chain-smoker," one of the officers who had been observing me remarked. He led me to the King and departed. Carol greeted me with the bored detachment of a man being fitted by his tailor. The camera, I noticed, was not kind to him. His features had more character than his official portraits suggested.

Carol's three Pekinese were then produced. Catching sight of his son Michael in the distance with his Great Dane, he beckoned him over. For a moment, there was an expression of tenderness. Michael responded with friendly diffidence. After some father-and-son pictures with their pets, the pets were disposed with. We took an elevator decorated with red plush and gold interlocked letter "C"s. The King operated the elevator and let his son off on the second floor. We went up another floor. Carol led the way to his study along a wide corridor. We were alone. "What an opportunity," I thought, "for one of Carol's would-be assassins."

The King's desk was massive. Neatly lined up were pictures of his son at various ages, a large bouquet of flowers, a sizeable dictionary, a perpetual calendar, a writing pad with two fountain pens. Behind him were bookshelves with bound editions and folders filled with documents. On a shelf, two more family portraits in curlicued frames flanked an elaborately ornate clock. The whole effect was darkly Victorian, in sharp contrast to the rest of the place where what looked like gold probably was. My last picture was a portrait. The moment I'd taken it, Carol turned to his papers without a word and never looked up again.

The politician I was most interested in was the one Dimonescu was adamant I should not meet: Juliu Maniu, the incorruptible leader of the National Peasant Party. The most popular political figure in the country, Carol kept him out of office. Shortly before Dimonescu left for London, I had a unique opportunity of photographing Maniu at his home with his collaborators. Fortunately, Dimonescu had one of his weekly rendezvous, from which he always turned up late. I therefore made a dinner date with him for 9:30, and planned that as the time I would be photographing Maniu. My alibi set up, I put on an overcoat, with my equipment stuffed in its pocket, wore a felt hat and borrowed a pair of prescription glasses. The two plain-clothes men on duty outside the apartment building scrutinized me closely but let me pass. Maniu was in his dining-room surrounded by his collaborators. I hurriedly took a group picture, then concentrated on the frail and fearless Maniu. By the time Dimonescu turned up for dinner, I had discarded my disguise and was settling down with a drink.

My story was now complete except for pictures of the Hungarian minority in Transylvania. Ever since Hitler had seized the Sudetenland, the Romanian government denied the existence of this minority. I approached Under-Secretary Titianu on the subject. He looked pained. Pointing to the map behind his desk, he gestured towards it vaguely. "There are barely a few thousand scattered around," he told me. (A more realistic estimate was closer to one million.) I therefore waited for an opportunity to present itself.

It came the week Titianu led his entire English-speaking department to London, leaving Mme Cataggi, who spoke no English, in charge. She asked to see me and appeared embarrassed at first. The United Press wanted a statement from Carol regarding his impending state visit. "You must understand that we simply can't bother His Majesty," Mme Cataggi told me. "I don't speak English. I can't ask the United Press to write it. But you can." I agreed on condition that I got to see a Hungarian village in Transylvania.

I produced the statement Mme Cataggi asked for, and she kept her word, in a manner of speaking. I was driven to my Hungarian village through such bad roads and lengthy detours that I only reached our destination at nightfall. This didn't really bother me. I had flashbulbs and shot interior pictures.

Four or five years later, I got a phone call at *Life* in New York. The speaker had a strong Balkan accent. He informed me that he was the uncle of the little boy in the photograph *Life* had used as a cover. I knew at once that he wanted money. "That's something for *Life*'s lawyers," I told him. "Call them up—and be sure to tell them what the Tsar said about Romania."

Children, Transylvania, Romania, 1938

Mickey Mouse Club, Birmingham, Alabama, 1940

Carmen Miranda, Brazil, 1939

The
Americas

New York

"You're sailing aboard the *Bremen* for New York on December 7," Dave Ritchie, *Life*'s London editor told me. Although I was very grateful to *Life* for the opportunity to get away from Europe that dismal winter of 1938, I was not enchanted by their choice of a German liner. Edgar Anstey, the documentary film maker who had been to the States set me straight. "When Americans want to see you, they want to see you at once and book you on the first ship for New York. Americans don't think politically the way we do. So get on the bloody boat and see they don't throw you overboard."

Possibly on account of the season, few passengers sailed with me. At my table were two American engineers from J & L Steel on their way home after supervising the completion of a steel mill in Russia.

"You're building steel mills in Russia?" I exclaimed incredulous.

"Why not?" one of them replied. "They're paying for it." From what they told me, J & L was not the only American company setting up plants in Russia. There was Lockheed, and also several others. I was to remember this conversation in June 1941.

We landed in New York to a chilly dawn. I hailed a cab. The first thing the driver asked was, "Many passengers on board, bud?" He sounded anxious, which I put down to his fears for his fellow countrymen left in a Europe moving inexorably towards war. "Who says Americans aren't politically conscious?" I thought to myself and reassured him we were only a few.

"Darn it," he said. "I hoped I could get back and pick up another fare."

"What d'you think of the situation?" I asked.

"Business is okay," he told me.

I said that I meant the world situation.

"Things look kinda punk in Asia," he replied.

"I mean Europe," I said.

"Why don't you guys get together and stop stirring up trouble?"

I tried to point out it was not us but the others, nevertheless he lumped us together and created a European unity Europeans were unable to achieve. I gave up trying to argue, but what he said bothered me. I wanted no part of Nazi Germany, though I willingly regarded Beethoven as more proof of the superiority of European civilization. I had been taught that Western Europe was the center of the world and took it for granted that the United States was totally dependent upon Europe for her culture. But when I stared at the broad back of my driver, the first American I had had any contact with in his own country, I became doubtful. I had never come across such a cabby before. He called me "bud" and was very independent. He was awfully big, too, but so was his taxi, and everything else in sight.

As we leapt along, I thought of my friends who had seen me off at Waterloo. There had been something about the scene that reminded me of a newsreel about a European prizefighter who left for the States in search of a title and wound up getting knocked out. I wondered how I'd make out. All I knew was that I had a room at the Lexington Hotel and that *Life*'s office was in Rockefeller Center. I had also been given several names that meant little. All my dealings with *Life* so far had been through the London bureau. Everybody from head office sounded important to me.

The Lexington Hotel was the tallest building I had ever set foot in. I was therefore not prepared to be given a room on the third floor. Like most Europeans, it had never entered my mind that skyscrapers had a third floor. The hotel lobby, too, was different from any I had known, with its shops and news-stands scattered around. The porter had none of the dictatorial powers of his European counterparts. Never having had a radio in a hotel room before, I switched it on. Dance music at 7:15am. Amazing! In London, the BBC didn't believe in pampering its listeners—dance music was restricted to definite hours, the way drinking was. Americans aren't dedicated to gloom, I decided.

At nine I called up Ruth Berrien, the only person I knew in New York. She was *Life*'s foreign news researcher. Without regard for the hour, I launched into a dissertation on European politics, interrupting myself only to ask if we could speak freely over the phone. She burst out laughing. "You aren't in the Balkans now. We don't listen in here." This made me feel provincial, and the doubts that had assailed me in the taxi returned. If Americans were so provincial, why was I the one who was worried?

Out in the street, I felt like running to keep up. What I saw filled me with wonder. I stopped at a drugstore for a cup of coffee. My attention turned to a burly fellow who had been ripping up the avenue outside with a steam drill. He was still in his work clothes and wearing heavy gloves. He sat himself down next to a woman in a mink coat. That's going to do it, I thought. But she didn't seem at all concerned as he poured mayonnaise on a large turkey sandwich. In London the lady would have made a fuss or the workman would have been embarrassed by the surroundings. In New York, it seemed, this kind of scene was normal. The wonder to me was that the man could afford such a meal. There's obviously no class distinction when it comes to food, I concluded.

After coming across a Christmas tree decorated with tinsel in the street for the pleasure of passers-by, I thought nothing more could astonish me. I was wrong. At a skating rink at Rockefeller Center couples glided by to a Strauss waltz in the midst of skyscrapers. It was only in the elevator that the cost of such a fantasy struck me. A skating rink in the heart of Manhattan— it hardly matched the European conception of Americans as people only interested in money.

I got out at the 31st floor of the Time & Life Building and asked for a Mr Manthorp, who was expecting me. I had no idea who he was, but a quick look at his youthful appearance, his secretary, and his carpeted office convinced me he must have married the daughter of one of the owners. Mr Manthorp was friendly and relaxed. He called me John, instead of Phillips, and said his name was Jack. His detailed knowledge about my trip surprised me. You simply can't beat the Americans when it comes to organization, I decided. "You've seen Wilson, of course," he said at last.

"Wilson?"

"Wilson Hicks."

"He left a message that he wanted to see me, but I told him I was with you." Manthorp turned pale and rushed me over to Hicks's office as I wondered how, in such surroundings, I was expected to tell the difference between a man in charge of travel arrangements and an executive editor.

Wilson Hicks, the picture editor, looked very stern, wore his hair parted in the middle, and had a habit of peering out of the window when he talked. "D'you mind flying?" he asked.

"Why, no."

"Fine," he said, and handed me a plane ticket a meter long. It would take me around South America, where I was to report on Nazi and fascist infiltration there. Hicks's tone made me feel he was extremely disturbed by their activities. "You'll be on your way by the weekend," I was told.

"What about Christmas in New York?" I asked.

"Who told you about that?" he demanded.

"Mr Hulburd, when I saw him in London."

"Dave Hulburd's with *Time*," Hicks snapped dismissively. Now did not seem an opportune time to mention that I thought $48 a week was very little for the work I did.

Hicks led me into the office of the text editor. "John, I want you to meet Dan Longwell."

"You're going to South America for us," Longwell said. He was especially anxious that my pictures illustrate the great similarities between South America and the United States.

"I don't know the United States, Mr Longwell," I told him. "I landed here at six this morning, and am off in four days."

"Well, just look out of the plane window," he suggested.

By the time I was ushered into Mr Billings's office, I knew he was the managing editor, the towering figure on the 31st floor. I had been told he liked Shirley Temple, locomotives, and Cape Horn. I had also been warned not to mention Indians in his presence. "But I thought Americans were proud of…"

"Sure we're proud of our Indians, but Billings doesn't like them."

After shaking hands with this imposing man I sincerely hoped he would not take a dislike to me.

Now that I had met my employers, I was shown around the rest of the editorial floor. Walking down one corridor, I was overtaken by a writer on roller-skates. Someone from the layout department was trimming a Christmas tree made of photo-montages. Whistler's mother, disguised as Santa Claus, replaced the star at the top of the tree. In the picture department, I noticed that one of the young secretaries had an aquarium next to her desk, fitted with running water and full of goldfish. In Europe, employees approached their work in the manner in which they lived: diffidently. I tried to imagine the look on Neville Chamberlain's face if he ever came across an employee with an aquarium in his family's nut and bolt factory. I looked down at the skaters gaily waltzing below and wondered, why can't we live this way in Europe?

In the photo lab, I learned that the technicians were of Greek, Italian, German, and Hungarian extraction and still got on well together. Among the photographers were those born in Germany, Russia, Albania, and Hungary. Well, now they've got one born in Algeria, I thought. At lunch, I found I had a choice of Chinese, Swedish, Turkish, French, Italian, or "anything else you care to name".

That night I looked out at New York from the Empire State Building. I searched for the *Bremen*, my link with Europe, and found it, a speck among the carpet of dazzling colors spread out beneath me. I wondered how much larger the *Bremen* was than the boat which had brought over my mother's predecessors long ago. I tried to place my mother, with her quiet ways, in this land where she was born and found she fitted perfectly. New York seemed to have the gift of absorbing everything and giving a unity to the whole. I watched the blazing lights illuminating the night, a gaudy spectacle of violence and power. The firemen's sirens echoed across the skyscrapers like the scream of banshees. I felt in the presence of a colossus. In Europe a colossus was measured in brawn and steel and guns. This one laughed, and I heard the rumble of his laughter come from deep in the earth as the subway rushed by. From the top of the Empire State Building I felt as though I were peering down a mountain into the valley. But these mountains were man-made, and the valleys below, bathed in light, seemed a welcoming place to live.

The contrast between Washington and New York was unexpected. The streets were wide, the imposing white buildings were low, the sky was visible in all directions, without having to look up. The pace and the population was leisurely and easy-going. "We're a Southern town," I was told. The shock made me appreciate that in America, the capital was only concerned with politics and government. In Europe it was the nation's showcase. And there were other differences. The White House was the smallest and most elegant residence for a chief-of-state I had ever seen. It was not even called a palace.

I was in Washington to be briefed by the State Department's specialists in the ten South American countries I expected to visit. They were knowledgeable, authoritative, and extremely sincere in their concern over each country in question. They also made it very clear that the press created problems for the diplomats. Helen Lawrenson's humorous article "Latins Are Lousy Lovers", published in *Esquire* magazine, was very much a case in point. Although the article was over two years old, the fury it had generated among the macho-minded males still simmered.

"We're still feeling the after-shocks," I was told, while being admonished to keep clear of such sensitive topics. There was no trace of amused cynicism in their approach to South America, or a hint of the sophisticated advice a French diplomat had given me: "If you want to succeed in Brazil, remember this, Phillips: it's never hot in Rio even if it's 100°F at midnight."

I could hardly blame their seriousness. At the time, the United States was promoting "the good neighbor policy" to improve its relations with Latin America in view of a possible threat from both Germany and Italy in the uncertain future. Until then, there had been little effort for any cultural relations between these two totally different worlds: both were focused on Europe while spurning each other. This outlook had been chided by Oswaldo Aranha, Brazil's witty Foreign Secretary. He had stunned the Washington Press at the conclusion of a successful agreement with the United States by announcing, "I'm going to ask my government to honor Hitler with a statue. Thanks to him, the United States discovered Brazil."

Tom MacAvoy, *Life*'s White House photographer, who told me this story, asked what I'd wish to see while in Washington. "President Roosevelt," I said, aware of the foolishness of my request.

"Simple," Tom said. "Be at the White House entrance at 2:30 sharp."

I joined a group of onlookers as an open car drove through the main gate and got my wish. A smiling Roosevelt drove past within 15 feet of me with only a Secret Service man seated next to the driver. The lack of need for greater security stupefied me—America was indeed a different world.

In my brief two days in Washington, my sightseeing was limited to the Lincoln Memorial. Walking up its wide stairway, I was overcome by a mystical feeling—possibly due to the play of light on Lincoln's statue. There was no unbridled glorification of this great man. He was seated in an armchair. The look on his face was unforgettable. Quite unexpectedly, I became conscious of my American heritage. My mother's father had been a surgeon in the Union forces—my spiritual link to this memorial.

Later, I found out that the Union's Surgeon General, under whom my grandfather had served, was Doctor Billings, the grandfather of Mr Billings, my boss on *Life*.

Loading coffee in Santos harbor, Brazil, 1939

Carnival, Rio de Janeiro, 1939

Carnival, Rio de Janeiro, 1939

Carnival, Rio de Janeiro, 1939

Brasilian dictator President Getulio Vargas, Rio de Janeiro, 1939

Brazil

"Two hundred and fifty dollars in excess luggage?" Jack Manthorp exclaimed. "What will Wilson Hicks say?"

"That Rio's far away," I told Manthorp, who saw me off at the New York Terminal.

Although $250 represented six weeks' salary—my way of gauging prices at that time—I was not particularly concerned. I had learned aboard the *Bremen* that the values I grew up with no longer mattered in this new world. Taken aback by the enormity of a potato, I'd been asked, "Haven't you ever seen a baked Idaho before?" All things considered, $250 sounded reasonable enough for a six-day journey by air.

A blast of heat greeted me as I stepped off the plane in Rio. Being summer, it was raining. I found Brazil, the fifth largest country in the world, an exotic mixture of cultures: Indians, bypassed by civilization, still lived in inaccessible jungles, while Rio's sultry beauties languished on the white-sand beaches of Ipanema. Brazil's 22 states spread across four climatic zones: tropical, arid, sub-tropical, and humid. Great natural resources remained untapped. Success was a question of luck. An American businessman on his way to Buenos Aires stopped off in Rio. He liked the city, stayed, and started a Woolworth-type chain store. He made it a success. Most were not so lucky. Rio had a way of gagging entrepreneurs with red tape.

Besides the German and Japanese minorities who lived in secluded enclaves and only spoke their own languages, the vast majority of the population was of Portuguese origin. Although sharp-witted, they were languid—a quality which the "white elite" attributed to the early assimilation of the Portuguese with blacks and Indians. (Others believed the blacks and Indians had helped civilize the criminal elements deported from Portugal in the 16th century.) For me, the climate contributed greatly to the slow pace. Any mention of the weather was considered offensive and efforts to keep cool were ridiculed.

Ridicule, along with carnival, were the average Brazilian's main luxuries. When the Foreign Minister installed air conditioning in his office, he became the subject of great mirth. The day he developed trouble with his eyesight, the air conditioner was blamed. It was the same outlook that incited Rio's urchins—the irrepressible *cariocas*—to mock foreigners in tropical clothes. As most were passengers aboard such liners as the Normandie, they trailed anyone in white chanting, *"Je suis du Normandie."* Remembering the French diplomat's advice, I wore a tweed jacket and flannels. This obliged me to change shirts every few hours, but it fooled people into thinking I understood Brazil.

Besides fighting the heat, there was a permanent struggle with the Kafkaesque bureaucracy. Journalists had to submit six carbons of whatever they filed. Each carbon was scrutinized by the censor with the same lip-moving concentration as was the original. The inefficiency was such that state employees had to devote a full day to collecting their monthly salaries. There were cases in which employees were not paid for months. This prompted a judge in the Amazon to take out an ad in his local paper: "High court judge willing to give piano lessons for ten *milreis* an hour."

Coming from what was considered an orderly European society, I was overwhelmed by the prospect of trying to define in pictures this sprawling immensity. To get some perspective, I talked to a number of Brazilians. One in particular, the gifted painter Candido Portinari, impressed me. "We are simply a reflection of Europe which had no consideration for our local needs," he told me. "Everything in Brazil happened by accident."

He told me a story. "In 1500, the Portuguese navigator Pedro Alvarez Cabral set off for India and drifted here. Thinking he had discovered an island, he named it Vera Cruz. Finding out it was considerably larger, he renamed us Santa Cruz. When he came upon forests of *pau brazil*, a wood that promised great wealth, we then became Brazil. We remained a Portuguese colony until 1822, when Dom Pedro proclaimed himself emperor, and decreed Brazil's independence. Unfortunatel," Portinari sighed, "Portugal did not object and recognized this *fait accompli* three years later. We didn't have to fight a bitter war for independence, as the American colonists did. We never had to make terrible sacrifices for a cause that would become sacred and lay a solid foundation for our national unity. Liberated by accident, we accepted independence with indifference. In 1880, the empire collapsed and made way for a Federal Republic."

This first Republic was overthrown by a revolution in 1930. A junta of victorious generals sought out a temporary president. They picked a politico from the rural Rio Grande do Sul. He was so colorless, the *cariocas* nick-named him *"Xuxu"*—a vegetable marrow so tasteless, it takes on the flavor of whatever it is served with. His name was Getulio Vargas. Vargas was still in office eight years and two revolutions later when I landed in Brazil. Chubby and under-sized, he had an almost comical look about him. It was hard to remember this was the man who held Brazil's future and the United States' South American policy in his hands. And he certainly didn't look the type who would know how to deal with the belligerent National Socialists, the Brazilian German movement *Life* was interested in. As it turned out, rarely have appearances been more misleading.

I met Vargas soon after my arrival in Rio. He took me along when he went golfing. He never spoke, but allowed me to take all the pictures I wanted. Next day I was to photograph him at work. I was ushered into his office and told Vargas would see me shortly. I was then taken to a waiting room where I spent several hours before being escorted to a door that led into the street. Although I never did get a picture of Vargas at work, he gave me a clue as to how he operated. Brought up among Arabs, I understood devious thinking. Vargas wanted *Life* to publish pictures of him golfing, but he did not want to leave the impression he objected to being photographed in his office.

It was vintage Vargas. A South American dictator, he did not rule through faithful party henchmen but depended upon the army's good will. The army had put him into office in 1930 and could just as easily have dismissed him in 1938 (it would do so in 1945). The Brazilian army was not a war machine, but existed to keep the dicators it wanted in power. It maintained its presence in all government ministries by having soldiers act as receptionists. Their ignorance and stubborness simply aggravated an incoherent bureaucracy. On one occasion, after photographing the Foreign Minister, he amiably called up the Minister for National Defense to inform him that I was on my way to take his picture. To avoid any possible delay with the soldier on duty, he wrote a note I was to present. The soldier, who presumably could not read, put it under a large pile in spite of my tantrum. He then took me to a waiting room where a woman was breast-feeding her baby and a man was doing a crossword puzzle. At six, we were told to return the next morning. When I eventually got in to see the Minister, he said, "I've been expecting you for the past three days."

To govern under such chaotic conditions, Vargas required extra-ordinary political flair and an iron will to maneuver the army into policies no self-respecting South American military mind would normally tolerate. He achieved this by being both considerably brighter than his generals and by corrupting them. He had the army behind him when he put an end to the Nazi threat to Brazil, despite its greater affinity with National Socialist rather than democratic principles.

The Germans first emigrated to Brazil in 1848. They came seeking a better life. Most went south, to distant Santa Caterina and Porto Alegre and formed colonies. They were attracted by a setting, if not a climate, reminiscent of their homeland. They built roads and developed the land, but they never mixed with the other Brazilians, never intermarried, only spoke German, and generally remained isolated from society. The more enterprising stayed in Rio and Sao Paolo. They started modest companies requiring few employees, making such things as beer bottle caps and safety pins. Others saw an opportunity in importing German manufactured goods un-available in Brazil. Hard working, frugal, and peaceful, they were accepted by the rest of the community. All this changed with Hitler.

Brazil's Germans took to him as a matter of course. They also agreed with the Nazis about being the master race. (They had always looked down on the other Brazilians.) The stories in the German-language newspapers and broadcasts over the short-wave radio rekindled a pride in their father-land which over the years had faded with their inability to enjoy their parents' promise of a better life in a land they now called with some resent-ment the *Grüne Hölle*—the "green hell".

Euphoric over the brown shirts, black breeches, Sam Browne belts, Nazi insignias, fife and drums presented to them, they no longer felt fail-ures but transformed into dashing Germans with a Nazi mission. They para-ded and terrorised the neighbouring populations as they dreamed of an independent German community. They swallowed the propoganda that every good German was a good Nazi, and good Nazis contributed to the *Winterhilfe*, the welfare of the fatherland. This had been considerably sim-plified by the opening of a *Winterhilfe* account at the Banca Allemao Transatlantico in Rio. There the funds were transferred to Hans Henning von Cossell, the German Cultural Attaché at the German Embassy in Rio and the recognised Nazi leader in Brazil, whose staff then decided whether the contributors had displayed the expected patriotic zeal. A reminder was sent to those who faltered and retribution was swift if they did not mend their ways. In the colonies, the penalty was being ostracized, with all the dire consequences that would inevitably follow. In the city, an import company's license was transferred to a more deserving German. Thus it paid to be a "200 per cent National Socialist".

The crisis over the Nazis broke out during the presidential campaign of 1936. One of the candidates, Plinio Salgado, was the leader of the *Integralista* movement, the home-bred fascists. The *Integralistas* were underwritten by Hans Henning von Cossell, and although the Germans paid for the green shirts and offered ten *milreis* to those who joined, the movement was restricted to non-German Brazilians. Its mission was to destabilize the government.

In a show of strength, Salgado recklessly threatened Vargas by announcing he could put 100,000 stormtroopers on the streets of Rio at 24 hours' notice. Vargas immediately suggested he should do exactly that. Then, unknown to the *Integralistas*, he assigned pollsters to count the number of demonstrators. Forty-eight hours after learning they numbered only 20,000 including the women and children, Vargas banned the movement. On the same day, Rio's movie houses showed newsreels of Vargas waving to the *Integralista* demonstrators, appearing to mock them. This greatly appealed to the *cariocas* who admired his cunning.

Vargas then postponed the elections "temporarily" on the grounds they threatened national unity, substituting a new constitution which dissolved Congress called the *Estado Novo*. (It was established on November 15, 1937, but was retroactively dated to 1930, the year Vargas became temporary president.)

On April 18, 1938, Vargas took a major step, though the consequences were not obvious at the time. In defiance of the National Socialist Party and the Hitler Youth movement, he prohibited the wearing of uniforms and political badges. For Guilbert Landsberg, publisher of the Brazilian-German anti-Nazi weekly, it signalled revolution. "It was in the air," he told me.

The rebels struck on May 10. A number of palace guards who had defected killed the loyalists who were taken by surprise. Although the plans had been carefully worked out by the Germans, the over-confident

Brazilians neglected to toss a hand grenade into the palace's telephone switchboard as instructed. This allowed the loyalists to call for help. Meanwhile, another group of rebels went to arrest the chief-of-staff in his home. Intimidated by his rank, they allowed him to dress in the bathroom from which he emerged firing a machine-gun. Having wiped out his captors, he hastened to the presidential palace where Vargas had escaped assassination. By morning, the uprising was over. Five days later, Vargas took up golf.

Vargas' 1938 decree played havoc with the well-established institutions. Everything German was naturalized: the *Deutsche Gesellschaft* became the Club Germania; *"Giessen Stahl"* shovels reached the Brazilian market as "warranted cast steel." Condor, Lufthansa's South American feeder line, naturalized its German pilots *en masse*.

I took pictures of these newly renamed German companies to illustrate that Germany still retained an important economic presence in Brazil. No German executive allowed me to take his picture but I did manage to get a shot of Hans Henning von Cossell at an official reception we both attended. A friend had to point him out as I had never seen him before. Von Cossell never gave me a second chance.

My assignment now turned to the Germans in the South. From what I was told, they sounded like the fanatical Germans in Czechoslovakia, agitating for reunion with Germany, but the people I found in Santa Caterina were deflated and discouraged. They were now back to where they had been before their orgy of Nazism. Vargas's easy-going Brazilians had done their job.

At Blumenau, despite being German in both name and architecture, conditions had changed considerably. A Brazilian prefect now replaced the German one. All official transactions were conducted in Portuguese. Signs around town instructed the population to speak Portuguese. The German-speaking troops once stationed in the south had been sent north, while those from Bahia replaced them. The main street was renamed Rua 15 Novembre, a none-too-subtle reminder that the *Estado Novo* was alive and well. All the shop signs on the main street had been naturalized. Even the beauty parlor had become *Ondulaçao Permanente Bischof*, although *Damen Friseur Salon* was still discernible beneath a coat of whitewash. When the

Casa Lohner, the optical instrument and camera store, reverted to the old ways and advertised for an "Aryan messenger boy," a mulatto applied. When the man was turned down, a mob wrecked the store. The prohibition of Nazi paraphernalia, however, had proved to be the fatal blow. No longer allowed to parade and gather together in uniform so they could enjoy the camaraderie and the intoxication of being National Socialists, the Germans were devastated. They were once again human nobodies in the *"Grüne Hölle"*.

At the cafés they discussed how they had been betrayed, how a number planned to return to Germany—2,000 did while I was in Brazil—how the Americans had destroyed "their ideals". They no longer looked like fearful stormtroopers, but very average people. I was reminded of what somebody had said about the Ku Klux Klan when I was aboard the *Bremen*. "If you took away their horses, their white sheets, and their flaming crosses, they'd loose their mystique, and appear what they are: so very ordinary. No one would be afraid of them."

Vargas's idea of stripping away all of the trappings of Nazism had been a stroke of genius. He emasculated the National Socialist Party. They were still anti-Semitic and pro-Hitler, but they were no longer a threat. I sometimes wondered if there would have been a Nazi Germany without uniforms.

German schoolboys, Brazil, 1939

Swastika in the German community, Gran Chaco, Paraguay, 1939

New-born calf, Argentina, 1939

Argentina

Everything was bull when I landed in Argentina on a spring afternoon in 1939. It was impossible to escape the "baby beef" in Buenos Aires: he was on postage stamps; he crept into conversation and emerged sizzling on a platter. He was the soul and symbol of Argentina. It was hard for Americans to understand that the Argentines could be wealthy while not owning any stocks and bonds. Their reply, "beef", did not satisfy them. For the *Estancieros*, the wealthy class, their stock was on the hoof.

On a friend's advice, I simply said that *Life* had sent me to photograph Argentina because I was its Paris and London correspondent. I never explained that Argentina was part of a South American survey. Despite the fact that nature had placed them closer to the penguins of Antarctica, the frustrated Argentinians felt Bond Street and the Rue de la Paix were their spiritual homes.

Fanatically pan-Latin American at the conference table (mainly to aggravate the Americans), they disliked being associated with South Americans. They took great pride in their mild climate and their light complexions, boasting "We have fewer blacks and Indians today than during colonial times."

The only South American country with a middle class, they were ashamed of their neighbours whom they contemptuously dismissed: Brazil—a tropical Negro republic; Paraguay—a dependence; Uruguay—a summer resort; Bolivia—a vulture's nest; Chile—a land where the population hung on to the *cordilleras* by their eyelashes.

My own status in Argentina was never clear. An Englishman, I was obviously a gentleman. Working for *Life*, I had unfortunate connections with "the colossus of the North". Socially, I was a great success. Everybody suspected I was a spy.

The country had been spy-conscious ever since a fantastic plot had been uncovered: a German plan to seize Patagonia. However far-fetched this might appear, it was taken very seriously and produced unexpected results. Map makers were ordered to depict Patagonia on the same scale as the rest of Argentina, and no longer tuck it away in an inset. The belief I was a spy was due to my plans of photographing the Army, the Navy, and the Air Force. (This led to a spirited debate with an admiral who resented my telling him that all of his hardware had been purchased on the open market. Taking exception to the truth, he never allowed me near a naval base.) This made me "interesting" and resulted in a great many invitations by the *estancieros*.

The lives of these *Niño Bien* or *Gente Bien*, as they call Argentina's version of European aristocracy, I found to be humdrum-deluxe. Meals were social events. Cocktail parties and nightly dinner engagements started much later than in Europe, and even then it was considered chic to be late. Invited for 9pm, you showed up at 10, thus giving your hostess time to get back home from her cocktail party. Argentina was a man's country. The dashing *estanciero* kept a mistress without any family argument, though it would have been considered bad form for the wife and the mistress to meet. This was unlikely as they rarely belonged to the same social class. A wife, of course, could not take a lover with impunity. It was a far greater sin to be seen harmlessly flirting in public than to conduct an affair no one knew about. The husband would face humiliating ridicule in his exclusive all-male clubs. To have an affair was so complicated, many society women felt it was not worth the effort, though a few indulged in lesbian relations since it was fashionable in Paris and London.

A society woman's life followed a well-regulated schedule. As a child, she was sent to the fashionable Sacre Coeur School. There she was taught that one day she would marry and that her life would be dominated by a man. On leaving school, she drifted into the social whirl in search of him, chaperoned by a brother. The moment she ceased to attend parties, everybody knew she was about to become engaged. Married young, her honeymoon was a compromise between romance and cattle breeding. The couple visited both the pyramids and the Scottish moors—where the husband bought champion bulls to improve his stock. Back home, she went to live in the country on the *estancia* where she produced a family. In her late twenties, she returned with her offspring to a social life in Buenos Aires. The phone, which had once been her ideal medium of flirtation as it dispensed with a chaperone, came back into her existence.

After breakfast in bed, she phoned her friends, at a loose end until lunchtime. Lectures were a blessing. They took up the afternoons and became a rage for the women and a racket for the lecturers. Visiting celebrities caused a tug-of-war over invitations. They could, however, prove disappointing. An Argentine lady who had monopolized a successful French author was shocked after she had gushed, "I see, *cher maître*, that you think highly of my intellect," to be told, "I do not aim that high."

French, English, and American books were assured a devoted readership on condition they were bestsellers in Paris, London, and New York. By absorbing such scraps of culture, the women acquired enough education to realize it was totally lacking in most of their dashing husbands. Tied down by their cattle, their clubs, and their mistresses, husbands were rarely at home by day unless their wives entertained—which when they did, they did well and at home.

Their modern apartments were furnished by the leading Paris decorators. The latest issues of *Vogue* were displayed on the drawing-room tables. Picassos, Cézannes and Renoirs hung on the walls. The women were dressed in creations by Chanel, Schiaparelli and Lanvin flown over on Air France. The men wore Savile Row suits. The food and the wine were in keeping with the setting. The guests numbered 12 or more, but never 13. On occasion, the conversation took on an unexpected turn. At one lunch, the hostess asked a newly-arrived Frenchman what he thought of Franco. The *Generalissimo* was a great favorite of the *Niño Bien* as he was fighting "the Reds" in the Spanish Civil War. Apparently indifferent to this, the Frenchman replied, "Not much."

"So, you approve of nuns being raped?" he was admonished.

In the silence, a titter was heard from a countess who contributed to the Communist Party to please her lover. "This may well be true, my dear," another guest remarked. "Raping nuns is an old Spanish tradition. Remember Don Juan?"

The *Niño Bien* were conservative, more as a caste than a political faction, for both spiritual and material reasons. They viewed the army as their special police force, whose duty was to maintain their way of life. They did not even consider their sons joining the armed forces, as the officers were middle class. The officers resented this. They felt they were being manipulated. After all, they had carried off the 1930 Revolution, but a civilian had reaped the presidency. They were determined that the next time they'd hold on to the power—Peron was already in the wings.

Gauchos and cattle, Argentina, 1939

While the *estancieros* were devoutly pro-Franco, most of the country was not. I had occasion to observe the importance of the war in Spain when a friend and I were getting into a taxi and the driver turned and said to her, "*Buona noche, Signorina.* I remember your addressing a Spanish Republican rally three years ago. I was in the audience. You convinced me to go over to Spain and fight. I just got back."

The Argentinians have preferred the British over the Americans since George Canning, the astute British Foreign Secretary, recognized their emancipation from Spain, despite the fact they were allied with Spain at the time. But they still resented British ownership of the railroad that took their cattle to the slaughter-houses and packing-houses, and of the refrigerated ships that transported their beef to Great Britain. When it came to their disapproval of the US, it was mostly due to the American embargo on exporting their beloved "baby beef" in competition with Texas, and on the grounds their cattle would spread hoof and mouth disease. The *Niño Bien* also borrowed the superior attitude of the British upper classes and regarded the Americans as vulgar.

The French regarded the Argentinians with a witty condescension. I was introduced to the French Ambassador at a gala reception, and admired the splendor of his uniform. "It's not ambassadorial," he chuckled. "It's a left-over from my North African career. As it cost me 3,500 francs, I decided it was good enough for Argentina."

Half of the 12 million Argentines lived in Buenos Aires. The majority were called *porteños*—those from the port—and represented Argentina's middle class. The *porteño* was worldly in thought. His unfulfilled dream was to visit Paris. The one I photographed was stamped out of a pattern. He was a civil servant by conviction, liking the office hours of 12 to 6, which allowed him to get up at 10. He also liked the prospect of the pension that awaited his retirement. He was mesmerized by the municipal elections as his career depended on the results. (His interest in the presidential elections was academic. He knew they were rigged.) He considered Argentina a democracy and was inclined to believe that the US might be one too. He feverishly went through the foreign section of *La Prensa*, and gathered a smattering of knowledge. This allowed him to know most of the European statesmen by name and misquote them. His favorite subject was the beauty of the Argentine countryside, where he never set foot if he could help it.

Evita Peron visiting Pope Pius XII, Rome, 1947

He loved watching the horse races and considered himself a sportsman by belonging to the cheering section of his favorite soccer team. His great luxury was attending performances at the theaters in Corrientes Street which featured sexy revues where Evita Peron had performed. (I vainly examined my negatives to see if I had shot her on stage.)

Another of Argentina's most famous communities was now no more. Though the world links the tango to the *gaucho*—the nomadic *gauchos* disappeared and instead became *peones*—South American cowhands—who lived contentedly on the great *estancias*, handling the cattle. For the rest they were were mostly foreigners, Spaniards, Germans, and Italians, and the Argentinians had the good sense to leave them alone to develop the weath of this great country. There was one class, however, which did not benefit from the general prosperity. It remained nameless and poverty-stricken until Evita Peron came along and gave its people an identity: the *descamisados*.

Nothing about her feminine appearance or background suggested Evita's political genius. She first displayed her power after Peron was arrested on October 15, 1945. She took to the streets and led 50,000 marchers to the prison. Peron was promptly released. His recompense was to marry her and bask in her power.

Within two decades of a law allowing women to keep the money they inherited, Evita Peron, an ex-chorus girl, ruled over macho Argentina. She not only championed the poor, but gave women the vote and legalized divorce. She was ruthless with the *Niño Bien*. When they failed to realize that she did not appreciate their calling her a "slut", she struck back by ruining them. When the owner of a century-old caramel factory refused to contribute to Evita's fund, she had the factory closed down for sanitary reasons. Without Evita, there would never have been a President Juan Peron.

I had occasion to photograph her in Rome during the summer of 1947. I was at the airport when she landed there from Spain, where Franco had given her a regal reception. The Italians were much more ambivalent. On one hand, they did not wish to be associated with Peron and his fascism. On the other, there were many Italian emigrants in Buenos Aires who made generous contributions to their homeland and experience had taught them that Evita was not one to trifle with. This did not prevent the Romans from spreading a *barzelletta* about her: a crowd gathered outside the residence where Evita was staying, chanting *"Putana fascista!"* . She came on to the balcony and indignantly said, *"Fascista no!"* The authorities, for their part had to be much more circumspect. The Italian President retired to his country villa near Naples. The American Ambassador left town. As for the Pope, he granted her an audience. I stood in Saint Peter's and photographed her dressed in black from head to foot as she walked past me escorted by Swiss guards. I was not allowed to take pictures of the audience, neither was her personal photographer. The Vatican photographer, usually on hand, was nowhere to be seen. In this way, Evita Peron, whose European visit was an artful public relations exercise, did not get the one photograph which meant most in Argentina: the Pontiff and herself.

Evita, however, made sure the other important figures in Italy did not escape her. She announced she would travel to Naples for a meeting with the Italian President. The courteous elderly gentleman returned to Rome. There he got his picture taken with Evita.

The US Ambassador was also on the list. He was back in Rome as it was the Fouth of July when, according to tradition, the Ambassador held open house. Madame Peron showed up at the residence bearing President Peron's greetings. The Ambassador had no alternative but to receive Evita. He, too, got his picture taken with her. Evita Peron had perfected the photo-opportunity.

She did not limit herself to getting her way when it came to being photographed with statesmen. She also applied the principle to shopping. After her Italian tour, she flew to Paris as a guest of the French Republic. There she dropped by Cartier. She wanted to see some pearl necklaces. She took the most valuable. Asked about payment, Evita reminded the salesman she was a guest of France. The nephew of the French Ambassador to Argentina told me that his uncle received the bill for the pearls with instructions from the Quai d'Orsay to collect. Wearing his top hat, he paid the Argentinian Foreign Secretary a visit and was told, "I'm very sorry, but the Foreign Office is not responsible for Madame Peron's debts." Five years later, to the month of her European tour, Evita Peron was dead.

Indians of Fireland, Argentina, 1939

Seals, Patagonia, 1939

Shipwreck in the Magellan Strait, Patagonia, 1939

Back to the USA

"RETURN TO NEW YORK. WAR APPEARS IMMINENT." was the message that greeted me after my trip to Patagonia, where I hadn't found any German activity worth photographing. My South American assignment thus brought to an abrupt end, I left Buenos Aires and flew back to the States.

After eight months in vast, underdeveloped South America, I was now less surprised by the size of the United States, but more impressed by the way the Americans had overcome the barriers of long distance communications—something that had eluded all the other countries large enough to cover one continent. The Americans had created a sense of national unity the Soviets had failed to achieve despite their centralized government. And there was an immediacy about everything in the States that was unique. I was stupefied that a picture I took on a Saturday would be on every news-stand from Maine to California by Wednesday.

Offered a chance to work for *Life* in the United States, I jumped at it. (Until then, I had been employed by Time Inc.'s British company.) This meant getting a resident's visa before I was allowed to take any pictures.

Because I was born in Algeria and came under the French quota, I had to fly to Canada to pick up my new visa. On my return, we landed in Bennington, Vermont, where an inspector came aboard, called out my name, told me to follow him, and to see that my luggage was taken off the aircraft. I was devastated to be told that I'd have to submit to an examination to see whether I would be admitted into the United States.

I was led into a room where three officials, two men and one woman, were seated. They asked if I wanted a lawyer. I said no. I was then asked kindly, but persistently, why I wanted to emigrate to the United States, why I should be admitted, would I take someone else's job, would I become a burden to the States, or did I plan to overthrow the American government?

This went on until the female official said that she had no objection to my being admitted into the country. The two men agreed with her. We shook hands. They left for lunch and left me shaking. Even today, I can still recall my terror—the worst I ever experienced, which is saying something as I have since become quite an authority on the subject.

The next plane took off at 4:30. Anxiously I kept looking at my watch to see how much longer I had to wait, as though I could escape the authorities if they had a mind to detain me. During those hours, I reviewed what it would have meant had I failed to gain admission. I would never have set foot in the States again and, very possibly, I would never have taken another picture for *Life*. I'd no longer be able to take care of my father and mother, who depended on me entirely. Although my father came from country gentry, a class that usually led a life of leisure on the proceeds of their land, his extravagance had made it necessary to sell much of his land and mortgage the rest.

I had never really known security, but insecurity was not something you became accustomed to, and I sat at the bar trembling. What had terrified me about these immigration officers was not their behavior, but the implication of what could happen if they had found me an undesirable.

During the three years I worked in the States, I shot 172 stories and got married twice. Through the kaleidoscope of pictures I took, I got to see something of the country. Through my marriages, I learned something about myself.

I also found out that taking pictures in the States was much easier than in Europe. Americans welcomed the *Life* photographer. They posed so naturally there was rarely that dreadful sense of staginess which had to be overcome in Europe. On a hot summer day, President Roosevelt, for example, appeared so elegantly at ease in shirt sleeves and bow tie in his White House office, he did not mind being photographed. Thinking of my encounter with his counterpart in Britain, I could imagine Neville Chamberlain's scrawny Adam's apple bobbing nervously up and down inside his wing-collar at such a prospect.

Being new to America often provided fresh insight on a story, but my ignorance also led me astray. On my first trip south to Atlanta, I sat at the back of the airport bus, much to the annoyance of the driver who asked me to move forward. Since I'm tall, and I was able to stretch my legs, I refused to move. The driver, for his part, refused to drive off, and I sensed a hostility from the other passengers I could not understand. Finally, since the driver was becoming incoherent, a passenger, more worldly than the others, broke the deadlock. "Can't you see he's a foreigner and doesn't know that niggras sit in the back."

Democratic Convention, Chicago, 1940

Democratic Convention, Chicago, 1940

Macy's Parade, New York, 1941

Confederate Civil War veteran, Birmingham, Alabama, 1940

Presidential election, Thomas E. Dewey, Wisconsin, 1940

Bathhouse at Homestead Hotel, Hot Springs, Virginia, 1941

Homestead Hotel baseball team, Hot Springs, Virginia, 1941

Guests of the Homestead Hotel, Hot Springs, Virginia, 1941

Alfred Stieglitz, New York, 1943

Charlie Chaplin at Condé Nast party, New York, 1940

Striptease act during a star-spangled benefit at the Astor, New York, 1940

Car hops, Corpus Christi, Texas, 1940

Designers drawing up war plans, Corpus Christi, Texas, 1940

Association of Machinists' float on Defense Day, Birmingham, Alabama, 1940

My first story took me to Massachusetts where I photographed the Republican Congressman Joe Martin, the minority leader of the House. Before leaving, Wilson Hicks had instructed me to visualize Joe Martin as a latter-day Abraham Lincoln. "He may be presidential timber."

The Republicans were anti-New Deal, and since as a European I greatly admired President Roosevelt, I felt apprehensive about Joe Martin. To my ignorant surprise, he turned out to be so friendly that I told him I had just been admitted to the United States. He promised to help me get my citizenship, should I need assistance. I was taken aback when he told me that he was a lapsed Catholic. (One thing I knew was that no Catholic had ever been elected President.) That decided me to let Wilson Hicks know that his Abraham Lincoln was a lapsed Catholic. When he heard this, he ordered me right back to New York.

He was not at all impressed when I grandly showed him what I considered a very unusual picture: Joe Martin eating apple pie with a scoop of vanilla ice-cream. I was thinking of how I'd been put in my place on board the *Bremen* over the giant baked potato when Hicks snapped, "Haven't you ever heard of apple pie *à la mode?*"

As 1940 was an election year, Hicks assigned me to the campaign, assuming that everything would be such a novelty I would be bound to come up with original shots. The country was concerned over the possibility that President Roosevelt might consider a third term. According to Republican pundits, this would mean the end of democracy and free elections; no longer the land where George Washington, in his infinite wisdom, had turned down a third term and made two terms sacrosanct.

The Republicans discussed the subject in ominous tones. The sense of impending doom was heightened by my mother's elderly first cousin. He had been the commodore of the exclusive Edgartown Yacht Club in Martha's Vineyard and was a devout Republican, like all the members of my mother's family. He now brooded about "that man in the White House who had betrayed his class".

The possibility of a third term hung heavily over the senior editors of *Life,* but didn't bother the smaller fry. I felt there would be no tragedy, owing to the American propensity for humor. When a Democratic spokesman asserted you couldn't change horses in mid-stream, a photographer shot a horseman doing just that for a full page in the magazine.

What enlivened an otherwise sedate campaign were the stunts set up for candidates that backfired. The dignified Senator Taft had been convinced to let himself be photographed catching a dead fish. The story ran in *Life*, much to his embarrassment.

Editors had to be wary of their photographers. Mr Billings, the managing editor, was about to run a full page on Thomas E. Dewey, the former district attorney-turned-presidential candidate, when he became suspicious about a round white mound in the background. Discovering it was the rear end of a white horse, he was amused, but the picture did not run.

I was assigned to the Dewey party when he toured Wisconsin. Dewey was small in size and neat in appearance, with a well-groomed black moustache which attempted to make him look mature. It failed, however, to overcome the widespread understanding that he "had tossed his diaper in the ring". A smoker, he would never be photographed with a cigarette as he set himself up as a role model for youth. For a time, his entourage referred to him as "the gang-buster" for his successful prosecution of the mobster Lucky Luciano. This nickname was soon dropped and he became known as just "Buster". In my total ignorance and on an admittedly superficial appraisal, Thomas E. Dewey did not look to me the man who would defeat Franklin Roosevelt should he consider running for a third term.

I joined the Dewey party in Milwaukee where they had boarded a train with an observation coach. We journeyed to Madison, stopping at every small town. There we remained for five minutes at the depot where the faithful awaited their only chance to see the candidate. Before Dewey addressed the crowd, the politicos who were aboard briefed him about the local personalities and conditions, reminding him to mention that he loved Wisconsin cheese: simple enough as Wisconsin was a dairy state. My job was to hop off the train and get shots of Dewey addressing the crowd before hopping back on before the train pulled out.

At one station, I recall an onlooker asking Dewey if he liked the cheese they made in this town. When he told them it was his usual fare, his reply was greeted in total silence. As I climbed aboard the observation car, I heard a member of the audience say, "Doesn't he know we don't make cheese in this burg?"

I was then switched from Dewey to Wendell L. Willkie. Willkie was not officially running for president, but he had attracted Harry Luce and a number of his friends as a possible candidate. As a try-out on the radio, he appeared on the most popular quiz show called "Information Please", which had highbrow overtones. I shot the broadcast. Willkie was a success.

Early in May I was pulled off the Willkie story and flown to Fort Benning, Georgia, to cover the greatest American military maneuvers to date: 80,000 troops were to be trucked to the Sabine River area in Louisiana and Texas where exercises were to take place. Three hundred B-17s, practically the total number of US bombers, would participate. I was assigned to the 1st Division, which had been first to see action overseas in World War I. Now a streamlined division, it was commanded by Brigadier Karl Truesdell, who gazed out on the world through a pair of gold-rimmed *pince-nez*.

His vision turned out to be remarkable. After dinner at the mess, with chilling clarity he outlined the moves he expected Hitler to make in the West, sweeping through Belgium and Holland with disastrous results for the Allies. Three days later, on May 7, Hitler unleashed his *Blitzkrieg*, achieving just what General Truesdell had predicted.

The 1st Division drove out of Fort Benning heading for Mississippi. At the time I noted what seemed—at least to a European—almost incredible: the smalltown scenes of this great country. Crowds lined the road waving affectionate signs. One was held by a Mr James Edgar Chancellor, a wealthy businessman. It read: "Goodbye 16th Infantry. God Bless You. We love you all from Colonel Chas. H. Rice to buck private, and wish you a safe trip and quick return to Fort Benning."

There was also: "We damn country villagers like you all, Sgt Soutner, Sgt Lepski, Sgt Conrad, and my friend, Staff Sgt Eddie Miller."

The most original was held by William Grant, a grinning black man from Bob's Bar. An empty Scotch bottle dangled from the sign: "Bob's— That's all."

On the first leg of the journey, 1,288 motor vehicles transported some 8,400 men 103 miles in seven hours. When we got to Mississippi, I had heard the expression, "like Grant took Vicksburg". And so I went to see the statue there commemorating the event. An American officer was gazing at it. Not a bad picture, I thought. Before I could shoot it, the officer turned on me and shouted, "Don't!"

Several days later I found the same man in a Shreveport bar. "You must have thought me rude," this Colonel said.

Republicans, Wisconsin, 1940

"Why, yes sir."

"Normally I'm not."

"I'm sure of that, sir."

"Have a drink with me, and I'll tell you why I didn't want that picture taken. My grandfather was Robert E. Lee."

On my return to New York, a cable awaited me from France. The cancer my mother had been fighting had been diagnosed as terminal. The trip to the States I had planned for her would do her good, but she should come right away. As both my father and mother had their visas, and a ship was sailing for New York from Liverpool, I didn't anticipate any problems with their coming immediately. I had the $1,000 in the bank required by the authorities, and as I had turned over my entire bank account in England where my salary had been paid for the past 16 months, my parents had the money for the sea journey. At least I thought so, until my father cabled for the amount for the passage. He had spent everything I had sent him. Very embarrassed, I requested a loan from *Life*, which was graciously granted.

My parents got the money in time to sail. Mother got back to her native land, and saw her sister before dying. My father's extravagance continued. It only came to an end with his death in Rome on January 15, 1951—just at the time I could finally afford him.

I got back to Willkie in time for the Republican Convention in Philadelphia. Willkie had been a Democrat until he changed his affiliation to the Republican Party. A self-made man, his fortune had earned him the ironic sobriquet from the Democrats, "the barefoot boy from Wall Street". I found him likeable and not stuck up like Dewey. Although he was not the favorite at the start, he gained steadily in each one of the breathtaking ballots to encouragement from the galleries: "We want Willkie! We want Willkie!" Finally Willkie clinched the nomination in a frenzy of enthusiasm, and committed his first mistake: called upon to make an acceptance speech, he didn't appear and the crestfallen public was told,"Willkie's gone to bed."

The Democratic Convention in Chicago turned out to be far less high-minded than its Republican counterpart. The Roosevelt faithful were planning the third term for the President. The New Deal powerhouse—the Federal Loan Administrator, the Attorney General, the Secretaries of the Interior,

Labor, and Agriculture —were all on hand. Harry Hopkins, the social worker-turned-politico, and "Boss" Kelly, as the notorious Mayor of Chicago was called, were busy at the Blackstone Hotel, which was linked to the White House by a direct phone line.

Assembled in Chicago to nominate the presidential candidate, the delegates enjoyed themselves in the city bedecked with pictures of Roosevelt. A number of them sought revelry at the famous Club 606 at 606 South Wabash Avenue. The house specialty was non-stop striptease. A sense of intimacy was created with the tables right up against the stage at the same level. I shot Tiger Lily performing her bumps and grinds before a mesmerized delegate. (*Life* ran the picture, and the week it did by coincidence I met the delegate on assignment. Fortunately, he didn't realize I was the one who'd shot the picture, as his wife was in a fury.)

Harry Luce, the founder of *Life*, did not attend the convention. He thoroughly disapproved of the third term. *Life*'s description of it as "the cynical end-justifies-the-means alliance" of New Deal reformers and self-seeking city bosses to engineer the draft left an exceedingly sour taste.

My assignment was to illustrate *Life*'s sentiments by getting a picture of Harry Hopkins and Boss Kelly together. My problem was Hopkins didn't want such a picture taken. The two were never seen together conferring. Boss Kelly remained in an adjoining room, where he worked the telephone, and Harry Hopkins went in to consult with him whenever the need arose. I simply sat in Harry Hopkins's suite while journalists and politicos milled around. After two days, no one paid any attention to me while I waited. Then came a phone call apparently so important that Boss Kelly joined Hopkins. The pair, deep in conversation, never noticed me. Then the flash reminded Harry Hopkins the "*Life* guy" was still here. "You had better leave now," he said curtly. And I did.

Will Lang, the *Life* reporter with me in Chicago, notified New York I'd got the picture they'd been hoping for. I caught the next plane to New York and went straight to the lab, before going home to get some sleep. An hour later, I got a frantic call. The Hopkins-Boss Kelly picture was missing. I called up Lang in Chicago. He went to my hotel room. By chance, it had not yet been made up. In the middle of the bed was my missing film. It made the flight to New York and the *Life* issue. It didn't, however, prevent Roosevelt from being swept back into office.

Democratic Convention, Chicago, 1940

Wedding in Birmingham, Alabama, 1940

Some stories are doomed from the start. The worst I can recall was a wedding in Birmingham, Alabama. *Life*'s fashion department had come up with the nuptials of the year. The bride had ordered some 40 dresses from I. Magnin in Los Angeles. A wedding counselor would come with the trousseau. I was to shoot the bride in every one of her dresses so that the magazine could run them in a strip.

The problems started as soon as I landed in Birmingham. Our stringer, who met me at the airport, told me that owing to a confusion in dates, I had arrived in mid-morning of the wedding day. To add to my irritation, he insisted on putting me up in his home—something I hated, much preferring to stay at a hotel.

We reached the bride's house shortly before she her hairddressing and manicure appointments were due. Her trousseau, she told us, was already on its way to Havana. All she had left with her were the eight dresses she planned to wear on her wedding trip.

Realizing there was no story I wanted to cancel the assignment, but the mother and daughter were so eager for me to take their pictures, and our stringer was so anxious not to displease such important people, I agreed to stay. Enthusiastically the bride quickly made eight dress changes so as to be punctual at the hairdresser, while I shot banal pictures.

In the middle of this ordeal, I felt a tap on my shoulder. It was the father of the bride. He was tall, imposing, and extremely annoyed. He had never wanted his "baby's" wedding to be photographed by *Life*. He had only reluctantly given in, at his wife and daughter's insistence. He was nevertheless prepared to sue if the magazine did not do right by his baby. So, dressed in white tie, tails, and sporting a topper, as had been ordained by the bride's mother, I showed up with the stringer at the club where the wedding was to take place.

A large drawing-room had been set up as a chapel. On the improvised altar a golden crucifix emerged from a sumptuous bouquet with two large candelabras on either side. The three windows behind the altar, in fact all the windows in the room, were partly masked by large floral arrangements. The spaces between the windows were taken up by more candelabras. I have no idea if the wedding ceremony was conducted by candlelight as the bride's father had informed me I could not attend the church ceremony or photograph the buffet supper.

I got one shot of the bride standing in front of the altar ready for her official wedding picture. Her long train had been perfectly arranged by the wedding counselor, herself an image of perfection. Tall, slim and extremely chic, she radiated a heady fragrance of what I immediately recognised as Schiaparelli's "Shocking". While the official wedding photographer set up his camera, I got another picture of the bride just as a black mess boy was sweeping away the flower petals that littered the parquet floor.

Annoyed with myself for not calling the story off and for accepting the stringer's hospitality when I might have been enjoying a drink at the hotel, I sat feeling sorry for myself, when I overheard the best man and two of his cronies. They were the worse for drink and louder than they imagined as they gloated over a prank they had set up for the young married couple. The best man had called up the police, given the license number of the newly-weds' car and reported it as stolen.

While the dancing was in progress, the married couple prepared to leave. I took the bride's father aside and told him about the best man's prank. "You, of all people, warning me," he exclaimed.

"I certainly didn't do it for you," I assured him. "But I thought it would be a shame if your daughter was the victim of such a prank on her wedding night."

"I should have allowed you to photograph the wedding," he said.

"It's bit late now," I replied.

As I was leaving with the stringer, the attractive marriage counselor stopped me. "Don't you think it's sad going to bed alone after a wedding party? Why don't you join me?" I offered her a lift with us in the stringer's car, damning Southern hospitality in a haze of perfume. We dropped her off at her hotel. Very reluctantly, I bid goodnight to what could have been the only redeeming feature of the assignment.

Wedding in Charleston, South Carolina, 1941

Wedding guests outside the bride's home, Charleston, South Carolina, 1941

Wedding in Charleston, South Carolina, 1941

The official wedding picture, Charleston, South Carolina, 1941

On President Roosevelt's 59th birthday in January 1941, I had occasion to observe a fundamental friendliness in the American character. That morning, a 14-year-old girl named Anna Sklepovich showed up at the White House gates. She had just got off the bus from Gary, West Virginia, where she lived with her parents and older brother. She was clutching the usual form letter sent under the President's signature, thanking those who had wished him a happy birthday. Anna, born on the same day as the President, had done just that. The letter she held, however, was unusual. Beneath the signature was a hand-written postscript inviting her to visit Washington as the President's guest.

This being America, Anna's parents saw nothing unusual about the invitation. They put their daughter on the bus for the 400-mile journey to Washington. The idea that this might be a prank played by Anna's older brother never occurred to them.

The White House guard, realizing that Anna was the victim of a hoax, called up the President's secretary. She notified the President. The President received Anna and invited her to be his guest for the birthday celebrations, which was how Anna Sklepovich, now rechristened the "Cinderella Girl" by the press, became my assignment.

I first photographed Anna leaving the White House. She was heavy-set, and her long pointed nose accentuated her sharp Slav features. She described the President as, "Grand. Looking young, and not formal." We then drove to the Lincoln Memorial where she gazed at Lincoln's statue with the same lack of expression she displayed at the Washington Monument, and at the Tomb of the Unknown Soldier in Arlington Cemetery. She did express surprise, however, during her visit to the Library of Congress when she discovered that blacks were allowed in the reading room.

After lunch, Police Officer Myrtle Richards, who had been assigned as Anna's chaperone while she was in Washington, bought her a pair of slippers to go with the evening dress she had brought with her. She then visited John Kee, the Congressman from her district in West Virginia, who gave Anna passes for both the Senate and Congress. Above all, he recommended that she be sure to tell "the good people from his district" that he wished them well. The Congressman's wife gave Anna a short black fur coat. On her way back to the Mayflower Hotel, Anna granted NBC a brief sidewalk interview, repeating her views about the President.

Anna Sklepovich getting an autograph from Lana Turner, Washington, 1941

That evening, Commissioner George Allen, Washington's official greeter, who had squired the King and Queen of England during their state visit to the United States, was Anna's escort. He arrived at the Mayflower in full evening-dress to take her to the various benefits celebrating the President's birthday. Anna wore her full-length white evening-dress completed by with the camellia corsage the debonair Commissioner had sent.

Wearing a black tie, I trailed after the pair with two reporters, all of us trying to create the illusion of escorting a celebrity. At every hotel, Anna was introduced to the guests and received a round of applause. Self-conscious at first, she gained confidence as the evening wore on. By the time we reached the Wardman Park, Anna was signing autographs as she went. Very composed, she was introduced to Deanna Durbin and Lana Turner and got their autographs for herself. Along with the two film stars, she joined Mrs Roosevelt on the stage where a huge birthday cake was to be cut for the photo-opportunity.

Following Police Officer Richards's orders, we got Anna back to the Mayflower by midnight. There, she obligingly signed her last autograph for a dazzled child barely four years her junior. About to step into the elevator, she spotted the actor Tony Curtis and shook hands with her last celebrity. Escorted to her room she removed her slippers and wrote letters to her friends on Mayflower stationery.

At nine the next morning, Police Officer Richards saw Anna Sklepovich to the bus. Four hundred miles away Gary, West Virginia, was about to welcome back its most illustrious citizen.

Secrecy was never an American forte. I was reminded of this when I photographed Colonel William Donovan the head of project COI. Donovan, a man of very considerable vitality, had been asked by President Roosevelt to create a new department. The Office of Co-ordinator of Information was described to me as "the world of information applied to intelligence, rather than propaganda". I was assigned the story within days of Colonel Donovan's appointment.

As soon as I began following the Colonel around, I became suspicious about what the COI was really about. We first went to the Navy Department building, to see Frank Knox, the Secretary of the Navy. Donovan's opening words were, "As you know, we're preparing for war…"

Isolationists at an America First rally, New York, 1941

Yale University, 1942

Student fascists' day, Staten Island, 1941

General Patton, Fort Benning, Georgia, 1941

This meeting over, we then visited the poet Archibald MacLeish at the Library of Congress, and Nelson Rockefeller, the co-ordinator of Inter-American affairs. In those early days, the atmosphere at COI was urgent and makeshift. The Colonel's temporary office at the old State Department building did not even have a telephone. I photographed the Colonel at all hours on the phone in his living-room and bedroom as he made notes on his yellow pad. He would hold morning meetings over breakfast, conduct afternoon interviews on the porch, and entertain his staff at late candle-light dinners in his elegant Georgetown mansion.

In one of the last pictures I took of him, he was in the back seat of his car, wearing his old Panama hat, which made him look benevolent. Resting on the empty seat was a large manila envelope and some other mail. The Colonel was deep in a copy of *Madame Bovary* in the original French. This surprised me as I'd been told that he didn't speak it. Why, then, pose reading a book in French? To have the picture published in *Life* and create the illusion he was fluent in French. But for whose benefit? Eleven months later I got an answer of sorts. By then, the US was at war, COI had become the OSS—the Office of Strategic Services—code for the American intelligence service—and its boss was Colonel William Donovan.

Back at Fort Benning, the Corps of Engineers I was sent to photograph had no regard for secrecy. They were eager that *Life* make public their latest invention: a rubber pontoon bridge. It had been specially designed for armoured vehicles and could be assembled in no time, I was told. In addition, this bridge could easily be concealed from the enemy while in transit. Its simple parts could be transported in a normal army convoy. The engineers were true to their word. A 28-ton tank rumbled across the 315-foot Chattahoochee River on a pontoon bridge they had assembled in just over two hours.

This bridge was made up of a number of rubber pontoons strung together (20 in the case of the Chattahoochee). They were inflated on the river bank by a compressor truck. To prevent the pontoons from being destroyed by enemy fire, each one was compartmentalized into ten sections. Each individual section weighed 600 pounds and was carried to the water's edge by eleven men. A steel treadway was lifted into place by a light motorized crane. Beneath each treadway, a steel frame and a plywood saddle were installed to distribute the weight over the float. Each pontoon section was propelled into position by an outboard motor. The low-riding pontoon made the usual abutment work unnecessary. "It's quite an invention," a gleeful engineer told me.

While photographing the pontoon bridge being assembled, I had noticed a general observing the operation with undivided attention. I had rarely seen anyone look so satisfied. There was something so striking about him that I took his picture, and once the pontoon was assembled, I went to find out who this general was. I came up to him while he was conversing with two young officers and overheard the tag-end of a remark by one of them. He had expressed surprise that the general was in favor of court-martialing some officer who had disobeyed orders. "But you approved of Sheridan disobeying orders at Missionary Bridge during the Civil War," he told the general. The general agreed. "The difference was that Sheridan had been successful."

I learned that the general's name was George S. Patton Jr, which meant nothing to me at the time. He apparently had some future plans for that pontoon bridge. He had a similar bridge with him when he unex-pectedly appeared on the banks of the Rhine on March 22, 1945. With neg-ligible opposition, he bridged the Rhine in 48 hours and put four divisions on German soil with only 34 casualties. As the engineer had said, the pontoon bridge was quite an invention.

I was in Tennessee with the Corps of Engineers on Sunday, December 7, 1941. They were about to blast several bridges which had become obsolete owing to the Tennessee Valley Authority's project of building dams and flooding the area. After spending the morning photographing them blowing up bridges. I drove with the conducting officer back to Knoxville. We were on the road a good hour before he asked me what I thought about the rumor a sergeant had picked up on the radio that Pearl Harbor had been bombed by the Japanese. "It can't be a rumor," I said.

"You know how these guys are," he argued.

"We must be at war," I insisted. The captain believed me only after we reached Knoxville and found out I was right.

My first thought had been for my wife Peggy. We had been married for 18 months, and her father was Japanese. This news meant he would be regarded as an enemy alien. Peggy wasn't at home when I called and I got no reply from her parents' house in White Plains. Back in New York, I found her at the office. She said she had been with her parents when the radio carried the report of the attack on Pearl Harbor. Her father's words were, "That's the end of Japan," as he walked off to pack an overnight bag in anticipation of being detained, which he was.

Peggy's father was a tragic misfit. He had come to the States a young man and never returned to Japan. A distinguished architect, he married a Scottish-American woman and lived according to a strict Japanese code which his friends regarded as archaic. Desperate for a son, he never got over having a daughter and this led to a classic type of parental cruelty.

I met Peggy at *Life* where she was Wilson Hicks's secretary. She was slim and extraordinarily elegant. Her Asian heritage simply added an exotic touch to her beauty, and a few freckles made her look the delightful person she was. A graduate of Smith College, she had originally been slated to be Hicks's assistant, but he had managed to have her side-tracked as his secretary. She cheerfully handled the photographers and became their lifeline to the magazine. They all liked her. This annoyed Hicks, who knew that he was unpopular with his photographers, and didn't care. The reason was simple. He never stood up for them. He would never comment about the assignments he sent them on until he found out what the managing editor thought. In some cases, this meant waiting for months. Hicks had tried in vain to get rid of Peggy and replace her with a more compliant secretary.

We had married in August, 1940. Peggy was so self-possessed that I never got the impression she might be disturbed by the anti-Japanese sentiments prevailing at the time. She had never been to Japan, and her Asian background rarely seemed to affect her. She remembered how at Smith, a counselor planning a promotional picture had asked her to pose in her national costume. She appeared in shorts and sneakers, much to the irritation of the counselor who demanded to know why she didn't wear a kimono. As she seemed amused by the story, I didn't perceive a more somber emotion. I was first made aware of Americans' attitudes towards Asians when we planned to move into a new apartment, but were turned down because "Asians were not welcome".

When I caught up with Peggy on December 8, she was calm. Her father was in detention on New York's Governor's Island pending a hearing that would determine whether he'd be interned or released as trustworthy. (He had built barracks for the army during the First World War, and Jessie Jones, who had been the powerful head of the RFC—the Reconstruction Finance Corporation—eventually vouched for him and gained his release.) Meanwhile, Peggy took the boat to Governor's Island once a week to visit him. On these same boat trips was a captain in the US Army who was also visiting his interned father.

The war provided Wilson Hicks with an excuse to get rid of Peggy. In January he asked for her transfer to another department, claiming that her presence in his office would create an unfavorable impression in wartime America. Hicks, lacking the courage to say this to my face, went through management, who took his word. It was obviously unfair as all the people Hicks had dealings with knew Peggy and liked her. Hicks's fears that employing a Japanese in wartime would damage *Life*'s reputation was a shameless excuse. Peggy refused to take on another job; working with photographers had been her life. She resigned, came home, and never went out of the house after that.

My work kept me away most of the time, and Peggy remained alone. I realized how much I had failed her when I suggested having a child. With terrifying calm, she told me that she would never let a child go through what she was going through.

I was on a story in Chicago when I got word she was in hospital with a bad fever. Beyond that, nobody seemed to know what she was suffering from. Specialists were called in, but they couldn't find the cause of the illness. Her fever never subsided and Peggy died three weeks later. The young doctor who had been in attendance asked me if I would authorize an autopsy since they had no idea what had caused her death. He said, with no sense of irony, that it would be in the interests of medical progress. I agreed on condition she would not be disfigured. She had died of septicemia, which was fatal in those pre-penicillin days.

I was miserable over Peggy's short and very sad life, feeling that I had failed her. Soon after her death, I met the executive who had hired Peggy at *Life*. She recalled meeting her in the elevator and remarking on her very handsome new coat. "My husband gave it to me," Peggy said with a happy smile. That small story made me feel perhaps I hadn't been a total failure after all.

I was miserable and lonely, too, shooting stories while awaiting my military clearance to the Pacific theater of operations. Partly because of my character, partly because of my work, I got to meet a lot of people briefly, but made no friends. I could never make definite appointments because I could be sent on an assignment for days, even weeks, at an hour's notice. The only people I really knew were colleagues who kept the same type of schedule I did. I grew increasingly lonely. Before I was to leave for the Pacific, the Allies invaded North Africa. As I had grown up in that part of the world, my assignment was switched. While I waited for my clearance, I did something foolish. Out of loneliness, I married a tall California blonde. It was a serious mistake. We had nothing in common and I would be responsible for the inevitable break-up of our marriage. Humiliated, she cleaned out my bank account, and left me with only a summer suit and my father's debts.

The "Hoopla" booth at an RAF benefit, La Guardia Airport, New York, 1941

The Tabian

"I'm assigning you to the Middle East," Wilson Hicks said. "You're to join Montgomery's 8th Army for its link-up with the United States 5th Army in Tunisia." *Life*'s picture editor took a martial tone when sending his photographers to the war zones.

On March 3, 1943, I reported to the Brooklyn Navy Yards in uniform, but unaccustomed to saluting. I signed a postcard addressed to my family announcing my safe arrival at a destination left blank to be posted whenever I reached that destination—wherever it might be. I then joined a group of 24 awaiting embarkation. All but four were in uniform. A cutter took us to our ship, which was not the Queen Elizabeth, as Wilson Hicks had predicted, but the motor ship *Tabian*, an ancient 8,000-ton Dutch freighter, chartered by the United States.

The decks were crowded by massive ambulatory cisterns which left little room to move around. We were six in a cabin for two. My room-mates were a rabbi, a Protestant missionary, a representative of Lend-Lease, the organisation Roosevelt had set up to give aid to the Allies, and two members of the Office of Strategic Services. Captain Prisen, the *Tabian*'s skipper, briefed us in the small wardroom where we'd have our meals in two shifts. "There will be no boat drill," he announced. "It's unnecessary. Our cargo being explosives. It'll all be over in three seconds if we're torpedoed."

Turning to the missionary, I asked, "What are you doing here?"

"I'm on my way to Ethiopia to convert heathens."

"Heathens?" I echoed in disbelief.

"There is a lot to be done there," the missionary sighed. "Fortunately, my wife Pansy will soon join me."

Life-jackets were then issued. "They will come in handy on chilly nights," Captain Prisen said. "But what you really need are parachutes."

The Dutch crew might be philosophical about their cargo, but they were intransigent when it came to liquor, and Bols gin was plentiful. Cooks, cabin boys and stewards had jumped ship in New York, but Immigration produced enough Javanese deserters to fill our quota. The *Tabian* was equipped with Oerlikon anti-aircraft guns and a cannon at the stern of the ship. The American gun crew was under the command of Lieutenant Pickard. "Our enemy is the U-boat," he told us. "At all times be on the look out for periscopes."

"What does a periscope look like?" I asked.

"To be honest, I've never seen one myself," the lieutenant said, "but, I'm told it looks like a glass watermelon."

The most nervous person on board was one of his gunners. At the slightest sound he'd be out of his bunk and up the companionway. He had watched a munitions ship blow up. Asked what it had been like, he said, "One minute the ship was out there. Then there was a huge orange ball of fire and a tremendous bang. Then there was nothing, and you've no idea how nothing nothing can be."

We sailed out of Brooklyn Navy Yard on a sunny winter morning. Our convoy was made up of 27 freighters escorted by destroyers. Blimps provided a festive touch. The *Tabian* was so far back from all the other ships we were part of the convoy in theory only. "Why is that?"" I asked Captain Prisen.

"In the First World War, a munitions ship blew up in Halifax and practically wiped out the harbor. Just imagine what we'd do to this convoy if we got hit and the ships were not at a safe distance."

A sign was posted on the bulletin board: "From dark to daylight, don't throw anything overboard. It will leave a trail. Day and night don't speak of the trip or the cargo. The enemy is always listening. Don't ask to be sunk." We got a reminder when we came upon wreckage floating on the surface along with a dead Airedale.

Our Javanese cooks paid no attention to the warning. They regularly dumped garbage over the side. "The closer you get to the front, the more the restrictions fall off," Lieutenant Pickard said, and an exchange I had with Colonel Goodrich, the senior officer of the field grade group, while we were both on the lookout for glass watermelons certainly bore this out. Like all his officers, Colonel Goodrich was not regular army. A lawyer in civilian life, he told me that all the members of his team were specialists. For his part, he was the commanding officer of OCCA's Team One. I wasn't particularly interested in the initials until he explained what they stood for: Officers in Charge of Civil Affairs in Occupied Areas.

"What do you mean by occupied areas?" I asked, baffled.

"Italy," he said.

"Italy?" I repeated, stupefied. And in this casual way I learned that Italy, in some near future, was to be invaded by the Allies, and that the members of the occupying mission were passengers aboard the *Tabian*. They represented, under their official titles: Fiscal and Financial Affairs, Public Safety, Public Welfare, Public Health, Public Works and Utilities, Public Relations, Communications, Justice, and Education. What struck me was the contrast between the care with which the team had been selected and the haphazard way they traveled. (In Rome after the war, I ran into Colonel Weber, the judicial member of the team. He had dealings with the Italian Justice Department. He told me everybody on the team had worked out except Goodrich, who had been dispatched to Marseilles as Provost Marshal.)

Though Captain Prisen had been all too explicit concerning our possible future, he wasn't at all forthcoming about our destination. We were traveling under sealed orders. We reached Guantánamo Bay, the US naval base in Cuba, on a Sunday. A convoy conference was called, attended by all the captains. The sealed orders were opened. We finally knew our course was set to Egypt. The Straits of Gibraltar were still closed to Allied shipping, so we would take a southern route via the Panama Canal, along the Southern Pacific coast of South America, around Cape Horn, into the South Atlantic, around the Cape of Good Hope, into the Indian Ocean, through the Gulf of Aden, down the Red Sea, into the Gulf of Suez, finally reaching Port Taufiq in Egypt. This 18,000-mile journey at an optimistically estimated speed of eight knots an hour would mean the *Tabian* was going to be home for the next two months at least.

With this prospect in mind we grumbled at not getting shore leave. Only our gunners were allowed to visit Guantánamo. They returned disgruntled, having failed to find any female companionship on the base. Only two of them reported for prophylactics—to the astonished envy of all the others. But the pair had simply gone through the formality to make their buddies believe they had got laid.

Less than 24 hours later, our convoy was on its way to the Panama Canal. There was a full moon when we reached it, and we could not seek its shelter because the defensive mine fields had been activated. Instead, we were put on alert for a U-boat pack in the area. I spent a nerve-wracking night on the upper deck with the financial advisor to the military mission. He confided in me about his business deals with Joseph P. Kennedy. His candor was embarassing. It was as if he was making a confession to a priest rather than conversing with a journalist. The next morning, while we sailed through the Canal, he avoided me sheepishly.

The *Tabian* required engine-room repairs. The Canal authorities, aware of our cargo, ordered them made at sea. Once outside the Canal zone, we cut our engines and drifted in silence beneath the full moon which lit up the south Pacific.

For weeks I lay in my bunk, two feet below the bulkhead, reflecting on Prisen's words: "It'll be over in three seconds." I imagined the crunch of a torpedo smashing through the hull and thinking, "This is it." Running the palm of my hand over the bulkhead's rough surface , I wondered whether I'd end up splattered against it. It took me several sleepless nights to realize that I'd be dead without even knowing it. This helped me sleep, but I haven't been quite the same since.

On our third Sunday at sea, William Gordon of Lend-Lease told me that a number of our traveling companions were in serious need of a church service. The ship was too small to accommodate the outbreaks of bad temper caused by idleness and the stressful conditions we were living under. So we approached Rabbi Ben Zion and Mr Russell, the missionary, and got their agreement to conduct services on alternate Sundays. Crossing the Equator provided an occasion for the traditional baptism at sea, with Lieutenant Pickard acting as Neptune.

We also started a number of other activities. I gave French lessons. We held a chess tournament. We had a morality play performed by a member of the OSS with a facility for reeling off bawdy poetry. We even put on a variety show, "The Tabian Follies", in which all of us were both participant and spectator. When not involved in group activities, we 25 were a class-conscious society. The young lieutenants shot craps. The field grade officers played poker. If they were short of a player, Colonel Goodrich, asserting his rank, would send a major to rouse me out of my bunk for an all-night game.

My usual companions were Bill Gordon and the three members of the OSS—in civilian life, an archeologist, a professor of ancient history, and a museum curator. Several of us made friends with the Dutch officers. I'd drop by and have a couple of gins with the chief engineer in his cabin when he was off duty. One evening, on his daughter's eighth birthday, he became emotional. He had not seen her for over four years. He produced a large box from a drawer beneath his bunk. Inside was a doll: "my daughter's fourth anniversary present."

Brons, the friendly electrician, enjoyed entertaining us. He not only told the worst jokes I'd ever heard, but had an irritating habit of repeating them. One night I stupidly told him he was a bore. Peering at me through his heavy bifocals he said, "When we reach Egypt you'll get off the ship. I'll be stuck on board with a prospect of being torpedoed. What have I to look forward to as I'm half-blind and can't swim? To sit in my cabin and go down with the ship. Please, be a little more considerate."

I got to know Captain Prisen who showed me a cutting from *Life* of the pictures I had taken in Patagonia. Captain Prisen had been the skipper of a 30,000-ton transport bound for the Netherlands when he picked up the message Rotterdam had fallen to the Germans. He promptly headed for the nearest British port. Ever since, he'd been sailing for the Allies.

Ironically enough, we were safest when under the worst conditions. The time we ran into such a fierce tempest rounding the Horn, the *Tabian* had to reduce its speed to three knots an hour and drift to prevent our deck cargo being ripped off. Those four days were the safest of the entire journey. No U-boat was lurking around the Horn to destroy a small Dutch freighter.

We entered the South Atlantic and prepared to dock briefly in Cape Town. Colonel Gevers, the education officer on the military mission, and I were determined to get rid of an obnoxious Javanese cabin boy bequeathed to us in New York. When I suggested he jump ship in Cape Town, he refused to do so unless someone took his precious guitar on shore for him. He knew the duty officer would detain him if he did so himself. Colonel Gevers was the only one with both the authority and the willingness to oblige. With great solemnity, he carried the guitar ashore. That was the last of the cabin boy.

At Aden, our next port of call, Mr Russell was to leave us for his heathens. He had been such a good sport, we decided to hold an auction for his mission. Having nothing of value, we auctioned off the home-made song-sheets used for the religious services. Along with the ship's seal there was a handwritten mention: "These sheets were sold at auction on May 9,

1943, for the benefit of the work of the United Presbyterian Mission in Ethiopia in appreciation of our friend Mr Russell." Using methods Mr Russell would not have approved of we sold all 25 sheets and raised $125. "It's a real body-blow against Satan," Mr Russell told us, almost in tears.

When I said goodbye to him, he offered me a drink. Knowing him to be abstemious, I asked for a lemon squash. Stopping the waiter, Mr Russell said, "Bring him a gin," adding, "I don't think it will hurt you."

On May 12, while in the Red Sea, we picked up the communiqué that the Afrika Korps had surrendered in Tunis. The 8,000 tons of highly volatile explosives we had all perched on for 73 days were no longer required by Montgomery's forces. The campaign I'd been assigned to cover was over.

Four days later we put into Port Taufiq. The authorities there were surprised to see us. We had been reported sunk by the Germans. Leaning over the side of the ship waiting to disembark, I reflected there was no satisfaction in photographing a munitions ship. If nothing happened, you had no story. If something did, you had no photographer.

Shadow of a minaret, Egypt, 1948

To the
Middle East

King Farouk's escort in the streets, Cairo, 1943

King Farouk in his Palace, Cairo, 1943

King Farouk

"Put on a *tarboosh* and try to look Egyptian," instructed Commander Atif Bey, King Farouk's grinning aide. "His Majesty doesn't want the British to know he's taking you along." So I obediently donned a fez and presented myself at Cairo's royal palace, ready to leave for Lower Egypt and witness Farouk's newly regained popularity.

Our procession consisted of a car for me, followed by Farouk's bright-red Rolls Royce sedan, wedged between two convertibles filled with armed aides and brought up in the rear by a truckload of soldiers waving rifles. This whole ensemble was surrounded by outriders who looked like curried shrimp as they leaped along on their saffron-colored motorcycles.

The passionate support for Farouk became apparent even before we left Abdin. Across the square, a crowd in filthy *jellabas* had gathered to gaze at us in awe, feverishly waving green banners that praised Allah and Malik Farouk in flowing Arabic squiggles. They were joined by a seven-piece brass band awaiting our departure to beat out the national anthem. The minute we crossed the palace gates we were swamped. The crowd, howling, dancing, prancing, unable and unwilling to contain itself, let out a long, raucous scream: *"Ash el Malik!"* (Long live the king!) We never got away from that howl the rest of the day. Wherever we drove there was a mob. In small towns across the countryside people overflowed the streets which were sprinkled with yellow sand where *gamouses* (water buffalo) were pinned down, their hoofs thrashing wildly in the air. At our approach, butchers hacked at the beasts' throats to the chant of *"Ash el Malik!"* The blood, mingling with the yellow sand, matched the color of Farouk's car as we drove past. This cattle, gifts from the local pashas to the populace, were to feast on in honor of the King.

Our first halt was in front of a gold-and-blue marquee specially erected on the side of the road to provide cool shade and refreshments—iced lemonade in wide, frosted pitchers, pastries of all kinds, including Turkish delight in confectioner's sugar, were spread out on trestle tables behind rows of large, red plush armchairs and more rows of bowing notables. No sooner had we slowed up than throngs broke through the police lines and surged toward Farouk. The soldiers in the truck fired wildly into the air to create a diversion, while the aides barely managed to get Farouk back into his Rolls before the *fellaheen* hurled themselves against it, sweeping away the bowing pashas in their black *stamboulines*, like driftwood in the midst of dirty white foam. The scene kept recurring along dusty roads and beneath a sun that invited sunstroke. Finally we reached Tanta and parked in front of a stone building strong enough to withstand Egyptian enthusiasm and cool enough to refresh the 24-year-old monarch.

"Well, am I popular with my subjects or not, John?" King Farouk demanded.

"I would say dangerously so, sir."

For Westerners unacquainted with Egypt's colonial background and the Egyptians' mercurial character, this fanatical devotion to a hitherto unpopular sovereign might appear strange. But even for a newcomer to Egypt like myself, it did not take long to understand the two very different perspectives on the British presence in Egypt.

For colonial Britain, struggling to maintain its position in the Middle East, Cairo was a very pleasant place to live, with its imposing Moslem architecture and tumultuous population riddled with *gulla gulla* men (magicians), who produced chickens from out of nowhere, and unctuous *dragomans* (guides), who were as difficult to get rid of as flypaper. If you were a WASP and resided at Shepheard's Hotel, the rambling rococo institution which still kept officers' luggage from the Boer War in its cellars, then you enjoyed a life of privilege which revolved around the Long Bar, where Joe mixed "Suffering Bastards" to soothe the brows of the Cairo Cossacks—the rear-echelon officers recovering on the terrace in immaculate desert boots that never trod sand, waving their obligatory fly whisks.

From the Egyptian *fellaheen*'s point of view, colonial life in Cairo was rather different. They were increasingly restless over Britain's "temporary occupation" of their country, now in its 61st year, and they had prayed for a German victory. With the Afrika Korps' defeat they no longer expressed pro-Axis sentiments—at least not publicly. But all the unsettling and unsettleable problems still remained and the Egyptians simply waited for another opportunity to break away from British control.

Lord Killearn, the British Ambassador to Egypt, polarized the hatred of the "natives" for the colonial system. Beefy and blustering, he roared around Cairo in his yellow Rolls Royce with two very large Union Jacks flapping from the mudguards. He was escorted by four outriders, their sirens blaring, in an outdated display of power reminiscent of Victoria's reign, during which the occupation has started, in 1882. Thirteen years after the completion of the Suez Canal, Egypt had been turned from a cul-de-sac into a funnel, making it a British wayside station on the road to India.

Although the colonial system did mold the cotton-owning pashas into hereditary peers, it utterly failed to turn the teaming mass of *fellaheen* into good-natured cockneys. These *"gyppos"* despised British rule and made them suspect and hate everything Western—which would have dire consequences in the future. Xenophobia, hysterical nationalism, violence and frequent political assassinations increased and were now only held in check by the British army. The British had been compelled to walk a tightrope until the United States entered the war, and army supplies poured into Egypt. After that, Lord Killearn decided take his revenge on the Egyptians and on Farouk in particular.

Lord Killearn held a personal grudge against Farouk, and he thoroughly distrusted—possibly with good reason—Farouk's closest confidant, Pulli Bey, the son of an Italian electrician who had worked at the royal palace when Farouk was a child. On one occasion, Killearn, who had an Italian wife, ordered Farouk to get rid of his Italian. "I'll get rid of mine when you get rid of yours," Farouk had replied.

With all the pent-up fury of a Tory whose authority had been flouted, Killearn marched on the royal palace in a crude and foolish display of force. American tanks, manned by British gunners, surrounded the palace. A military plane stood by to fly Farouk into exile should he prove difficult and refuse to appoint a pro-British nominee to the premiership. Farouk wasn't difficult, merely prophetic. "You will regret this day," he told Killearn.

Jewish settlers, Palestine, 1943

Palestine

"If you think conditions are terrible in Egypt, just wait until you get to Palestine," I was told. At first this warning struck me as greatly exaggerated. Palestine looked like the dream it was for American airman on leave from the Western desert. The mandate was British, colonial, proper and clean. The atmosphere was western for the most part. Moslem Palestine was picturesque with its camels and donkeys. Tel Aviv was a modern resort, with tropical plants lining wide thoroughfares that ran between white buildings influenced by the Bauhaus. There were theaters, movie houses, smart shops, restaurants, and terrace cafés. The waterfront and beaches rivaled Florida. The average temperature was 60°F.

The new part of Jerusalem, built since the mandate, was dazzling and its peach-colored stone edifices provided a sedate air of well-being which was epitomised by the King David Hotel, affectionately called "the KD", and built in the tradition of the grand international hotels. A notice in its lobby informed guests that "the object was to evoke the glorious period of King David".

Archeological remains from that same period were in strolling distance of the hotel within the confines of the Old City, whose walls also enclosed the Christian Quarter, the Armenian Quarter, the Moslem Quarter, and the Jewish Quarter, each mentally and structurally isolated from the other very much the way it had been in the Ottoman era.

The Dome of the Rock was visible across the wide square from the *rauda*, on the Via Dolorosa, which would become the Arab Legion's headquarters during the Arab-Israeli War in 1948, from where I would speak over the phone to my colleague, Bob Capa, on the Israeli side before the lines were cut.

This was in the not-too-distant future as I stood with Moshe Shertok, the Jewish Agency's foreign affairs spokesman, who was about to shatter my peaceful vision of Palestine. "It took a world war to bring peace to Palestine," he told me. Within days I would come to understand the complex political and religious situation which divided the country I had come to photograph.

The hostility of the Arabs towards the Jewish settlers in Palestine had built up steadily since the Zionists had been promised a National Homeland there by the Balfour Declaration in 1917. By 1939, the situation had reached the pitch of armed rebellion across the mandate and was only temporarily contained by draconian censorship and the British Army.

Although the Balfour Declaration was British-inspired, it soon became apparent that colonial Britain, with its interests in Iraq's oil policies, preferred to keep Palestine in the the somnolent state it had enjoyed for centuries under Turkish rule. This policy met with the full approval of the wealthy Arab Sheiks. Both parties saw the disadvantages of progress and were only too aware that the Zionists with their Western know-how would bring changes and create unrest among the Moslem masses.

"Don't ever forget," Moshe Shertok had told me. "We've come here as settlers, not colonisers."

Nothing was done to encourage the Zionist efforts to have friendly relations with the Arabs. On the contrary, Herbert Samuel, Palestine's first High Commissioner, backed the feudal-minded sheiks, aware that their antagonism towards the Zionist settlers offered a perfect opportunity to control Jewish emigration. Meanwhile, he pursued a policy of divide and rule among the Arabs, playing off the two most powerful tribes, the Nashashibis and the el Husseinis against each other, backing the el Husseinis in a bid to reduce the authority of the Nashashibis who controlled Jerusalem's civic affairs. It was Samuel who appointed Hadj Amin el Husseini as Mufti of Jerusalem—making him Palestine's Moslem leader, despite the fact that he had failed the Islamic philosophy exams necessary for anyone holding such a privileged religious office. Soon afterwards, Samuel bolstered Hadj Amin's spiritual standing by appointing him President of the Supreme Moslem Council with full financial control of over $400,000 a year.

Through his religious authority and financial clout, Hadj Amin built a powerful political machine. He wiped out the Nashashibis and brought Zionist emigration virtually to a halt. Herbert Samuel, who had advanced the career of the Middle East's most implacable anti-Semite, just happened to be Jewish.

It was shortly before the outbreak of war that the colonial authorities woke up to the fact that the Mufti had forsaken their cause for Hitler. They decided to arrest him, but allowed him to escape to Iraq, where he staged an unsuccessful anti-British coup instigated by the Germans. Again threatened with arrest, the Mufti was rescued by Hitler who sent a plane to pick him up. In Berlin, Hadj Amin became *"Der Grosse Mufti"* and enjoyed ever-increasing popularity among the Palestinians, whose resentment could only increase in the presence of 585,000 Zionists whose *kibbutzim* covered over 400,000 acres of land which had been purchased by the Jewish Agency.

Jewish Palestine had its own legislature and council, backed by the executive board of the Jewish Agency of Palestine, chaired by Ben Gurion—which I photographed in session. This board was elected by the World Zionist Organization, whose president was Dr Chaim Weizmann, and which was financed by Jewish people all over the world. In those pre-oil days, the Arabs received nothing.

I illustrated the difference between the two Palestines with four pictures, showing first the similarity of the Arab and the Jewish children at school, before hatred set in, and the stark difference when it came to adults. On the one hand there was the Beersheba sheik in his Bedouin outfit with a Mauser slung over his shoulder; on the other, the commissioner of the Betar youth, the tough revisionist organization which would produce Menachem Begin. The only links between their two worlds were the asphalt roads that stretched out past the Arab conglomerations and Zionist *kibbutzim*.

The administration of these settlements depended on the political complexion of the *kibbutzniks*. On a labor *kibbutz*, like Ain Hashofet, which I photographed, the children were raised communally and played with their parents for a few hours in the afternoon. They would grow up to be the blue-eyed, blond-haired fierce *sabra* fighters of the future. What struck me most at Ain Hashofet were the different nationalities, personalities, and classes. There was Dov Vardi, the cattle herder, who seemed to me as American as Brooklyn, where he had lived until five years before. The fat lady in bloomers driving the tractor had been one of Berlin's leading hostesses, whose musical salons had included the pianist Arthur Rubinstein. In those early days uncluttered by religious factions, *kibbutzniks* saw nothing wrong with breeding hogs for export.

The Hebrew language was increasing at the rate of several words a day as new ones were created to bring up to date a language which had been considered dead for centuries. (The Hebrew for electricity, I learned from the Palestine Post, translated into "bottled lightening".) At that time, the Zionist IQ must have been one the highest in the world since its population contained so many intellectuals.

Jewish Palestine, it became clear, with its dynamic enthusiasm, was the future. They built everything from a modern irrigation system across land which had never known water to a forest in the wilderness (at the rate of $1 per tree). The most modern industry I encountered in Arab Palestine was soap-making, where one Arab stirred a large vat of liquid with a huge ladle and another stood on a ladder neatly piling up pillars of soap. The lethargic East was being humiliated by the dynamic West—and one day the West would have to pay.

By the time I left Palestine, I had also become fully aware of the intrigue that prevailed. On a personal level, I attracted the suspicions of the British authorities after they'd got wind I had surreptitiously photographed a unit of the anti-British Betar Legion. I caught my Jewish guide going through my papers. And the Arabs, who had at first eyed my camera with a cool indifference, were finally so suspicious of it that it drove them to the point of trying to lynch me.

On a more international level, the American Consul told me he was fed a steady stream of information about the activities of the Nazis in Europe via a Jewish network working out of Poland. The disorganized Palestinian Arabs were united in their devotion to the Mufti. The thoroughly disciplined Zionists were divided into two irreconcilable factions which remain to this day: the revisionists, who were irreconcilably anti-British; and, the Haganah, the Jewish secret army, which not only suspended anti-British action but even co-operated with the British, at least until the end of the war.

Moshe Shertok's parting words before I left Palestine would turn out to be prophetic. "Peace in the world," he said, "will bring war to Palestine."

Golda Meir, Palestine, 1943

Abdullah observing maneuvers, Aqaba, Transjordan, 1943

Abdullah

I was offered a ride to Amman for the inauguration of a British-sponsored club and jumped at the opportunity to photograph Transjordan, now known as the kingdom of Jordan, where Lawrence of Arabia had fought the Turks during World War I. As a teenager, I had read his account of the Arab revolt, conjuring up visions of warriors sweeping across the desert on their camels in clouds of sand as they drove on to Damascus.

What made this junket all the more irresistible was that I'd have occasion to meet Abdullah ibn Hussein, the son of King Hussein of Hedjaz, who had proclaimed a holy war against the Turks and launched the Arab revolt.

In 1914, after Turkey entered the war on the side of Germany, forming an alliance which was seen as a threat to India, it became imperative for the British to "knock the Turk out of the war". To this end, a group of young intelligence officers in Cairo conceived a plan in which the Arab provinces—today Syria, Lebanon, Israel, Jordan, and Iraq—would rise up in revolt against their Turkish masters. This required Abdullah's father, as the Sherif of Mecca, to proclaim a *jihad*—a holy war. To strengthen Hussein's resolve, a slight, lantern-jawed young archeologist named T.E. Lawrence was despatched to negotiate with him. After long and tortuous debate, there was finally an exchange of letters: promises for independence and loopholes, high ideals and money.

When it came to a leader for the revolt, Lawrence passed over Abdullah for his younger brother Faisal, making Abdullah Foreign Minister of the rebellious Bedouin government. Only belatedly did he discover that the British and the French had agreed to divide the Arab territories promised independence among themselves. This led to a series of misunderstanding usually only found in a French farce.

Faisal set himself up as King of Syria according to one agreement and was booted out by the French in accordance with another. Abdullah threatened war on France to avenge his brother's honor, only to be offered a stretch of barren land known as Transjordan, originally earmarked for the Zionists, by Winston Churchill, then Colonial Secretary (the Zionists were left to purchase land from the Palestinians). Faisal was given Iraq in compensation for losing Syria and a young Arab chieftain named Ibn Saud grabbed Hussein's former kingdom. Lawrence unexpectedly quit when British colonial interests prevailed. Thus the Arab aspirations for independence remained unfulfilled, producing repercussions still felt to this day. No wonder I was eager to meet Abdullah, a participant in such an extraordinary epic.

We crossed Allenby Bridge which connected the mandate of Palestine to the Emirate of Transjordan. In those days, Transjordan stretched from the Red Sea to the carp-filled lake Tiberius before fading into the Iraqi and Saudi deserts. An artificially-created state, it had no natural resources, no industries and no goods on its market. The Bedouin population was estimated at half a million, as no census had ever been taken, and these Bedouins provided soldiers for the Arab Legion, the only real reason for Transjordan's existence. This Middle-Eastern Sparta, British-created, British-trained, British-financed, and British-controlled, was a blend of fairytale and *Realpolitik*.

The winding barren road to Amman overlooked a *wadi* along whose slopes sand gazelles fed on dark-green scrub. Amman itself perched on seven hills. Combined with the local architecture, this gave the capital an appearance of lopsided unreality.

Along Amman's dusty streets, pensive moth-eaten camels loped along; eager little donkeys, undismayed by the bulk of their riders, trotted briskly, and barefoot figures in shapeless gunny sacks staggered under heavy loads. Cross-legged tinkers in small booths turned gasoline cans into pots, pails, and funnels. Cobblers carved dyed goat-hides into pointed *babouches*. Storekeepers and customers haggled in harsh, loud, guttural voices which, combined with their violent gestures, gave the erroneous impression that almost everybody in Amman was angry.

Along Faisal Square's sidewalks, wild-eyed Bedouins in the red and-white-checkered *kouffiehs* of the Arab Legion, strolled in twos and threes, pistols flapping against their hips. The air was filled with the insistent mechanical honking from dilapidated and overcrowded buses. Nasal songs from old Victrolas drifted all the way to the open-air cafés, shaded by trees where customers sipped Turkish coffee and studied chessboards as they sucked the large wooden mouthpieces of their *narguilehs*. It was as if I was being transported back to the days of the revolt.

The purpose of the club, whose opening we were here to attend, was to instil a greater sense of kinship among the more affluent "natives". However, when I arrived to photograph the inauguration ceremony, I discovered it had been called off. That morning, as Abdullah was being shown around the square stone building, he had taken a fancy to a framed painting of a "Scottish moor" and walked off with it.

"Unfortunately," I was told, he had replaced this cultural *pièce de résistance* with a gaudy oil portrait of his late father, King Hussein, which was judged "quite unsuitable" for the reading room. Unable to remove it without enraging the Emir, the British Council had postponed the inauguration while it debated what to do.

The inaugural tea party, however, had not been canceled. Seated next to Brigadier Ronny Broadhurst, the Arab Legion's second in command, I was disappointed to hear that the Emir would not be there. He had been whisked off to Aqaba where military maneuvers were being held. Seeing my regret at missing the opportunity to photograph him, Brigadier Broadhurst offered to take me to Aqaba the next day.

We sped across the desert spewing sand. The road followed the old Turkish railroad line which once had linked Damascus to Medina and which Lawrence had sabotaged 28 years before. All that remained of the once-thriving line were the abandoned and rusty tracks which I photographed as skinny black goats nibbled on the scrub. We drove on through M'an and Wadi Rum, for a time Lawrence's headquarters during the revolt, before reaching Aqaba. There I met Emir Abdullah ibn Hussein, descendent of the Prophet and the head of the Hashemite dynasty, whom junior British officials irreverently nicknamed "Ab".

"You look like a man from Aleppo," was his greeting.

"I was born beneath the sky of Islam, *Sidi*."

The Emir nodded solemnly "You can always tell," he observed.

He was seated on a low divan in a mud-framed building whose walls and ceiling were made of reeds that allowed the cool sea breeze to seep through. He wore a spotless flowing *abaya*. His skin was as smooth as a baby's and the colour of a Havana cigar.

He was a diminutive figure, a fact which he tried to conceal by conveying an air of dignity through his bearing and distinguished features. Although his black eyes sparkled, his carefully trimmed beard and moustache lent him an austerity he occasionally dispelled by sticking his tongue out as when I took his picture. At times like this, although he was over 60, Ab looked a mischievous child.

When he couldn't get his way, which was almost daily, he flew into terrible rages like the Oriental potentate he fancied himself. In his more composed moods, he was affable and gently stroked the wide gold dagger that only the descendants of the Prophet were entitled to carry. Its heavy blade had been soldered to the sheath to prevent Ab from injuring himself when he became excited. Although Ab professed to speak no English, I soon noticed he grew fidgety and interrupted his secretary's translation to reply directly.

Because of his devotion to Islam, Ab did not share the Crown Prince's predilection for martinis. He was a great drinker of bitter coffee and sweet tea which we were served alternately that afternoon.

At Broadhurst's suggestion, I told the Emir what the captain of the munitions ship had said as I was issued a life jacket: "If we're torpedoed, what you'd really need is a parachute." Ab listened intently. Slowly raising his eyes toward the fluttering reeds on the ceiling, before inquiring "how high would you have gone?"

"Too high, *Sidi*."

Ab chuckled and, looking out towards the Bay of Aqaba unusually filled with transports, asked, "How many ships can New York Harbor hold?"

"I've seen six of the largest liners in the world berthed there at the same time, Sidi, and there was still lots of room."

"I like boats," Ab said, and he scratched his foot, a sign that he was deep in thought

"I certainly do like boats," he repeated, before asking, "How long is the Queen Mary?"

"Twelve times the length of your palace, *Sidi*."

He nodded approval. He was to associate me with boats for a long time after that. On later meetings he would recall, "Do you remember the good time we had at Aqaba? I said to you, 'How high would you go?' and you said to me…"

The Emir also enjoyed enticing his visitors to a game of chess then gleefully checkmating them. "Nobody in Transjordan can beat me," he chuckled as he proposed a game to me and nimbly moved his pawns. A fast player, he got bored if he did not win in ten minutes. In the middle of our third game, my attention was distracted by the appearance of General Sir Henry Maitland Wilson, the British Commander-in-Chief Middle East at Aqaba. The presence of "Jumbo" Wilson surprised me as much as mine did him. As the General paid his respects to Ab, I wondered if the forthcoming maneuvers were more important than I'd thought.

After Wilson left, a tablecloth was laid on the floor and we all squatted around it with Ab at the head of the carpet. A four-foot copper tray appeared bearing small fried fish. Next came a tray heaped with rice spiced with fresh pistachio nuts and raisins. On top of this mound rested a whole roasted sheep. Ab was the only one provided with a small knife and fork, which he wielded expertly as he busied himself at his corner of the sheep, stopping only to tell me not to photograph him eating. I imitated the others by placing my left hand behind my back and eating with my right, rolling rice into balls, swallowed between bites of mutton. When Ab was through, he rose. We did likewise. The platters were dragged off to the harem, set up behind Ab's camp. When the wives had dined on our leftovers, what remained went to the servants. Drowsy with food, Ab gave the signal for us to retire.

The sound of gunfire woke me up in the middle of the night. Going out, I found we were illuminated by flares. The maneuvers had started. In that theatrical lighting, I saw armchairs lined up outside Ab's camp. He sat in one, cross-legged and barefoot, holding a pair of large naval binoculars. Next to him was a small man in an ill-fitting general's uniform I had never seen before. In this fleeting light, I first made the acquaintance of Glubb Pasha. Offered an armchair, I sat back and watched the operations, which turned out to be the secret British rehearsal for the landing in Sicily.

Glubb Pasha, Amman, 1948

Glubb Pasha

Jumbo Wilson was not particularly fond of journalists. He had been both surprised and annoyed to find me playing chess with Abdullah and I later learned that British security had contemplated holding me incommunicado until after the landings in Sicily had taken place. Fortunately, Glubb Pasha had a better idea. He took me along with him on an inspection tour of the outposts of the Arab Legion.

The first night we camped at Wadi Rum, where the purple and red granite formations rose straight out of the dried shrubs like nature's pyramids. Carpets were spread out on the sand in a square formation and the Bedouin legionnaires sat around cross-legged and silent, gazing at Glubb, their checkered *kouffiehs* hanging loosely. The desert armchair—a camel saddle—was produced for Glubb and myself to rest on either side of. In the center of our square, a Bedouin corporal, *kouffieh* tossed back and pigtails dangling, leaned over a low brazier making bitter coffee which he passed around, everybody drinking out of the same small cup. As twilight set in over the desert, the legionnaires began conversing in low tones, out of respect for Glubb.

John Bagot Glubb, a deceitfully mild-mannered man, looked like a civil servant even in his general's uniform. He was frequently called the successor to Lawrence of Arabia, a comparison he did not appreciate. I discovered this as I listened to him talk at Wadi Rum, the same place Lawrence had once dreamed of Arab independence.

Glubb, I soon realized, shared Abdullah's feelings about Lawrence. While Ab impishly ridiculed the pink-cheeked Englishman who spoke poor Arabic and was afflicted by carbuncles, Glubb offered more serious objections in the sing-song voice his legionnaires imitated by the hour.

"Lawrence, you know, threw away a great opportunity for really helping the Arabs," Glubb said. "He held great prestige with them after the revolt. But he was cynical and did not want to risk his fame by doing an honest job of work. Now, he is completely forgotten by the Arabs. All they know about him is second-hand, through his book. He also loved publicity and was ruined by an American journalist's exaggerated praise. Went to his head, you know. Lawrence should have rolled up his sleeves and done a job of work." This was precisely what Glubb did when the British Imperial forces failed to bring peace to the desert and thus protect the oil pipeline. His job was to find a way to stop Bedouins from raiding caravans.

"These raids were not at all sound economically," Glubb explained, "as there were few foreign caravans. All the Bedouins did was rob each other. So I suggested turning the thieving Bedouins into policemen. When they heard this, they were greatly offended." Eventually, though, Glubb got his way. The Imperials were withdrawn from the desert. "And we all waited."

Notified that a tribe was planning a raid, Glubb sent his men to their camp during their absence and confiscated their camels. "I was lucky," Glubb recalled, "because their raid failed and they got back empty-handed to find that they had now lost their camels. Several days later, crestfallen, they came to see me in the hopes of getting at least some of them back." Having made a show of force, Glubb could now afford to be generous and returned their camels with a warning. "So they left feeling very pleased with themselves. That's the way to deal with Arabs. They have their brains in their eyes." Glubb sounded very much like an English nanny. He then set out to make the Arab Legion attractive, explaining that, "Arabs being romantics, they raided as much for glamour as for profit."

When it came to uniforms, Glubb displayed a Paris designer's skill. The more demanding the service, the more handsome the kit. The most sumptuous went to the camel corps who patrolled the Saudi border for two weeks at a time. They got crimson coats with white wool linings. Soon every able-bodied male wanted to be in the Legion to swagger around Amman. Glubb drew volunteers from Italian Cyrenaica to the Turkish border.

Though Lawrence might be forgotten by the Arabs, his myth still gripped young Englishmen who rushed out to serve as officers. Through their efforts, scruffy Bedouins appearing at the depot in filthy *abayas* were turned into smart-looking *jundies*. Those who took to mathematics were initiated into mechanized warfare and warned to keep their pigtails out of the cannon's breach. Within six months, Glubb had restored peace in the desert. He built his forts around the water-holes. "Because you see, whoever controls the water, holds the desert," he said mildly as he fingered his amber beads. The success of his policy was demonstrated during the war. Although the British were being driven back across the Western desert during the early stages of the campaign, Glubb's Bedouins remained loyal and protected the pipeline in spite of their conviction the British would be defeated.

"The Arabs", Glubb explained, again sounding like a nanny, "react well to good treatment, and not only to force." Then as an afterthought: "They respect it, though you must never forget, Arabs do not have the European's sense of patriotism, which is only recent with us. Remember how feudal knights thought it was quite all right to join a foreign prince against their own countrymen?" He paused while the coffee maker passed around the bitter brew. "You see, the Arabs became acquainted with Europe second-hand, through their Turkish masters. What appealed to the Turks were the superficialities of the West—felt hats, nightclubs…The Turks decided to go European all of a sudden and decreed the Napoleonic Code for everybody. While the law worked in the cities it failed with the Bedouins and created anarchy."

"How come?" I asked him.

"Bedouins have their own laws suited to them. Take murder, for instance, the Bedouin does not consider this a crime against the State, but an offense to the victim's family. The family must seek revenge. They do not simply hold the murderer responsible, but his entire family back to the fifth cousin. Now, with the Napoleonic Code, bewildered city officials saw the relatives of the murdered man swear to the assassin's innocence, then kill him when he left the courthouse acquitted."

Glubb re-established the old law, but streamlined the procedure to keep mortality down. When a murder was committed, the entire guilty family, down to the fifth cousin, was banished to another part of the country. This was a deterrent in itself because of the serious problems of finding food and water. After the family had moved, negotiations would start over the financial compensation. A great deal of discussion had to follow before the money was paid. Everybody knew from the outset the amount which would be agreed upon, but there had to be a face-saving ritual of accepting money for a life. Finally, when all was forgiven, the reconciliation feast could take place.

As I listened to Glubb that night, I felt in him an inner anxiety when hc wistfully talked about the future, the number of years he had spent in the desert, and his hopes that his work would not be undone. "Because, you see Phillips, it's been a lifetime after all."

Camel corps, Syria, 1943

The Levant

When I heard the suspicions of a French officer, that *les Anglais* were planning to take Syria and Lebanon away from the French, I felt his fears might well be justified. Ever since the British had defeated the Vichy French in 1941, for allowing the Germans to take over the Syrian airfields, they had troops stationed there. The arrival of Major Spears and his mission to the Levant made a takeover increasingly likely. Major General Sir Edward Spears, with his ruddy complexion, cold blue eyes and imperious manner, was the image the world has of a British Imperialist. Before assuming full military and diplomatic control over the Levant, he had been a director of 30 British corporations, was a personal friend of Winston Churchill, and had flown DeGaulle to England in June 1940. Spears seemed quite capable of taking over Syria and Lebanon to me.

The French were even more disturbed to see Syrian tribesmen serving in the British Army and marching to a new tune, the lyrics which translate as follows:

> May ye be permanent, ye strongest of kings.
> May ye be victorious, ye whom the troops adore.
> You are the guardian of democracy, hence the sword of God.
> May ye be permanent, King George.
> Ye guardian of the country.

This none-too-subtle proselytizing was the work of a friend, Colonel William F. Sterling, once Lawrence of Arabia's chief of staff. Sterling was organizing another Arab revolt, this time against the French, and was considered by them to be a British agent. All I knew was that he was the best-informed man in the Levant.

I traveled about Syria and Lebanon while the crisis was brewing, photographing the pillars of Baalbek, Palmyra, founded by Solomon and sacked by Tamerlane, Damascus, whose origins are lost in antiquity and possibly the oldest city in the world, along with Aleppo near the Turkish border. While in Northern Syria near the Euphrates, our staff car broke down. Harry Zinder of *Time*, an American conducting officer and myself were stranded in the desert until a French army patrol found us and put us up for the night in their camp. With our luggage back in Aleppo, a barber was produced the next morning to give us all a shave. Zinder went first. He had a peculiar look when he rose from his chair and made way for the conducting officer. When my turn came, I noticed the other two exchanging glances. The barber's cut-throat razor swept across my face and throat in broad strokes. It was the fastest and most unpleasant shave the three of us ever had, and I said as much to a French sergeant. "I suppose the barber was nervous," he said, and shrugged. "He's about to be executed, but I thought in the meantime he could still be useful."

The crisis in the Levant came to a head that summer, and would trigger an unrest still felt to this day. Looking over one of my stories which appeared at the time, I noticed the headline was "Trouble in the Mid-East—Syria Simmers as Lebanon Boils". Although these two French mandates wanted their independence, they had little in common. Lebanon, with its capital Beirut, had a Maronite Christian majority and a Western tradition through its seaboard civilization that went back to the Phoenicians. This had made them brilliant tradesmen and allowed them to survive five centuries of Moslem rule.

Syria, with its capital Damascus, remained profoundly Moslem and Oriental-minded. I realized this when I drove from Beirut to Damascus, more a journey through time than distance as I left the West behind at the Lebanese mountains and entered the world of Islam.

The Lebanese elections of 1943 brought the crisis to boiling point. The British candidate for the presidency, to no one's surprise, defeated the French candidate. He promptly declared the French mandate at an end. In response, the French military arrested him. A press conference was called in Cairo. We were told that the Lebanese president had been arrested by "Senegalese". Violence was intimated. This was neither an official handout nor a communiqué, we were told—it was merely for our edification. For once, Cairo's political censorship was broadminded. Everything the correspondents filed was passed immediately. The mention of the president's arrest by Senegalese raised loud protests abroad. The French general's denials that he had used black troops was ignored.

Exaggerated versions of the riots and casualties piled up. British censorship in Palestine denounced French censorship in Lebanon. Arab demonstrations took place in Cairo. It was a touching spectacle to see Moslem Arabs so upset over the fate of Christian Arabs. "You always find a mob willing to break windows," an Egyptian diplomat remarked. "It's simply a matter of a few pounds and the car fare."

The crisis was temporarily halted by Sir Edward Spears and George Wadsworth, the American diplomatic agent. They asked the French to release and reinstate the Lebanese president. Soon after that, Syria declared its desire for independence. By August, I had photographed the newly-elected President of Syria, Sukri Bey Kuwatli, making his maiden speech in parliament. His main point: Syrian independence from France and alliance with other Arab states. The inscription above him—"Affairs shall be arranged by consultations among ourselves"—was a further slap in the face for the French. But if the British colonials believed the Levant was moving within their orbit, they were mistaken. France's loss of Syria and Lebanon started the countdown to the foreclosure of the British mandate of Palestine.

Death in Aleppo

"Anything cooking in Syria?" I asked the American Military Attaché in the Levant. "Nothing special this month," he replied. But they've got an execution coming up September 29th."

"That's a month away. I thought spies were tried one day and shot the next morning at dawn?"

"That's right. They'll be court marshaled the 28th and shot the 29th."

Which is why I was waiting for a truck at the rifle range of Abu Fares outside Aleppo. We were a small gathering besides the two firing squads—a dozen officers, several correspondents, and a man in white ducks. The man in white ducks, especially, looked miserable.

I had trapped myself into the privilege of watching two men killed and I felt ashamed. Since the morning before, as I drove to Aleppo, I was haunted by the knowledge that the last 24 hours of their lives were running out. At sunset, I wondered what it must feel like never to see the sun again. Now, in the chilly dawn of what promised to be a hot Middle East day, I shivered. The silence of our small group was broken by a know-it-all voice, which announced: "All you hear about executions is bunk. I've just spoken to an officer who set me straight: It all goes according to the book. This romantic stuff about being shot at dawn! There's no special rule. Question of convenience is all."

"Pretty civilized, these Frenchmen," another voice remarked quietly. "They only heard the sentence this morning when they were woken at 5:30 and given a cup of coffee. There were several grains of morphine in the coffee — which helps."

"According to regulations," the know-it-all went on, "the sentences must be carried out within two hours of hearing the verdict. Now take that famous blank shot you always hear about. That ain't so. According to regulations, there must be six live shells by firing squad, but nobody knows who's got the live ammo because after the rifles are issued, no one is allowed to open the breach to see who's got the blanks. The firing squad must aim at the chest. Better not miss at 18 feet, because Doc is going to count the bullet wounds after the execution."

Time dragged on until I began wonder if the inevitable would not happen. I stared at two lengths of rope lying on the reddish earth between the two stakes and noticed for the first time the olive green ambulance parked near the rustling weeds. "Gallows humor?" I asked the American military attaché.

He didn't smile. "That's the hearse. And if you're interested in the details, the coffins are of rough, unvarnished wood, lined with sawdust to stop the blood from oozing through."

A group of Senegalese soldiers in red fezzes squatted around the ambulance. Though they all looked identical to those I'd seen as a child, right down to the last slash marks on their cheeks, they appeared somehow different. They weren't grinning like children and I missed their milky white teeth. Their faces were sullen, like shuttered houses.

"The blindfold is optional," our know-it-all proclaimed, "and the *coup-de-grace* is administered point blank, a bit above the ear."

The Englishman in white ducks said nothing. His loose clothes fluttered in the breeze and gave his gaunt body a ghoulish appearance. He stood alone on a bluff against the pale-green sky.

"He doesn't look too happy," I remarked.

"Would you, if you'd promised to save their lives in exchange for becoming double agents?" the American Military Attaché asked. I was about to reply, when we all jumped at the sound of an engine in the distance. It was going to happen after all.

I was now conscious of an extreme lucidity, and everything that followed seemed to happen in slow motion. The truck, raising dust, bumped into sight along the narrow dirt road. Slowly, it swung round and backed up. The tailgate was dropped. I glanced at my watch: 6:32. In three minutes, it would all be over.

After the military escort had poured out, a tall Nazi in a loose brown shirt and shapeless blue pants rose from a bench. His arms were bound, and I noticed he ducked the tarpaulin to avoid banging his head as he lightly jumped to the ground without assistance. The last one left in the truck wore baggy shorts and a dirty yellow sweatshirt. He had to be dragged out. His wobbly legs were unable to support him.

Defiantly, the Nazi strode between the two firing squads with only a quick glance at the men about to kill him. In a few brisk steps, he reached the left stake where he was bound. Helped by two officers, the figure in shorts tottered toward the other stake.

The Nazi refused the blindfold. The figure in shorts did too. But, like an echo, he changed his mind, and the cloth was removed. Very pale, a young French officer, the attorney for the defense, went over to them and kissed each on both cheeks and muttered a few words of encouragement.

"Oh, I say, that's really a bit too much…"

This outburst was interrupted by the voice of the prosecutor: *"Le vingt-huit Septembre dix-neuf cent quarante-trois, le tribunal militaire d'Alep…"*

"A bas l'Angleterre!" the figure in shorts cried out. But his protest was drowned out by the Nazi who, upright and glaring at the man in white ducks, started to shout. The words themselves were hackneyed slogans, but what gave them their special quality was the inflection of hate in his voice. *"A bas la perfide Albion!"* he spat out as his voice rose in fury. *"A bas l'Angleterre! Vive la France victime de la perfide Angleterre!"*

Even those who did not understand the meaning understood the hate and reacted to it. "You lousy bastard!" someone shouted.

Pity made way for rage. I could now watch the execution without qualms, although I would have nightmares later.

The prosecutor droned on, *"…condamné à mort…"* But the end of the sentence was sliced off by the non-com's sword which swept down. The command to fire was lost in the volley. The sound of the shots was lost on me at the sight of the two suddenly swept off their feet, dancing wildly on their toes as though performing a frantic jig before they crumpled. The bullets which crashed through the Nazi's chest blew a funnel of flesh out of his back and snapped off the upper part of the stake he was fastened to. This left him limp and sagging forward. The figure in shorts slithered to the ground, disarticulated and grotesque. Burly non-coms, pistols drawn in their gloved hands, stepped over, stooped and two shots rang out like dry coughs.

It was all over except for the formalities. The ropes binding them were cut and left where they fell. The dry earth sucked up the trickles of blood. The Senegalese peeled off the ripped and bloodstained shirts so that the doctor could make notes on the gaping wounds. The ambulance pulled up. The Senegalese dumped the bodies into the coffins as I took close-up shots. One wiped his bloody hands on the Nazi's chest. Another hummed as he nailed down the coffin lids. A French non-com scribbled a name in pencil on each lid. The ambulance drove off without clanging its bell.

The problem now was to get my pictures cleared by the censors in Beirut. I first went to see the French, on whose territory the executions had taken place. Initially, the major I talked to objected, saying such pictures published in the States could create an unfavorable impression about France. He gave me an amused look when I pointed out that it was well known that captured spies were always executed. He finally relented when I told him that Americans had executed Nazi spies captured in the States.

Next I had to clear the pictures with the British at the Spears mission. The walls of the office I was ushered into were bare except for two sketches. One showed an eye peering through a triangle with the words "Abu Ali, the all-seeing eye." The other was simply a fist wringing out the last drops of juice from a lemon. In view of the surroundings there was something sinister about those sketches.

This was the office of a British major. He was young, athletic and expressionless, until he crinkled his nose in disgust at the sight of the two dead spies: "Those two were scum." He had no objections whatsoever to the publication of most of my pictures, although he did censor the two dramatic head-shots of the dead men in their coffins. While having a drink with the American Military Attaché, he explained why those two pictures had been withheld.

These spies, controlled by German intelligence in Athens, had both infiltrated Egypt via neutral Turkey. However, they did not belong to the same network, and didn't even know each other. Captured in Cairo at different times, they had been turned around and sent out false information until Athens realized they had become double agents. Their only usefulness now was to court martial them together and mislead German intelligence that another pair of agents had been executed. "That's why your close-ups—which clearly identified the pair—were censored." Seeing the look on my face, the Military Attaché concluded, "Who ever said war was pretty?"

Execution of two German spies, Aleppo, Syria, 1943

Stalin, Roosevelt (with his head of security) and Churchill, Tehran, 1943

Tehran

"Report within the hour to the Ministry of Information and bring along four-days' supply of warm clothes for a journey East. Your destination is top secret, but chilly," I was instructed in a dark hallway. "No one's to know you're leaving Cairo."

It was still night when a command car whisked me off to the airport along Egyptian roads guarded by sleepy American troops. My group was made up of secretaries in slacks and fur-lined coats and junior officers. On the field we hung around our plane, saying little, not even speculating among ourselves as to our destination.

We were first off in a twin-engined Dakota. We flew over Jericho, the Euphrates, the Tigris, and the Hamadan range before landing in Tehran seven hours later. Our trip had been kept so secret that the first the Shah himself knew about the impending summit meeting to be held in his capital was the roar of our planes over his palace. This summit had not only been kept from the Shah, but from everyone not directly involved with the conference. Even the foreign correspondents in Egypt, who were aware there had been a conference in Cairo, had no idea about the one in Tehran. These impressive measures were the result of the anxiety over the success of an enterprise that filled all concerned with a mixture of awe and terror: the much anticipated moment when Roosevelt and Churchill would at last confer with Josef Stalin.

The commotion which now descended on Tehran after our arrival left the population dazed. In spite of the imposed secrecy, rumors were rampant. Bazaar gossip had it that Iran was about to be divided up. When the radio went off the air, the long-distance phone calls went dead, the trains remained in the stations and no one was allowed to leave the city limits, this rumor spread to the provinces.

On first impression, Tehran, a blend of crumbling glory and present-day shabbiness, appeared a poor setting for the coming together of three great powers whose grand schemes included the planning of the second front and laying the ground work for world peace. But looking back, Tehran was a symbolic choice: the East and the West met there and clashed.

The Iranians, who were Islamic in their religious beliefs, were casually Western in their attire. *Tarbooshes* had made way for gray caps and their loss of Oriental color was replaced by the drabbest aspects of Occidental culture. Water in open drains gushed down the main streets for people to drink, wash and defecate in. Innumerable street pedlars hawked their wares on their heads while chanting praise for the quality of the goods they sold. There was even one slouching at the front gate of the British Legation as our car drove up, while his merchandise—a dozen turkeys—strutted around him.

The Legation, now called "the compound," was a hive of activity. Convoys of cars swept down the driveway past bivouacked troops. The Sikh sentries sprang to attention as Churchill alighted, followed by his daughter, Sarah, and his son, Randolph. British marshals, admirals, and generals leisurely sought their quarters. Anthony Eden, the Foreign Secretary, hurried past, trailed by aides swinging briefcases. Harried secretaries sorted out their files from the luggage rapidly piling up in front of the rambling Victorian buildings.

In the middle of this diplomatic confusion a mild-looking man with a pair of beetling eyebrows calmly eyed the pedlar and his turkeys. "Six should about see us through," he said aloud.

"I beg your pardon?"

"I said, six should see us through."

"If you say so…" I agreed without knowing what he meant. This being a top secret conference, cryptic conversation seemed reasonable enough.

"I'm a state secret," beetle brows remarked affably after a lull. "It would never do if the Germans had an inkling where I was, because, you see, Hitler knows that wherever I am, there Mr Churchill can be found."

"Fair enough," I agreed.

"Now take the name on my passport," he went on. "K - R - A - M. Well, it's really not my name. Oh dear no. It's really M - A - R - K—if you see what I mean..? So now I'm Mr Kram," Mr Mark concluded.

"And Hitler's fooled," I volunteered, keen to oblige.

"This is extremely confidential, of course. Wouldn't say word if you weren't one of us."

Confidence for confidence, I now admitted that although no one had fiddled with my name, I was not the civil servant I was supposed to be, despite being the 70th and last member of Churchill's official delegation to the summit. (I had been transferred from an accredited US war correspondent to the American Office of War Information before being loaned to the British Ministry of Information to act as Churchill's photographer at Tehran.)

Gossip, I soon realized, was something Mr Kram simply could never enjoy in the normal course of his work. It was only on occasions such as this, where absolutely everything was bound by secrecy, that he could indulge himself. Mr Kram, I now learned, was a petty officer in the Royal Navy who had been assigned to Churchill when he took over the Admiralty in 1939, and then had moved with him to 10 Downing Street in 1940. Mr Kram was considerably more than a valet—the job he performed during the conferences. He also handled such exacting chores as keeping Churchill supplied with cigars and liquor.

Taking advantage of our conversation, I asked Mr. Kram about the Prime Minister's drinking habits. "He never has a drop of whiskey before 9am," Mr. Kram said.

"And before that?" I inquired, half-seriously.

"Vermouth."

At this conference, Mr Kram was also to undertake the most nerve-racking task of his career: supervising Churchill's 69th birthday party. It used to be that Churchill, who always demanded the highest standards, had taken care of such details himself. Now he left it to Kram. Nothing disturbed Kram. He did not even suffer from frustration. Churchill was quick to criticize and slow to compliment, but Kram knew the Prime Minister and philosophically accepted silence as praise.

The conference meetings took place at the Soviet Embassy, a logical choice as the Russians had the only suitable accommodations for the plenary sessions. This was no concession to Stalin, who had turned it over to Roosevelt—while he himself moved into a smaller house at the far end of the garden. This arrangement spared the American President the commuting to and from the American Legation and allowed the Big Three to meet more frequently as Churchill was over the road in the British Legation. It also considerably simplified the necessary security measures.

As I was on the list of those admitted into the Russian Embassy, I joined a convoy chaperoned by Colonel General Arkadiev, the Russian chief security officer at the conference and a senior member of the NKVD (later the KGB). We swung out of the compound into the street that led to the Embassy. At every street corner, Russian sentries stood guard, totally expressionless, their flat caps perched on their wide, shaved heads, their massive hands gripping Russian-made machine guns. The Embassy gates opened at our approach, manned by Russians dressed in black from head to foot. A few hundred yards up the winding driveway, we entered the American zone guarded by American military police.

I photographed Churchill, Roosevelt, and Stalin on Monday, November 29, 1943. The setting for this historic event was the front porch of the Russian Embassy, a Greco-Marxist temple with six columns topped by a hammer and sickle.

At the foot of the steps that led up to this porch was a gravel driveway where the lesser members of the conference milled around, eager to see Stalin in person. Most of them, however, missed his entrance as he casually emerged from a side door. "He's no taller than Hitler," I thought, suddenly aware of him near me. His movements were rigid to the point of clumsiness, possibly because of his brand-new beige uniform which hung stiffly on him. His pockmarked face had the texture of granite. His hands were those of a laborer. The fingers of his shriveled left arm peeked out from under the wide cuff of his uniform. Unlike his marshals, Stalin was not festooned with decorations. He was satisfied with the Order of Lenin, the Soviet Union's highest award. As he mingled among the onlookers he was seemingly unaware of the curiosity he attracted. Watching him, I was reminded of a peasant from Eastern European in his Sunday best strolling through a market, slow-footed, but shrewd.

"Delightful old gentleman," a British officer behind me remarked.

"You'd never suspect the old boy has done in four or five million people, would you?"

Winston Churchill appeared from inside the Embassy and slumped down in his armchair. Before Roosevelt appeared, Mike Reilly, the head of White House security, said no pictures were to be taken before he gave the instructions and his tone of voice left me in no doubt that he meant what he said.

Although all of us knew Roosevelt was a victim of polio, there was a gasp when he appeared. The President, his legs dangling, was carried to his armchair by two of the White House security guards, his cigarette holder jammed in the corner of his mouth at a jaunty angle. He was seated with legs crossed. A foot swayed helplessly until a guard's hand steadied it. At that moment, he was the image of a helpless cripple.

When the guards who had screened him withdrew, we all gave another gasp. Roosevelt, completely relaxed, his *pince-nez* in his left hand, cigarette holder in the right, was casually chatting with Churchill. Although his steel braces were clearly visible around his ankles, we looked at one another, willing to doubt what we had just seen.

For their historic portrait, the President of the United States sat between the two Prime Ministers, Stalin on Roosevelt's right, Churchill on his left. The chairs the three sat in were different from one another but reflected each occupant's outlook on life. Churchill's was padded and completely upholstered, Stalin's was solid wood—hard, ungainly and uncomfortable, Roosevelt's was a compromise between the two, with neither the easy-going quality of the one or the rigidity of the other, the seat was padded while the back was firm. Churchill slumped comfortably, looking like a bad-tempered cherub. Stalin leaned forward stiffly, gazing straight at the camera. Roosevelt was perfectly composed.

November 30, Churchill's birthday, was marked in the morning by an incident which was characteristic of Stalin. The three statesmen had decided to make up for the slight they had inflicted upon the Shah by landing on his empire without notice. Roosevelt had therefore been nominated to invite the Shah for a chat—a breach of etiquette justified by his infirmity—and Churchill and Stalin had agreed to take this opportunity to meet the Shah. When the time came, Stalin never showed up. But on the day Roosevelt and Churchill left Tehran, Stalin pointedly visited the Shah at his palace, according to protocol.

On that morning of the 30th, however, I presented Mr Churchill with my gift to him—a Persian lamb hat. In the evening we assembled for Mr Kram's birthday banquet.

Half an hour before the guests were due, I found the residence ablaze with lights. British sentries had replaced the colonial Sikhs. Stewards fluttered around the "Yellow Room" where cocktails were to be served under the sedate full-length portraits of King George V and Queen Mary. Across a wide hallway was the dining-room. There, below a large painting of

Edward VII, stood the unperturbed Mr Kram. "This must be the most important feast since the Last Supper, if that's not too sacrilegious a comparison," I said to him in greeting.

"The Tehran dinner," Mr Kram replied, eyeing the long table with its brittle flower bed of long-stemmed glasses softened by the dancing lights they reflected from the crystal chandeliers above, "is indeed the most important of my career. Though I must admit the one I like to re-member best is the Atlantic Charter dinner served aboard the *Prince of Wales* in honor of President Roosevelt. We had grouse brought all the way from Scotland."

Looking at the portrait of Queen Victoria and suddenly taken aback to find she had once been a young woman, I asked him about the menu.

"We will have oyster patties, consommé, boiled salmon..."

"All the way from Scotland?" I suggested, but Mr Kram wouldn't be interrupted. "...as I said, boiled salmon, roast turkey, ice-cream, and a cheese soufflé for savory."

I asked about the turkey, adding facetiously, "Surely not the ones loafing outside the compound?"

"Oh, yes," Mr Kram replied, mistaking my tone for admiration.

"As I told you at the time, six would about see us through." He gazed thoughtfully at the open hearth. "But, of course, I didn't purchase them myself. Dear me, no."

We were interrupted by the arrival of Churchill, wearing a silver "V" on the lapel of his dinner-jacket, followed by his daughter Sarah, who was acting as hostess. Talking all the while to her, Churchill carefully scrutinized each place, making a change here and there. Then smiling broadly and without a word to Kram, he ambled off to the Yellow Room, a female section officer in his wake.

"Dear me, no," Mr Kram repeated. "They would have overcharged me, you know. Thought I was a foreigner. So I ascertained what was proper to pay in advance and sent out a local lad to buy them. As you can see, Tehran will be an English dinner." He paused while the birthday cake was carried in. "Because, after all, the guests will come expecting you to serve food from your own country. Won't they?" He paused, as if to reflect further on the assumption. "Because you can do that best, can't you? I have made only one concession to internationalism."

Churchill's birthday, Tehran, 1943

He paused again. His tone suggested this had been a very great concession indeed. At that moment Churchill, hearing his cake was in the
dining-room, trotted back. He beamed at his cake, 15 inches wide and
2½ inches high, covered in icing, decorated with a "V" and overloaded with
candles. This "austerity cake" had been decided upon after it had been
thought in poor taste if my photographs revealed a "really splendid one" in
a country where sugar cost $12 a pound.

Spotting me, Churchill inquired in a hoarse whisper, "Are you planning to photograph Marshal Stalin?"

"Why, yes," I replied, equally in a whisper, realizing I, too, was overcome by excitement. On the spot the Prime Minister drew up a plan. On
receiving Stalin, he would find out if he had any objections to having his
picture taken, If he did not, Churchill would immediately transmit the message to a British colonel standing at this side that I could go ahead. This
colonel would then wave his handkerchief, signaling that I could carry on.
Having settled that, he departed, leaving me dubious as to whether he
would remember.

"My one and only concession," Mr Kram went on, "are the toasts; they
will be Russian-style. You know, that means they can be proposed all
through the meal. It will make the service a bit awkward because courses
must be slipped on and off without interrupting the rhythm of the meal."
He gestured with his hands, as though beating time, then hurried away as
the first guests began to arrive.

Averell Harriman was among the first, struggling with the birthday
gift from President Roosevelt, a fragile 13th-century bowl. The greetings on
a card read: "With all my affection. May we be together for many years."
Harriman's own present, a 17-century brocade, was tucked under his arm.
He was explaining to an aide that the gifts should be placed on the dinner-
table without Churchill seeing them, when Churchill appeared. Promptly
Harriman clamped his old felt hat over the bowl, while Winston Churchill
greeted him, his eyes shut tight, announcing genially, "Haven't seen a thing."

Ambassador Winant came next, followed by President Roosevelt, who
was followed in turn by a flock of secret service men. Reilly posted security
men all over the place, and left three of them in the lobby. One of them, a
chap with a sensitive face, a small well-trimmed moustache, and a maroon
suit, struck up a conversation. He wanted some pointers on a typical

souvenir for his wife. "I haven't got time to look around," he explained, keeping his right fist in the pocket of a bulging jacket, while his eyes swept the hallway like a lighthouse beacon.

The guests were now pouring in. Among them, Anthony Eden, the Foreign Secretary; US Chief of Staff, General Marshal Sir Andrew Cunningham; Admiral of the Fleet, Lord Portal; Air Marshal, General Alan Brooke, CIGS, and Admiral King, US Chief of Naval Operations. Churchill went from one to another to greet them, making wild dashes to the hallway to see if the last guests—the Russians—were arriving.

Ten minutes later General Arkadiev appeared, looked us all over and, unsmiling, departed. There was an uproar in the vestibule; Stalin had arrived. Churchill greeted him, the British colonel waved his handkerchief frantically, and I tried to keep cool. All the guests were now reassembled in the Yellow Room, and I wondered what would happen to history if a bomb landed on us

It was a mind-boggling spectacle, so many important figures gathered together; it was as if a wax-works show had come to life. The mood was extremely cheerful (the final details of Operation Overlord, the second front, had already been agreed upon.)

President Roosevelt, in his wheelchair, sat in the center of the room mixing martinis. Cautious, Stalin took a sip, while Churchill tossed his down. Molotov, holding his cocktail, chatted with Anthony Eden. The British and American officers formed clusters of red tabs, gold braid, and stars. The three security chiefs were in a mellow mood. Stalin even let out a couple of belly laughs, his jaws snapping apart then shut, while his eyes remained wide open.

Dinner announced, Mr Kram stood to one corner like a conductor waiting in the wings for the audience to be seated before coming on stage. The table slowly filled as the 34 guests took their places. Roosevelt, Churchill and Stalin sat side by side, and I was only allowed one photograph of them. Facing the Big Three across the table were Molotov, Eden, and Harry Hopkins, who I'd photographed in Chicago at the Democratic Convention, and who was now Roosevelt's right-hand-man. Randolph Churchill sat next to Elliott Roosevelt, while Commander Thompson, who was to Churchill what Hopkins was to Roosevelt, sat next to Sergeant Robert Hopkins, Harry Hopkins' son.

With the oyster patties came the toasts: 17 in all. The first was to the King of England, then the President of the United States, and the President of the Soviet Union. Facing the portrait of Queen Victoria, Churchill got up and proposed a toast to "Stalin, the Great," and "Roosevelt, the Man." Stalin repaid in kind, calling him "My fighting friend Churchill". The double doors closed on what sounded from outside like a lively party.

Long afterwards, when the guests had all left and Churchill was ready for bed, he turned to Mr Kram, who was gathering up his clothes, and said, "A very fine effort. Good night."

Conference with Ibn Saud, Jeddah, Saudi Arabia, 1943

Ibn Saud, Jeddah, Saudi Arabia, 1943

Saud, Sand, and Standard Oil

Major General Ralph Royce was the Commanding General of the United States Air Force in the Middle East, to which I was accredited. "Beat it over here," Royce's aide, Major Putman, instructed me one morning. The last such summons had been to buy souvenirs in Damascus. "What is it this time,?" I asked warily.

"It's different, this time," Putman said. And indeed it was. Royce was about to confer with Ibn Saud, the ruler of Suadi Arabia, in Jeddah, just north of Mecca. Few foreigners had been allowed into the huge subcontinent that stretched between the Red Sea and the Persian Gulf. Until recently, its sole resources had come from pilgrimages to Mecca. But now the situation had changed radically. The largest oil deposit known to man had been discovered beneath the hundreds of thousands of miles of its barren desert. Oil was the purpose of our mission.

A solemn State Department official prefaced his briefing with a warning that our mission was top secret. Abdul al Aziz ibn Saud, he explained, was the absolute ruler of the greatest part of the Arabian peninsula, which he had snatched from King Hussein, Abdullah's father, and named after himself. The most impressive Arab since the Prophet, Saud unified the desert by conquest and in the course of the fighting slaughtered several hundred enemies himself. One of his favourite means of communication reportedly was to line up twelve prisoners, carve the hearts out of eleven, then order the twelfth, "Go back to your tribe and tell them what happened."

Having unified the disparate tribes, Saud consolidated his power by marrying, in turn, a daughter of each of the leading chieftains. The Koran allowed him four wives at a time. This provided him not only with solid family ties but over 30 male heirs. For a man of Saud's stature, the administration of his desert kingdom had presented no problems—at least until oil was discovered.

Saud, however, proved equally adept at foreign affairs. Although he had never been out of Arabia or seen a Western city, he had a clear grasp of world events, which explains why he was the only independent ruler in an area coveted by the British and its minions, Transjordan, Iraq, and Aden.

Also the name "Shell Oil" was not unfamiliar to him. It decided Saud to grant oil concessions to the Americans, thus assuring for himself dollar revenues from a country which was not involved in Middle East politics and also guaranteeing his country's independence, as he speculated the United States would not allow Britain to swallow him up. For this reason Ibn Saud was eager to see General Royce. The war in the Middle East was over; the oil war had now begun.

The Royce mission was to supply expert advice on strengthening Saud's army and protecting his borders. Saud's tribesmen were to be equipped with Italian rifles, purchased from the British, allowing them to push back the Iraqis across their border. In addition, a powerful transmitter was planned to enable Saud to communicate directly with the Americans. This was the first time the US took military action against Iraq over oil.

As our briefing meeting was breaking up, a voice called out, "Don't forget to bring your passports. We're going to get ourselves some swell visas!" This put me in a predicament—although I was an American war correspondent, and had American papers, I still carried a British passport. This was due to *Life* getting me accredited to the US armed forces and shipping me off to the Middle East before I got my final papers. Now, however, wasn't the time to mention the anomaly.

Although Saud was a stickler about obeying the Koran, which prohibits the making of graven images, he made an exception when it came to having his portrait taken. Before leaving, we had been instructed that, in Ibn Saud's presence, "Your breath should be clean of tobacco and liquor. You should also refrain from crossing your legs, since by doing so you show the soles of your feet, which is considered offensive to an Arab."

All the way down the Red Sea, General Royce played gin rummy. He was remarkable in many ways. He could never understand why Egyptian and other Arab leaders made such a fuss over him. He simply considered himself an army man with a command, temporarily stationed in Cairo because of a war, and therefore failed to see himself as the Arabs did—as the representative of United States military power, a new force in the Middle East. Royce baffled the Arabs with an amiability they could not associate with one so powerful.

On the plane I sat next to a nervous, talkative major, a medical officer, who explained that he was on rather a different mission from our own.

He had once taken care of Ibn Saud, and the king had been was so satisfied that he had decided to add his harem to the major's practice—an unprecedented honor as well as a big job. No wonder it was making him fret. "I'll be there three months," he said gloomily. "What's going to happen to my regular practice?" He seemed totally unaware of the diplomatic importance of his task. Americans are reluctant conquerors, I thought, as I considered how differently the British would react under similar circumstances.

Months later I was to learn how justified the major's gloom had been. He had not been allowed to see the faces or even to hear the voice of the patients he was examining. Instead, he stood at the far end of the long gallery from where the four veiled women stood, with an Arab translator halfway between them. It took him about half-an-hour to get the medical history of each one. Then he went to get the necessary medicines. On his return, he found the veiled quartet had mingled together, and as he could not distinguish them from one another, nor recall in what order they had been examined, he had to start all over again.

General Royce left his card game to land the plane, flying in low as requested by Saud so that our profane eyes would not contemplate Mecca. We landed on a stretch of desert near several light planes chartered by wealthy Moslem pilgrims.

A guard of honor was lined up and a Saudi official, his Bedouin costume fluttering in the wind, was seated at a rickety table ready to inspect our passports. I was at the end of the queue, wondering how to avoid him, when everybody's attention was diverted. A limousine appeared from nowhere racing toward the Royal palace, its two Union Jacks flapping wildly. "Guess we caught the British Ambassador flat-footed," somebody remarked as I sidestepped the passport inspector.

General Royce was dropped off at a brand new guesthouse he was inaugurating. It stood out alone on a stretch of desert, like some displaced Florida villa. At the foot of the stairwell were two door mats inscribed "Welcome". The rest of us were driven into town and put up at the Hotel Jeddah. The windows of my room were black with flies. I brushed my teeth and gargled, as ordered, before being driven off with the others to Saud's palace.

The throne-room, the size of en enormous ballroom, took up the entire ground floor of the palace. Except for carpets scattered on the floor and heavy armchairs lining the walls, the room was bare. Saud's throne was a gilded armchair, upholstered in floral brocade. Next to it was a low table on which rested an antiquated telephone. We were presented in turn to the mighty ruler, who stood in stockinged feet before his throne.

With my hand in his powerful paw, I had a good chance to observe this impressive 73-year-old, who stood an erect six feet despite his numerous battle injuries, majestic in his flowing Bedouin robes with a heavy gold woven *agal* resting on his head as a crown. Deep lines scored his dark features and he looked as if he rarely smiled. He was a man of the desert, gaunt and impassive, and despite a very obvious blind eye, still managed a searching gaze. We took our armchairs in order of precedence and, resisting any impulse to cross our legs, waited, as instructed, to be served the traditional cup of coffee before the meeting began.

General Royce sat on Saud's right, while the interpreters, cross-legged at their feet, translated the small talk. James S. Moore Jr, the American plenipotentiary to Saudi Arabia, sat on the King's left in formal dress, from top hat to white kid gloves, painfully aware nobody was paying him any attention. Next to him was Mr James Terry Duce, Vice-President of California-Arabian Standard Oil. The most influential person after Saud, he sat back with a contented smile.

Royce was enjoying himself hugely. Despite the taboos, he sat with his legs crossed, one foot practically on the king's lap. As for Ibn Saud, he giggled like a schoolboy. The General, in his bluff way had made a hit. When Ibn Saud complained that he couldn't stand long on account of an old leg wound, General Royce said he shouldn't have got himself into so many wars.

I now slipped out of my armchair and on tiptoe started to take pictures, wondering what would happen. The American minister had been doubtful about this, but General Royce, who seemed to have his own ideas, was unconcerned. Ibn Saud's aides believed the king would not object as long as I did not make his blind eye obvious. They weren't positive, however, and Saud wasn't the kind to bother with such trivial questions. I therefore slowly made my way around, and each time my flashbulb went off, I felt like someone with whooping cough at a concert. The members of the mission watched me with amusement as I stood out alone in the center of the immense expanse. The king, I also noticed, was following me with deep attention. I watched him rest both hands on his cane and lean over toward the interpreter. In the silence which fell, the interpreter spoke to General Royce who, in turn, leaned over and nodded. Both he and Ibn Saud then looked in my direction and the General beckoned. Although I felt very much alone where I stood, I pointed to myself inquiringly. General Royce nodded impatiently. Not sure what was up, I started to tiptoe toward the side carpets, but noticing General Royce's scowl I decided this was not time for protocol and clattered over directly.

"Ibn Saud wants you to take his portrait," General Royce told me.

I glanced at the formidable face now draped in a beatific smile.

"Now?" I whispered.

"No, tonight at the state banquet."

After more brushing of teeth and gargling away traces of bourbon we arrived that evening to be led out to a large white terrace overlooking the desert. The full moon, which bathed the terrace in a pale, greenish light, was so large it seemed to hover over our heads like a lantern. Ibn Saud sat facing the moon, surrounded by chairs in a square formation. His fierce guards in green and red, rattling sabers, faced their monarch. The British Ambassador sat on Ibn Saud's right and General Royce on his left. The rest of us were wide-eyed in wonder.

Slaves, their heads muffled in *kouffiehs*, served us coffee, disdainfully flicking the dregs on the heavy carpets. Again the King nodded to me. Again he felt the time was inappropriate, and told General Royce to bring me along with him the next morning before we left.

The feast that night was an Oriental buffet, spread out before the seated guests. Mounds of roast lamb were piled up on platters; innumerable plates with various cuts of meat and mixed vegetables basked in different sauces. There was pitta bread and a pyramid of oranges stacked up in front of each guest. The dessert was *crème caramel.* The beverage was water. The retainers standing behind the King either fanned him, held goblets of water, or awaited his wishes. Carried away, I took far too many pictures of the dinner, forgetting all about my appointment in the morning.

Shortly before we were due to leave, aides of Ibn Saud presented every member of the mission with a royal Bedouin costume. (As chief of the mission, General Royce also received a watch with Saud's name inscribed on the face, and a sword.) The State Department official who had escorted us then paid the Saudi aide a hundred dollars tax for each member of the mission.

Next morning, the General and I drove to see the Ibn Saud. I felt doubtful. My flashlight equipment was working erratically, my bulbs did not always go off, and I had only three left. Saud left the picture suggestions to me. Fingering my bulbs, I proposed three shots—a portrait, a full-length study, and a picture of him on his throne. Saud beamed agreement, drew himself up to his full height, stared straight into the camera and waited. I slipped my first bulb into the battery case while General Royce glowered at me. My battery case held high in my left hand, I stepped back to frame Ibn Saud's towering figure in my camera, and shot the three pictures in quick succession.

One of Farouk's 98 cars, Cairo, 1943

The Man Who Had Too Much

"Atif," King Farouk told his aide, "Now that John has photographed my palace, you've seen more of Abdin that you did in ten years." Until then, only Farouk, his family and his servants had seen the recesses of Abdin. In the months I spent in Cairo, I also discovered more about the King. There were two Farouks: the official one, the Oriental potentate I had encountered during that first tempestuous drive in lower Egypt, and then there was Farouk the democrat.

At the time, Farouk was tinkering with the notion of becoming the Caliph of Islam—the office of Moslem Pope—which had disappeared with the Ottoman Empire. There had been no suggestion of reviving the office until Farouk got eczema on his face. Then, unable to shave, he grew a conventional beard and moustache which his courtiers told him gave him a striking resemblance to his illustrious ancestor, the Khedive, Ismail the Magnificent. After the eczema disappeared, Farouk kept his beard. Given the appearance of a Caliph, he attempted to become one.

To demonstrate his piety, every Friday (the Moslem Sunday) he led the noonday prayers in the mosque wearing a fez and a full-length dove-gray *stambouline* coat with matching silk lapels straight out of Ottoman tradition. With his heavy, drooping eyelids and pouting lips, fingering his amber beads, he projected the very image of a sulky and distant Eastern potentate.

The other Farouk was for American consumption. He wore Bermuda shorts, slapped his thighs as he burst out laughing, and cultivated what he considered more democratic ways.

As far as the British were concerned, Farouk the democrat was no more acceptable than Farouk the autocrat, his change of ideals being solely due to the United States' presence in the Middle East.

Farouk was impressed by the way the Americans did things on a grand scale. They did not disembark, they flew in. They landed in smart uniforms and with a bouncing stride. They brought with them bombers, fighter planes, Hershey bars, Camel cigarettes and, especially, Coca-Cola. Although they sometimes blundered in their friendliness, like the officer who graciously greeted passers by with *"Saida wog"*, unaware this amounted to

"Good morning, you son-of-a-bitch," their desire to see everything and then buy it soon made them popular with the suave *dragomans* and a favorite with the urchins, who called them "Joe".

For Farouk it was a new experience to meet representatives of a powerful nation who did not behave arrogantly. Possibly he assessed them as easy to fool. Yet there was a genuine admiration in his judgment. Once, when we were discussing the Tehran conference, he observed, "You know, John, America has no foreign policy, but —" he grinned "—she has awfully powerful hind legs, and with those you can kick." Shrewdly, Farouk saw that the United States, with her powerful hindquarters, was going to play an ever-increasing role in shaping the future. He was delighted that most Americans did not approve of the colonial ways they found in the Middle East. He saw an opportunity to infuriate the British and gain considerable advantages for himself. If only he could induce the US to take the same interest in Egypt that American oil companies displayed in Saudi Arabia, the three stars of the Egyptian flag would find themselves bolstered by all those of the United States. He therefore set about wooing the Americans.

Unfortunately, the US was solely interested in winning the war and impervious to his blandishments, although its representatives enjoyed his company. Farouk's charm stopped at no one, from Patrick Hurley, President Roosevelt's roving ambassador, whom he called "Pat", to the sergeant from Baton Rouge who trained the royal bodyguards, whom he greeted with a "Hiya, Sarge".

It was Farouk's determination to impress his new friends which had landed me with the job of photographing the Abdin Palace in Cairo.

I was led into a throne-room with brown walls covered with colored Arabic squiggles that reminded me, incongruously enough, of a fruitcake. There, reclining on an extravaganza of gold and red plush, was Farouk. He pointed to the Arabic motto overhead: "A King supported by faith remains. A faith supported by a King is strengthened." This, Farouk said, inspired him. He then reminded me that Farouk meant, "one who distinguishes between right and wrong".

Thinking I'd taken his point, I proposed taking Farouk's picture on his throne. He objected. It was, he said, far too modest for him to be photographed sitting on it. This was exactly the kind of thing that summed up Farouk. But I cheerfully complied with all his suggestions having learned that photographing people the way they wanted to be seen usually offers the best reflection of themselves. Farouk enjoying himself too much, wallowing in excess: that was my story. It explained why, after the British gave up Egypt, Farouk was forced to abdicate. There was no one left there to hate more than him.

In addition to Abdin, Farouk had three more palaces: Koubbeh outside Cairo; Montazah, and Ras el Tin in Alexandria; he also had a hunting lodge at Inchass with its stable of white racing camels, and a pagoda at the Cairo zoo. His wife, Queen Farida, was relegated to Ras el Tin, and Farouk led a solitary life. With little to do, he supervised my work, which I encouraged by admiring his outrageous way of life. He even thought up possible pictures. He had his champion Alsatian, Loretto, which he kept in Alexandria with his keeper, specially brought up to Cairo to pose with him. He recalled having shot on August 4, 1940, a champion ibex with horns that measured a record 51 inches. The mounted head was brought from Inchass to Cairo by its keeper for me to photograph.

Abdin was a gaudy version of Buckingham Palace. The front entrance to the royal grounds contained offices looking out on a noisy square. High walls on the other three sides isolated the palace from the teeming slums and the dusty heat of the city. The palace buildings were surrounded by gardens complete with a marble bandstand, a swimming-pool, and an open-air movie theater. The whole scene was given an East-meets-West flavor by drooping palms, carefully trimmed evergreens, clusters of wild tropical plants, and tidy lawns and flower-beds neatly divided by sandy paths.

Inside, rich carpeting snaked up the palace stairway and along endless miles of halls and corridors with their bizarre accumulation of objects of great value and junk. The Red, the White, the Diplomatic and the Suez reception rooms were of regal proportions and filled with larger-than-life portraits of male members of the dynasty. The private theater, where Farouk enjoyed watching magicians perform, was a miracle of indirect lighting. The Queen's box, in discreet *purdah* at the back of the house on the second floor, looked down on 400 delicately shaped chairs and four armchairs for the monarch and his male relatives. The State dining-room—not to be confused with the wing where buffet suppers for 600 were served, or the private dining-room, or the emergency snack bar set up for Farouk just off the kitchen—had a horseshoe-shaped table. The combination of

Farouk's breakfast, Cairo, 1943

dim lighting, richly upholstered leather armchairs, white-gloved Nubian waiters in red and gold livery and solid gold plates made it grandly oppressive and I wondered whether Farouk's guests felt satiated before the meal had begun.

The King and Queen's private apartments were crammed with Louis XIV and Louis XV furniture. Seen *en masse*, it went a long way to explaining why the French Revolution came with Louis XVI. From the walls, portraits of female members of the Khedival Dynasty looked down on busts of their consorts. On the ground floor were the vaults with entire cabinets stacked with gold plates and sterling silver flatware, tiers of glasses of all varieties, from delicate Baccarat to massive Bohemian cut crystal, each embossed with the dynasty's crest; forests of silver confection stands, rows of tea and coffee services, everything, in fact, to entertain guests by the hundreds.

Just off the vaults was Farouk's "hobby room" where, like a child surrounded by new toys, he gloated over his treasures. His collecting was not limited by quantity or quality. With equal joy, he contemplated the finest collection of razor-blade wrappers in the world or fingered his precious gems for the tactile pleasure it gave him. His worldwide assembly of automobile license plates were kept up to date by his diplomatic envoys—including one from every state of the Union. He estimated the value of his collection of coins, which included at least one example of every gold coin minted in the world, at $10 million. His stamp collection was valued at $17 million. Peering over his shoulder while he sorted out some newly received stamps, I noticed they came from Nazi-occupied Europe. My surprise made Farouk roar with laughter. "Hitler sends them to me," he explained airily. But when I tried to take some pictures of him with his stamps, he refused, giving me a sound piece of collector's advice: "If it gets around I'm interested in philately, prices will go up."

Farouk's mania for acquiring objects belonging to others for the improvement of his own collection would have been considered kleptomania were he not a Moslem. He revived for his own benefit an archaic law which stipulated that whatever the guest admires the host must offer. Farouk accepted these gifts with great charm and was thoughtful enough to bring along palace servants to do the packing and crating.

To keep the smell of food out of the palace, the royal kitchens were in a semi-detached wing. The first time I gazed upon this white-tiled splendor, awaiting the regal whim, I told Beta Ali, the Escoffier of the Moslem world, "This is a finer kitchen than Buckingham Palace's"

"You're right," Beta Ali agreed casually. "We were there." His office was located next to the emergency dining-room Farouk used whenever he got peckish between meals. Just as the captain and crew of a battleship are aboard solely to get the guns into firing position, Beta Ali and his staff were stationed in the kitchen to keep Farouk fed. Children spent their youth peeling fresh almonds by the bushel, then crushing them to extract the milky substance which, mixed with a pound of sugar, provided Farouk with his favorite beverage. After sampling this chilled concoction, I asked, "Isn't it very fattening?"

Beta Ali rolled his eyes and sighed.

Nubians prepared vegetable dishes; seafood specialists handled the lobsters; the roast chef spent hours in the cold room carving fresh cuts; the pastry cooks baked croissants; there was even a royal Turkish coffee-maker.

Preparing Farouk's lunch was a mammoth gastronomic production. The menu that day was broiled lobster, grilled chicken, sole *vol-au-vent*, mutton chops, mashed potatoes, peas, rice and artichokes, fruit compote, fresh peaches, pomegranates, mangoes, jellies, flans, exotic-flavored ice-creams, and a carafe of chilled almond milk.

After I had praised Beta Ali's talents, Farouk gave me a sound piece of advice on how to handle cooks. "I keep my chefs," he said good-naturedly, "so long as they build only two houses and own only three cars. First car or house after that, out they go." It was not greed, however, but religious zeal that brought about Beta Ali's downfall. This otherwise happy man had one ambition. He wanted to make a pilgrimage to Mecca, and become the "venerable Hadj Beta Ali", entitled to wear a green scarf around his red *tarboosh*. Feeding Farouk left him no time for his pilgrimage until opportunity knocked at the kitchen door. King Ibn Saud planned to visit Egypt, and Farouk was sending his royal yacht, the *Mahroussa*, to pick him up at Jeddah. This quick trip offered Beta Ali a unique opportunity of getting to neighboring Mecca and becoming a Hadj. He took the chance that his assistant would not offend the royal palate. Unfortunately Hadj Ali, on his return from Mecca, found himself out of a job. His assistant had overcooked a steak.

In addition to the *Mahroussa*, on which he would eventually sail to exile, Farouk had a river yacht that could accommodate 250, several smaller boats, innumerable cars, and a silver-painted diesel train which had a large kitchen and two sections, one for the menfolk and one for his harem.

The royal garage adjoined the palace. There, Farouk's 98 cars were serviced. They came in all shapes, shades, and nationalities: two red Rolls Royces for state functions, two red and black cabriolets for desert journeys, a black bulletproof car for times of unrest, a maroon Mercedes from Hitler, a green Alfa Romeo from Mussolini, a brace of jeeps from the Allied generals, and a whole line of American and continental cars. The first model of any car imported into Egypt had to be delivered to the royal garage so that nobody could claim to have a new model Farouk did not own. I was about to take pictures of his cars when Farouk called out from the palace balcony, "John, be sure and photograph my eight favorites."

Farouk always kept a car 24 hours a day beneath the archway of the Palace's back entrance. It looked like a mummy under its protective covering adorned by a foot-high initial "F" He whimsically picked and chose from his array of cars and enjoyed testing them recklessly along deserted highways at odd hours. That is how, one dawn, he collided with a British Army truck. At the Army hearing, the cockney driver explained, "It all happened so fast, your honor, that the next thing I knew, there were three wogs sprawling on the highway, and the one in the middle was King Farouk!"

Laid up in hospital, Farouk missed meeting the most important American of all: President Roosevelt, who had come to Cairo for a conference with Churchill and Chiang Kai-shek. His only participation in this historic event was loaning his bulletproof car to the President, who in return sent him an autographed picture: "From your friend, Franklin Delano Roosevelt."

When Farouk grew bored by the lonely immensity of Abdin he spent his evenings out, thus it was a standing practice for every nightclub to hold the best table in case "HM" dropped in. (In those happy days, when he was popular, he did not require a second table for his bodyguards.) Although the lights were dimmed to make him less conspicuous, his loud laughter usually gave him away. One evening at the Club de la Chasse, Farouk spotted a group of us with several USO entertainers and summoned the company to his table. As usual, he greeted us while remaining seated—much to the annoyance of a blonde, who growled, "Got no manners, that King of yours?" Later, when Farouk heard she was a singer and asked for a song, she stared at him coldly and said, *"Naah."*

"You won't sing for me?" Farouk exclaimed surprised. "Why, that's a royal command."

"Not if you don't get up for me!" the blonde spat back, sending Farouk into gales of laughter.

Other times he would pay unexpected visits to General Royce at his apartment. He liked to listen to the latest recordings from the States and raid the refrigerator for cold cuts, which he ate sitting on the kitchen table. Farouk's habit of keeping late hours drove the General to distraction. He would finally bring the evenings to an end with a blunt, "I'm sorry, but I work for a living and I've got to get up early."

Shortly after the birth of Farouk's third daughter, which left him so desperate at having another girl and still no heir, he suggested calling the child Fiasco and shaved his beard. This vital bit of information was kept from the public on account of Farouk's pretentions to the Caliphate. Before General Royce heard this news, Farouk entered his apartment building unannounced, wearing sneakers, slacks, and a turtleneck sweater. Accidentally stopping off at the wrong landing, he barged into the apartment of Royce's chief-of-staff and breezily demanded, "Where's Ralph?"

"*Major General Ralph Royce* lives on the floor below," the chief-of-staff snapped. "Okay, okay," Farouk answered cheerfully as he departed.

The consternation of the Egyptian servants made the chief-of-staff realize what had happened. He promptly called up General Royce to warn him and got his aide on the phone, just in time. He was heard to say with a sigh of relief, "This certainly *is* a surprise, Your Majesty."

The face that emerged from behind the beard looked aged beyond its years. I realized the strain he was under on the winter evening in 1944 when I went to bid good-bye to Farouk. We were in the Victorian expanses of his office in Abdin. Farouk was in such high spirits that even his aide, Atif Bey, was misled. Farouk said, "So, you're leaving us for the Italian front, John?" At this, Atif blurted out, "He's leaving for the land where kings are losing their thrones." Farouk's smile was wiped from him face. "Atif!" he barked, turning on him. "I won't have talk about kings losing thrones," and strode out of the office without looking back.

A Native's Return

The airport in Algiers where I landed in the winter of 1944 had changed considerably since I had last seen it 20 years before. Then my father had taken me out to a deserted field on which a small shack stood and a windsock fluttered. We had come to applaud a pilot making a test flight across the Mediterranean. The bi-plane, however, never showed up and I was very disappointed. Now Algiers' airport was the hub of the Italian campaign and the runways were crowded with four-engined DC-4s you disembarked from by a rope ladder which dangled from the doorway.

A GI drove me to the Hotel Aletti, which did not exist in my youth and was now an American billet nicknamed "the rich man's kasbah". I checked in with an American sergeant, and an Italian prisoner of war carried my luggage up to my room. A colleague showed me the ropes. He took me to Le Berry, a restaurant converted into a temporary mess hall, and told me the PX was at Les Dames de France, once Algiers' largest department store. So far nothing reminded me of my childhood.

To fit my vague recollections into present-day reality, I took a stroll and stepped into a dream. As I walked I began to recognize places and remember where streets led. The long narrow arcades along the Rue de Constantine were familiar, and I knew they would take me to the Square Bresson, which for a child had been the emotional heart of the city. My mother used to take me there, and on special occasions bought me a balloon. I would get very excited as the vendor hauled down the multi-colored cluster attached to white threads which fluttered nervously as though trying to escape. Only when the sale was completed would he attach the thread to my wrist as mother firmly gripped my other hand. One time a large red balloon slipped away and slowly drifted over the square heading for the open sea, a cherry in the blue sky. I chose another one through my tears. It was not the same thing. I became acquainted with sorrow.

I looked around for a balloon salesman and found only donkeys with ribbons round their necks trudging the square with short determined steps, nodding as they went, just as in my time donkey boys led them while parents walked proudly alongside, gripping their terrified children.

Crossing the square, I reached the boulevard overlooking the harbor where mother had taken me to meet my father when he came back from the war. I suddenly recalled the bright-yellow wooden spokes of the carriage which drove us home.

On a corner of the boulevard was Gruber's, once the most elegant restaurant in Algiers. After Sunday walks around the port, we stopped there while my father and mother chatted with friends and I toyed with an ice-cream. Now Gruber's terrace, littered with peanut shells, was a forlorn sight. Street cars of a more recent vintage traveled the same routes. One sceeched past the sinister Barberousse prison every Thursday, transporting the prisoners' relatives with their wide Arab baskets filled with food.

The *kasbah* remained a honeycomb of damp, narrow streets lurching uphill, while the smell of leather, fritters soaked in honey, and sweat drifted down. Arabs sat cross-legged drinking *café maure* out of small cups, arguing in guttural voices in which occasionally words like "jerry can", "Hershey bar", and "six-by-six" could be recognised. The main trolley line traveled up the rue Michelet to the *bois*, where all of Algiers flowed on Easter Sunday to eat *mouna*, a fluffy sponge cake. Our old apartment was off that street, so I started along it, wondering at how narrow it seemed. When I reached the old photographic shop where my mother had had my picture taken, I remembered the intersection ahead which led to my school.

First I stopped to look round the square framed by tiny shops once filled with marbles, spinning tops, water pistols, candy, and slot machines. Here we used to hang around waiting for the school gates to open. The school building hadn't changed, though it was no longer called the Petit Lycée but the Lycée Emile Gautier, and had been temporarily converted into a hospital for venereal diseases. I set off to reach our apartment by a short cut, picking my way by guesswork because so much had changed.

Some landmarks, however, remained. The Cinéma du Plateau, no longer the converted stable of my youth, was now the modernized heaven of another generation, but I could still imaginge the smell of celluloid and hear the grinding of the projector. The public garden had undergone improvements. There was a merry-go-round, while our big sandpit had made way for a tiled pond. The large earthenware vases I used to climb into when we played hide-and-seek were gone. The bright-yellow uniforms of the guards had been replaced by blue ones.

Leaving the square through a side gate, I recognized the bench where my aunt had let me take a picture of her with her vest-pocket camera. Afterwards, with a child's persistence, I had asked to see "my picture". Finally I was shown a contact print where a ghostlike image of my aunt emerged from a building. I don't remember the explanation which left me believing I'd done something wrong, but to this day I clearly recall that contact and now know my aunt had forgotten to rewind her camera and made a double exposure. So much for my first picture! Halfway down the steps, I stopped, realizing I couldn't remember where she was buried. I could see in my mind her grave close to a wall. There was a stretch of road I could not place, somewhere past the *bois*, lost!

I found the English library in the grounds of the Holy Trinity Church. A sign read: "Ring the bell and come in boys." I did. The room was dark in the early winter evening. Servicemen flicked through magazines. A middle-aged lady walked up to me smiling pleasantly. "I was here as a boy," I told her. "I'm just looking around." Going up the steps leading to the church, I felt the need to talk to someone and found a padre. "I was here as a child," I explained. "And I was christened in there." Like the librarian he smiled politely. "In that case you will want to attend Sunday service," he said, and I watched as he hopped into his jeep and drove off.

It was not what I wanted. I gazed down on the Bay of Algiers and the American liberty ships and realized I was reliving my memories. Nobody could share them with me. Algiers held nothing personal for most of those I spoke to. Just another stop, another town on which the United States had superimposed itself on its march to victory. Tomorrow, somewhere else, I would be like these others. But today I was a native.

I walked towards our old apartment. There it stood: a five-floor building with a wrought-iron doorway. The second-floor balcony had been ours. I read the names on the brass plates of the letterboxes and found the Decaille family still lived there. I rang their doorbell. A white-haired lady opened the door. "Your face is familiar," she said, pausing for a moment. Then she said: "You are the young English boy who lived on the floor below us." She told me that her son, who had been my playmate, now worked for the gas company. As I was leaving she asked me, "Where have you been all these years? Oran?"

Jean Gabin, Algiers, 1944

Partisans near Litija Bridge, Slovenia, 1944

Looking for Tito

First communist-socialist meeting after Mussolini, Rome, 1944

Shoe vendor, Eboli, Italy, 1944

Italy, 1944

In February 1944, Naples harbor was clogged with sunken ships; the water-front *bassis*, where the poor huddled, lay in ruins. Stores on the fashionable Via Roma displayed signs which read: "OUT OF BOUNDS TO ARMY PER-SONNEL". No less prominent were the ones that read "DANGEROUS. VD". In spite of its unique setting, with Vesuvius peering down over the wide sweeping bay and out to the Island of Capri, Naples looked forlorn in winter. To make matters even worse, the city formed the rear echelon of a front which was bogged down at Monte Cassino, the fortress-like monastery the Germans had occupied, and from which they commanded the surrounding plain. The Allies' drive North had so far been stalled there.

American GIs of Italian origin felt humiliated by their country's part in the war. They would say, "My old man won't tell me about Italy anymore." For their part, the Italians heartily disliked the GIs, finding them *antipatico*. The Italian Americans seemed to forget that their ancestors were part of one of the longest unbroken civilizations in history.

I made this mistake myself in April 1945, when I was sent to Washington by General Eaker, Commander of the Allied Air Force in the Mediterranean, to report on the US airmen who had been rescued by Tito's Partisans in Yugoslavia. I reported to John McCloy, the Under-Secretary of War. After disposing of Yugoslavia, McCloy asked me about Italy. My pessimistic description of the devastation and the all-too-obvious misery matched his own views. Asked how long it would take for Italy to recover, I was at a loss. At his insistence, I ventured "50 years?"

"You're an optimist," Mr McCloy said.

Within 18 months of this conversation, the Italian miracle was under-way. For all the contempt once heaped upon it, the country would soon once again become tourism's pet.

But meanwhile, during that winter of 1944, everybody was hoarding food and trying to keep warm. Much of the action took place at the US Army's dump, where yesterday's garbage was smoldering.

Sunk in a wide ravine on the outskirts of town, the rising mound of trash looked like an infernal lake. It was encircled by barbed wire to keep

out the starving Neapolitans, who waited impatiently for the day's supplies
to arrive. They milled around the top of a steep slope where the trucks
backed up to unload. The moment the convoy appeared, weary MPs
cracked their rawhide whips to keep the dirt road clear. As streams of garbage noisily cascaded down the slope, the Neapolitans dived right after it.
Up to their hips in cans, cardboard boxes and crates, they scavenged. Some
ate on the spot, gulping down whatever they found. Others pushed crates
on to which they piled their scraps. These starving people simply couldn't
understand why the Americans tried to prevent them from helping themselves to all that wasted food simply because it was rotten.

With high prices, low salaries, nothing much to buy, and no money to
buy it with, the black market flourished. Created out of necessity, it overtook the economy of liberated Southern Italy. Everything was pilfered, from
the supplies the army trucks carried to the trucks themselves. Here
Neapolitan ingenuity came in. Organized gangs of kids would wait in a
dimly lit tunnel for an army vehicle to drive past. Then one would stretch in
the middle of the road, forcing the driver to stop with a jolt. As he did so,
members of the gang unbolted the back panel and let it down. The kid on
the road then scampered away. The truck started up and the stacked-up
goods slithered on to the road, to be snatched up by teams of juvenile
delinquents. The goods were soon peddled all over Naples. Checking up on
the black market, an American officer found that it was so well organized,
the Neapolitans ordered by brand names.

Twelve-year-old urchins, homeless and war-orphaned, who washed up
in Naples were already accomplished pimps. Their pockets bulging with
army 'script, they accosted GIs, offering them their "sister," while puffing on
American cigarettes. Thirteen-year-old girls willingly complied, and house-
wives, too, to make ends meet.

At the time I made frequent trips to Monopoli, the Italian harbor on
the Adriatic where the Yugoslavs had a naval base, trying to get accredited
to Tito's Partisans. When I was in Naples, I stayed at a very large apartment
in the residential district of the Vomero. It had been taken over by colleagues on *Life* and was shared with several paratroopers from the 82nd
Airborne. The windows for the most part had been blown out, but the paratroopers had fitted a stove in the living-room. It was propped up on bricks
and the chimney stuck out of the window. The kitchen was large, and the

Tito playing chess, Island of Vis, Yugoslavia, 1944

(Joza would have been sent to live with an aunt in Cleveland had his father been able to raise the boat fare. When asked what he'd have done in the States, Tito said to me, "become a millionaire".) At 15, he went to work as a waiter before becoming apprenticed to a locksmith. After serving the required three years, Josip traveled around Germany and parts of the the Austro-Hungarian Empire, picking up languages and a variety of experiences (such as test driving Daimler cars) as he went. He did his military service in a Croatian regiment stationed in Zagreb. Putting into practice his theory that it is better to learn something useless than do nothing, Josip took up fencing and became the regimental champion. He was also the youngest sergeant major in his regiment.

When World War I broke out, Josip Broz, like most members of the Empire's peasant minorities, dreamed that the Hapsburgs would be defeated and Croatia would become independent. Nevertheless, he proved himself a good soldier when his regiment was sent to the Carpathian front. Severely wounded when they was overrun by the Russians, and taken prisoner, Sergeant Major Broz spent over a year in a hospital on the Volga recovering from wounds aggravated by pneumonia and typhus. Although it was not mandatory for captured NCOs to work, Broz applied for a job, finding idleness intolerable.

By the time the Tsar abdicated in the spring of 1917, Broz was in charge of a work gang on the Trans-Siberian railroad. In the chaos which followed, feeling a strong affinity for the Russians as Slav brothers, Josip Broz participated in the revolt by joining the Bolsheviks. Arrested once again, he managed to escape and crossed Russia to Petrograd, where he took part in the July demonstrations. In the crackdown on the Bolsheviks which followed, Broz attempted to reach Finland. Caught at the border, he was returned to Petrograd and interned at the fortress of St Peter & St Paul before being shipped back to Siberia under guard. Finding himself on a crowded station platform, he jumped on a train heading for Omsk and escaped. There he became a member of the Red Guard and took part in the October Revolution until the Whites Russians occupied the city in 1918.

Broz then went into hiding with a nomadic Kirghiz tribe, where he learned to be an expert horseman. After the Whites were thrown out of Omsk he returned and married a young Russian. These were the adventures he would recall in Kumrovec when he got back in 1920. Home was no

longer a part of the Austro-Hungarian Empire. Croatia had been incorporated into a new state: Yugoslavia. During the years which followed his
return, Broz was a metal worker and a union organizer. Elected head of the
metal workers union in Zagreb, he showed the coolheadedness which had
enabled him to survive in the past and would serve him in the years to
come.

When the police broke into the union headquarters in search of Josip
Broz, he pointed to a door on the left, saying, "He went that way," then
leapt out the window and landed two floors below. Eventually he was caught
and tried for communist activities. His defiance earned him the maximum
five-year sentence. On his release from prison, he was considered so dangerous, he was put under house-arrest in Kumrovec and ordered to report
daily to the police. Within days he disappeared. For over ten years nothing
more was heard of him until he re-emerged as the leader of the Partisan
forces.

Our visit coinciding with the third anniversary of the Partisan uprising. Tito took the afternoon off. He played chess with General Jovanovic.
While the general played with brooding concentration, Tito had a good
time and cheerfully checkmated his chief-of-staff.

Then we went for a swim. In single file we trooped down to the road
where two jeeps awaited us. At the waterfront we boarded a large fishing
boat. Selecting a suitable beach was a problem, as the coast was mined. Tito
left the decision to General Jovanovic. "He's the chief of staff. Let him
worry." He did keep a firm grip on Tigar so that the dog wouldn't leap off
the boat and blow himself up.

Once the beach was selected, Tito retired to a small cabin and changed into a bathing suit. Each in turn did the same. As I had no bathing
trunks with me, I told Stojan, "I'll go in the raw."

"No you won't," Stojan warned me.

"Why not? We're all men."

"You would scandalize them."

"Scandalize Tito?" Somehow, this had never occured to me.

Life at Macmis

Captain Evelyn Waugh took his constitutional pacing the path that led to the Allied Military Mission's villa on Vis. He reminded me of an English schoolboy, and the villa "Macmis"—Maclean's Mission—and its grounds, might well have been a setting for one of his novels. It overlooked a beach where the members of the mission swam, despite the fact that the vineyards surrounding the villa were booby-trapped. Copies of the *Sketch* and *Bystander* lay on tables on the large veranda. A slogan, "*Zivio Drug Tito*" (Long Live Comrade Tito), was painted on the whitewashed walls and translated by members of the mission as "Tito's civic drugstore". Guests frequently flew in from Bari for an afternoon dip, as the regulars brooded over a possible shortage of limes for the gin.

One of our guests, an earl, had been on leave in London when the Allied landings in Normandy had taken place in June. Curious, I asked him what it had been like. "My butler woke me up, announcing, 'Kippers for breakfast my lord, and the landings have started,'" the earl recalled. The atmosphere was somewhere between British country club and Balkan conspiratorial.

Brigadier Fitzroy Maclean, the chief of the mission, was the link between Tito and the Western Allies. He had come to Vis with Tito for a brief spell that summer of 1944.

Nicknamed "Little Gibraltar" by the British troops, Vis was a colorful Allied fortress. A large British commando force and and American OSS operational group were stationed on the island to help in its defense. The US Air Force had built an airstrip for damaged heavy bombers unable to return to their Italian base on their return from raids over Austria and Eastern Europe. Whenever the bomber was damaged beyond quick repair, it circled over the island while the crew bailed out. After that, the pilot ditched the plane in the Adriatic where he was picked up by one of the air-sea rescue boats. These crafts, which could cruise at 60 knots, were also used for night raids on German-held islands and the Yugoslav mainland. The commandos called these night operations "battles". One memorable character who participated in them was a Colonel Churchill—no relation to the Prime Minister. Churchill was convinced he could kill someone with his bow and arrow, and to prove it, he went on battles wearing his kilt and playing his bagpipe while stalking "Huns." Before he could demonstrate his theory, he was wounded and taken prisoner.

Lieutenant Sherman, a freckle-faced Texan, was a specialist in sabotage. His interest in explosives dated back to the Christmas he was given a chemistry set and blew off part of the family's back porch. Unwilling to wait for the United States to enter the war, he had joined the British Army and was sent to the Middle East assigned to Special Services. After Pearl Harbor, he decided to serve in his own country's army, and very nearly received a military discharge: the medics found that he had an unusual heart beat, flat feet and was blind as a bat. In charge of the Partisan sabotage academy, he wrote to his mother that he had a desk job in Cairo. "They moved my academy to the outskirts," Sherman recalled happily, "after one of my demonstrations blew out most of the windows in town".

Sherman trained his Partisan students how to rig locomotives with time bombs activated by photo-electric cells. "It's simply great," he beamed. "Just think. One of these locomotives is traveling in German-occupied Europe, then on a beautiful, sunny day, it enters a dark tunnel. Two seconds later, the electric cell sets off the fuse. What a mess to clean up."

Sherman also instructed his students in the art of blasting bridge abutments, and setting off all types of booby traps. (His favorite was an artificial cow turd scattered on country lanes.)

A perfectionist, he reprimanded his students whenever they used too much explosive. "It's not elegant," he'd tell them. "With a quarter of the charge, you'll kill just as dead."

While he welcomed all these foreign allies, Tito, who was a cautious man, nevertheless maintained a Partisan force twice the strength of the Anglo-American units on Vis, and thus the community there was a strange mosaic of political and social contradictions, ranging from Marx to Waugh.

Curious about the novelist, I joined him on his constitutional. He talked about education. "My father was better educated than I am, and I am better educated than my son." This he put down to the decline in Greek studies. "What about engineering?" I asked.

"Do you expect my son to be a taxi driver?" Waugh demanded sharply, then abruptly changed the subject, "Have you met her ladyship?"

"Her ladyship?".

"Tito." Waugh stated.

"Tito?" I echoed in surprise.

"Didn't you know Tito was a woman?"

"He's a man. I've met him. Besides, he's married," I insisted, feeling foolish.

"Whose her husband?" Waugh wanted to know.

"But he's got a son named Zarko who served in the Red Army and lost a hand at the Battle of Moscow."

"Well who was his father?" Waugh persisted. This weird conversation was interrupted by the sound of bagpipes—Brigadier Maclean liked to have his meals to the accompaniment of pipes.

Later that evening I told Stojan about my encounter with Waugh. "It was just like being in one of his novels."

A few days later, Stojan, to my surprise, mentioned my conversation with Waugh to Tito. I watched him sit back as he shook with laughter. After he had removed his glasses and wiped his eyes, Tito said, "If only Captain Waugh was not an English gentleman. I'd prove to him unmistakably that I am a man."

About a week later, Tito came down for a swim at Maclean's villa. He wore a very tight bathing suit which made him appear unmistakably masculine. As Brigadier Maclean introduced Tito to his lined up officers, he came to Waugh. Tito scrutinzed him, then turned to Fitzroy Maclean, and said, "Could you ask Captain Waugh what makes him think I'm a woman?"

Tito bathing, Island of Vis, Yugoslavia, 1944

Destroyed village, Slovenia, 1944

Welcome to Titoland

"For Christ's sake, Sir, be careful or you'll castrate yourself if you have to jump," the cockney sergeant warned cheerfully as he harnessed a parachute on me. I had just been stripped of my identity to become part of "Picadilly Club", en route to join "Flotsam", making me marvel at who in the middle of this war could think up such code names. For six weeks I had been on alert in Italy, waiting to be dropped into Serbia to photograph the Liberation of Belgrade. Twice a day—at noon and at six—I phoned my British contact to find out if I was "on". For six weeks, the same reply: "Call again".

During those weeks I had slept on the sixth floor of the Oriente Palace Hotel in Bari, where I had a cot and a bidet. My contact's office was on Via Mello, where both British and American intelligence services were located. Everything about that street was secret and illegal. Any unauthorized person caught lurking around was hauled in for questioning.

Although I was not a member of the OSS, I had drinking facilities at their bar. I had been granted this courtesy as I was accredited to the Yugoslav Partisans, and the OSS was in the business of dropping men and material to all such resistance groups in Eastern Europe. Owing to the kind of guerrilla warfare the partisans fought, the territory liberated by them shifted continually, making drops in specific areas erratic.

I was also eligible to draw supplies from the British since Yugoslavia was in their theater of operations. Had I taken all the supplies offered me by the OSS, I could have opened a small PX. I turned down a full medical kit, and only kept a supply of morphine in case I was wounded. I did put in a requisition for a gross of condoms, amidst much hilarity due to the notorious chastity of the Partisan women. "Pretty ambitious, aren't you, eh?" Actually, I wanted them to slip my exposed films in, because once knotted they were waterproof.

I spent my evenings at the OSS bar, which was frequented by men of a wide variety of nationalities and backgrounds from archeologists to professional killers. You never asked personal questions or inquired about foreign accents. The closest I ever came to being confided in was by a lusty Hungarian. "In my branch," he explained, "we deal in fuck or shit. I'm in shit."

He was referring to the nebulous world of propaganda, deceit and dirty tricks performed by Allied agents in the German-occupied territories, known as "black" activities. By two in the morning the explosives specialists were usually back to their favorite topic: how many Bangalor torpedoes would it take to bring down the Eiffel Tower? To these men, there was an elegance to blasting and a chic in the minimum use of explosives.

Frequently fights broke out between the Americans assigned to the Partisans and those with Mihailovic's Serbians. I not only kept out of those free-for-alls, but went to see William Joyce in charge of these operations. "I've only one question. Is Mihailovic collaborating with the Germans?" I asked.

"And how," Joyce replied.

"That's all, thank you."

One evening it had been unusually quiet—no fights had broken out. I was sitting alone when a swashbuckling blond captain strode up to me. His name I was to learn was James Goodwin. He had just come out of Slovenia, where he was part of Fitzroy Maclean's Allied military mission. Facing me, hands on hips, Goodwin said, "If it's war you're interested in, instead of hanging around the bar, I will gladly see to it that you get a taste of it." He was about to be parachuted back to Yugoslavia carrying instructions for a combined Allied-Partisan operation. "If you've got the guts," he added before stalking off, "I'll take you to Germany."

As Goodwin recalls it, he heard a knock on his door the next morning and found me standing there. He assumed I'd come to pick a fight over his aggressiveness the previous evening. "When do we go into Germany?" I asked. Four days later I was on my way to "Flotsam." That morning I had asked a serious young bank clerk, newly drafted into the OSS, to exchange some of my dollars for gold napoleons, the only currency acceptable to Eastern European peasants in case you needed their help.

"Don't you realize this is a federal offense in the States?" the clerk lectured me, adding bitterly, "But here, the more illegal things are the better." He waved a bundle of German marks at me and shook his head. "See what I mean? Enemy currency!" I wondered how he would find his bank when he got home or, more to the point, how his bank would find him.

C-47s were lined up on the airfield. Ours was the first to take off. The doors had been removed as we would be dropping leaflets. Banking over

Bari Harbor as dusk set in, we headed out over the Adriatic, leaving the Italian coast behind—one of many lonely planes flying towards Eastern Europe to drop men, leaflets, supplies, and pick up the wounded, maintaining a link with widespread islands of resistance.

The other passengers—two Yugoslav Partisans and a British sergeant who sat facing me on crates of ammunition—slowly faded from sight as night fell. A full moon rose on our left and cast reflections on the sea below. Inside it was so dark I saw nothing except the lines of white static fluttering near the open doorway and sparks flying past from the port engine. Chewing a piece of gum, I thought about the long-drawn-out nights at the OSS bar, arguing about fear.

Unlike Captain James Goodwin—who had gone in two days ahead of me—I did not intend to not jump. My status was the same as the crates I was sitting on: a consignment to be delivered, if possible. For the next few hours I had no control over my life, which depended on such extraneous factors as not meeting a German fighter plane and crumpling before his guns like a cat under the wheels of a truck. Of one thing I was certain, in three hours I would be in Slovenia or I'd be dead. I caught myself glancing repeatedly at the phosphorescent dial on my watch. Time went by very slowly. The plane lumbered along, its engines ticking off the seconds. From time to time, I peered out to see whether the shiny surface of the Adriatic had given way to the looming mass of central Europe. With growing excitement, the two Partisans did the same.

Anxious to keep my mind occupied, I asked myself what had prompted me to join Picadilly Club. My stock reply had been: "I'm convinced that Tito's successful uprising in the middle of occupied Europe is an important event of the war, and I want to photograph it." However true, it sounded somewhat pompous when perched on a C-47. There was more to it than that, of course. For a young Brit like myself, educated in Europe, there were all kinds of precedents to kindle a sense of adventure. There had been the romance of Lawrence's revolt in the desert. Then there had been Malraux's and Hemingway's books on the Spanish Civil War, which had seared the minds of my generation. Then there was the fact that I am a loner. Being the only Allied photographer on his way to Greater Germany appealed to me. I sat there in the dark, thinking over the events of my life so far. I hadn't been so introspective since my days on the munitions ship.

One of the Partisans nudged me and interrupted my train of thought. I looked out and saw land below, lost in total darkness and sinister. "Dalmatia", he whispered, patting me on the back. The co-pilot lurched toward us and started tossing the bundles of propaganda leaflets out of the plane. Some simply tumbled. Others, their wrappers torn, went out screaming into the night, leaving a shower of paper in the sky. A few blew back into the plane, flinging themselves wildly at the co-pilot before they fell limp. *"Serai tu l'ultima victima?"*—"Will you be the last victim?" the leaflets read.

Clouds drifted by, white against the dark monotony of the land. Finally, in the blacked-out continent below, a light blinked, feeble but reassuring, signaling us to land. Down we spiraled, the moonlight sweeping us like a lighthouse beam while we sank slowly into a valley. The flare path came into sight and grew more distinct as we circled the field. A white dirt road loomed up larger and larger.

I braced myself for a bump that never came. The C-47 taxied towards voices. I listened intently for an American accent—my only connection in this wilderness surrounded by Germans. Jumping out of the plane I landed on Slovene soil, within walking distance of Hitler's Greater Germany. The flares dimly lit a field filled with short stocky men in a variety of uniforms and squat garrison caps with red stars. Shouting hoarsely, they came running toward the plane. In their midst was a lanky American officer in jump boots that I recognised as Jim Goodwin. "Welcome to Titoland!" he called out.

The Partisans clambered aboard the plane and started unloading the ammunition with obvious satisfaction. "Must be off in ten minutes to get back before daylight," the pilot said. "We've got plenty of wounded," Jim warned him. "How many can you take?"

The wounded were spread out on the field near the oxcarts which brought them. Practically naked and shivering from cold and fever, they had been stripped of their uniforms so others could wear them. The first to be evacuated were mostly cases of gas gangrene. Grim-looking nurses stood around, Sten guns slung over their shoulders. The commotion of our arrival caused one wounded man to prop himself up and call out hopefully, *"On parle français?"*

"Naturellement", I said, going over to a Frenchman who had lost one eye. *"Ça fait plaisir!"* he exclaimed. *"Une cigarette?"* he begged. "It's been so

Wounded Partisans, Slovenia, 1944

long since I last smoked. But you'll have to light it," he added, waving his right arm which ended at the elbow. He had been a forced laborer who wound up working in Klagenfurt. "The first Partisan I ever saw," he recalled, "was skiing through the forests early one morning. 'A Partisan patrol in German territory. They have some balls.' I thought."

He had not joined there and then because the Partisan did not speak French. "When I fight I want someone around I can talk to," the Frenchman explained. *"C'est naturel."*

Finally he met one who spoke some French. But again he did not join up right away. "I had saved up marks, and as their goddam money won't be worth a thing after the war, I decided to spend mine right away. I got myself put on the sick list and in two weeks spent everything on good food. I realized it wasn't going to be chicken in the pot every Sunday with the Partisans. Wearing two pairs of pants, I met my Partisan pal at the clump of trees where we'd agreed to rendezvous. Unfortunately he got killed a few weeks later. After that I fought in silence until a German grenade got me." As they lifted him into the plane he waved his good arm and called out, *"Salut vieux!"*

The overflow of wounded was hoisted back into carts while the engines revved up. The C-47 rose in the moonlit sky. The flares were put out and the carts, with nurses at their sides, slowly faded into the night to wait for another plane to come in. "Look, we're prosperous," Jim said. "Got a jeep, six cans of beer and a bottle of Scotch. Let's drive to the village."

Half a mile from the airstrip, our village stretched between low rolling hills reminiscent of Switzerland. We were some 12 miles from the Germans in one direction and 15 in the other. Nothing about this peaceful setting suggested war. Peasants worked in the fields and horse-drawn carts rattled along dusty roads while the smell of freshly cut hay filled the air. But when night fell Yugoslavia belonged to the Partisans. Through the trees, over the hills, across the gullies they came, bringing silent terror to the enemy. When day broke they were gone, leaving dead Germans and miles of uprooted railroad track as proof they really existed. Once again the countryside became deceptively peaceful.

I was put up at a farmhouse. On the whitewashed wall hung a print of the Virgin Mary with pictures of Stalin and Roosevelt tucked in the frame. I was to share it with an elderly RAF squadron leader who was in charge of the gooseneck lamps used by the British when their planes came in. He was especially proud of these lamps, which he had designed, but his pride was to get him into trouble later on. When the squadron leader mentioned to Major Nikolai Patrahalcev that his goosenecks were far more efficient than the bonfires the Russians lit to guide their planes in, Colonel Patrahalcev was so insulted he demanded the squadron leader's dimissal. "They gave me my bowler hat," he told me when I met him again some months later.

He was a pleasant, if eccentric, companion during the time I stayed at the farmhouse. He informed me that we were in a village which had been sympathetic to the pro-German White Guard. "Why only a week ago a couple in a horse-drawn cart drove up with a corpse. Not too unusual, I was told, in this part of the world. The chappie had died in a neighboring village and was brought back to be buried in the cemetery here. The sticky thing was that the Partisans found a letter in his pocket. It was addressed to our landlady, and was written by her son, who was with the fascist White Guards. He asked her how much we paid the peasants for working on our airstrip. Our landlady, her daughter, and all her grandchildren were rounded up. Before being led away, she asked if I could help. Well, as it turned out, she was innocent and they were all back the next day. But not the couple with the corpse. They were shot. Our landlady was ever so grateful. Can't tell you how the cooking has improved. I don't know if you noticed, but she's added caraway seeds to the coleslaw."

The estimated time of arrival that night was 1am. Three planes were expected. Along with the wounded, a group of 50 American airmen shot down over Yugoslavia and rescued by the Partisans were to be evacuated. As we made our way to the airstrip, a young pilot told me about his experiences. His B-24 was so badly shot up, he ordered the nine members of his crew to bail out over liberated territory. He jumped last and lost contact with the others. Hoping to make the Allied lines in northern Italy, he started to walk and came to the German-occupied naval base of Pola. Boldly, he entered the city wearing light summer pants and a gray sweater. In an empty street he saw a German officer headed his way. As the German came toward him, he stared at the American GI boots. Their eyes met momentarily before the German walked on without a word. He also went unchallenged by the sentry guarding the road out of town. On three occasions he stopped at farmhouses, identificd himself as an American, and was given food and drink. At the fourth farmhouse, an Italian woman listened to him in silence before closing the door. He was about 200 yards away when a man came running after him shouting, *"Amerikanec! Amerikanec!"* The captain dashed into the underbrush with the man right behind him. He turned out to be the Italian woman's husband—and a Partisan. He fed the captain and led him to other Partisans who in turn sent him down the line until he reached our village and found the other nine members of his crew. They all got out that night.

We stayed on in the village waiting for the explosives needed for the operation to be flown in, before Jim reported to the Slovene headquarters with the orders from the Mediterranean command. A few nights after my arrival, two planes came in. From one, eight officers in American uniform alighted—a captain, a lieutenant, and six second lieutenants. Only the captain and the first lieutenant spoke English. The six second lieutenants only spoke German. They were Austrian communists who OSS was sending into Austria to establish communications. "Usual *snafu*," the captain complained on hearing that they had landed on the banks of the Sava instead of the Drava. "Can you beat it?" he added bitterly. "Now we'll have to walk across this country, lousy with Krauts, carrying all our gear. Some picnic!"

Unmoved by this outburst, the second lieutenants unloaded their equipment under the bug-eyed gaze of Partisans who could not understand why the six *"Amerikanecs"* spoke German. "Jesus!" the captain exploded anew when he heard how many miles lay between us and the Fourth Zone. "And I've got to get these guys into Austria real fast so we can set up communications. Do you realize," he said with total disregard for security, "we aren't receiving any information from there right now?"

"Wunderbar, dieser Krieg", one of the second-lieutenants chuckled, eyeing the heap of equipment being hauled into carts.

"I'm certainly glad someone finds this war wonderful," I remarked.

"But don't you see," the second lieutenant explained, "we have everything. Ask Karl what the Spanish Civil War was like."

"In Republican Spain, we had nothing," Karl said. "It wasn't anything like this," he added, surveying the pile of supplies affectionately. To make his point, he produced a handful of gold napoleons. "See?" Karl was right. They had everything: cartons of cigarettes, tubes of toothpaste, shoelaces, and rolls of toilet paper to spare.

The next morning, waiting for the Partisans to drive them across the country, the Austrians sat around stripping down their Marlin sub-machine guns. There was craftsmanship in the soberness of their movements and the way they handled their weapons. An old farmer walked past leading a cow. Karl looked up. A grin cut across his sharp features. "Beefsteak!" he shouted as the others took interest. They had not been impressed by the food and decided to do something about it. Stopping the old farmer, Karl tossed a gold napoleon in the dust at his feet and pointed to the cow. The old man let out a scream, so Karl tossed a second napoleon. The farmer screamed again, but the anguish had gone out of his voice. I cannot recall how many times he screamed, but finally Karl held the cow on the lead and took her behind a barn. There was another scream. We all had meat for lunch.

But even Karl's gold napoleons, backed up by cartons of Chesterfields, did not help him locate any liquor. There was none. The day before, Jim and I visited the local commander in a nearby village. He had promised us a drink. It was tepid when we drank it. I felt lightheaded as we walked along the dirt road toward our jeep. Coming to a large farmhouse where several Partisans stood around idly, guns slung around their necks, I noticed a young man eagerly watching for us. He wore baggy clothes with large patches and his socks peered out from battered felt slippers. Stopping us, he addressed Jim in a chanting tone. "I'm sorry," Jim told him, "but you're in bad trouble. You're going to be shot."

"Why, this is dreadful," the young man exclaimed, rubbing his hands together nervously as he shuffled at Jim's side. "Dreadful! You must notify the British military authorities in Italy immediately."

"I'm sorry," Jim repeated. "These are their orders."

The young man stopped, stunned. "We were betrayed, my mother was killed. I was very lucky to escape, and now you tell me I'm going to be shot!" He wrung his hands.

Jim walked on in his easy lope and I watched the young man staring at this back, still rubbing his hands and repeating, "This is dreadful!" Shocked by what I had heard, and the way it had been said, I demanded, "D'you really mean it?"

"Yeah," Jim replied. "It's a hell of a story. He's an Italian seminarist who worked for British intelligence behind the lines in Friuli. I wish he wasn't a priest. Something went wrong, but it's not clear what it was. It never is when you're operating behind the lines. Anyway, information stopped coming out, the contact was lost and several people got killed. Then this guy shows up here. Bari holds him responsible, so…I wish they would have him transferred to Bari and court-martialed there instead of ordering me to have him killed here like a cow behind the barn."

We found Giga, the Partisan liaison officer, standing by the Jeep.

"I got orders," Jim told him. "The priest must be shot."

"Yes, Captain Goodwin," Giga agreed, his face a blank.

"I know it's none of our business. But frankly, I don't like it, Giga. What's the Vatican going to say when it finds out? Because you can be certain the Pope is going to hear about this after the war. Who knows? He may even blame the Partisans, especially if they find him buried here."

Giga said nothing.

"You can be sure the Catholic church is going to investigate, Giga, and when they find out he was shot by Partisans, it's not going to sound very convincing to say it was on orders from the British. It would be much better if he was flown out to Italy under guard." Jim paused. "Giga, do you think the Partisans can spare two men to escort him out on the next plane?" he asked.

"Certainly, Captain Goodwin," Giga said.

"Well, let's do that."

Jim turned to me. "I feel much better," adding with a grin, "I'd be very surprised if they shot him in Bari."

The Battle of Litija Bridge

The Slovene headquarters were hidden in the forest, invisible from the air. The British and Russian missions stood side by side along an uphill path. These wooden huts looked like diners from the outside, and Pullman cars from within. At the British mission, where Jim and I slept, there were four bunks, two uppers and two lowers, with enough space for a long table where messages were decoded. We ate our meals in the open.

One of the other two occupants of our hut was a second lieutenant in the commandos. He had come out of the siege of Tobruk with his jaws clenched together from bomb blast. His front teeth had to be knocked out to unlock them. He was always cheerful. The decoding corporal, named Raffles, had a bristling shock of curly red hair and a jovial appearance. He was also unexpectedly tough beneath his grin. To his considerable disgust, he spent his life between his bunk and the decoding table, a matter of three feet. "I've had this bloody office life," he frequently complained with a superb disregard for the forest which peered in through the window and the Germans who prowled around.

Two interlocked roses with a Union Jack in between were tattooed on his right arm, the result of a drunken spree in Portsmouth during leave. Sobered up, he liked his tattoos, but fretted whether his display of taste was due to circumstances or good breeding. "You see, Cock," he explained, "I worried if I'd behaved like a gentleman simply because there were no sporting tattoos to tempt me." On his next leave, he had returned to Portsmouth to find out. "Lord lumme, I was a gentleman all right. I could have had a fox hunt around my body, ending you know where. It was a lark."

The Russian mission, just down the path, was under the command of Nikolai Patrahalcev, the Red Army officer who had objected to my squadron-leader. He was a stocky man of middle age who displayed a set of steel teeth when he laughed. He introduced himself as "Colonel Nikolai Patrahalcev from Kiev". A certain amount of backwoods diplomacy was called for in dealing with him. Whenever the British mission attended an official function within driving distance, Jim always made sure the colonel was notified that a seat was available in the British mission's jeep, to which—just as invariably—Colonel Patrahalcev would return the compliment by offering the British Army the pillion seat on the Red Army's motorcycle.

Captain Petrov, the second-in-command, also had steel teeth, and was a boor, riddled with complexes (though he was totally unaware such things existed). On Jim's return, Colonel Patrahalcev and Captain Petrov, loaded with bottles of vodka, visited the British mission to celebrate the event. In exchange for this courtesy, Jim offered a can of beer to each. Patrahalcev shook the can and listened to it gurgle with delight. "Colonel Patrahalcev from Kiev has seen many things," he announced, "but never beer in boxes." Captain Petrov said nothing.

Seated around the decoding table, we tossed down the vodka Captain Petrov doled out. Having little to say, we drank a lot and after a while, Jim and I said we had just about had vodka. Patrahalcev displayed his steel teeth, and so did Captain Petrov, but his smile was not exactly cordial, "So the American Army is scared," he said.

"Not at all. Not at all," Jim replied. "The American Army was just about to offer you some whisky." He got up muttering something which sounded to me like wasting good liquor on a son-of-a-bitch. Captain Petrov gulped down the first slug, remarking that whisky was very good although a bit light. By the third tumbler, Captain Petrov announced he was through with whisky. "Don't tell me the Red Army's scared," Jim said.

At this, Colonel Patrahalcev and Captain Petrov reached for their glasses. Soon afterwards, Petrov was sound asleep, his head resting on the decoding table. While I watched Patrahalcev rattle his can of beer happily. He was swimming before my eyes like a reflection in water.

The main headquarters office was located in a larger hut at the end of a narrow lane. From there two men, both under 5ft 4in, exerted a political and military influence over liberated Slovenia. They were Commissar Boris Kraigher and General Stane (who was born Franc Rozman, a veteran of the International Brigade in Spain). Unlike Kraigher, Stane was known to laugh heartily. Kraigher never let himself go beyond a pinched smile.

To be honest, there was little ground for levity in Yugoslavia then. The Germans were waging a merciless war against the Partisans, and although the Partisan command was entirely communist and conducted indoctrination courses for the recruits, over 80 per cent of the rank and file were non-Marxist. They were Yugoslavs who took up arms to defend their land from the Germans and their collaborators. This was the basis of Tito's success. He had stirred their pride in being Yugoslavs, not Serbs or Croats or Slovenes or Montenegrins or Bosnians or Herzegovinians or Macedonians—and awakened a patriotic yearning for a Yugoslav nation many had been dreaming of for the past twelve centuries. The nation responded heroically. Men, women and children joined the Partisans. Women, in particular, were swept up by this patriotism. For the first time they had rights.

One of the nightly operations of the Partisans in Slovenia was hacking at the German railroad lines. It was a task without end. The Germans rebuilt as fast as the Partisans destroyed. This was why the Allied Command chose Litija Bridge as the target for the Partisans as part of an all-out attack against the railroads leading to northern Italy. The destruction of the bridge at Litija, which spanned the wide Sava River, would put out of action the strategic Zagreb-Ljubljana-Trieste railroad line thus paralyzing German supply lines to Italy during the weeks it took to repair the bridge. The operation was coded "Rat Week." We were the rats.

This was such an important target that three brigades were to be committed on our side of the river while the same number would synchronize their attack from the opposite bank. For the first time Partisans would have air support—six fighters from the Mediterranean Command would lead off the attack to soften up the strong German positions. Jim had managed to convince the Allied High Command of this, arguing that since we would be in Greater Germany, we required additional support for the operation. At first Jim was told we were out of fighter range, but eventually he proved persuasive enough to get six Mustangs.

Jim and I went on the operation. When we reached Zuzemberk, we crossed the German-controlled road which led to Ljubljana. Jim and I climbed out of the jeep and kissed it good-bye. From now on we would travel on foot. We hiked to Poljane, a village in White Guard territory, and joined the Fourth Partisan Brigade which had marched 75 kilometers to participate in the operation. We rested at Poljane for two days as our patrols combed the hills. Only once was there any excitement: a peasant woman who had two brothers in the White Guard was caught smuggling out information about us. She was shot trying to escape.

As meat had been plentiful, everybody suspected something big was up, although they didn't know what. In anticipation the Partisans spent all their free time sleeping, sprawled about the orchards under the autumn sun. They cleaned their weapons and our 50-mm Howitzer. They packed the explosives needed to blast the bridge, deloused themselves, washed, got shaved sitting on tree stumps while barbers wiped the lather off their cut-throat razors on to the leaves.

It was on one such occasion that I became aware of the truly egalitarian nature of the Partisan movement. Along with a group of fighters, I was scrubbing my face on the banks of a stream when I noticed an amazon in her late teens stride up and calmly strip to the waist. Through widening soapy eyes I saw her washing her powerful breasts in front of a hundred-odd men. And though she was lovely, nobody made a move or let out a whistle. There was something defiant in her matter-of-factness.

We got our orders at dusk. The carts were loaded with explosives and soon the Partisans could be seen swarming down from the hills. The commander stood at the crossroads of Poljane and Zuzemberk. At his side two fighters stood; one held the Slovene flag, the other played *"Lepa Nasa Domovina"* ("Our Wonderful Land") on an accordion.

There was something about these marching men that I could not figure out. It wasn't so much the fact that everybody was on foot carrying his own weapon in a time of mechanized warfare. Nor was it the extraordinary variety of people: boys who should have been in school, old men who ought to have remained at home, a mechanic from Trieste, a cobbler from Ljubljana, women with big red hands, city people toughened by fresh air, sturdy wood-cutters, a hollow-chested student, a coal miner with a pronounced stoop, a father whose son had been shot by the White Guards. The patchwork of uniforms —some had been donated by the Allies, some captured from foes and some left over from civilian life —produced an odd color scheme: the khaki of British battle-dress, the Wehrmacht's dark green, the Alpini light green, the tight-fitting black breeches of the Gestapo, maroon plus-fours, and tailored blankets. The weapons were long-barreled French Lebel rifles dating back to 1907, lobster-shaped Schmeisers, Germany's latest sub-machine gun, the Italian service rifle, Luger pistols, Berettas, and the occasional .45—gifts of rescued American airmen; they also had English Mills grenades, German "potato mashers",

Italian "red devils", and a species of home-made grenade which looked like a shiny apple. While all this gave the Partisans a strange, revolutionary appearance, there was something else which was different about the long line of marching men—something I could not place, and it nagged at me.

"We're going to be as green as a couple of lilies fresh from the garden," Jim observed as we swung down towards the Dolenjska Valley. "The Partisans have been at it for three years, and they believe their war of liberation will be remembered for a thousand." He'd given me the image. "That's it!" I thought. "An epic!"

We walked side by side talking mostly about the pleasures of life. Conversation kills time. Night crept up and the hills took odd shapes. The stars came out but we could still see ahead the dusty white road we hoped to stay on, but weren't sure we would. Our exact route was known only to the man leading the column and the man bringing up the rear,—a very effective security measure.

We marched until we were drained of conversation, sweating profusely in spite of the chilly air. With nightfall we formed a single column along which call words were passed from one to the other in order to keep 800 men in contact marching in the dark. Suddenly one of the signals was passed on to us: *"Celo stoj."* ("Vanguard stop.") We passed it down the line.

Jim sat on the steps of a wooden shack by the side of the road, saying, "I think we've got time for a smoke." Around us figures lit butts that were passed along, puffed with relish and passed on again. Others rolled green tobacco in newspaper. The orders came through: *"Kolona!"* ("Single file!") *"Tisina!"* ("Silence!") *"Naprej!"* ("Advance!") One by one we got up and filed past the battered Italian frontier post.

A hundred yards ahead, behind wide-open gates as massive as those leading into concentration camps, lay Hitler's Greater Germany. We marched on the side of the road in a long, well-spaced single file. On reaching the first village occupied by the Germans we left the road to bypass the garrison and took a winding lane through orchards. We groped for apples, but too many men had already passed ahead of us. The stars shone brightly but we soon lost them when we entered the forest, dark as a tunnel. Suddenly feeling alone and unable to hear the footsteps of Peter, our interpreter, behind me or Jim's ahead, I started to run and fell over him. Jim held on to the raincoat of the Partisan in front, I grasped the strap of his carbine, while Peter grabbed my musette bag. I could feel the strap of Jim's carbine tugging in my hand as if urging me to walk faster, and again I quickened my step. I could not see where we were marching. My feet trod soft, uneven earth. I did not know how wide the path was and sometimes my face brushed past branches. I knew we were going downhill when the carbine would nearly be yanked out of my hands and I would break into a trot to keep up. When we went uphill I usually stumbled over Jim, whose pace had slowed up. I could feel if we were going right or left by following the direction the carbine would jerk. Ceaselessly the mouth-to-mouth query traveled up and down the line: *"Ali je vezaI?"* ("Is there contact?"), with the usual reply, *"Je veza."* ("Contact.") And so 800 of us, hanging on to one another, unable to see where we were running so fast, plunged forward. This was called *pokret*—literally, "movement"—a horrifying word conjuring up hours, days, months and years of forced marches before and after battles as brigades struck out 50, 100 or more kilometers across the country to strike the enemy when least expected and then vanish, reappearing again 50, 100 or more kilometers away. Phantasmal to the enemy, it was also a hallucinatory experience for the Partisans. From 800 mouths, the anxious question and reassuring reply swept along the column: "Is there contact?" "Yes, contact."

In the midst of this furious pace, a shout was heard in the distance, followed by a volley of curses, the hysterical whinnying of horses mingled with the sound of crashing wood and the abrupt command: *"Stoj!"* ("Stop!") Was it a cart carrying our explosives that had overturned or was it our Howitzer that had tumbled down the ravine, or was it one of the oxen we would eat before the battle that had lost its footing? Passing on the command to halt, we flopped down in the moist underbrush. Sweat streamed down our faces as we tried to catch our breath. From this point on nobody talked whenever we stopped. Jim and I chewed on the black bread we had brought with us. Some even tried to snatch some sleep. Men and animals were growing tired. The carts were overturning more frequently, forcing us to march faster in order to clear the last German garrison before dawn.

It caught us marching up a hill which overlooked a fog-filled valley where the early morning sun cast a pale-pink border around the green hills, turning a beautiful landscape into a bad painting. We had cleared the last German garrison. It had taken us close to 14 hours to reach the village from which we would launch the attack. Below us the forest hid the Sava River from our sight. There, in a few hours, we were going to fight. The headquarters was set up in a farmhouse. I was too tired to marvel that almost a thousand men could be within two miles of the enemy without their being aware of us. Jim and I crawled into a hayloft. As he was saying, "Look, the hen just laid an egg…" I fell asleep.

Minutes later, it seemed, we were awakened and joined the headquarters' staff to hack at boiled meat with our spoons. The Partisan commanders, their mouths full, speculated on when the air attack would come off. From the walls color prints of Christ and the Virgin Mary gazed peacefully down at us.

Jim and I moved into the forest along with the detachment when it took up position. Crouching behind trees with their weapons on their laps, the Partisans dozed, smoked or just waited, looking like men about to play some terrible child's game. We joined Captain Jesen, the commander of the Fourth Brigade, who was wearing a brightly checked shirt. He was sitting with the divisional commander and his commissar nonchalantly munching overripe pears. They argued and laughed, waiting for the air attack Jim and I knew was due anytime after four.

"How far are we from the bridge?" Jim asked Jesen.

"One kilometer," Jesen said, describing a line in the air with a half-eaten pear. "But the bomb line is one mile," Jim had the interpreter tell him. "One kilometer…one mile," Jesen laughed, shrugging his shoulders with such indifference that Jim stared at me with raised eyebrows and shrugged, too.

Finally, at 4:30pm, we heard the faint sound of planes. Jesen leaped up, grabbing his Schmeiser, and ran to the clearing. Partisans, leaving their positions, also came running up to look, but Jesen, shouting, ordered them back. Six fighters came over very high. Everybody gaped at the sky. I could feel excitement rising. The enemy guns were still silent, still unaware of who was overhead and what was about to happen. Hardly had the six Mustangs vanished from sight when the first was back, diving, as the anti-aircraft guns opened up. From its wings I saw two black grapes detach themselves and hurtle down. The crunch of the explosion mingled with the ack-ack fire as the second plane came in. Under the pines the Partisans were laughing and slapping each other on the back, shouting while the next four fighters unloaded their bombs and were gone. Now, it was up to us. Gunfire broke out everywhere. Jim was humming: "The woods are alive/ With the yodeling jive…" Jesen eyed his men, tossed his Schmeiser in the air, grabbed it, and bellowed, *"Juris, hura!"* ("Hurrah, attack!") Then he tore through the trees followed by all of us.

Although the air attack with its small bombs had been mainly aimed at demoralizing the Germans, the six planes had produced such a drunken enthusiasm nobody bothered about what lay ahead. Now the grim job of destroying the bridge belonged to the Partisans. Coming to a clearing, we got our first look at the bridge. Jesen fired a clip as I took a picture. A farm-house on the opposite bank of the river was wrapped in yellow flames. We swept on. This was to be the only look I got of the bridge, stretching spider-like across the Sava River.

Galloping through the trees, I saw the road leading to the bridge. The Partisans were slowly moving up as the first wounded were being carried back. Panting, we reached the road just as German mortar shells started coming in. After taking a picture I flung myself down at Jim's side. "You're earning your salt today," he said, handing me a cigarette. With the excep-tion of the communists—who prided themselves on never taking cover— the rest of us hugged the sides of the road. An old man next to me was reloading an equally ancient rifle. I noticed he was oozing sweat. So was I. Looking around at the trees in front, the steep embankment behind and the road on either side, I felt that anything could happen. I must have taken three puffs on my cigarette when I was rocked back. Jim looked as surprised as I. A youth next to him looked at us. Something had happened, but nobody knew what. The youth's eyes widened as he became covered with blood. "I was sure somebody got hit," Jim said.

Fifteen meters up the road the Partisans had set up a Russian anti-tank gun and were firing into the castle, hidden from our view. The brigade commander was urging his men on. A young kid got up and slowly made for an open space. He was pale and tense. Jim and I moved up the road. As I looked up I could see the top window of the fortified castle. Nobody was peering out. "Let's take the castle before they get reorganized!" Jim shou-ted, and with that he dashed toward the field that led to it. Mortars were covering the road and Jim vanished in a puff of black smoke. He was dazed. "If St Peter had said 'Congratulations, you've made it,' I wouldn't have been a bit surprised," he called out as he got to his feet.

Litija Bridge, Slovenia, 1944

Mortar fire made me take cover. A Partisan photographer was also lying on the road taking pictures of me photographing a German sign tacked on a tree trunk: *"Eintritt verboten!"* ("No admittance.") A Partisan voice kept repeating, *"Rusi, Amerikanci, Anglezi, so nasi zavezniki!"* ("The Russians, the Americans, the English are our allies!") The beautiful amazon I had seen washing at Poljane stalked up the road carrying a sub-machine gun. Getting her first look at the castle, she stopped and, leaning back with an air of indifference, fired her gun from the hip. A crouching figure, trying to pull her down, grabbed one of her pant legs. But she kicked herself free and strode up to a Russian anti-tank gun set up 20 yards or more ahead of me. Mortars smeared the road. I scrambled up an embankment where Jesen stood grinning. A young commissar was singing, "We got a tank! We got a tank!" as he hopped around nursing his bleeding hand.

I stood there a couple of minutes trying to catch my breath. Then a shout came up: "The *Amerikanec* is wounded!" I ran towards the castle, passing half a dozen Germans being led off, and found Jim still holding his carbine, supported by a Partisan. He was very pale and the left leg of his pants was soaked with blood. I threw my arms around him, shouting in the midst of the din, "You're okay, Jim, you're okay."

"Don't let them cut my leg off, John," he said. "Don't let them amputate." We helped him towards the embankment and seated him there. A young nurse in a large *Feldgendarmerie* overcoat that almost dragged on the ground slit open the leg of his pants and started to bandage the wounds. "I got it after we got into the castle and were fighting room to room," Jim explained wearily. "Firing was going on all over the place and someone tossed a grenade."

I lit a cigarette and passed it to him. It was only then I noticed the middle-aged German soldier seated next to Jim. He had been wounded by the same grenade. Blood streamed down his face but he was laughing, happy to be alive. When the Partisans marched the prisoners off they had overlooked him. He had stuck close to Jim, believing that was the safest place to be. Without thinking, I handed him a cigarette also. *"Danke schön, Kamerad,"* he said. Someone gave Jim an apple. "The one good thing about this," he said with a smile, "is that I won't have to make that long march back on foot."

Jim's leg bandaged, I slipped one arm around his waist and we started up a trench, followed by the German. Slowly we made our way as shells pounded the embankment. Peter, our Partisan interpreter, appeared and hurried back to find a stretcher. "You're such a heavy man, Jim," I sighed. An oxcart jogged down toward us. "That's just what we need."

"No," Jim said. "There are some who can't walk."

Peter arrived with a stretcher and as we laid Jim on it I noticed that his face was drawn. He looked considerably older. "Much pain?" I asked. "Not much."

It seemed to take us hours to reach the village. When we got there it was night. A Partisan produced a chair and a bottle of *rakija*. After taking a long swig, Jim passed me the bottle. We started off for the first-aid station set up near the headquarters, the German still following. "Say, that was a pretty good charge we made," Jim remarked as we passed some Partisans going toward the bridge with their carts of sickly-sweet-smelling explosives, "It was lucky I was wounded and not you," he said thoughtfully. "You couldn't have gone on taking pictures."

I laughed. It seemed a silly thing to say. At this moment he was the one person in the world I felt closest to.

We found the first-aid station in a small farmhouse at the end of a dark lane and carried Jim in. There were two low-ceilinged rooms. A Partisan followed the doctor around with a kerosene lamp. The floors were covered with hay and crowded with wounded men. The doctor, middle-aged and civilized, apologized that there was no bed for the American officer. "He doesn't expect one," I said in French, a language we had in common. As an aide started to remove Jim's bandage the doctor was called into the other room. He excused himself. Following him, I noticed the German sitting between two Partisans. He smiled at me and said, *"Kamerad"*. Here was this man who a few hours before had crouched in the old castle waiting to kill us, just as we were ready to kill him. And yet, in this hell hole of a hospital, he—the very symbol of the misery his countrymen inflicted upon us—had called me *kamerad* and I had offered him a cigarette a few minutes after my own comrade had been wounded. Was it that he too, wounded by the same grenade, wanted to dissolve the bloody barrier which separated us? Those who had never seen any fighting would probably have been shocked, even found it immoral, that I had given him a smoke. But in its terrible way, war produces a strange kind of dignity in men.

In a corner of the farmhouse, the youth who had been wounded earlier lay unconscious. His nose was pinched and he looked so pale I wondered if he was dead. The doctor glanced at him and shrugged. "What can I do? I have nothing." He removed his glasses and wiped them carefully. I looked around at the other unconscious figures groaning in the flickering light of the kerosene lamp. "Horrible, isn't it?" he said with quiet fury. "We have only a small supply of morphine to ease the pain, and we are lucky to have that. Amputations are performed without anaesthestic, our bandages are made from old shirts, and when a man dies we remove them because we need them for others." After this outburst he blushed. "Could you give me a cigarette, please?" He examined Jim's leg and again looked embarrassed when handed the first-aid packs issued by the American Army.

"We're out of touch here," he told Jim. "I don't know how to use this type of medication or what to do if anything goes wrong. Let me treat you the way I know." And he skilfully proceeded to clean the 23 wounds.

At headquarters I learned that the Partisans were still fighting their way to the bridge, which they hoped to blow up during the night. The brigades would then withdraw in the morning. As it was impossible to get the wounded back to liberated territory before dawn, they would be moved to a hiding place sometime during the night and the following night we would make our breakthrough into liberated territory.

"Can't we keep the wounded where they are?" I asked the colonel. He shook his head, "They wouldn't be safe. The enemy tries to kill our wounded. It's studied terrorism," he went on. "We'll have to hide them." I returned to Jim at the makeshift hospital and told him the news.

"The Germans are hot on the wounded," he said. "They'll take losses in order to capture prisoners and then kill them. Don't let me be captured!"

Next to Jim a man in a traction splint was dying to a chorus of delirious moans. "I can't spend the night here," he said. "It's terrible."

"I'll take you outside," I said. I got a bale of hay to keep him warm and packed him between the outer wall of the farmhouse and myself. The cool air made him feel better. "They haven't got the bridge yet, have they?" he asked. "Not yet," I said, " but they hope to."

He fell asleep. I was so tired I slept too, only dimly aware of the Partisans carrying the wounded stumbling over me in the dark. Towards dawn the cold woke me. I found that a couple of horses harnessed to a cart had eaten most of the hay which I'd used as a blanket. Kicking them away, I fell soundly asleep to the continuous sound of gunfire until awakened by the deep rolling rumble of explosions. I was so excited I shook Jim. "Listen!" I shouted as one explosion followed another. "The bridge, Jim, they got the bridge!"

"We sure did, John." He sounded happy.

I got up stiff but wide awake. The horses were still chewing our hay. Three bodies, stacked face-down, were in the horse cart. The breeches of the body on top were in tatters, revealing flesh that looked so very white and delicate in the uncertain light. Then I saw her face. The amazon was frail in death.

"We will move as soon as we've buried our dead," the doctor said. "The brigades will start pulling out at nine. By then we must be in hiding."

Jim was given some tea laced with *rakija* and placed in the last cart of the column. "What's happening to the German?" he asked. I went to find out from the doctor and passed the sleeping German.

"As he's wounded, we'll leave him behind. His friends will take care of him when we've left," the doctor said. When Jim heard this he asked, "Sure we can't take him with us?" The doctor shook his head. "We have more wounded than we can take care of properly. We have practically no supplies. This man would only be a burden we cannot afford."

"Tell the doctor he must be shot then. He's picked up too much information about us," Jim said thoughtfully.

"I understand," the doctor said softly.

"*Pokret!*" a voice called out.

Ahead of us lay the long march and the breakthrough. We had just started to retreat when a shot rang out from the farmhouse we had left behind.

For hours the oxcarts rattled along with only one guard for each. Yet here we were in Hitler's Reich and our protection was that we would not be betrayed by the peasants. In fact they gave the wounded food—a loaf of bread in one place, apples in another—I can still recall the old man who galloped after us with a bottle of *rakija* he had dug up from his cellar.

As dawn broke the oxcarts zigzagged down into the valley to the faint sounds of music. A blind Partisan, his face swathed in bandages, was playing "*Lepa Nasa Domovina*" on his mouth organ.

We stopped in a small village and got Jim into bed. I tried to sleep. In the afternoon a heavy rain started. Headquarters issued orders to move that night as the Germans were becoming increasingly difficult to contain. Their trucks were racing up the roads bringing reinforcements. The doctor told the headquarters officer that they would have to hang on. Traveling in such weather would kill his patients. So we stayed the night. Though they had little, the peasants gave us eggs and cider. The doctor came and examined Jim's leg, producing a strange picture: a farmhouse in Germany, its walls covered with religious paintings, a wounded American officer having his leg bandaged by a Partisan doctor while our host, a cobbler, sat in a corner repairing a pair of shoes.

"We'll be leaving at four this morning," the doctor said.

Out of the night, a stranger, soaking wet, appeared at the farmhouse. He turned out to be one of Jim's OSS operatives who reported on German troop movements in the area. I have no idea whether he'd been tipped off that Jim was in the farmhouse or whether it was merely coincidence. In any case, his cordial reception made it clear he was welcome. Interestingly enough, the cobbler displayed a surprising knowledge about the German occupiers. What made me marvel was that their gossip about seven armored cars and trucks filled with German troops would become top secret information by the time it reached the Pentagon.

At four we were on our way, the oxcarts jolting the wounded as they bumped along the rocky road filled with potholes and puddles. The doctor and I marched behind. "We've lost 30 doctors," he muttered, "and that is more than we can spare. But Slovenia, which has had no independence for over 1200 years, has been magnificent."

We found the brigade waiting for us. The men were better dressed than when we had started out on the operation. The brand new uniforms of the German *Gendarmerie*—light-blue with brown cuffbands and orange piping—could be seen on a number of them. They had cleaned out a *Gendarmerie* post en route. As we were about to pull out, a mortar shell fired from a church across the valley in German-held territory killed two men and wounded four.

Our progress was slower. Units of the brigade fanned out, protecting our convoy of wounded. Behind came 11 Austrian prisoners clad in rags the Partisans had given them in exchange for their uniforms. We were traveling along the good roads for the sake of the wounded, but they had already become quagmires and everybody was slipping. The oxcarts got bogged down. Some overturned. Night came. With flashlights we tried to catch sight of the sharp hairpin turns we were taking. An order came down the line: *"Stroga tisina!"* ("Absolute silence!") We were coming into a village where a strong German garrison was stationed. At the first house of the village we cut into the fields. Heavy gunfire broke out. The order for contact was traveling up and down the line as the rat-tat-tat of the Breda guns could be heard. Peter, our interpreter, whispered, "A Partisan patrol is simulating an attack on the German garrison to give us time to clear the village."

At 4am we had marched 24 hours and had not yet crossed the border. Each time there was a break, the weary men fell onto the wet soil. I was falling asleep on my feet. I rubbed moist fern leaves over my face to stay awake. Finally we passed the border. We were too weary to look back and catch a last glimpse of the Reich. At dawn we reached Klanec. I fell asleep on the floor of a farmhouse.

"Mr Phillips, Mr Phillips!" Peter shouted a few hours later as he shook me. "We must get out of here quick. The White Guards are attacking the village." We hurriedly got Jim into the oxcart and made for the woods. Following the last cart came two girls lugging a huge Italian container of hot food they had not had time to serve the wounded.

All day we camped in the forest. That night we traveled along the main Ljubljana road patrolled by German tanks during the day. As dawn broke, we crossed the Sava River into liberated territory. It was going to be a lovely day. Church bells rang. It was Sunday.

At Slovene headquarters orders awaited Jim. He was to be hospitalized in Italy. Anxious to get my story out, I went along with him. Because he was on crutches, Jim asked me to take care of a bulky package wrapped in old newspapers and fastened tight by a cord. "That's $450,000 in cash," Jim told me. The money was for special operations, he didn't specify what.

We spent the next few days at a farmhouse near the field where our plane was to pick us up. While waiting, we played cards. Having no chips we used gold napoleons from my stash of currency, dutifully returning the napoleons to their bag at the end of the evening, when Major Patrahalcev from Kiev ordered the bonfires along the runway put out as there would be no plane that night.

Finally a C-47 with a red star and a Russian crew landed. By then we had grown to a pretty large number of passengers. The plane was over-loaded. Jammed into my bucket seat I was amused by the irony of cluching $450,000 wrapped in old newspapers under such conditions.

Just as we were about to take off, a motorbike was added to our cargo. It wasn't battened down and I hated to think what it would do to us caree-ning around if something went wrong while we trundled down the mini-mum-length field on take off. I said as much to the Russian pilot. "Afraid to die?" he replied, as he headed for the cockpit. Without even revving up the engines, the plane bumped along and slowly gained altitude as we cruised for the next couple of hours over occupied Eastern Europe.

When we landed at Bari, I returned Jim's $450,000 and he was driven off to hospital. I kept an appointment with a British colonel and a major from the SBS (Special Balkan Service) and gave them a rundown on the battle of Litija Bridge. In that bantering tone the British occasionally take when expressing a serious thought, the colonel told me that Jim deserved a decoration for his bravery and the British were anxious to award it. For such a decoration, however, a witness was required to corroborate the action. Would I be that witness?

We met at the colonel's office and with great formality went through the entire procedure, from my giving my name and stating my status before answering the questions regarding Jim's participation in the operation. That over, we had a couple of pink gins. Jim got his medal.

Partisan amazon, Slovenia, 1944

Schönbrunn Palace, Vienna, 1945

Pontoon bridge, Vienna, 1945

Europe
Divided

Austria, Summer 1945

The war in Europe was over. American armies, non-existent at its outbreak, had linked up with the Red Army and brought the fighting to an end. It was clear to Europeans that the victory was due to outsiders whose armies, sprawling across Europe, would shape their future.

What would happen in Central Europe was of special interest to me. These small, violent countries, once precariously held together like delicate mobiles by the Hapsburg Empire, were in total disarray. All that remained was a hopeless tangle of conflicting nationalist emotions and aspirations. Feudalism faced Marxism: large estates faced expropriation and grandeur faced abject misery. I wanted to record the confusion of a thousand-year-old world as it crashed down, while another groped through the rubble to establish itself. For eight months I roamed through Austria, Czechoslovakia, Poland, Hungary, and Romania. I scrounged film to feed my camera. I became a bootlegger to feed myself and keep one step ahead of regulations that would force me to lose the thread of the lunacy I was now a part of. I pushed on in the midst of a world hit by a hurricane which was uprooting all the old values.

"Tell him he is being detained for making the glorious Red Army look ridiculous," the Russian officer said. He was sitting behind an empty desk in an equally desolate office as he gazed with open admiration at my boots. I was back in Vienna, and back in trouble. "And besides that, it is forbidden to take pictures in the bazaar," he added.

"They call that flourishing black market a bazaar?" I asked the Viennese cyclist who had volunteered as an interpreter.

"Didn't you know?" The cyclist coughed, shifting unhappily in a suit several sizes too big for him. "The glorious Red Army shops there."

"All I did was try and take a picture of a fat Russian lady officer inspecting a black brassière she was swapping for a mound of butter she had clutched to her bosom, and five green caps pounced on me!"

"You don't consider that would make the glorious Red Army look ridiculous?" he asked with a grin.

"Well how does the glorious Red Army think it looks when it takes one NKVD officer and four green caps clutching pistols to parade one of their allies through the streets of Vienna?" I countered.

The cyclist ignored my question. "I must go now," he said, and after some hesitation: "You won't consider it excessive, I hope, if I ask for one American cigarette for my pains?"

"Why, not at all," I said. Fortunately the American provost marshal soon got me released and from then on I was given a Soviet escort to make sure I didn't ridicule the Red Army again.

Like the rest of Austria, Vienna was divided into four zones: American, British, French, and Russian, but unlike the rest of Austria, in mid-July Vienna was still run by the Russians, as the final protocols governing the administration of the city had yet to be signed by the four Allied commanders. The Russians, as a matter of course, had put Vienna on Moscow time, even though Vienna was normally two hours behind. Except for those caught up in the middle, however, the change presented few difficulties: the Viennese stuck to their time and the Russians to theirs.

Unfortunately, Colonel Stanley J. Grogan, generally acknowledged to be "the oldest colonel in the US Army", was assigned to set up a press billet. The Hotel Weiser-Hahn, adjoining Max Reinhardt's old Josefstadt Theater, was selected. Grogan went by the book. He put our billet on Moscow time and created chaos. Since there was nowhere else for a correspondent to eat, I would either skip breakfast or have it at 8:30am (6:30am Vienna time). I would then hang around for two hours waiting for the Viennese to get up. By then, it was 11am Moscow time, the hour my GI driver was fed. As soon as he was he through, it was my lunchtime. By the time I'd eaten, it was lunchtime for the Viennese. Since the situation could not improve in the afternoon, I became curious to know how the Russians coped.

"You want to know at what time we eat lunch?" the Russian officer pondered. "Why any time between ten and four."

The Russian soldier's main preoccupation was acquiring watches the GIs sold at exorbitant prices. It was not uncommon to see GIs with several watches on each wrist. The Mickey Mouse was a favorite; it sold for 50 times its PX price.

The Russian authorities' main occupation was plundering Vienna. Passing by the telephone exchange, I watched Russian soldiers shoveling stacks of phones piled in the street onto a truck. Endless freight trains, bulging with everything that was removable, headed east, closely guarded by armed Russian soldiers sitting on top of the loot.

"It wouldn't look right," the Russian major in charge of constructing a pontoon bridge told me as he prevented two of his men from having their picture taken while sawing a log. "I don't see why I'm building a bridge across the Danube when Kiev, my home town, suffered worse damage than Vienna."

I walked round the city with the journalist Mike Fodor, who was an authority on Central Europe. He dismissed the destruction as a "mere detail", as he went on to explain. "People say that the Viennese have no character," he chuckled. "Why, Vienna is like a weeping willow. Its branches bend in the storm, but don't snap." We came to a huge statue of a Russian soldier, a gift of the Red Army to commemorate Vienna's liberation. "That," said Fodor, "is the Memorial to the Unknown Looter."

We visited the city's landmarks: the buildings and cemeteries where the great composers were either born or died; Sacher's Hotel, home of the *Sachertorte*; Demel's, famous for its *Schlagobers* (whipped cream). "All these places survived the war," Fodor told me. He also found kind words for another survivor, the Academy of Creative Arts, for rejecting Hitler's paintings: "A terrible man, and a worse painter." he said.

"Vienna," I was told by a more critical observer, "has convinced the world that Hitler was German and Beethoven was an Austrian."

"I'm from the *Kommandatura*," the woman guide assigned to me snapped: "These two seats are not good enough for us." She glowered at the columns behind which the Austrian director of the concert hall had thoughtfully placed us. We got better seats. My guide relaxed. "This is really beautiful," she said looking around. "Have you anything as fantastic in New York?"

"Why yes," I said. "We have a Park of Culture called Radio City Music Hall every bit as fine as this, in its own way. It was there I saw a symphony orchestra of over 50 musicians emerge from the pit, be swept across the stage and lifted the height of two floors into the air without missing a beat of Beethoven's Fifth."

"I know," my guide said. "New York is wonderful,"

"Who told you?" I asked.

"I know," was all she would say.

The lights dimmed, the makeshift curtains flew open as two dancers pirouetted against a red backdrop. "She is the famous Ulanova," my guide whispered. "I know her." Below us the klieg lights were switched on as a Russian film unit went to work. They did not film the dancers, but the audience, where Austrians and Russians mingled. They concentrated on the two front rows filled with Russian officers with large bouquets on their laps ready to be enthusiastically presented to the entertainers.

We listened to pianists and violinists, watched gypsy dancers and all the talent that could be crammed into a Russian transport plane to impress the Viennese. Before the intermission, a baritone sang. My guide, unable to restrain her pride exclaimed, "Imagine! He sings in Italian!"

During the intermission, she led me backstage. Mme Ulanova ignored her. The baritone, smiling broadly, mopped his brow. The other artists charmed the groups of admirers which surrounded them. The most popular was a statuesque figure in a tight-fitting, white evening gown and long kid gloves that reached practically to her pale-pink shoulders. With brisk authority she signed autographs with a signature about the size of the paper she wrote on. "A singer?" I ventured.

"And very famous," my guide sighed.

When I tried to coax these artists on stage for pictures, they either turned their backs, walked away or ignored me.

Colonel General Blagadatov, in temporary command of Vienna, made the most of his short height in a splendid white tunic. Stopping before the imposing singer, he bowed and, about to kiss her glove, was brushed aside by a feverish lieutenant who dumped a bouquet on her bosom. He then enthusiastically kissed her gloved hand as she smiled benignly while holding her fountain pen as though it were a cigarette holder. Catching sight of Mme Ulanova, General Blagadatov hastened over to her. Without even a nod, she pirouetted on stage. Treated like an American photographer, the general sadly departed while the American photographer, behaving like a Russian general, followed Mme Ulanova on stage and took her picture in spite of her shrill protests.

My flashlight had a magic effect. All the artists suddenly took interest, and followed me as though I were the Pied Piper. They patiently queued up on stage to be photographed until the curtain flew open prematurely.

Madame Ulanova was extremely nervous when she arrived at the Hotel Sacher to meet Nijinski, the mad genius, after her performance. As she entered the room, he walked over, kissed her hand and said, *"Vous étiez magnifique, madame."* He then hurried off to scowl at the wall in the far corner of the room for the rest of the evening.

I took this once great dancer and his wife for some fresh air in my jeep. My GI driver looked askance when Nijinski, lean and supple with piercing, expressionless eyes, obediently followed his wife from the terrace of Sacher's, where they had been waiting for me.

"Viens, mon petit Vaslav," she instructed her husband, cautioning me at the same time not to speak to him. He stalked up to the jeep, moving with the controlled step of a caged panther. Halfway to Schönbrunn Palace, Nijinski let out a raucous growl, which was somehow pathetic in spite of its fury. My driver leaned forward and peeked at him through his rear-view mirror.

Nijinski growled again, louder this time, then chuckled to himself as he sniffed the air. "Vaslav is very happy," Mme Nijinski explained. "He loves to be driven around." The unhappy silence that followed was interrupted by the driver, who turned to me and muttered, "This guy's nuts!"

I left Vienna for Salzburg. Physically I found the city of the pre-war Festival-goers was undamaged. The Nazi occupation and American liberation, however, had brought changes. The Residenz was now the US Army head-quarters, the Osterreichischer Hof, a billet. The Café Bazaar was closed. Lanz of Salzburg, famous for its *dirndls* and *lederhosen*, only a memory. The Marabell Garden was operated by the Red Cross. GIs now drank Coca-Cola where I once photographed the Countess of Oxford and Lord Asquith sipping beer through a straw. English was spoken as much as ever, but now the speakers were in uniform.

Within three months of the armistice in Europe, the Music Festival opened. Although the American policy had been to let Austrians organize their own festival, aid coming from the wings helped to make it a success. This led to a certain amount of *gemütlich* buccaneering in the name of culture: the symphony orchestra, which had been reduced to string-quartet proportions after de-Nazification, was miraculously restored to its requisite number of musicians; star performers were smuggled out of other zones;

unobtainable sheet music appeared; musicians collapsing from starvation at rehearsals were beefed up with K-rations; lodgings were made available in the midst of a housing shortage.

With Salzburg in the American zone, General Mark Clark played host to the British, French, and Russian commanders. He drove them to nearby Germany to visit Hitler's house at Berchtesgaden, now a tourist attraction. On the way to our jeeps, Colonel Grogan, my conducting officer, approached General Clark and nodded in my direction. He must have told the general that I had been accredited to the Fifth Army in Italy. The General told me how happy he was to see me again, unaware we had never met.

At Berchtesgaden an arrow pointed to "Hitler's Home". The generals, followed by a retinue of armed MPs, made their way to the famous bay window where Hitler had his picture taken. There I photographed them in the midst of the Berghof's debris.

We then drove to Hitler's "Eagle's Nest", perched on top of the mountain and only accessible by an elevator inside the mountain. The elevator man had served Hitler. He volunteered the information that the cost of the Eagle's Nest had been entirely underwritten by the royalties from *Mein Kampf.* I had never thought of Hitler as a best-selling author.

Looking out from the balcony, I couldn't see a thing. We were above the clouds that blanketed both sound and sight. The silence became even more oppressive when I thought that in this sealed-off solitude Hitler made his fateful decisions. Mist drifted in through the broken windows. The place was bare except for a large, circular table covered by hundreds of signatures. The four generals, like the GIs before them, scribbled their names.

The Music Festival opened that night. A thrill of pride drifted across Austria. The opening ceremony took place at the Stadtsaal. The guests were gathered on either side of an aisle shaped like the outer edges of a double bass: Austrians on the right, American officers and their guests on the left. The Austrians sat with their hands in their laps as they listened attentively to General Mark Clark, about to govern their lives.

In the midst of their respectful attention, I tiptoed around, flashing bulbs as I went. No sooner had I sat down then my name was whispered as a white-gloved hand tapped my shoulder. It was Captain von Ripper, whom I had last seen in Naples. Over drinks, he told me that he had parachuted into Austria on an OSS mission. When his mission was completed, he was detained by the Germans in Linz and hadn't had new ID papers issued after he had landed in Austria. His forged papers, supposedly issued in Salzburg where he was born, were in the name of Rudolf Ritter—close enough to Ripper for him to respond instinctively,

A German sergeant vainly tried to get Salzburg on the line to get confirmation on Rip's identity. "I knew what would happen the minute he got a connection," Rip told me. "Having been tortured by the Gestapo once before, I knew that I could not take it a second time." He had slipped a cyanide tablet in the space between two teeth the Gestapo had knocked out previously. "During those six hours, I kept my hands in my pockets so that no one noticed they were shaking."

Fortunately, the sergeant quit his attempts to call Salzburg when it was time for him to go off duty and left his replacement to handle the case. After two more unsuccessful attempts, he let von Ripper go.

By the end of the war, Rip had located and captured the German forgers who had been printing British five pound notes. And by the time General Mark Clark arrived in Austria, von Ripper also had one of Hitler's Mercedes' waiting for him with the compliments of the OSS engraved on a nameplate.

The first concert took place at the Mozarteum. I was there after a flirtatious WAAC told me that I'd see a beautiful woman I was bound to want to photograph. This turned out to be Princess Rethy, the morganatic wife of King Leopold of the Belgians. Accused of appeasement by his subjects, the King had spent the war in Austria under SS guard. Liberated by the 106th Cavalry, his family now lived in an elegant villa on the Sankt-Wolfgang lake.

The Princess had been born Lillian Baels, a commoner who, despite her lowly birth and lack of money, climbed to the top of Viennese society. The perfect dinner guest, she had successsfully graced what diplomats call the "ends of tables" and thus found herself in great demand. In 1938 Lillian Baels entered the royal household as lady-in-waiting to the Leopold's children from his first marriage. In 1941, she married the King at a time when his father was collaborating with the Germans.

At the concert I photographed the Princess surrounded by American officers. When I asked for their names, there was some hesitation. "The ones with the Princess de Rethy," I specified. "You know who she is?"

"Yes."

I then asked the liaison officer who had escorted the Princess, if I could get pictures of her at home. "Call me tomorrow," he said, but he didn't sound too hopeful.

When I rang the next morning, I was told: "You're expected this afternoon."

The American sentries who guarded the entrance to the royal villa, checked me through. A Belgian aide led me to a large drawing-room, which gave onto a terrace overlooking the lake.

"The Princess and her children will be down presently," I was told. "His Majesty does not wish to be photographed."

A man who seemed prematurely old was on the terrace. He was gaunt, his hair was thin and graying. On seeing me, he walked away.

"A tutor," I thought. But of course it was the King. He showed up later while I photographed the princess and the royal children, keeping well clear of my camera but offering advice. He wanted me to photograph his son with the Princess, along with the children from his previous marriage.

When the photo session was over, Leopold produced several filters for his Contax camera and asked me how to use them. He then produced his Contax. The film was jammed, and he could not get it out. He led me around the house preceded by an aide who threw the doors open as we sought a substitute for a darkroom. The best I could find was an armchair. Crouching in front of it, the King put a large pillow over my head while I removed his film from the camera. When I asked if I could load the Contax for him, he admitted to having no more film, so I gave him several rolls.

Some of the guests in my makeshift hotel had the most unusual occupations. Colonel Simmonite's mission, for example, was to recover the Holy Hand of Saint Stephen, Hungary's most revered relic.

Since time immemorial this relic of Hungary's first monarch had been paraded through the streets of Budapest on August 20 amid national rejoicing. This year, with the parade only three days away, the relic was not in Hungary. It had been taken out of the country by the fanatically pro-Nazi prime minister when he escaped from Budapest with his mistress as the Russians stormed the city. A few days before the Americans reached his Austrian hiding place, he married his mistress "to offer her the protection of his name," and at the same time abandoned the holy relic on the altar. It was found by a US lieutenant who reported his finding to Captain George Selke of the military government, who in turn notified the Archbishop of Salzburg, who took possession of it. Colonel Simmonite had to recover the relic before August 20. His mission had a top priority since the communists were against the Holy Hand being returned in time for the procession.

When Colonel Simmonite and his escort reached Salzburg, the Archbishop refused to return the Holy Hand. The matter was then referred General Clark, who, as time was running out, referred it directly to the Pope. His Holiness notified the American Ambassador to the Holy See that it would be fitting for the relic to be returned to Budapest at once. The Ambassador telegraphed General Clark, who then told Colonel Simmonite to expect the relic in Budapest in time for the procession.

Armed with this document Colonel Simmonite, followed by members of his mission, a US chaplain Father Ralph J. Difenbach and myself, trooped into the great hall of the Archiepiscopal Palace of Saint Peter on August 17 to take possession of the Holy Hand.

We were received by the Reverend Johan Schreiber, the Archbishop's secretary. He told Colonel Simmonite to call again in a few weeks, as the Archbishop was out of Salzburg on a retreat. "Weeks!" wailed the Colonel's driver, Sergeant Smergel, suspecting that the Austrian clergy intended to keep the Hungarian relic. Eventually the secretary's ample body was eased into a staff car and the mission drove off to the mountain village where the Archbishop was staying. Here Sergeant Smergel wailed some more before the Archbishop agreed to return the relic.

At 11:15 on the night of August 18, with just time enough to get back to Budapest for the procession, we stood once again in the Palace of Saint Peter while Reverend Schreiber drew up the necessary protocols. Once signed, he withdrew to fetch the relic.

He reappeared carrying a gold and crystal reliquary in which rested a tiny, shriveled black hand covered with jewels. Chaplain Difenbach kissed the reliquary and became the first American to touch the relic. The Holy Hand was then carefully packed in the same wrapping in which it had left Hungary. It was turned over to Father Difenbach, who slowly walked across the great audience hall to the car in which Sergeant Smergel drove him back to Budapest in time for the procession.

Allied soldiers posing in front of the Johann Strauss monument, Vienna, 1945

Displaced Persons, Austria, 1945

Two members of the Red Army, Vienna, 1945

Nijinski and his wife, Schönbrunn Palace, Vienna, 1945

Allied generals signing their names on Hitler's table at the Berghof, 1945

Flowers for the assassins of Heydrich at the Church of Saint Cyril and Methodius, Prague, 1945

Lidice, Czechoslovakia, 1945

Czechoslovakia, Summer 1945

At first sight, Prague had changed little in appearance over the past eight years. This was thanks to Messrs Chamberlain and Daladier delivering the country to Hitler. If it hadn't been for a few Russians and American GIs in the streets, parked jeeps, brand-new war memorials, pictures of Stalin and Benes in shop windows, UNRRA signs (United Nations Relief and Rehabilitation Administration) in the department stores, the burnt out medieval *Rathaus* and several damaged modern apartment buildings, it might well have been 1938.

Crowds bustled as usual in the center of the city. The shop windows were filled with goods, although mostly for display. The book stores were well stocked. The movies were just as popular, as were the several exhibitions of modern art. The food situation was not brilliant, but no one starved. Rationing functioned smoothly. The black market was practically non-existent. (Extra ration coupons were available, but only for those who performed heavy manual work.) The hot-dog stands were back on street corners. There was beer, but it was watery. Cigarettes were rationed to two a day, for men only.

On Sundays, as in pre-war days, the citizens of this middle-class democratic republic queued up for the streetcars which took them to the football stadium, the family graves at the cemetery, or the banks of the Moldau, where they rented rowboats or sailed up the river aboard the steamer *T.G. Masaryk*. Barandov, the café with many tiers of terraces overlooking the river, remained a great favorite.

Memories came back to me. There was Fritsek, the gnome-like barman at the Alcron Hotel. He had grabbed my hands, delighted to greet a foreigner he had known before the war. Pointing to the empty bar, he wailed, "Look what they have done to me! They now expect me to serve tea and pink lemonade!" There wasn't a bottle of liquor on the shelves.

Fritsek had been less teary-eyed the time a drunken German had grabbed him by the lapels so that his feet dangled like a puppet's and called him a *"Böhmischer Hund"* ("Bohemian hound"), an insult no Czech would tolerate. Clearing his throat, Fritsek spat in his face.

The hotel lobby reminded me of where I had met Monika, a lively Czech from Brno. She appeared to be at a loose end and was wonderful company, although her English was pleasantly chaotic. A Prague friend believed that Monika was with Intelligence. With Czech thoroughness, he reasoned that as I worked for the most influential magazine in the States, it was vitally important for the authorities to know whether I was being influenced by the very efficient and effective Nazi propaganda. "You tell me of a better way for the authorities to know how you really feel about our country than your having a Czech girlfriend," he concluded. I never asked Monika whether she was an agent. She would never admit it if she was. So I cheerfully enjoyed her company.

At times I forgot that eight years had gone by and half-expected to run into her. I never did. The last time I saw her was at the airport after the Munich Agreement in 1938. She had then told me, "You've left many times before, Johnny, but you always come back. Now I know you never will return. It's all over for us without a fight."

The Ambassador Hotel also evoked memories. There, the great foreign correspondents of the time gathered in the evening after filing their despatches. They were the original dirty-trenchcoat correspondents who traveled from crisis to crisis. There was H.R. Knickerbocker—"Knick"—the Hearst press star with his brick-red hair, green shirts, and gold-rimmed glasses. Through him I was admitted to their club, although I was only 23 and a photographer. He was the highest-paid journalist of his day, and to my astounded admiration, earned in one year what it would take me to earn in 12.

I can still recall him passing along historical titbits, such as the time he was filing his story from Vienna after the Anschluss. In his piece he had reported that Adolf Hitler exerted a greater influence on the German people than Jesus Christ. Though the censor had agreed with Knick, he nonetheless refused to let this pass. Knick's great pal was John T. Whitaker of *The Chicago Daily News*, a newspaper famous for its foreign coverage. There was Hungarian-born Mike Fodor, and Raymond Swing, then unknown, but who would become a major radio commentator of World War II.

The most colorful correspondent of this small group was an Englishman, Claud Cockburn. Cockburn had switched both conviction and newspaper during the Spanish Civil War. A star correspondent of the conservative London *Times*, he had quit to write for the communist *Daily*

Worker. A brilliant conversationalist, Cockburn liked to observe that he was the first member of his family to return to Washington since his ancestor Admiral Sir George Cockburn had burned the down both the White House and the Capitol during the Anglo-American war of 1814.

Being very much the junior in this group, I was frequently their legman as I rushed around Czechoslovakia while they reported from Prague. I was the only one to have covered the Czech evacuation of the Sudetenland, and Knick and Whitaker were eager to file a story about my exodus on the last truck. Foolishly, I asked them not to. Covering the Nazis was my bread and butter. I didn't want to attract their attention now that visas were required to enter Germany. It was only when I got to New York that I appreciated my stupidity. Had such a story been syndicated across the States, *Life* would have been overjoyed, and would have run a lead story instead of the one picture they did print.

I was now confronted by the fact that war did strange things to people. Decent people in 1938 had become criminals by 1945. Colonel Letov, the tough Czech soldier who had taken me around the Skoda works while I photographed the Czech armament industry, and who had cried over the Munich Agreement, was now in jail awaiting trial at the People's Court. An obedient soldier, he had ended up running a Czech concentration camp.

In the summer of 1945, ironically, the popularity of a nation was in direct relation to its absence from the scene. The Americans occupied the Pilsen area, and the Russians were sprawled across the rest of the country. The dream of the Czech population in Pilsen, therefore, was to have the Russians, instead of the Americans.

Nothing could ease the relations between the American forces of occuption and the Czechs. The GIs hated the Czechs. The source of their antagonism was their fraternisation with Sudeten German girls. For these girls, not surprisingly, having a GI boyfriend was a bonanza. They provided both food and entertainment. They took the girls out at night and enabled them to flaunt the curfew imposed on other Germans. The GIs, for their part, knew there was always a warm welcome awaiting them in a German girl's bed, and, feeling lonely, took advantage of it: the boudoir was much more effective propaganda than the Czech posters denouncing the Nazis. For the GIs, stories of Nazis murdering Czech patriots belonged to a world which had ended on VE Day. The stories they heard from their German girlfriends was far less easy to dismiss. They were personal tragedies concerning people they knew. The GI's girlfriend would soon be evicted with her family from their home in Czechoslovakia and sent off to Germany. Her grandmother would be forced to leave the house where she was born. The GIs were appalled.

These land expropriations and the expulsions from Czechoslovakia were the price the Sudeten Germans had to pay for becoming Nazis. Their properties were earmarked to be broken up into lots of no more than 30 acres, although this was not done immediately as it would have been disastrous in the middle of the harvest. In the summer of 1945, labor shortages were made up by employing Nazi-sympathizers who were kept in concentration camps and taken to the farms daily to work. There, they received two hot meals a day. The apparent lack of bitterness between Czech and German peasants was truly surprising. The Germans I photographed ate at the same table as their Czech employers. It was impossible for me to find in these Sudeten peasants the exalted Nazis of 1938.

The urban population was far less forgiving. I witnessed this at the trial of Dr Josef Pfitzner. Pfitzner was a Czech national of Sudeten German origin. A distinguished professor of history at the German University in Prague, he was the author of several notable books. When Hitler occupied Czechoslovakia, Pfitzner wired Hitler offering his services. He was made deputy mayor of Prague and once in office put into practice his belief that Prague was a German city. He set about removing all traces of Czech influence, beginning with the Czech universities, which he closed down and sent the Czech students to the gallows.

On the last day of the three-day trial before the People's Court, Pfitzner pleaded for clemency in perfect Czech. The prosecutor, who was a concentration-camp survivor, demanded the death penalty for the betrayal of his own country. Normally the execution would take place within two hours of the sentence. The judge, however, granted Pfitzner a reprieve of an additional hour. The American journalist, Maurice Hindus, after much soul-searching, came along reluctantly as I joined the president of the court in his office. From a window there, I got a view of the gallows. The scene looked medieval. Three gibbets stood on a platform, its framework covered with scarlet cloth. As word had spread throughout Prague, 55,000 onlookers had gathered outside the prison. They were silent and so orderly that only 13 policemen were required to keep the crowd away from the gallows. Although I had been granted permission to photograph the execution, the president was worried about the impression it would create with the American public.

I noticed a young man in uniform with the emblem of the twin-tailed lion of Czechoslovakia on his right arm. He wore white gloves and was listening attentively to the President and repeated a gesture he had just made. He brought his hands up and made as though he was gripping something. Then he gave a sharp twisting motion to the left. The president nodded assent. This young student was the executioner.

The president looked at his watch. The time had come. He led the way. We all fell in line. Maurice Hindus at my side was still worrying. Having seen an execution before, I was less shaken than he was. I did, however, set my camera shutter at a fast speed in case my hands shook. We left the courthouse and entered the enclosure where the gallows were erected. Three men stood astride, their arms behind their backs. Pfitzner stood behind us. He seemed very calm.

The president once again read out the death sentence, listing every one of Pfitzner's titles and decorations. Then the executioners propelled him up the gallows' steps. When the crowd caught sight of Pfitzner, a sound like the roar of the tide was heard. A harness was fastened to his chest while his feet were bound to a rope connected to a pulley. Hoisted up by the harness, Pfitzner came up to the level of the young executioner. A noose was slipped around his neck. When he felt the noose being fitted, Pfitzner cried out, *"Ich sterbe für Deutschland!"* ("I die for Germany!") The executioner slapped his face with the back of his gloved hand. When the noose was tight, the man who had fastened Pfitzner's feet started to pull the rope. The young executioner placed both hands around Pfitzner's head and repeated the twisting gesture I had watched him make in front of the judge. Pfitzner had a quick spasm as though gasping for air. His handcuffed arms came up slightly and slipped back. He never moved again. Once the doctor was satisfied Pfitzner was dead, the crowd slowly made its way home.

When it became known that the execution had taken place in public, there was such an outcry that all further executions were held in the prison yard. Fortunately, the film of Pfitzner's execution was censored. I had been all too obviously on the gallows.

To appreciate fully the deep hatred the Czechs had for the Nazis, I visited Lidice. A rough cross with a crown of barbed wire stood in the hollow of a large rolling field. A path led up to it and vanished over the low crest. "You are standing where the church used to be," the priest told me. I looked down at the grass round my feet. I searched for a stone, for any solitary remnant that might have survived. There wasn't even a pebble.

On June 10, 1942, the Nazis massacred all the adult males in the village of Lidice and deported all the women and children to concentration camps. The village was then shelled, the debris blasted, the rubble completely removed, and the land plowed up. Lidice had disappeared so irrevocably that those born there now came from nowhere.

The destruction was an act of revenge for the assassination of Reinhard Heydrich, the acting protector of Bohemia and Moravia. Heydrich, known as "the hangman", was one of the most ferocious and dangerous of Hitler's henchmen and Czech intelligence in London had decided to eliminate him. Two agents were assigned the job. They ambushed Heydrich as he was being driven in his open Mercedes to the Hradschin Palace on May 29, 1942. The assassins managed to escape and hide in the Church of Saint Cyril and Methodius in Prague, where they fought off the Nazis until they were killed. I photographed the bullet-splattered exterior wall of the church, which had become a memorial where wild flowers were placed. Nothing was known about the assassins' identity.

Maurice Hindus was the kindhearted journalist who had been mocked for publishing a book predicting that Germany could not defeat Russia at the time when military experts said that the Red Army had ceased to exist. I was with him when I covered one of those wonderful stories we call "a natural".

Jeromir Vejvoda had played the violin in his father-in-law's Prague inn for over ten years. His 11-piece orchestra was made up of amateurs who had regular jobs but enjoyed music. They also performed Jeromir's compositions. During the war, Jeromir listened in secret to the BBC news broadcasts, which was punishable. One evening he heard a march which was very familiar. He had composed it. It was called the "Beer Barrel Polka" and was the most popular march of World War II with both the Allies and the enemy. Jeromir had no idea how his composition became so famous. I asked him if he had ever received any royalties. He said no.

Lukas was a Czech photographer. His was a small man but he had a natural elegance about him that you also found in his work. Ever since 1939, Lukas had dreamt of the day he would photograph the liberation of Prague. Prague was Lukas's town and he felt for it the deep and quiet love Czechs have for their land. Unfortunately, necrosis of the bones attacked his legs. He could no longer walk. He was a cripple when I visited him.

Lukas looked very young. With great effort, he rose to greet me. Pointing to his feet, he made a vague gesture of apology. He gathered some of his work and showed it to me.

"His best work isn't here," a friend said. "We gathered it up to make a book.."

"A memorial book," Lukas corrected.

I looked away and gazed at the modern paintings on the walls. "You're admiring my paintings," he remarked softly. "They are very beautiful. Too beautiful for me to afford if the artists had not been my friends." He named them, one after the other, along with the concentration camps where they had been sent, and where some of them had died.

"I heard that you were having trouble finding film here," he said. "Film is unobtainable now, but I happen to have a few rolls." He got up and hobbled to a drawer. Bending over, he pulled out a cardboard box and took out some rolls of film. I could have sworn he caressed them.

"For six years," he said turning his back to me, "I saved them for the liberation of Prague. But," he pointed to his legs, "I am not allowed out of the house now. I haven't even seen Prague."

There was no bitterness in his tone, simply despair. Then he handed me a dozen rolls of film. "They're of no use to me now. Please accept them. You will take the pictures."

Execution of Dr Josef Pfitzner, Prague, 1945

Warsaw, 1945

Warsaw Ghetto, 1945

The German battle cruiser *Schleswig-Holstein*, whose fire opened World War II, Danzig, 1945

Poland, Autumn 1945

"Amerikanski! Amerikanski!" the guards at the Polish border shouted in delight as we drove up. Hurriedly, they raised the barrier to let our jeep through. We slowed down to show our visas which had required some diplomacy to acquire. The guards expressed no interest in our documents. All they wanted to know was whether we were the vanguard of the American Army they hoped would come to Poland and boot the Russians out.

At dusk we reached a deserted *Autobahn*. "Look it! Just look it!" Paul exclaimed, eyeing the surrounding scorched earth with distaste. "Get me back to Yonkers." I had been loaned Paul and his jeep for the duration of my Polish assignment.

He had the round, open face often associated with Poles, but his appearance was deceptive. He was born in Chicago and had been a butcher in Yonkers, outside New York, until drafted. He not only spoke Polish, but Russian, and had been called upon to act as interpreter whenever an American and a Russian general socialized. It required an extremely elastic mind to keep a pleasant conversation flowing as the American insisted upon talking about sex and the Russian about the glories of the Red Army. Paul's solution was to conduct two parallel conversations, which he did to the parties' mutual satisfaction. I soon found out he had a keen sense of observation. He frequently made notations on the map he kept by him, especially when we drove past airfields. We came to a large Russian military cemetery filled with endless rows of white obelisk headstones. Still there was no one in sight.

We eventually reached a city. Breslau had been a thriving German town in Lower Silesia of some 700,000 before being turned over to the Poles and renamed Wroclaw. Now 30,000 Germans and 15,000 Poles rattled around in it. Driving along a wide avenue, we passed rows of stone façades covered with creepers which looked reassuringly residential, wealthy and solid. Yet there was something eerie about their appearance. There was no one, not even a stray cat to relieve the autumn gloom. I stopped and looked into the windows. It was like staring into blind eyes. The façades were only roofless shells.

I walked up the wide stairway of one house and went in through the half-opened front door. The inevitable desolation greeted me. Little had survived the owner's hurried departure, or the Russian soldiers' occupation, or the Polish carpetbaggers' looting. Stuffing spilled out from slashed mattresses. Tattered books, magazines and newspapers cluttered the floor. Fishing around with my boot, I uncovered a publication with a picture of Gypsy Rose Lee clad in fishnet I had taken some years before. Published in *Life* and stolen from that magazine, it now adorned the cover of a Nazi propaganda publication called *USA Nackt* — Naked USA.

We parked in front of an official-looking building in the center of town. Paul went to find out where we could spend the night. He soon returned with two militiamen in faded uniforms to act as guides. The hotels in the vicinity of the station were filled with Polish emigrants from the East. We drove to the Polonia. The hotel was deserted except for an old man in a threadbare coat sitting behind a long reception desk in a very large hall which suggested its past grandeur. He gave us a room with two beds. Paul ordered sheets. They were produced from the cellar as we were *Amerikanski*.

Anxious about our jerry cans of gasoline, he ordered the militiamen to get a sentry to guard our jeep. A youth hardly taller than his rifle was produced. We left him seated on the trailer and followed our guides to a restaurant.

Silence fell when we arrived at The Krakow. We were led, like prized booty, to a table vacated in our honor. *"Amerikanski"*, people whispered, as they stared at our uniforms. Most tried to catch our eyes and nodded, grinning. Enormous schnitzels appeared, along with coleslaw. Glancing around, we realized this was not something special for us.

A young man who spoke English joined us without being invited. Apologetically, he produced half a bottle of brandy. "It's all I can afford," he said, "but it's good." He was one of the emigrants from the East settling in the West. Unable to find work, he had fallen back on an old standby, the black market. He immediately offered us what he considered the best prices in Wroclaw for cigarettes, chewing gum, rations, uniforms, dollars, and whatever else we had to sell. The older of our two militiamen signaled Paul not to deal with him, though he was fully aware we had no local currency. "I'll pay for the meal," he whispered. "We'll settle later."

The young black marketeer, having run out of proposals, launched into what I soon realized was the Poles' favorite topic: when would the *Amerikanski* toss the Russians out of Poland? Discouraged by our response, he departed. The older militiaman explained that this young man was a *szaber*. The immigration to the newly acquired German land in the West had given birth to *szabers*—Polish carpetbaggers. They arrived from Warsaw with a land grant and empty cardboard suitcases. Before leaving with everything they could pack, they notified the local authorities they were going back to Warsaw to fetch their families, never to return.

A skinny man with a shaved head, wearing a worn-out uniform daubed with white paint, climbed on the music stand. "He's from a concentration camp," the militiaman remarked casually. "A political."

Having ordered silence, the emaciated figure launched into a lengthy monologue, which built up steadily to a passionate climax when he stopped short, exhausted. Everybody applauded.

"Sounds like a communist." The militiaman tore open the pack of Chesterfields I had given him. Keeping one smoke for himself, he passed the others around. "We're cultured Westerners like you," he said, lighting his cigarette and taking a puff. "The Russians are neither."

The band struck up and couples began to dance. A Russian soldier, whose turned-up nose and close-shaven head accentuated a comic appearance, went from table to table soliciting a dance. The women coldly declined. One even grimaced in revulsion and turned her head away.

Having unsuccessfully gone around the room, he stopped at a table next to ours and was about to sit down, when a man shouted that it was occupied. The Russian stared at him, pushed his cap back, scratched his head and went away. He soon returned with several chairs. "Chairs, chairs, chairs," he chuckled. "Here are some more chairs for you." Then he slowly left the restaurant.

As the band came to the end of a tune, sporadic shooting could be heard outside. The militiaman glanced at his watch. "It's getting close to curfew. The hunt is on. We'd better go.

"Night," he continued, picking up his rifle, "is when we stalk them."

"Them?" I inquired, but he merely winked at Paul and nodded. Our final settlement with the militiaman next morning belonged to the new era of bartering. He paid for our meals and hotel bill and accepted a worn shirt as reasonable compensation.

"Warsaw has splendid ruins," I had been told by an Englishman before I left for Poland. In every respect, they lived up to expectations. All that remained of the Ghetto I had photographed in 1938 were mountains of red brick. The Christian neighborhoods had not been spared, either. Wild plants grew on what had once been a cornice on the second floor of a house, a steering wheel emerged like a lightening rod from a pile of rubble three floors' high. Dud shells and empty coffins lay in side streets. Whenever it rained, walls collapsed, killing passers-by. Everybody walked in the middle of the street. The pockmarked houses had become shrines, reminding pedestrians that every day for six years, men were shot against them. During their occupation, Poles made it their patriotic duty to disobey the Germans, even to the point of defiantly selling white bread beneath signs prohibiting its sale on pain of death.

Hitler had decreed that Warsaw would be wiped off the face of the earth. The Poles were all the more determined to rebuild their city. With their customary vitality, they set about surviving in the midst of chaos. Nothing illustrated this more than the small wooden shack advertising "Pedicure and Manicure" in front of the once magnificent Alexandre Church, now a spectacular ruin.

Open-air stores selling siphoned water by the glass and cigarettes by the pack were at most street corners. Shops sprang up in the rubble selling aluminum pots and pans, electric irons, cameras, and even watches. Tricycles were converted into taxis. A nightclub emerged on the ground floor of a wrecked house, decorated with a painted palm and coconuts. Its owner, Micky Fogg, called the "Bing Crosby of Warsaw," had made a name for himself during the city's siege when he gave 104 recitals on the barricades, singing "*Warszawa*"—the "Marseillaise" of the Polish resistance. "Isn't it remarkable," Albert Harris, its Jewish composer remarked to me, "how they love my song and loathe my race?"

In all of Warsaw, one building remained undamaged: the Hotel Polonia. The Polonia had been the billet of the SS, whose duty it had been to dynamite Warsaw out of existence. Before the war it had been listed as a second-class hotel. Now its 215 rooms bulged with representatives of the diplomatic corps, who both resided there and set up the chancellories of their embassies, legations, and consulates there, along with UNNRA, trade delegations and influential Poles. The Americans were spread over two floors. Ambassador Arthur Bliss Lane expressed relief when I showed up. He had been worrying that all of Warsaw's destruction would be cleared up before a photographer recorded the damage. I though he was cynical at first. But he was right. The citizens of Warsaw soon made you forget the damage and only notice their reconstruction feats. Cavendish Bentinck, the British Ambassador, however, really was a cynic. I found him in an armchair with Angus, his Scottie. As he told me Angus was a pedigree, I assumed the Ambassador had brought him along from England. "Not at all," he told me. "I got Angus at a Krakow kennel."

"A champion Scottie in a Polish kennel?" I exclaimed.

The Ambassador nodded, amused at my stupefaction. "Survival of the most expensive," he smiled.

The only quiet spot in The Polonia was the news-stand in the lobby which sold second-hand books. Along with the bedrooms and the breakfast-room, the news-stands were administered by Poles. The restaurant and the bar were leased to a Soviet concern: Osobtorg. Osobtorg came as something of a surprise. Private enterprise was allowed to flourish in the midst of this socialist food combine. Cigarette vendors went from table to table, peddling American, English and Swiss brands. Red Army truck drivers, criss-crossing Central Europe supplying the Soviet forces in Germany, gave a big lift to the black market. Tempted by the many good things out of their financial reach, the drivers satisfied their craving through "vodka money", speedily transporting both goods and marketeers across the borders.

What surprised Paul and me the most was the food. The hors d'oeuvres in the Osobtorg-run restaurant consisted of chicken salad, tomato salad, herring salad, Russian salad smothered in mayonnaise, cold cuts of all kinds, and two varieties of caviar. The black caviar cost five *zlotys* more than a cup of coffee, the red caviar five *zlotys* less. "I know meat," Paul said, his round face beaming as he eyed the large steak the waiter had served him, "and this is good. Remember how everyone said we'd starve?" Polish vodka and beer were plentiful, too. The vintages inscribed on the labels declared the beer was three days old and the vodka nine. My bill amounted to $350 at the pre-war exchange rate, $17.50 at the official quotation, and $8.50 on the black market. Having no money, I signed, like everyone else.

In Danzig I remembered that the Polish consul in Prague had told me about a human soap factory there. I had dismissed this as propaganda, refusing to believe even the Nazis were capable of this. But when I asked my guide if there was any truth about such a factory, he said there was, So we went to visit it. On our way there, I decided to have a witness. It's sometimes wise to have an unbiased observer to call upon. Walking through the docks, we came to an UNRRA ship from Boston unloading horses. I asked the captain if he wanted to see a human soap factory. He joined us.

The smell of formaldehyde hit us as soon as we entered the building. Skulls and bones were stacked on two tables. The skin was salvaged and used to make handbags. We went into the room where the vats were located. They were covered by metal lids which were hoisted open by a pulley. When the captain saw the contents of the first vat, he doubled up, vomited and rushed out of the building. I did something I had never done before. I ordered the lid lowered, set up the camera on a tripod, turned my head away, asked for the lid to be hoisted again and shot the picture. In one vat, three bodies, two of them decapitated, lay partly immersed in a blood-red liquid which reeked of formaldehyde. The arms and hands that emerged at strange angles either belonged to bodies which were invisible in the red liquid, or were simply detached from their bodies. All were naked. In a final insult to humanity, a dead monkey had been tossed in with the bodies. The second vat was a variation on the same theme.

Although I knew that *Life* couldn't publish such pictures, I took them for the record. I'm glad I took them now that I hear there are revisionists around the world who claim the holocaust was merely Jewish propaganda. My only regret that these people were not with me in Danzig. They would then have shared the nightmares which have haunted me ever since.

Back in Warsaw, Paul handed me back the dollar he had borrowed the previous evening. This had become a routine between us. The first time Paul had said, "Lend me a dollar bill for the evening." I told him, "You won't get very far with only that."

He had proved me to be mistaken. Paul's technique was to produce the bill and shout to the group he was carousing with, "I buy the drinks!" Everybody shouted, "No, no, Paul!" Paul would then put the bill back in his pocket. But as he pointed out, he needed one bill to make it convincing.

"What sort of an evening did you have?" I asked

"Some evening," Paul grinned. "We all sat in a café where a Russian soldier was doing a Cossack dance. I jumped up on the table and did a Cossack dance, too. This made the Russian cry, 'He comes from Chicago, and he does better Cossack dance than me.'" Paul pondered this for a bit, his face deceptively naive. "Also, I got our jeep's spare tyre back."

"How?" I asked.

"How do you think?" Paul replied and casually changed the subject.

Now we were ready to leave Poland, I faced the problem of paying my bills. My cables to New York had all gone through Moscow and, as I later learned, never reached their destination. I still had my watch, having refused to sell it in Vienna for ten times its value. Now that amount looked good, and my scruples were gone. But so had the opportunity.

"Bottom's fallen out of the watch business," Paul yawned. "But we still have fine assets. You're the only correspondent with transportation. Bill Mueller, a nice fellow from Chicago has dough, but no transportation." I borrowed from Bill, paid all my debts, and gave him a ride to Prague.

When we reached Krakow, our last stop before Prague, Paul said, "Borrow more dough from Bill. I know how you can repay what you owe him." With Bill's additional loan, we loaded our trailer with cases of vodka purchased at $1.50 a bottle. Back in Prague, I soon disposed of the vodka at $17.50 a bottle wholesale. I then took four cases I had kept for my friend Colonel Chrystal, who had loaned me Paul and the jeep. This was an additional benefit to Paul's survey of the Russian airfields in Poland.

"Did you have any trouble getting in and out of Poland?" he asked me.

"They didn't even ask to see my passport."

"How about taking in four of our trucks to Krakow and have them loaded up with vodka? It's pretty thirsty around there."

I turned down the offer. I was on my way to Budapest for the election.

"How much do you think we would have made out of that deal?" I asked Paul as he drove me to Pilsen.

Paul thought a moment. "About a quarter of a million bucks."

Life's book-keeping department was taken aback by my accounting. It wasn't used to having bootleg money put as an advance against expenses.

Human soap factory, Danzig, 1945

Human soap factory, Danzig, 1945

Hungary, Winter 1945

"You don't want a gold watch?" the man in the street asked. "Not even the kind that tells you the phases of the moon?" He sounded incredulous. The watches disappeared into one coat pocket and a silver cigarette case emerged from the other.

"No."

"How about a case of champagne at 25 cents a bottle?" he proposed, leaning comfortably against the jeep, ignoring the fact that I had simply asked for directions.

"No!"

"Maybe some *pâté de foie gras* ?" He watched my reaction ."No *foie gras?*" he shook his head. "Okay, okay. I have Leicas and Rolleiflexes?"

"No." My complete lack of interest left him undisturbed.

"Don't you need binoculars, or golf clubs…nearly new?" He paused. But as we drove off, he called out, *"A villa!* Don't you want to rent a villa?"

I was in Budapest. When I naively asked a waiter at the Park Club if villas were really up for rent, he offered to have me settled in the time it would take to move the present resident into the cellar.

The Park Club was tucked away behind high railings in the residential part of Pest. It dominated the wide avenue lined with villas, most of which were requisitioned. The club looked out towards the Varosliget Park where statues of the great figures in Hungary's thousand-year history could be contemplated. There was Arpad, the barbarian chieftain of the Magyar tribe, who swept in from the East; Sandor Petöfi, the patriotic poet, killed in the 1848 revolt, and Archduke Rudolf, heir to the Hapsburg Empire, who committed suicide with Baroness Maria Vetsera at Mayerling, leaving behind them an aura of mystery and decadence. Yet this exclusive club, which appeared serene from the outside, was in emotional turmoil.

The Park Club's transition from pre-war to post-war exclusivity went considerably further than transforming the tradesmen's entrance into the main gate so that you went through the dining room to reach the cloak-room. Hungary's nobility, for whose delight the club had been created, were no longer members. It had been turned over to the small group of officers on the Allied Control Commission, journalists and their friends, people the ex-members would never have associated with in the good old days.

For its titled former members, the Park Club remained the most glamorous spot in Budapest. The moment they stepped inside, as guests now, the outer world of land expropriation, ruins and Russian patrols was replaced by the gaudy luxuries organized for the entertainment of the new members. The aristocrats, now poor, recognized in their hosts at the Park Club what they themselves had once been: a tiny and privileged elite, in this case further subdivided into British personnel, paid in local currency, the Americans, paid in dollars, and the Russians, who lived off the land.

It was natural that these newly rich and newly poor, having luxury or its memory in common, got on. The Park Club became the rallying point where new members and old could, by eliminating the outer world, live in the present as though it were still the past. The outer world, however, was not kept out completely. It crept back in by way of the club staff. Forever faithful to the aristocracy, they obligingly flogged family heirlooms to the new members.

The center for this deluxe black market traffic was the bar with its soothing burgundy curtains and music by "The Two Georges", who played the latest American hits. While the ex-member sipped champagne, a waiter would tactfully whisper to a new member, "Have I got something special for *you.*" They would then meet in the toilet where deals were conducted over just about anything from golf clubs to diamond earrings.

Nothing delighted Hungarian society more than going to the Park Club for the most sought-out Friday night galas. These galas represented to them considerably more than a floor show with their supper. This was their last hope of picking up a weekend invitation to hunt, a sport which had been turned into a means of livelihood. When invited, they drove off in the army jeeps of their military hosts, directing the officers to their old estates, now owned by their ex-peasants. The party cheerfully tramped across the fields, hunting while the new owners, hat in hand and bowing deeply, greeted their former masters with a diffident *Kezét Csokólom*—kissing the hand. As hares and pheasants were plentiful, and the aristocrats were very good shots, the trailers were filled with game on the return journey. The sight of a countess delivering pheasants and hares to the restaurants was commonplace on Monday mornings.

Although these representatives of a feudal nobility, with titles as lengthy as their estates had been vast, suddenly found themselves ruined, they did not let themselves sink into despair. After watching their great, estates expropriated, they danced in the streets when the smallholders party won the first post-war election, as they had feared a communist victory. Abandoning their large country homes, they moved into apartments, single rooms, or even the basements of their requisitioned palaces in Budapest. They took along with them whatever could be salvaged from the war and its aftermath, even though it might only be a couple of pickle-jars filled with paprika, a fencing sword, or half a Louis XV armchair. They then set out to make money as best they could with a nonchalant grandeur. Several turned to drug-trafficking, which was a mistake. They got caught. All of them, however, displayed enormous resourcefulness in their day-to-day struggle for survival. This meant first converting whatever they still owned into dollars, as inflation was daily adding zeros to the local currency.

Count Istvan Karolyi, recalling that the buttons of his valet's uniform were solid gold, walked all the way to his former country estate to recover them. Others sold everything down to their most personal belongings without a tear. (In childhood, their English nannies had made them trot barefoot through nettles to form their character, and spanked them if they cried.) Now they sought regular employment and their wives did likewise, becoming barmaids and walking to work in their mink coats, at least until they, too, were sold.

Curious to learn more about this society, I hired Baroness Kati Shell—born Countess Taleki, from one of Hungary's great families. Kati knew everybody, and for a salary of $10 a week she helped me meet some of them. Kati was full of surprises. "Let me tell you my experience with a Russian soldier," she giggled, sitting down next to me at the Park Club one day. "'You don't look poor,' he said, looking at my clothes. 'But, I am poor,' I assured him. 'Why?' he asked. 'Because I'm Countess Teleki, and everybody knows that countesses are poor.' I said. 'A countess?' he repeated, as though he had no idea what that was. 'Are all countesses poor?' 'They are now,' I told him. His face brightened. 'You must be a victim of bourgeois class discrimination,' he said." She giggled some more.

"Do you know what the Foreign Minister said when he heard I earned $10 a week as your assistant?" she said when she told me my appointment at the Foreign Office was set. "'I only wish I had your job. I earn $7 a month.'"

In need of an anecdote to sum up the times, who better than Kati to provide one? She promptly came up with the one she got from the Minister of the Interior. "It's about democracy," she said. "The peasants of the small village of Hajduboszormeny had been hearing a lot about democracy. So they sent Pista to Budapest to find out what it was all about. Pista went to see Rakosi the communist leader and told him the peasants of Hajduboszormeny wanted to know what democracy meant. Rakosi took Pista to the balcony and pointed to his car below and explained: 'If I confiscate this car, that's communism. If the real owner keeps the car, that's capitalism. But if in ten years everybody owns a car, that's democracy.'

"Back in Hajduboszormeny, Pista, with no car in sight, pointed to a beggar and said, 'If I take his rags away, that's communism. If he keeps his rags, that's capitalism. If we're all in rags in ten years, that's democracy.'"

The Park Club regulars were full of such parables. "You want to find out what's our definition of morality?" Kati's friend the count said to me, "I'll tell you a story that happens to be true. Two brothers here in Budapest inherited a fortune after the First World War. One was extremely serious-minded. He invested his money wisely and never dipped into capital. His brother, on the other hand, liked to enjoy life and spent much time drinking champagne. It amused him to keep a record of his consumption, and he stored all of the empty bottles in the cellars of his different estates. When this war was over, owing to our terrible inflation, the thrifty brother only got a few meals out of his millions. As for his brother? There was a shortage of champagne bottles, so he sold all of the empty ones he had stored over the past 20 years and goes on drinking champagne."

Although this was the temper of the times, and the Hungarians had good reason to grow indignant with the Russians, interestingly enough, few blamed the Prime Minister, Bardossy, who had declared war and led them into this plight. In fact, a pall of gloom descended on Budapest the day he was executed for war crimes.

"Public opinion is for my husband," Mme Bardossy had told me when I was introduced to her. And naturally enough I'd dismissed these views as prejudiced. Yet she was right. The afternoon of his execution, the newspapers, afraid to publish his dying words, simply announced they had been lost in the volley of shots. By nightfall, the entire city knew them, as though they had heard him cry out. "God save Hungary from these bandits!" A few wild-eyed fanatics were convinced he meant the Jews. It never occurred to anyone that he might be thinking of the Americans, who had turned him over to the new regime, a fact he hardly seemed to resent. Everybody took it for granted he meant the Russians and the local communists.

These two were lumped in public disfavor. The landowning nobility hated them for expropriating their estates. The new beneficiaries, the peasants, also hated them because they lived in fear that the old land-owners would reclaim their land with the same brutality they displayed after the First World War. As for the working class, they saw no reason for jubil-ation, either. A textile worker whose salary had been increased 450 per cent now earned five cents a week.

In this terrible confusion, where no one knew what to think, two irre-concilable personalities were on a collision course. One was Matyas Rakosi, the communist leader—who would become Stalin's proconsul. He was a tough, bullet-headed man, and on meeting him I soon found out that while communists were comrades, it didn't mean they liked each other. When I mentioned that I had been with Tito during the war, Rakosi literally snarled, "Why, he spent only five years in jail. I was in for 19 years." The other was Jozsef Mindszenty, Cardinal of Hungary. The Cardinal had fired the first salvo on the eve of the November elections when he read a pastoral letter attacking the radicals. Everybody in the country knew he meant the Russians and the communists. The outspoken Cardinal later referred to the 1242 Tartar invasion in a sermon and made matters worse by insisting he didn't mean the Russians. When the communists did take over Hungary, the Cardinal sought asylum in the American Embassy and became Hun-gary's symbol of resistance against the Soviets.

During the time I was in Budapest, an evil past and evil future con-fronted each other. It was the price Hungary was paying for failing to make the needed reforms between the two wars, a failure brought about by the fear of communism, which now was going to land the country into the Soviets' grip. The Russians, believing themselves liberators, were continu-ally surprised by the fear they inspired. Intensely patriotic and insular, they did not understand the rest of the world, though they openly marveled at it in a way which must have worried their government. They took their superiority for granted, yet apart from their modern weapons, they were not an army in the modern sense of the word, but a medieval host. They did not have the niceties of a PX, or a graves' division to notify the relatives about their dead. These armies marched across Europe with the rear brought up by trudging civilians and children straggling along behind.

I met one of these children, a 12-year-old boy who had been swept along by the war from a place he could no longer recall. He wandered around Budapest dressed in a soiled and ill-fitting Red Army uniform. I invited him over for a meal when he sauntered into the restaurant where I was having lunch. I offered him a watch when he told me it was the dream of his life. To demonstrate his gratitude, he pulled out his pistol and illustrated the way different nationalities took aim. The Romanian trembled, the Frenchman closed his eyes, by the time he got to the brave Russian, the restaurant had emptied.

At the other end of the social scale was Marshal Kliment Voroshilov in his elegant uniform. Voroshilov had not only liberated Budapest, he had also taken over a defeated German general's residence and his red-headed mistress. Between these Russian extremes was an enormous variety of types whose behavior depended upon whether they were educated or not; what time of day it was, and how drunk they were.

Lee Miller came into my life when she walked into the Park Club and sat down at my table. She was one of the most beautiful women of her time— an American free spirit wrapped in the body of a Greek goddess. She was the third Allied correspondent to arrive in Budapest, and she was put up at the convent in the cell next to mine.

How I happened to be staying in a convent was due to complications Hungarian-style. On my arrival in Budapest I had been put up for one night in a villa requisitioned by the Allied Control Commission and occupied by an American officer and his staff. The next morning, my uniform pressed and my tie ironed, I was shown to my billet at the convent of the Sisters of Mercy. There I was given a cell which I would come to share with Sy Bourgin of *The Stars and Stripes*, and with Lee as our next-door neighbour.

Lee's father had been a talented amateur photographer who used her as a model. At 19, fate intervened in her life and changed it dramatically. One afternoon in 1926, Lee would have been hit by a car in mid-town

Manhattan had she not been rescued by a total stranger. He turned out to be Condé Nast, the publisher of *Vogue*. Soon she was modelling for his magazine. From then on, she would always be at the center of the action.

After modelling in New York, she went to Paris and captivated the photographer Man Ray. She starred in Jean Cocteau's *The Blood of a Poet* and Picasso painted her portrait. In 1931, Lee met the Egyptian Aziz Eloui Bey. In 1932, his wife committed suicide. In 1934 he married Lee. In 1937, she met Roland Penrose, the English surrealist painter who would later write a biography of Picasso and found the Institute of Contemporary Arts in London. In 1939, Lee left Eloui and went to live with Penrose. During World War II she devoted her considerable photographic and writing talents to bringing the conflict to *Vogue* readers. The war over, she traveled Europe covering its aftermath, eventually reaching Budapest.

Since we were not in competition, we worked together on the same stories. She was such a pro that I didn't hesitate to take her with me to an execution. She coolly shot from the prison balcony. She was good company and had an unusual approach to life. When we drew our month's ration of cigarettes: half Lucky Strikes, half almost unpalatable Hungarian smokes called "Virginia", Lee smoked the Luckies first. Her reasoning: always the best first. It was her philosophy in life.

Only a beautiful woman like Lee could have dreamt up the steel helmet she wore in combat. It had a visor with slits for the eyes, so that her face was protected when she was not taking pictures.

One evening, Lee, Bourgin, and I walked back to our convent. It was past the curfew time and the Russian patrols prowled the streets. We ran into a refugee family of five with nowhere to go. Afraid they would get nabbed by the Russians, Lee shepherded them to the convent and gave them her cell. She then picked up her sleeping bag and moved in with us. The next morning I was awakened by Sister Myrtle, who had broken her vow of silence to berate me. "First we had the Nazis." she said in anger. "Now, we have the Russians, but you, John Phillips, are the worst." I angered her even more when I asked if she had expected us to leave the refugees at the mercy of the Russians.

By noon, Bourgin, Lee, and I were asked to leave this unconventional convent that sold Palinka brandy, and *pâté de foie gras*. We moved to the Hotel Astoria, a billet for the enlisted men. There had been a fight there the night before. Two men, bringing in supplies from Vienna, had paid the girls they had picked up. "You *paid* them?" an indignant staff sergeant roared. "Want to spoil it for the rest of us?"

As a civilian, I was not subject to military regulations, which prohibited women from staying past 4am in the hotel. Since there was the fear that there might be an unexpected inspection, I was approached by the staff sergeant with a request. In the event such a surprise inspection occurred, would I put up the enlisted men's girls in my room until the all clear was sounded? This left me with a vision of chaperoning some 40 Hungarian dames in the middle of the night.

A pall of gloom descended upon Budapest after the American military personnel were notified that the War Department now allowed wives to join their husbands overseas. The night before their plane from the States landed in Budapest, members of the Park Club spent a teary last night with their Hungarian girls. The next evening, the officers showed up at The Club dutifully escorting their wives

The last pictures I took in Hungary were at the Benedictine Abbey at Pannonhalma. The Abbot showed me around, outlining the problems facing his abbey. This magnificent building housed a boys' boarding school which had produced many prime ministers and was still operating, although expropriation had whittled down the abbey's land to a mere hundred acres, making it uneconomical to keep up. This left the Abbot in a quandary as to whether he would be able to maintain the old standards.

Guiding me to the baroque refectory, he showed me the frescoes and translated the inscription, "He hunts for his master, not himself". He was very keen about the second fresco which depicted wine spilling out of a cask from which the barrel hoops had been removed. "Too much freedom is bad," he repeated several times to make sure I understood.

An elderly gentleman walked over to us briskly. "And how are my dear friends the Goulds and the Vanderbilts?" he beamed. His Highness Prince Lonyay Elemer posed for me below the painting of Emperor Franz Josef, whose daughter-in-law he married after Archduke Rudolf's suicide at Mayerling. "Hungary, my dear boy?" His Highness snorted at my naive inquiry "There's no such thing left today. All that remains is a Russian salad."

Execution of Lászlo Bárdossy, Budapest, 1946

Man selling newspapers during inflation, Budapest, 1946

Prince Lonyay Elemer, Pannonhalma, 1946

Romania, Spring 1946

Armed with the proper Russian credentials issued by the *Kommandatura* in Budapest, my driver and I, followed by Lee Miller in her sedan, set off for Bucharest. We reached the Hungarian border at dusk. There, the Russians (Hungarians having no control over their own frontier) decided to send us back to Budapest under military escort. This misguided display of authority was due less to ill will than to confusion and secrecy on their part.

The military permits issued in Budapest were of a certain color, and bore a signature recognized only by the army group in command of Budapest. As soon as we stepped into another army's area, the color of the permit changed and ours, however authentic, merely made us look suspicious. Thanks to this autonomy, compounded by an obsession with secrecy, we had no idea which Red Army unit we were dealing with, and by the looks of things, the Russian authorities in Budapest didn't either.

Unabashed at our reappearance in the city under guard, the *Kommandatura* issued new permits and sent us off again, this time via Arad, thus avoiding the frontier post from which we had just been sent back. This time our permits were signed in red pencil. Documents bearing signatures in red appeared to carry more weight.

We spent the first night at Arad, in a shabby room with three beds and a sofa which our interpreter had advised us to take, assuring us this was neither the time or place to be fussy. The next day we drove on to Oradea Mare and found rooms at The Park Hotel, which was a vast improvement on the night before. It was snowing the next morning as we drove off hoping to reach Bucharest before nightfall. Preferring. Lee's company to my own, I got into her car.

It was a long drive and the road was slippery. It was late in the afternoon and already twighlight when, suddenly, Lee's car went into a skid and shot off the road. We landed with a thud on a slight slope and ploughed through a clump of bushes that peered out of the snow. The car stopped 40 feet from the icy road.

"I'm awfully sorry, John," Lee said.

My driver, who had been following us in the jeep, came rushing up and looked relieved to see us unhurt. "I thought that sure as hell you were going to get killed."

The landscape was bleak and deserted. Fortunately, we found a milestone which read: "Sibiu 14 kilometers." Slipping about on the road, we waved down the first truck we saw crawling up the hill. It was some sort of shack on wheels, obviously Russian. When the driver peered out, I explained that we were *Amerikanski* and not Romanians. There was a roar from inside the shack as a dozen Russian soldiers came pounding out shouting, *"Yanks Goddamn sonovabich bastard okay!"*

They belonged to a Red Army unit which had met the Americans on the Elbe. They slipped a tow on Lee's car and we all pushed. The sedan began to lurch as the Russian truck threatened to skid into the ditch. But after a couple of goes we gave up and decided to carry on into Sibiu rather than attempt to dig the car out. The Russians drove off and I gave Lee a lift in the jeep. By the time we got back a few hours later with two Romanian gendarmes to guard the car, there was nothing for them to guard. The front wheels had been stolen and the sedan had been picked clean by one of the gangs of bandits that roamed the countryside at night. Lee abandoned her car and next morning we all drove off to Bucharest together.

The Athenée Palace in Bucharest had had a face-lift since I was there last. The alterations, however, were purely structural. The atmosphere hadn't changed. The bar was just as crowded, and it was still difficult to differentiate the "nice girls" from the "pros" as on first sight both looked equally flashy. The room I had reserved by phone turned out to be an apartment. From my bed I could order anything I wanted for breakfast except caviar, which was temporarily in short supply. The Romanians seemed ready to admit that the country had not suffered too much throughout the war, though they were inclined to overlook their appalling casualties suffered fighting the Russians.

The Germans had needed the Romanians' agricultural supplies, their oil, and their army too much to disrupt the country needlessly. Bucharest's worst damage had occurred after the coup organized by King Michael against the Germans as the Red Army approached the capital. The Germans, in retaliation, had bombed Bucharest indiscriminately. The

Queen Mother, who had always regarded King Carol's interior decoration of the royal palace as an abomination, admitted she had hoped it would get hit. She had been disappointed.

The main street was the mixture of American cars, slow ox-carts and barefoot pedestrians I remembered from before the war. The attractive women who once loitered there were now missing: their disappearance was unsatisfactorily put down to the weather. The shops were filled with goods. A Russian bookshop had sprung up sponsored by ALRUS, the association for strengthening relations with Soviet Russia. The books displayed included Russian authors and the works of Pearl Buck, Upton Sinclair and André Maurois. The British had rented a corner window of Capsa, still the leading restaurant, and though it looked shabbier than in my time, excellent meals were served in the private dining-rooms. I had lunch in one of these with a Romanian newspaper publisher. To keep the appointment he had requested permission to skip the "spontaneous demonstration", scheduled for the same time as our lunch to honor Anglo-American recognition of the new left-wing government. Slogans from all the political parties were in evidence: "*Traiasc Regle*" ("Long Live the King") was seen everywhere.

Conditions in Romania were far better than in Hungary. Although the large landowners who had survived the agrarian reforms decreed after the First World War did not survive the second reform which now left them ruined, the trading and business classes remained. The two great steel tycoons who had built up Romania's industries in the Thirties were still very much in evidence. Businessmen could still afford to entertain in their elegant homes. The dinner given by a shipping magnate I attended reminded me of the pre-war times. We were a dozen guests and enjoyed *truite au bleu* served with Sauternes, stuffed turkey with French burgundy, and *pâté de foie-gras* with French champagne. The conversation also had a familiar ring.

I had been seated next to an attractive young wife of one of the guests and we discussed the conditions in Hungary. When I mentioned the large supplies of silk stockings, she grew peevish. "You know very well that silk stockings are impossible to find." She gave as an example a friend of hers who had just returned from Budapest where he had managed to buy two pairs for her. "He had an awful time finding them, and the prices..." she raised her eyebrows accordingly.

I remarked that her friend obviously didn't know his way around, and was taken aback by what seemed unjustifiable annoyance until her neighbor kicked me under the table and whispered, *"You can't insult her lover like that and get away with it."*

For all this fraternization, there were international problems, such as the differences between the Russians and the Americans over American oil interests. The Russians claimed Romano-Americanó was a Romanian company, according to the books, and thereby eligible for war reparations. The Americans claimed that the total capital was American, in spite of the Romanian directorship. At the center of this row was a 240-acre refinery in Ploesti which had been bombed by the US Air Force 12 times.

I found my old friend Mr Dimonescu seated in the Athenée Palace bar, where I had left him before the war. "What's new, Mr Dimonescu?" I asked him. The last time I had seen him was on the eve of his trip to London, where he had been sent by the Romanian Foreign Office. "As you know," he said, "I was sent to London by Carol's government. When Romania joined the Axis, I resigned from the Foreign Service and enlisted in the British Army. Now, I'm back in the Foreign Service, and will soon return to my old job in London." This didn't surprise me as I recalled his having told me in 1938 that he had friends and relatives in every political party and could face with equanimity any emergency, "even democracy".

"What about King Carol?" I asked. For the first time, Mr Dimonescu displayed some emotion. He looked around, muttering, "that fascist dictator..."

"Speaking of fascists, what's happened to your old boss, the Foreign Minister?" Once again, he looked uncomfortable. "Please," he begged, "do not speak in that tone about Mr Tatarescu. He is our new Vice-Premier."

"How are you Mr Tatarescu?" I said when ushered into his office. "You may recall I visited your country before the war, in the days of King Carol."

"That fascist dictator," Tatarescu snapped. Then in sonorous French he made a speech for my benefit in which he portrayed himself as a fearless defender of democracy.

"That's what you told me the last time we met," I told him.

Tatarescu beamed. "As you can see, I haven't changed. I'm still on the barricades fighting for democracy."

"That crook Tatarescu," a Romanian communist growled. "Of all the people walking on thin ice…on thin ice! What am I saying? He's the first person since Christ to walk on water."

"Why did you communists pick him as Vice-Premier then?"

"We needed someone so deeply compromised he would do whatever we wanted. Tatarescu had the choice between being Vice-Premier or facing the firing squad."

I was interested in finding out how the left felt about being in power. I found a Romanian communist where I least expected to meet him: we were guests at the same social lunch. There, he was freely conversing with a friend who by leftist standards was a reactionary. Their only common ground was that they had worked together in the coup which liberated Bucharest from the Germans and brought Romania over to the Allies. This communist did not believe in the effectiveness of spreading stupid propaganda. He told me a friend of his had been sounding off in the presence of an American about how the left had staged a demonstration on the Royal Palace Square involving 600,000 people. The American took the measurements of the square, allowed a minimum amount of space per person, and proved it was a mathematical impossibility to fit more than 80,000 demonstrators in it. Propaganda, the communist had decided, didn't work with the Americans. "It only makes them them suspicious and inclined to believe the situation was worse than it is in reality."

I asked him if he felt they had made mistakes. "The fundamental mistake," he said, "was made by the Russians." They had assumed that most of Europe had emerged from this war with a wish for social changes. The shocking record of excesses committed by the right had been sufficient grounds for this assumption. But the unexpected had happened. Central Europe was desperately tired and bewildered. They were too worn out to have energy and interest in reforms. Basic principles, such as eating and sleeping, appealed to them. The Romanian left had no wish to assume power so soon. They wanted the rightists to take office and reap the harvest of discontent they had sewn, and which was bound to follow a defeat. "Within a year and a half," the communist said, "we would have rolled into power on a tidal wave of public opinion." The Russians, however, had preferred to deal with a leftist coalition. "We took office and inherited the blame for everything that went wrong, most of which we had no control over."

The Russians had made other mistakes. They had stupidly antagonised King Michael, who had friends among the communist leaders, and was inclined to be anti-militaristic. They had alienated the most popular man in the country. It was the same with the leaders of the peasant party.

The Romanian communists had made mistakes, too. "The reparations we had to pay Russia were a heavy drain on the country. We tried to minimize them instead of simply explaining we had to pay them for the damage our armies committed in Russia. But once the reparation figures were set, it was the duty of the communist party to see that more was not shipped out of the country. We should have opposed individual Russian commanders who came here to send back 200 per cent of what they were supposed to. The People's Party should have protected these national interests.

"I will grant you," he said, "that many of our politicians are not brilliant. But they are no worse, in fact they are much better than the men on the right. We who tried to give dignity to the left only succeeded in giving it to the right."

I drove out to Sinaia, the royal family's summer residence, to see King Michael, whom I had photographed in 1938. Michael lived in seclusion there with his mother since he had been savaged by Andrei Vishinsky, the notorious Russian prosecutor. Until then, as my communist friend had explained, relations between the King and the Romanian communists were tolerable since they had participated together in the coup against Marshal Antonescu, the Nazi puppet. Michael had taken the lead by summoning him to the royal palace. There he had locked up the spluttering Marshal in the vault where King Carol once kept his stamp collection. But whatever hopes these two Romanian sides might have harbored about the future were shattered by Stalin's pronouncement that the war of classes would resume. This meant the wartime alliance was over.

The palace at Sinaia would not have been out of place in Disneyland. The main building was now a museum, where I waited for Michael and his mother, Queen Helen. The Queen Mother was slim, elegant, and full of charm. Michael was still very youthful in manner, despite his wartime experiences. He showed me around the museum, bristling with suits of armor and weapons his forbears had used centuries ago. He then demonstrated what he called "jeeping"—driving down a wide stairway in a jeep.

In the modern house he and his mother lived in, Michael kept a large room for his gadgets. He owned five Leica cameras with every type of lens. He expressed profound contempt for the Rolleiflexes his mother and I used. He photographed everything from landscape to tabletops. His results were of professional quality. He also kept a movie projector. Both mother and son were movie buffs. During the war, they had only one feature film: a print of *Juarez* featuring Paul Muni. Although the pair screened the picture 13 times, "It wasn't at all a cheerful film," the Queen Mother said. "It was about the execution of Maximilian, the Austrian Emperor of Mexico."

It was in Romania that officialdom finally caught up with me. "At last," the American colonel at the Allied Control Commission exclaimed. "Vienna issued you a jeep and driver for two weeks, and that was 137 days ago. Vienna wants its jeep and driver back at once."

My task now was to make sure Lee Miller got back safely to London. While I was still in Budapest, I'd got a cable from Dave Scherman, another *Life* photographer and Lee's close friend. He had asked me to tell Lee she should get back to London as she was in danger of losing Roland Penrose's affection.

I'd shown Lee the cable but got nowhere. She was determined to drive on to Bucharest, which she had visited with Penrose in 1938. Although she knew full well that *Vogue* was no longer interested in anything connected with the war, she refused to regard Budapest as the end of the line for her career as a war correspondent. There was nothing I could do. She had Scherman's sedan and no one could prevent her from driving to Romania.

After the car wreck outside Bucharest, however, the situation was rather different. Lee couldn't carry on further to Bulgaria. She had no transportation. And there was no chance I could give her a lift, because I was due back in Vienna. The next morning there was a note from Lee. She had left for London.

I met up with her again in 1949. I was in London seeking treatment for amoebic dysentery (a souvenir from the 1948 Israeli-Arab War) at the Hospital for Tropical Diseases. Lee had a better idea. She recommended Doctor Goldman, a German refugee who had spent World War II in West Africa curing the same disease. Lee was right. Doctor Goldman cured me. He was also the man who saved Elizabeth Taylor's life by performing a tracheotomy while she was filming *Cleopatra* in London. He went on to become the Queen's physician. Lee always knew the right people.

By this time Lee was married to Roland Penrose (her Moslem husband having graciously helped dissolve their Islamic marriage by repeating "I divorce you" three times on a London street). I only followed her career sketchily after that. She had a son, who was called Anthony. Roland Penrose was knighted in 1966. And Lady Lee Penrose died on July 27 1977. Tony learned about his mother's career as a war correspondent when he came upon her neatly filed negatives after her death. His books, his television film about Lee's many lives, and the exhibitions he organised of her work, finally got Lee Miller the recognition as a photographer she deserved.

I left the jeep in Vienna, and hitched a ride to Rome in a staff car. Traveling with me was Sy Freidin of the *New York Herald*. On the second day, we crossed into Italy and stopped in Verona for lunch. "Mind if I take along a girlfriend I have here?" an MP driver asked. "Why, not at all," I said as I browsed over the menu.

This was my first chance in eight months to pick what I wanted to eat. In Budapest, we had been gorged with *foie gras*, and in Bucharest with caviar. There had been an exuberant folly in the food of those lands. You could only get steak in Poland, veal in Hungary, and pork in Romania. You could swim in mayonnaise, but you could not get a plate of pasta. Here was a sane and varied menu where I had a choice of less extravagant cooking.

"God, I'm glad to be back in a normal country," I said before realizing that I was in Italy, a country I had last seen through the clouds of war. How rapidly things could change, and for the better, too.

The driver returned with his young *signorina* and we drove off. Night had fallen. It was snowing when we reached the Futa Pass. Trucks blocked the road and for the last time, I used the influence of my uniform to get our staff car through. "Should be in Florence soon," the driver said as we skidded along the road. He held the wheel in one hand, and clutched his girl with the other. Sy took one look at the precipice below. Without a word, he took a large swig of brandy and passed me the bottle.

Several hours later, the bottle of brandy was almost empty when the driver repeated, "ought to be in Florence by now." Sy and I exchanged glances and refused to look at the precipice again.

Shortly before 1am, our driver announced, "We must have missed Florence." The brandy was gone and so was my lunchtime euphoria. Finally we came to a town encircled by red-brick walls. The fresh snow and the flickering light from the street lamps gave it an eerie appearance. We drove along deserted streets until we came upon an apparition: a large pig's head on a human body was leisurely making its way up the street. We looked at one another. The driver let go of his girl and pulled out his .45 when, a few minutes later, we came upon a horse's head. "The next one I see I'm gonna blast," our driver announced.

We drove on until there on a curb stood another horse's head. We slowed up so that I could ask where we were. I watched the horse's jowls slowly puff up before a sound came out. Finally a sad voice said, "You're in Lucca and it's the last night of carnival!"

Monarchists shortly before the abdication of King Umberto II, Rome, 1946

The Italian Election, Summer 1946

On Sunday, June 2, 1946, Italy voted in the first free elections since Mussolini seized power in 1922. Goodwill prevailed. In a holiday mood, over 80 per cent of the electorate went to the polls. Considering the turmoil Mussolini had put Italy through while defiantly proclaiming "*me ne freggo*" ("I don't give a damn"), there was a remarkable lack of rancor.

It was barely 14 months since Mussolini had been summarily shot before being strung up by his heels at a Milan gas station. The new Italy was now very much alive.

In Rome, out of the chaos, anguish, humiliation, and ignominy of defeat, the defiant voice of the film-maker Roberto Rossellini was heard. With no money, without an official permit to shoot his picture in the streets of recently liberated Rome, using outdated film stock, and a cast with no acting experience except two music hall performers (Anna Magnani and Aldo Fabrizi), Rossellini made *Cita Aperta*.

"Rome,Open City" was the ironic title of the film about life during the German occupation. With a neo-realist style that made no concessions to theatrical niceties, *Cita Aperta* was much more than a ferocious indictment of Nazi warfare. It revolutionized film-making.

This picture was not an accidental masterpiece, but the forerunner of a number of great pictures made by Italian directors eager to express themselves now that they were freed from fascism. Although these films have been called the most important post-war phenomenon in film making, they had limited success in Italy when they were made. Italian movie-goers preferred to pay their 200 *lire* to enjoy the gorgeous swimmer Esther Williams splashing around in living color, than to sit through the black-and-white existence they knew all too well. Abroad, however, the success of these films, which had the courage of self-criticism, helped to restore the prestige Mussolini had destroyed. This artistic pessimism, along with the country's industrial optimism, would achieve the Italian miracle.

On election morning the mood of the city was reflected by its graffiti. "Death to the king of thieves!"read one slogan—leading a high-spirited Roman to ask in another, "Which one?" Others were humorous or cheerfully scatological, such as the whitewashed sign on a men's public urinal: "The monarchy votes here."

Despite the superficially easy-going attitude, however, the election was extremely dramatic, due to the referendum. Would Italians reject the monarchy, the only form of government the country had known since its unification in 1861? Or, would they vote the Republic in?

With time on my hands, I visited the 86-year-old Vittorio Emmanuele Orlando, who had been Italy's prime minister during World War I. He had been one of "the big four" at the Paris Peace Conference at Versailles in 1919, along with the US President Woodrow Wilson and Prime Ministers Clemenceau of France and Lloyd George for the British. Only days before the signing of the Peace Treaty, Orlando was out of office—his punishment for having failed to secure all the enemy territory promised to Italy for reneging on her alliance with Germany and Austria-Hungary to join the Allies.

Now, a year after the end of the Second World War, the monarchy was defeated, and a royal crisis broke out. For the clergy, the monarchists, most of the aristocracy and the upper classes, a republican victory only meant one thing: communism. King Umberto refused to abdicate and remained secluded in the Palazzo del Quirinale. Meanwhile Prime Minister de Gasperi's government met several times daily, seeking ways to entice Umberto to leave the country.

On June 10, in the midst of the turmoil, I went to the Quirinale to photograph the four royal children at play in the palace gardens. There I found a group of mutilated war orphans who were either blind or missing a limb or two. They had been brought to play with the royal children, I was told. They hung back while the royal children attempted to make some contact with them. The pictures I got of the royal children and the orphans simply highlighted the Italian catastrophe.

The next morning at 10:30, I returned to the Quirinale to photograph the Queen. By the time I got there, she had already left with the royal children for exile in Switzerland, while Umberto still refused to abdicate.

I went over to the Viminale where the cabinet met. They were gathered in small groups, irrespective of political affiliation, chatting and laughing as they waited for de Gasperi, who was with the King, while a major domo passed round glasses of mineral water. No one paid any attention to me as I wandered around taking pictures.

De Gasperi showed up. The king still would not abdicate. The cabinet went into session as I shot one last picture. Meanwhile, the Romans had taken to the streets. Among them was a couple holding portraits of King Umberto II and Queen Marie José. A huge mob estimated at 200,000 now filled the Piazza del Popolo. Their friendly disposition was illustrated by a banner which read: "Monarchists of good faith join us to rebuild Italy."

Finally, on June 28, Umberto bowed to the inevitable and left for exile. I watched the faithful waiting to bid goodbye to their sovereign. Besides the senior naval officers, the only people there were members of the working class. Those who had benefitted most from the regime had not bothered to show up.

Much later, in 1954, Umberto and I met in Paris. My purpose was to convince him to allow the publication of his late father's diaries. I had been told about them by Filippo Ungaro, a Roman lawyer who had been close to the royal family. Ungaro felt these diaries were of such historical interest they ought to be published. Victor Emmanuel III had kept a caustic chronicle of the fascist era. I approached the Milanese publishing house Mondadori, which authorized me to offer the ex-king up to $100,000 for the book rights ($1 million today).

Umberto agreed that his father's diaries were of extraordinary historical importance, but said he could not allow them to be published. His father had been brutally candid about a number of people still alive. Umberto did not want to antagonize them. He also refused to have the diaries published in an edited form. Graciously, he turned down my offer.

I respected Umberto's decision all the more as I knew that $100,000 would have come in extremely handy. All his life, Umberto had been the dutiful son of a selfish monarch. In a last display of meanness towards his heir, Victor Emmanuel had abdicated only days before the referendum, leaving Umberto to bear the brunt of the monarchy's failures without ever having been given any responsibility over its policies. Had Umberto flown to North Africa when the Allies landed, he could have established an Italian government-in-exile. The creation of such a government justified whatever the risks: Italy would have attended the peace as an ally, not a defeated enemy. And who knows? Umberto might even have saved his crown.

Proclamation of the Republic, Rome, 1946

PEN's World Congress, Zurich 1947

The World Congress of PEN—poets, essayists, novelists—took place in early June, 1947. For the first time since the outbreak of war, this international group of distinguished authors were brought together in Zurich. Their purpose was "to promote friendship and intellectual co-operation between the men of letters in all countries…" The sight of Zurich's picture-postcard countryside and romantic lake left the 1,800 middle-aged writers, battered by war and restrictions, in a state of euphoria.

While their Swiss hosts endeavored to point out the hardships of neutrality, their delighted guests enjoyed its benefits with unbridled pleasure. These generally jaded *literati* displayed youthful enthusiasm as they trooped off on sight-seeing tours, picnics at country inns, and a cruise up the lake aboard a paddle-steamer as white as the swans they sailed past.

And then there was the food: awesome in its quantity, quality, and variety. For the delegates, who had subsisted on ration cards for the past eight years, the extravaganza of food was as breathtaking as fireworks in the night. With childish delight, Erich Weinert, the elderly German novelist, gazed upon the enticing stacks of ham sandwiches before helping himself to one. Then, with a guilty look, he took a second. Even Ignazio Silone brushed aside his anxieties about the fate of mankind to join his wife on the see-saw.

Silone was born Secondo Tranquilli in Abruzzi in 1900. Along with his comrades Antonio Gramsci and Palmiro Togliatti, he founded the Italian Communist Party in 1921. Sent to Moscow to direct the Cominform's clandestine activities against the fascists, he became greatly disturbed by what he found in Russia. He reported to Togliatti: "What they're doing here in Moscow is what we're fighting in Rome."

In 1930 Silone was expelled from the communist party. He then led an exile's life in Switzerland, where he wrote his masterpieces, *Fontamara* and *Bread and Wine*. (When I got to Rome for the Liberation in 1944, I found that Silone was totally unknown to the Italian public.)

In his opening address to the members of PEN, Silone said, "Nihilism, which was considered typical for national socialism, has not vanished after the military defeat. You find it, more or less violent, more or less dangerous, in all countries. I do not know a single party, a single church or institution which is not contaminated by this leprosy…Often we are summoned by one party to protest against injustices suffered by its fighters, but the same party remains silent and indifferent when the same injustice is done in countries of its friends…The crisis of our time cannot be fully understood unless we see the general character…It is not the way of thinking of the intellectuals which is in question, but their way of living and feeling. Salvation does not lie in theories. Decadence has affected men who are exponents of the most different theories, and there are decent men who stand for the most opposite conceptions on society and state. Salvation lies exclusively in the honest, straight and durable loyalty towards the tragic reality on which the human existence is based."

His speech was regarded as the keystone of this memorable congress. What might have been a brutal confrontation simply turned out to be a passionate debate: should German writers be allowed to reorganize their own national chapter of PEN?

The French Resistance writer, Vercors, expressed his reservations but in lyrical terms. "This is the most cruel question that can be put to a French poet," Vercors said. "Cruel, because it is hard to adopt an attitude opposed to the ideals for which we fought…" He then proposed that there be permanent control over the German PEN.

Thomas Mann, who had just arrived from the United States, where he had become an American citizen, weighed-in in favor of the anti-Nazi authors with the authority of Germany's greatest living writer.

This was followed by a debate over the Swiss radio. Five German-speaking authors argued whether poets and artists should take part in politics. The debaters were three Germans, Erich Kästner, Erich Weinert, and Johannes R. Becher, the Austrian Franz Theodor Csokor, and Silone, who had learned German during his years in Switzerland.

Kästner, Becker and Csokor believed the duty of every intellectual and writer was to be "political", and to exert their influence in that field. Kästner had lived in Germany throughout the entire Nazi period without making one concession to the regime. "Whether writers admit it or not," Kästner said, "there does not exist such a thing as a non-political author."

Weinert, for his part, claimed the right of every writer to be an artist and nothing else.

Silone, the Italian skeptic *par excellence,* accepted both possibilites. "A chicken doesn't bark," he said, "and you don't expect silk worms to spin an atom bomb."

Thomas Mann did not participate in the debate. His address was the most anticipated as Mann had an affinity with Zurich: the city had granted him asylum when he left German in 1933 and he had lived there until he left for the States in 1936.

The auditorium was overflowing when he made his appearance to an ovation. The president of the Swiss Confederation and Prince Wilhelm of Sweden, the congress's guest of honor, were among the audience eager to hear the great German writer's analysis as to how in 12 years Hitler had managed to reduce a once civilized nation to a barbaric state.

Mann's lecture was about Nietzsche, who he called, "a saint of immorality". It was academic and difficult to follow, even for anyone fluent in German. As my knowledge was schoolboy vintage, I relied on Henry Tanner, *Time*'s Swiss correspondent, to fill me in.

All Mann had to say about the recent past was that the German middle class had mistaken the Nazi movement for Nietzsche's dream of barbarism to renew civilization, which had been the worst of misunderstandings. The audience left disappointed. A Swiss journalist was so annoyed he complained to me that Mann, who had benefited from Swiss hospitality, had demanded 5,000 Swiss francs to deliver a lecture at Zurich University, and then was content to read from his books. "Typical of Mann," he concluded.

On June 6, the last day of the congress, I got a call from *Life*, instructing me to contact Mann and see if he would visit Germany and gather material for a 5,000-word article. I was authorized to offer him $20,000 for the American magazine rights. June 6 was also Thomas Mann's 72nd birthday. The American Consul General planned a cocktail party in his honor. As I made my way to the party, I felt confident that Thomas Mann would accept *Life*'s offer, which as far as I could see would not only meet his financial expectations, but would also allow him to give the most plausible explanation for the rise of Nazism.

The American Consul, aware of the purpose of my visit, saw to it that Mann and I were seated in a quiet corner. With considerable enthusiasm, I outlined *Life*'s proposal. Impassive, smoking his cigar, Mann listened to me. When I was through, he said, "*Ja, ja,* when I go to Basel I'll have a look at

Germany." Feeling I hadn't made my case well enough, I explained that what *Life* expected was more than general reflection gathered from a casual glance. What we wanted was an in-depth analysis of the situation. Failing once again, I regretfully told Thomas Mann that what he proposed was not good enough, and left.

There was something ludicrous about a 32-year-old photographer telling Germany's Nobel laureate that what he proposed to write wouldn't do. The only explanation I could give myself for my failure was that Mann might be reluctant to visit Germany and discover on the spot what had made Germans respond to Hitler the way they did. My failure, and his reluctance, has always bothered me. But during the time I was struggling to write this chapter, I had dinner with a distinguished German surgeon and, as the subject was uppermost in my mind, I mentioned to him how I had turned Thomas Mann down.

"You didn't turn him down," the surgeon said. "He simply didn't want to write that article and his response was his way of getting out of it without appearing to refuse."

"But why?" I asked.

"Mann," the surgeon went on to say, "came from a class which was passive during Hitler's rise to power, and while he himself was never openly pro-Nazi, and even sought asylum in Switzerland, he never was actively anti-Nazi. He apparently didn't want to write about the causes and consequences. Mann is one of Germany's literary giants, but he remains a small man."

Thomas Mann, Zurich, 1947

Rome, December 2, 1947

December 2, 1947, was one of those bleak autumn days you occasionally get in Rome. A threatening overcast sky had turned the ochre city to a dull gray. The light was flat and lifeless; the kind of day a photographer dreads. Driving towards the Colosseum, I came upon a large group of people. This size of crowd in the street during Rome's siesta hours was unusual enough for me to stop and take a look.

"It can't be a political rally," I thought to myself. It was too quiet and orderly. The demonstrations held outside of the Chamber of Deputies were noisy and disruptive and ringed by units of the *celere*—the anti-riot squads. Here, there wasn't a cop in sight.

I watched the crowd as it flowed from side streets to merge into a single column which headed towards the Colosseum. No onlookers, so it couldn't be a parade. It was Monday, and in Italy parades, like roast chicken, were a Sunday treat. On the off-chance something of interest might develop, I slung a camera over my shoulder and joined the marchers, who turned out to be Jewish groups from right across Italy.

We set off towards the Forum, and made straight for the Arch of Titus which glorified the destruction of the Temple in Jerusalem and the Diaspora—a monument no Jew would normally be seen near. But today was different. Two thousand years later, the United Nations General Assembly had just resurrected a Jewish state,.

"What a triumph for faith," I thought, as the procession trod cobble-stones dating back to the Romans. This was the end of a march across time which linked the biblical era to the atom age, a moment for which Jews had waited for 20 tormented centuries.

Aware of being an intruder, I pushed my way through this silent crowd in search of a look, a gesture, which would sum up the moment. All that I could see was the blurry uniformity of an anonymous gathering. The emotions of these people ran too deep for my alien eyes.

A rabbi and three other speakers stood beneath the arch. The crowd gathered around them to listen. In Italian, Hebrew, and Yiddish, the speakers recalled the Jewish people's long history. It seemed more an epitaph to a spent holocaust than the celebration over the birth of a nation.

A voice called out, "Titus, you didn't destroy the Jewish state. You Romans conquered the world, but one nation never bowed to your rule—the Jews! Three times we revolted. Each time, you defeated us. But we still went on. Today we place our flag on your triumphant arch, to show that we are victorious!" Who put up the flag? A Jew like me! The offspring of some captive you brought to Rome in slavery!"

In the back of everyone's mind was the knowledge that the Arabs had announced their intention of driving the Jews into the sea. Scattered fighting had already broken out. Barricades had been set up at the Jaffa Gate to besiege the Jewish Quarter in Jerusalem. Two buses had been ambushed in an orange grove near Tel Aviv. The passengers were all killed. Arab convicts in Acre jail, responding to the Grand Mufti's florid battle cry—"When the sword speaks, all else must remain silent"—had set upon their Jewish cell mates, starting a prison riot. It was clear that the Israeli state, brought back to life in Flushing Meadow, New York, must seek its survival on the battlefields of Palestine. Once more, the Jews would be on the march. This time it would be along rocky roads beneath a glaring sun where the cactus that had given its name to Jews born in Palestine—the sabra—grows. I knew these people were tough, but I wondered whether 600,000 of them could hold 30,million Arabs at bay.

With dusk, the ceremony at the arch came to an end. Before we went our separate ways, I had a last look at a bas relief on the arch which showed Roman legionnaires making off with the menorah. I had no idea that I would soon be photographing similar scenes.

Farouk escorted through empty streets, Cairo, 1947

Arabian
Nightmares

Abdullah's entrance into the Old City of Jerusalem, 1948

His Eminence Sheik Abdel Galik Eissa, a dean of theology at the
Moslem University of El Azhar, Cairo, 1947

Egypt

I was back in the Middle East to photograph the Arab-Israeli War, which was scheduled for May 15 when the British mandate for Palestine elapsed. On that day the Arabs, refusing to recognize the United Nations Partition, intended to "drive the Jews into the sea".

Cairo had changed a great deal since I was there in 1943. The British had left Egypt, which now made it a genuinely independent Arab kingdom. The withdrawal had not been the triumph Farouk had expected, however. With their army no longer available to keep him on the throne, Farouk found himself trapped.

A constitutional monarchy could never perform properly within the leftovers of colonial Egypt. Besides, there was no democratic leadership Farouk could depend upon. The pashas were too absorbed in protecting their own privileges, and were too few to offer any help. The middle class was non-existent; the army ineffectual. All that remained was the great majority, the ragged and ignorant *fellaheen*. And Farouk was not prepared to depend upon them, as he feared the consequences.

I had occasion to observe the changes that had come over Farouk's Egypt. One Friday morning at noon, I photographed him as he drove to the El Refai mosque to pray on his father's tomb. His escort was beefed up by six red army jeeps which sped along the deserted thoroughfares. There were no onlookers, only lined-up policemen. The sullen crowd was now kept out of Farouk's sight. It was a far cry from our tumultuous journey to lower Egypt in 1943.

I also got a chance for a closer look at Farouk the evening I was invited to a dinner on the roof-garden of the Semiramis Hotel. Suddenly, above the ripple of chit-chat, there boomed a raucous, mirthless laugh unmistakable to anyone who had once heard it. *"He's here tonight,"* my hostess whispered. Farouk was there all right, in a field marshal's uniform. The dark glasses he wore because of his impaired eyesight made him look sinister. To say that Farouk had aged in the last four years was an understatement. At 28, decay had set in. My hostess glanced around, adding, "He's got spies everywhere," before letting me in on Cairo's latest gossip.

"As you know," she said, "*Le tout Cairo* always attends the annual Red Crescent Charity Ball. This year, His Majesty arrived alone and unannounced. Without a word, he sat at a small table, with his portable radio turned on full blast. After peering at us, he ordered the air-conditioners, which are usually only used in summer, turned on. You can imagine how we felt, all of us in sleeveless, low-cut dresses without our furs, especially as His Majesty just sat there laughing."

May 15 was three months away. In the meantime I tried to figure out the Islamic mind. Although I had grown up among Arabs I was still baffled by the way time appeared to mean nothing to them—and yet time invariably worked out in their favour.

Egypt was the right place for such an inquiry. For a thousand years, Cairo has been the center of Islamic theology. El Azhar was the oldest university in the world. Any Islamic decision made at El Azhar carries the same weight for Moslems as a Papal decree does for Catholics. I found out that a good Moslem, irrespective of his nationality, reads the Koran in Arabic, since any translation is considered sacreligious. This common language has created an indestructable bond among Moslems that dates back to the years Allah made his revelations to Mohamed around 652 AD. The Koran contains everything a Moslem needs to know. To enroll at El Azhar, foreigners must be proficient in all its teachings. Egyptians, for their part, must know the 490 pages by heart when they enter the classes at eleven. No wonder Moslems are inflexible in their convictions.

Since "infidels" are not allowed to visit El Azhar without royal approval, I asked Atif Bey, Farouk's friendly aide, if Farouk would grant me such a permission. A few days later, a jubilant Atif announced, "HM allows you to take pictures at El Azhar. It will be the first time," he assured me.

I photographed classes in the Koran at a mosque that goes back to the earliest period of the university. There, in the midst of colonnades rising up to oval archways, a group of students sat cross-legged on carpets as they listened to the sheik who looked down upon them from his bench.

The library, with its 100,000 manuscripts relevant to Islamic matters, was next to the mosque, as were a number of offices built to the proportions of another age. There I came across Sheik Ahmed Abdullah El Eugaiby—the Wakil El Rowak—chief of the Moorish section. When he learned I was born in the land of the Moors, the Wakil called me "brother",

Students at the University of El Azhar, Cairo, 1947

and had me escorted around in the hope of getting me involved in the internal politics of the university: he imagined I could help his cause by influencing Farouk who, as monarch, would select the next rector.

At the Faculty of Theology, I listened to a student read his thesis which earned him the title of Doctor and made him eligible for a professorship at El Azhar. I was briefed about the University's three faculties: Arab literature, Moslem law, and theology, and introduced to the Dean of each one. I was also taken to youth hostels for foreign students who came from as far away as China.

Finally, I was ushered into the office of the acting rector where, after he had ordered coffee, I photographed him as he elegantly held the saucer with three fingers of his left hand while he slowly enjoyed the Turkish brew in its small cup. I would never have suspected that this kindly old gentleman had decreed a *jihad*, a Holy War against the Israelis, the equivalent of Anathema for a Catholic.

A few days later, I found out how potent his words could be when I photographed the Friday noon-time prayers along one of Cairo's main streets. Because the faithful overflowed the mosque, a great number of them prayed in the streets. They lined up, row upon row, removed their shoes, produced newspapers or small mats to pray on, then knelt. I was taking their picture and off-guard when I was grabbed from behind and became the object of a tug-of-war. Fortunately, this occurred near a police booth where an anti-riot unit was stationed. They rushed out carrying their rattan shields and brandishing their long bamboo clubs. I was lucky to escape.

The announcement spread across Cairo. "The Mufti's back! The Mufti's in Cairo!" The years Hadj Amin el Husseini had spent in Berlin collaborating with the Nazis during the war had simply increased his prestige in the Moslem world. He was now by far the most important figure in Arab politics and the obvious leader for the future Palestinian State.

The Mufti, however, could not enter Palestine while the British were still there. He was wanted as a war criminal. Unable to campaign personally and arouse the masses with his rhetoric, he relied upon a relative, Abd el Kader el Husseini, who commanded the Mufti's forces.

On hearing the Mufti was in town, I sought him out. Hadj Amin was a wily fellow and had managed to escape from Berlin on May 7 the very day the Nazis gave up the war. After landing in neutral Switzerland, he re-appeared in France, confident he would never be brought to trial for his war crimes. He was not mistaken. De Gaulle's provisional government, mindful of the Mufti's popularity among the North African Moslems under French rule, put him up in a luxurious villa near Paris where he ostensibly waited for the British to demand his extradition. The British, however, con-sidering the consequences among the Arabs in Palestine if they hanged him, did nothing to disturb his French sojourn. Thus the Mufti vanished once again, to resurface in Egypt.

As a guest of King Farouk, he was provided a with a large villa in the outskirts of Cairo. The entire neighborhood was patrolled by Egyptian troops. Suspicious about his safety, the Mufti relied upon his six burly Palestinian bodyguards who never left his side.

After being checked out by the Egyptians and scrutinized by the Palestinians I was ushered into the Mufti's presence. He wore a flowing black robe with a gold brocade border and shiny black patent-leather shoes. His distinctive *tarboosh*, shaped like a flower pot, was firmly planted on his head. He had ginger hair and white bristles flecked his neatly-trimmed goatee. Unlike most Arabs, the Mufti did not gesture. He had an expressive face and a warm, disarming smile which made him look mis-chievous until you noticed that his eyes were a cold cobalt blue.

He was surrounded by an entourage of friends. Setting up my camera, I noticed that one of them stared at me and grew purple in the face. Coming over, he exploded, "You are the one who photographed Jewish Palestine in 1943!" Forgetting where I was, and flattered for a moment, I readily agreed that, yes indeed, I was the one. "And you have the audacity to take pictures of our Mufti when you photographed Ben Gurion!"

The Mufti, however, gave me a benevolent smile, and although he spoke perfect French, told me via an interpreter that I could take his picture, but should not write anything harmful to the Arab cause. When I was about to leave, he asked me in perfect French, "Do you speak Arabic?"

"I did when I was a small child," I told him. He nodded approval, and appeared satisfied that I was born "in the land of the Moors". The Mufti must have found that out from the Wakil El Rowak.

Fawzi with his staff, outside Damascus, 1948

Fawzi, The Lion of Damascus

A howl came out of Damascus: "The time for deeds has come..!" The voice in this case belonged to Fawzi el Kawukji, the field commander of a National Army of Liberation now being raised in Syria. For the Grand Mufti of Jerusalem, who had plotted and committed murders and treason for the past quarter of a century in the hopes of becoming the President of an independent Palestine, this was bad news. The Mufti had no political base from which he could raise an army and compete with Syria. He was now reduced to depending upon Farouk and the Egyptian army. For the first time, with an independent Palestine almost within his grasp, the Mufti was no longer the most effective force.

His suspicions regarding the National Liberation Army in Syria were well founded. Syria saw in the forthcoming struggle for Palestine the opportunity to recreate the greater Syria of the Ottoman era, which had covered what was now Lebanon, Palestine and Transjordan. Such a prospect depended upon the military achievements of the National Liberation Army and its field commander Fawzi el Kawukji, the man of the hour I set out to meet in Damascus.

Although the war was still three months away, with no invasion of Palestine by a foreign power possible before that time, I found Damascus on a war footing. Recruits in their black-and-white checkered *kouffiehs* were very much in evidence in the crowded streets. Recruiting posters were displayed all over town. Damascus was now the headquarters of "the drive against Zionism".

Tracking down Fawzi in Damascus was not easy. Everybody knew he was in town, but no one would say where. "The British still have a £10,000 bounty on his head," I was reminded. All I knew about the man affectionately known as "the Lion of Damascus" was that he would periodically make unexpected appearances on the balcony of the Orient Palace Hotel and roar that the time for deeds had come.

Getting nowhere in my search, I visited the Syrian Minister of Defense with a request to be accredited to the National Liberation Army. Although he had studied engineering in Boston, the minister loathed Americans. It hadn't prevented him from operating the Chevrolet dealership in Syria with a Jewish partner who vanished after the announcement of Partition, but he was non-committal about the possibility of either meeting Fawzi or being accredited to the National Liberation Army for its march into Palestine. "Just wait and see," he advised. (His was arrested when he attempted to leave Syria on May 15 with the contributions collected for the war chest.)

I was pondering this uncertainty at the bar of the Orient Palace Hotel when Mr Kaizi entered my life. Mr Kaizi belonged to the *Sureté*, a relic of the French administration in Syria. Each correspondent in Damascus had a plain-clothes man assigned to him. Mr Kaizi was mine.

When he first found me at the Orient Palace bar, he announced that he, too, was a journalist. From then on, he dogged my steps. There was a certain ceremony between the two of us: Mr Kaizi allowed me to pay for all his meals and was happiest when I took him to the Oasis, the smartest restaurant in town. It had three primus stoves in the kitchen and a waiter who had once lasted two weeks at the Café du Dôme in Paris. He insisted, however, in producing his police card at the movies so that I would not have to pay for his admission. As Mr Kaizi's duty was to report on me, I obligingly let myself be pumped about my ambition to meet Fawzi.

In appreciation of his meals, Mr Kaizi introduced me to Captain Mahmoud Rifai, Fawzi's executive officer. Mahmoud Rifai expressed himself in impeccable French and promised to lead me to Fawzi!

The Lion of Damascus's den was on the ground floor of a bungalow. Ducking under his child's diapers strung out on a clothesline, I eventually met him face to face. "I am a man of action," he roared, "and the time for deeds is near."

"How near?" I asked.

"Just wait and see," he said.

Fawzi's mouth was full of gold teeth, which he liked to display while he ground his molars and scowled. He greatly enjoyed talking German out of admiration for that country's military soul, and his third wife, Tarfa, was German. "She's a Moslem German, of course," I was told, to allay any suspicion the peope's hero had married an Aryan. "Saladin freed Jerusalem from the Crusaders and Fawzi's going to root out the Jews," was the saying. Meanwhile his favorite pastime was listening to Tarfa read him *The Arabian Nights* in German.

Fawzi el Kawukji, Field Commander of the National Liberation Army, Damascus, 1948

Fawzi's military career had so many turns, it almost defied credibility, despite the 80 wounds he boasted of as proof of his bravery. Born in Lebanon, he served as a Turkish officer in World War I. This did not prevent him from joining the French Special Services in 1920 when they took over the mandate of Syria, just as being a French officer did not prevent him from joining the unsuccessful Druze revolt against the French in 1926.

In 1928, he became a military instructor in Baghdad. This did not prevent him from joining the unsuccessful pro-German revolt against the pro-British Iraqi government he was serving. Escaping to Berlin with the Mufti aboard a plane Hitler sent to their rescue, Fawzi collaborated with the Nazis. Less crafty than the Mufti, he was captured by the Russians and tossed into a concentration camp. At the Syrian government's requests, Fawzi was released by the Soviets as they made their first downpayment on the Arab-Israeli war. Fawzi then assumed the field command of the Arab Liberation Army, whose commander-in-chief was none other than the Iraqi general he had betrayed in 1941.

Not long after our first meeting, I got word that Fawzi was about to move into Palestine. I reached him at dawn in the outskirts of Damascus. He allowed me to photograph him with his staff, but wouldn't permit me to join him. "Go and see Sabri Pasha Taba in Amman and ask him for a *laisser-passer* to our Palestinian headquarters," his executive officer told me. This required some delicate diplomacy since Fawzi still had a price on his head. The British, however, did not seem to recall this when he crossed over into Palestine and announced, "I have returned."

Fawzi's contact man in Amman was glowingly described by my Arab interpreter as having "the grace and hospitality of an Arab untouched by Western civilization". Sabri Pasha Taba handled the supplies, arms, and volunteers on their way to Palestine. I found him plump and superficially jovial as he sipped Turkish coffee, and smoked his *nargileh* among his bales of rice. "Just wait and see," Sabri Pasha Taba told me when I requested my pass. He then offered the three traditional cups of coffee.

In spite of Sabri Pasha's secrecy, everybody knew that Fawzi was at Jaba in Samaria. So without bothering to get an official clearance, I drove there.

The only security was Fawzi's bodyguard, an overweight Palestinian. Fawzi didn't appear surprised to see me when I walked into his office. He put on his pith helmet, picked up his binoculars, and took me to a balcony where shriveled geraniums were struggling to grow in gasoline cans. In the glaring sunlight he swept his right arm across the rolling countryside of hills, olive groves, cacti, rocks and dust. "The time for deeds has come," he said and took me to lunch.

Fawzi's mess was the hodgepodge I suspected his army to be. Around his table was his personal dentist (for his gold teeth), his personal doctor (he suffered recurring sinus trouble), along with Iraqi, Syrian, and Palestinian officers—all in as many different uniforms. Their table manners were as feudal as their mindset. There was a crudeness and bestiality about them that did not belong to our times, despite their automatic weapons. There was something wrong about it all.

I sat next to a gaunt, surly figure who wasn't an Arab but a Bosnian Moslem from Sarajevo who, like a number of the other Yugoslavs, had volunteered to join the Liberation Army. He suggested we have coffee together so that we could talk. When we were alone, his contempt was obvious: "What a rabble!" he said. "They have no idea about organization. Yesterday the Jews came over and dropped anti-personnel bombs. Do you think these people dug slit trenches? No! These louts don't know what a real fighting outfit looks like. Now when I was with the Waffen SS, it was different. That was a real outfit!" He sighed as I prayed he would never find out I had been with Tito.

The Arab strategy, I now learned, was to starve out the 100,000 Jews bottled up in Jerusalem and to force them to surrender when the mandate ended on May 15. The Jews, however, were supplied by convoys fighting their way up the winding Tel Aviv road below the Judean hills. Fawzi, although he was ready to "pounce" on Jerusalem, made a wide detour from the north across bad roads to avoid the two fortified Jewish settlements, Atarot and Neve Yaakov, strategically barring direct access to Jericho.

"Why doesn't he storm those settlements?" I asked the SS. He shrugged, spat and said, "You just wait and see."

Transjordan Arab Legion, Amman, 1948

Amman

The Road to Utopia was attracting big crowds at the Emirate Palace cinema. Amman was not in the psychotic mood in which I had found Damascus. It was noisily enjoying its post-war boom. The Emirate of Transjordan had been upgraded to the Hashemite Kingdom of Jordan and rated a British Legation with a minister: Sir Alec Seth Kirkbride. Amman's population had swollen to 70,000. The once-sleepy village was now a thriving capital. Real estate was becoming increasingly valuable. Large American cars obeyed traffic-lights alongside donkeys. Pedestrians wore sanforized shirts. Ray-Ban sunglasses protected eyes dripping with trachoma. Deeds were still signed by thumbprint, but the ink was squirted out of Parker 51 pens.

This prosperity was due mostly to smuggling, and the British government's decision to shore up Jordan. Although the kingdom was in the sterling block, dollars were plentiful. This hard currency, along with a total lack of government restrictions, had turned Amman into a city of opportunity.

Fortunes were made as merchandise flowed in and was smuggled out—East to Syria, West to Palestine. Goods unobtainable in England and difficult to find in the US were over-abundant in Jordan. Amman had everything except bordellos, which Glubb Pasha considered immoral.

In keeping with the prosperity of the times, Abdullah had a six-seater Humber limousine, a Daimler sedan, and a black Cadillac. (An American oil company had given him the Caddie, though his subjects were told it was a present from King George of England.) Whenever he ventured out of Raghdan Palace, one of these cars was sandwiched between two jeeps armed with machine guns and crowded with Arab legionnaires. A large sign on the first jeep read, "Royal Vehicle Approaching." The sign on the second was, "Royal Vehicle Ahead. Do Not Overtake."

Arrows indicated the direction, "To the Royal Palace". Raghdan stood aloof on a hill, surrounded by lawns and flower beds. The entire façade was covered with electric bulbs which gave the impression on sunny days that the building suffered from chicken pox.

Abdullah's aged Circassian guards, in dashing uniforms now two sizes too large, ambled round the grounds in a gouty shuffle. Their once-fierce moustaches, now Santa-Claus white, gave them a benevolent appearance they only suppressed when chasing away Abdullah's horses when they ventured down from their hillside pasture. The real security was undertaken by smart young Arab legionnaires.

Abdullah's first two wives lived on the upper floor of the harem in a separate wing of the palace. His third wife, an Ethiopian beauty, had her own home in town, listed in the Amman phone directory as "the White House". Her phone number, in accordance with etiquette, came after the first two wives', who were listed in order of seniority. The first wife was a Turkish princess. The second was his first wife's former lady-in-waiting. The third was the second wife's former maid. Abdullah visited them in the reverse order of his marriages.

Boredom of any kind offended Ab. From the moment he got up at 4am until he was safely tucked in at 9pm he needed to be entertained. While he expected his visitors to remain diffidently silent when first ushered into his presence, he soon got rid of them if they proved tongue-tied. He spent his days in the company of a wide variety of visitors with whom he shared coffee and endless chat, covering an unbelievable range of topics — all the more incredible when seen through his imaginative eyes. On the rare occasions when he found himself alone, he would hurry over to his secretary's office, which was over-flowing with panhandlers, to find someone to talk to.

I was early for lunch and strolling in the grounds one day when I heard myself called and saw Ab leaning out of the window waving frantically for me to join him. He then rushed to his throne to greet me there. It was on this occasion that he told me that being a King, he now required a more suitable throne. He had ordered one from an old Jewish carpenter in Jerusalem, he said, and was worried that the prevailing conditions would prevent it being delivered to him in Amman.

"*Sidi*," I suggested, "the Haganah will be only too happy to see that you get it."

"I know," Ab sighed, "but it wouldn't look right. I'm an Arab king."

It was his rule to gather as lunch guests all the visiting Sheiks, British officials, foreign diplomats, and interesting personalities, including women if they weren't Moslem, who happened to be in Amman, along with his regular male retinue, which included his favorite, a beautiful ex-stable boy with fluttering kohl-dyed eyelashes. (The one person rarely seen at these functions was the man closest to the King: Glubb Pasha. The Pasha liked to observe a certain reserve towards Abdullah, and preferred to eat a sandwich in the open air and make his appearance with the coffee.)

This habit of open invitations caused a daily domestic crisis, as there were always more guests than available china, glassware, and cutlery. The four crystal goblets, engraved with the royal seal, went to Ab and the three most distinguished guests. The others drank out of heavy kitchen glasses. Towels replaced napkins. The conversation was carried on to the gurgling sound of running taps which drifted from the adjacent pantry, where dishes and cutlery were hurriedly washed after each course. Ab ate heartily, picking small helpings from each of the six courses and delicately maneuvering his knife and fork to show off the flashing heavy cabochon ring on his little finger.

He directed the conversation, and the topic depended mainly on the guests' nationalities. When I was around, he tweaked me over the United States' refusal to establish diplomatic relations. But he was far more caustic towards the United Nations, which had also turned him down. He called the UN "the graveyard of diplomacy".

"Can you imagine?" he'd complain, "the United Nations airs their problems publicly!" Statesmanship, Abdullah believed, was based on secret treaties and shady alliances. "How do you know I haven't got a pact with Russia," he asked a startled Foreign Office-type. He then announced he was awarding Jordan's highest decoration to the King of Greece. "To scare Russia," he explained in the puzzled silence that followed. Such an act, he felt, would make it clear to the Soviets that he stood firmly behind the royal Greek government in its civil war against communism. "A world without a court," Abdullah would sigh. "How sad that would be."

Twentieth Century reality struck Jordan early one spring morning. A bomb was placed outside Glubb Pasha's window. While the blast caused minor material damage, the angry bark of the explosion jolted Amman out of its complacency. Suddenly, the Arab belief in their "invincible superiority" over the Jews was shaken. On April 4, Fawzi's National Army of Liberation undertook its first military operation against the Israelis. They attacked the Kibbutz Mishmar-Haemeck on the Jenin-Haifa road. Although Fawzi caught the Israelis off-guard—they were playing soccer—his forces suffered such a humiliating defeat that an observer remarked, "Fawzi has proved himself to be a menace to the Arab cause."

A few days after this disaster, qualms turned to real alarm when Fawzi participated in another Arab debacle, at Kastel. There, Abdel Kader El Husseini, the Mufti's relative and one of the most charismatic Arab commanders, ran out of ammunition and turned to Fawzi for help, aware that he had just received large supplies of military equipment from the Arab League. Abdel Kader pleaded in vain. Fawzi did nothing. Abdel Kader was killed, Kastel turned into an Arab rout and precipitated the collapse of the Mufti's forces in Palestine. Fawzi had simply wanted to get even with the Mufti, whom he held responsible for his arrest by the Nazis when both of them were in Berlin collaborating with Hitler.

After the massacre of Deir Yassin, alarm turned to panic. This small Arab village near Jerusalem had a non-aggression pact with the Haganah, the Jewish defense force, which both sides respected. With no regard for this agreement, Irgun, the Jewish guerrilla movement, and the Stern Gang, the anti-British Zionist militants, in a calculated act of terrorism, murdered the entire population, 245 men, women, and children, successfully destroying the Palestinian Arabs' morale. In panic, some 200,000 of these Arabs took the road to Amman. Down to the Dead Sea and Jericho they streamed in hysterical confusion spreading wild rumors, partly which they believed in, partly as a means of justifying their flight.

Now all the attention was focused on Abdullah and his British-trained army in the awareness that this was the only Arab force capable of opposing the Israelis. Delegates from Palestinian towns escorted by scruffy bodyguards came to plead for assistance. Azzam Pasha, the head of the Arab League, visited Amman to confer with Abdullah, as did representatives of the other Arab states. But although they made the pilgramage to Amman, none of them really trusted Abdullah. They considered him a British puppet. They also knew that he stood to gain by collaborating with the Jews.

This suspicion was not limited to outside Arab countries. It included Abdullah's own Bedouins, and even his son, Crown Prince Talal, who once complained to him, "As an Arab patriot, I wouldn't follow the British lead blindly." Abdullah's outraged reply summed up his political philosophy: "You talk about patriotism. But you don't know a thing about it. I will not

King Abdullah of Jordan shortly before crossing into Palestine, 1948

Arab volunteer training, Palestine, 1948

antagonize everyone to gain applause from the ignorant masses. I know what I'm doing.

"It is obvious we need a strong ally. Russia is out of the question because it is the enemy of God and kings. America takes no interest in us. Only the British know us well enough to help us. Though they have let us down in the past, they are the ones we can trust most!"

The break between father and son was the break between two Arab points of view. Abdullah felt that the Arabs were not prepared for democratic rule and favored a benevolent despotism backed by strong a Western power—in his case, Britain. The Crown Prince wanted Arab independence without any foreign domination and saw the war as an expression of pan-Arabism. For Abdullah, the coming conflict was an opportunity to extend his kingdom.

"What Abdullah really wants," the French Ambassador wryly observed," is to play both Saladin and Richard the Lionheart in this crusade." By this he implied that the Arab Legion would only fight a war serious enough in appearance to dispel Palestinian doubts and make them accept his annexation of the Arab territory of Palestine. Abdullah perceived the lack of any common purpose among the Arabs trapped in their fanaticism. He was equally aware that the Jews were in Palestine to stay.

Acceptance of the Israelis was not a new line of thought for Abdullah. Like King Faisal, who had led the Arab revolt, the Hussein brothers were not fanatics.

At the Paris Peace Conference of 1919, Lawrence of Arabia had arranged a meeting between Faisal and Chaim Weizmann. The two came to a visionary agreement based on "a most cordial goodwill between Jews and Arabs". Faisal agreed to encourage Zionist emmigration to Palestine. Weizmann promised Zionist assistance in Arab economic development. This little-known agreement was signed on January 3, 1919, and was conditional on Arab independence in accordance with the Hussein-MacMahon Agreements. Soon afterwards, the French expelled Faisal from Syria in accordance with their secret agreement with Britain. The agreement fell through.

Abdullah, for his part, maintained friendly relations with Abraham Rutenberg, who was permitted to build the Palestine Electric Corporation power plant on Transjordanian soil in 1932. For Abdullah, reaching an understanding with the Israelis would not only be beneficial for the Arabs, but it was the only option.

In the midst of the prevailing pandemonium, panic gripped Amman's city fathers. In a war which had not yet started, they were worried that Abdullah might transfer his capital to Jerusalem and expose them to a real-estate disaster. Journalists were now arriving from everywhere. While the Foreign Office appointed a press attaché to facilitate their work, the prime minister ordered their mass expulsion.

Three weeks before the mandate ended, the Haganah took a calculated risk. Surrounded on all sides by Arab countries, the Israelis would have to rely on shipping for their supplies. With the only docking facilities concentrated in Haifa, it was imperative for them to gain control of that harbor.

Like every city where the Jews and the Arabs co-existed, Haifa was divided into two fortified armed camps. It was also garrisoned by the British Royal Marines. The Haganah took a chance that the marines would not fight as the inevitable casualties would be difficult to justify in the House of Commons shortly before the mandate ended.

The British were notified well before the Haganah launched its attack. They withdrew from Haifa, and moved into the enclave around the harbor. The National Army of Liberation was also notified. Fawzi's Iraqi commander hurriedly left Haifa to get reinforcements. He was never seen again.

It was a strange experience for me, passing from the Arab road blocks towards the Jewish ones as I drove to Haifa. For months now I had seen the Jews from the Arab perspective and heard them mentioned only as "the enemy".

Although every Israeli I knew in Palestine most certainly belonged to one of the illegal armies, I still did not know them as fighters, but as civilian friends. As I drove, I tried to recall a face I could place in relation to those I would now see in Haifa. The only one was Lieutenant Allen, a Palestinian commando serving in the British Army I had met in Yugoslavia when we were both in Nadlesk, a small Slovene village behind German lines during the war. He had told me then that the Jewish Agency encouraged young Jews to volunteer in the commandos to get experience "for after". I had often wondered what had happened to Allen "after".

By the time I reached Haifa, the battle was over. Rushmiya Bridge and Stanton Street, the main objectives, had been stormed during the night producing an Arab rout. Its 60,000 Moslems were now refugees. Stunned and speechless, they tramped towards the docks to await evacuation to Acre across the bay. Youthful members of the Haganah, showing themselves for the first time in the open, stood guard outside these docks. Alongside stood Royal Marines, studiously ignoring them. As long line of refugees limped past, a member of the Haganah shouted to me, "We had to evacuate Egypt two thousand years ago."

On Stanton Street, I came upon a Haganah sentry relaxing on a chair wearing a sun helmet. Other members of the Haganah directed traffic as they had taken over control of the city. Palmach commandos in their late teens and early twenties, wearing *kouffiehs* as trophies, raced along the deserted streets in jeeps flying the Israeli flag: a blue star of David on a white and blue field. The *sabras* for the most part were stocky and tough, not at all the frail and cringing image the Arabs had of the Jews.

In two houses near a British roadblock, the Haganah had set up the headquarters of the Palmach commandos. Some of them, wearing the badges of military police, were moving Arab prisoners to a more secure jail. The first two were blindfolded. They were Poles who had done sabotage work for the Arabs, the commando in charge told me, "They'll be tried for illegal entry into Palestine."

At Rushmiya Bridge, I photographed a Haganah officer. He wore civilian clothes with a gun in his belt. He said his name was Ronnie, which he also told me was one of twelve pseudonyms. He was the officer in charge of the Palmach commandos I had photographed earlier. He told me he had been fighting since 1936, and had served as an officer in the Jewish brigade during the war.

I also photographed the marines herding the Arab refugees making their way fearfully to Gate 10 at the docks. They hurried with their belongings down a narrow street, apparently unaware of the body of a small Arab boy blown out of his shoes, a pack of cards spread out around him. His face was covered with flies and already swelling from the heat. The usual stench of death was missing, however, as one of the Arabs had dropped a large bag of mocha which had split open at its fall and filled the street with the cheerful aroma of fresh coffee.

Transjordan Bedouins marching on Palestine, 1948

Israeli sentry on duty after the Haifa victory over the Arabs, 1948

I asked a sentry to contact the Haganah High Command for me. "They're still underground," he told me, although their troops were clearly out in the open. But he took down my name and hotel address, promising to notify his superiors of my request.

On the docks, I photographed hapless refugees and their bundles; pyramids of humanity and belongings stacked on the lighters ferrying them to Acre. I was so caught up with photographing this spectacle of human misery that I missed my phone call at the hotel, and only got the message I'd been left: "If the John Phillips who tried to contact the Haganah is the one who was in Nadlesk during the war, tell him that his old pal took Haifa this morning."

The feeling of terror increased as May 15 drew closer. Past that date, no appointments could be made "because of the war". Arab volunteers now poured into Palestine by the thousand. Jordanian Bedouins in their *jellabas* and equipped with ancient muskets forded the Jordan for skirmishes on its West Bank. Weapons were peddled at street corners in Arab towns like Nablus as though they were Jaffa oranges. Much more discreetly, officers from the Liberation Army, stationed in the Jenin area, disposed of their self-propelled guns, armored cars with two-pounders, and Bren-gun carriers for American dollars offered by Israeli agents. British equipment was openly transferred to the Arab Legion. (I photographed Glubb Pasha as he walked across Allenby Bridge to inspect units of the Arab Legion stationed in Palestine.) The Arabs hired British deserters, Polish, German and Yugoslav mercenaries, to perform acts of sabotage. Although this conflict was over a stretch of barren land *without oil*, and militarily speaking was a minor event, it was no local incident. The repercussions would be felt outside Palestine, and would ripple in ever-widening rings until they circled the globe. The world powers with their conflicting interests watched Palestine, located at the crossroads of *Realpolitik*.

A number of countries had definite stakes in the war. The British, seeing their influence in the Middle East dwindling, banked on keeping a foothold there through Jordan. (They expected Abdullah's British-trained army to occupy Arab Palestine and become a major force in the Middle East. This scheme accepted Partition and never considered a Palestinian state.)

456

Syria hoped that the Jordanian Legions and the Israeli Haganah would destroy each other and both Palestine and Jordan would fall to Damascus. (Aware of this, both Jordan and Israel had undertaken secret talks which, although not entirely successful, prevented such a head-on collision.)

Lebanon, the only Arab state with a Christian majority, was increasingly alarmed over the growth of Moslem fanaticism. A war against the Jews was a ready-made solution to divert Moslem fury away from them. The most belligerent in their threats, the Lebanese found excuses for not enlisting in the Liberation Army. They prayed that history would overlook their very shaky Middle-Eastern Monte Carlo, where all the taxis were Packards.

In Saudi-Arabi, Ibn Saud, having lost none of his genius for remaining neutral through two world wars, publicly subscribed to El Azhar's *jihad* against the Jews, but did nothing to disrupt his kingdom's conflicts of interest as Saudi-American oil flowed freely beneath his realm that included Mecca and Medina, the holiest cities in Islam.

Faced with catastrophic internal troubles, Farouk saw in the war an opportunity for giving his subjects others than himself to hate. Ditto Iraq.

Some of the non-belligerent nations were no less involved in the war. The Moslem Turks, fearing that an Arab victory would bring territorial claims from their religious brethren in Syria for the annexation of Alexandretta, favored an Israeli victory.

"An Arab victory," a French diplomat told me, "would simply mean that Algeria, Morocco and Tunisia would demand independence." A defeat would calm them for a decade. The US, anxious lest Russia find an excuse to interfere in the Middle East, hoped for peace.

All of these extraneous considerations obscured the real issue. Until now, the Middle East, despite its cloak of colonialism, had remained essentially feudal. It now found itself confronted with the realistically ruthless Western Jews, who knew that their only alternative to victory was the refugee camp. The more I traveled around the Middle East, the more it became clear to me that I was witnessing events as important as any I had seen in Eastern Europe. Here, as there, an antiquated order was collapsing in the midst of confused aspirations. Where it would lead I had no idea, but the Middle East I had known was about to vanish forever.

Battle of the Jewish Quarter, Jerusalem, 1948

The Battle

On May 13 the Arab Legion's British officers threw a party before joining their units. At one point in the evening, a flushed major rose and toasted, "Gentlemen: The King! May he be victorious!"

"Does he mean George?" I asked my neighbor.

"'Course not, old man. Ab!"

On May 14 the stage was set. Early that morning the British High Commissioner, Sir Alan Gordon Cunningham, left Government House on the Hill of Evil Counsel outside Jerusalem. Sir Alan was driven to Kalandia Airport in a bullet-proof Daimler. Landing at Haifa, he boarded the cruiser *Euryalus* as a band struck up "The Minstrel Boy". On the stroke of midnight *HMS Euryalus*, floodlit by her destroyer escorts, crossed the three-mile limit into international waters. The British mandate in Palestine had ended.

All that day, the Arab Legion had wound their way down into the valley toward Allenby Bridge. At dawn on the 15th, my Arab Legion *kouffieh* flapping, I drove into Palestine.

For the first time since February I had no fear of getting lynched by a Moslem fanatic. The Arabs mistook me for a British officer in my Legion uniform. This reduced my chances of getting hurt by 50 per cent, the other half was in the Israelis' hands.

I drove to the settlements of Atarot and Neve Yaacov, which controlled the access to Jerusalem—the two *kibbutzim* Fawzi studiously avoided when I last saw him. Atarot, which had been evacuated the night before, was still smoldering. Airmail letters from the States and sheet music from Mozart's *Magic Flute* were scattered around. The Holstein cows left behind had been killed and were about ready to burst. At Neve Yaacov I came upon a group of British deserters. They were led by a man called Frank.

"We're what you might call unofficial transfers," I was told by Titch, a spokesman for this uncommunicative gang. Frank was responsible for screening the deserters who volunteered. "If they ask about pay and food, Frank doesn't want them," Titch explained. "'Ask no questions,' is our motto."

Frank and his band stood around the entrance to Neve Yaacov. Turning to the Arab constables who were beating off impatient looters, Titch shouted, "Keep the buggers away mon! The whole place is mined." He calmly removed the fuse from a milk churn crammed with nuts and bolts. "Stop that bugger," Titch warned as a reckless Arab clawed his way past a guard. There was a bang and a howl. A hush came over the crowd as the wounded Arab was carted off.

"That'll keep 'em quiet," Titch shrugged. Frank and his men then efficiently defused mines and booby traps. One of them was a 21-year-old German SS who had escaped from a French prisoner-of-war camp. "*Verdammter Hund!*" the German shouted, trying to reach for his gun with his left hand while fighting off a German Shepherd dog whose teeth were sunk in his right wrist. Looking for valuables, he had found instead an angry police dog.

On hearing the German language, the dog let go and wagged his tail. "*Was ist los?*" the German exclaimed in surprise.

"His owner must have been a German," I suggested.

"*Ach so*, a German Jew," he said thoughtfully as he wrapped a handkerchief around his wrist.

"This is thirsty work," Frank remarked. "Have a beer." He fired into a can of Budweiser and a column of foam shot up. The young German came out of the house holding a gray suit on a hanger. "Frank," he called out. "Do we take?"

"Don't be daft, mon," Titch advised him. "If it doesn't fit, it's worth at least three *quiddels*.

"I couldn't wear it," the young German said. "Although, I need a suit and this one looks clean." He held it at arm's length and stared at it, as though puzzling for an explanation. "It's my upbringing," he said at last. "Come on lads," Frank ordered as Titch carted off a case of liquor. "Let's get out of here before these buggers run wild and it gets dangerous."

They departed and I climbed on the roof of a house which commanded a view of the lane which led up to the village gates. No sooner had I got there than the Arab looters arrived in a frantic rush of screams, sweat, and rags, stumbling over each other. Their eyes were popping out of their heads as their bare feet pounded the ground. Those in front dived into the houses. Those following them rushed on. They milled around Neve Yaacov like ants picking a bone clean. They emerged from homes carrying desks, chairs, pots, pans, and beds. Here one grabbed a parasol, there another had a pair of boxing gloves around his neck; a third, balancing a sewing machine on his head, tried to grab a blanket from a fourth. Those loaded with loot fought their way against the stream of newcomers. They broke off door-knobs, unhinged doors, and tore away aluminum roofing. One, unable to yank open the steel door of the high-tension box, fired into the lock. The ricochet hit an Arab who was trampled by others as they rushed around screaming, "Snipers, snipers!" In this frenzy, two more Arabs got wounded. I left in a hurry.

The Arab Legion was besieging the Jewish Quarter. Major Abdullah el Tel, the Legion's commanding officer for the Jerusalem area, had established his headquarters at the First Station of the Cross on the Via Dolorosa. In civvies, the Major would have passed unnoticed in the City of London. His moustache was very British and so was his composure. Dr Moussa Husseini, the Arab civilian representative, also had an office at the headquarters. He was suavely continental, and wore a white linen jacket.

The pair had nothing in common with the Arabs hanging around: the hysterical young Egyptian "Moslem brother" who kept taking off and put-ting on his ammunition belt; the swashbuckling Iraqi irregulars with *kouf-fiehs* draped like turbans; the pudgy Amman city fathers anxiously inquiring about the progress of the war. In the midst of this hubbub, Turkish coffee was served as the telephone rang incessantly. When a call came through from Abdullah, Major el Tel stood to attention, wearily ordered silence, and informed his agitated sovereign that the Jewish quarter still held out.

I got some idea of how the operations were going when a British deserter reported on an attack of a synagogue by the Liberation Army. "It's so jammed with looters, there isn't any elbow-room to fight off an Israeli counter-attack," he said before turning to me adding, "You should see the silly bastards." That's how I met Peter.

On first impression, he looked younger than he was, due to his slim, boyish build, but this was quickly belied by the tired, almost haunted look about his eyes. Dressed in army pants and a windbreaker, he wore his woollen scarf with a certain elegance. His rifle was slung over his shoulder. Peter disapproved of looting. He was a killer. All he owned was on his back and he slept where night and fatigue caught up with him. He would disappear without a word and show up a day or two later without a word about where he had been. He vanished at mealtimes, and I don't ever recall seeing him eat. He knew his way around the maze of the Old City on the darkest night. Light-footed like a cat, he picked his way through the debris as he led me where he knew I would get good pictures.

From a spot near the Wailing Wall he took me to, I saw Porat Josef Synagogue rising in the distance across no-man's land. The synagogue, with its adjoining Talmudic schools and academy, was disintegrating behind billows of smoke. The massive walls were coming down in a rolling cascade of rubble. Stunned by this wanton destruction I wondered just how many more tons of TNT the Liberation Army would squander to reduce this seat of learning to dust.

On the window ledge, a pink bromeliad bloomed. From behind it, two Arab irregulars fired away. A third jammed a fresh clip into his rifle. A fourth was slumped on a chair, sound asleep. I had no idea where I was. Peter had led me here via a zigzag course from the Legion headquarters. Hurrying down narrow streets, we had passed barbed-wire entanglements at intersections guarded by tense brooding irregulars. We had crawled over the rubble of houses which had collapsed into the streets and trudged ankle-deep through mounds of broken furniture, piles of newspapers, rags and smashed crockery. We had ducked beneath low archways and sneaked from one building to another through gaping holes in walls. Whenever we paused to catch our breath, all I seemed to see were ruined synagogues.

"They must have 50 and everyone is a fortress," Peter said in disgust.

With no more idea where I was and what the irregulars were shooting at, I asked to look out of the window. Obligingly one of them stepped aside. There in front of me rose a massive synagogue awesome in its proportions and astonishing in the extent of its damage. I was contemplating the famous Hurva—which means "the ruins"—which had earned its name during the 150 years it had stood neglected between the laying of its foundations and its eventual completion. Now the Hurva lay in ruins once again.

On May 19 I watched Arab Legion *jundis* in full battledress stream into the Old City and take over from the bedraggled National Liberation Army.

Something was up, and nobody was talking. I finally found out what was going on from Peter.

On the night of May 18, the Haganah had broken through the Zion Gate and reopened communications with the besieged Jewish Quarter for a few hours. They had brought in medical supplies, ammunition and re-inforcements. Glubb Pasha, convinced that the irregulars could not prevent the Israelis from taking over the entire Old City, had committed the Legion, which until then had been held in reserve. The Israelis now had a fight on their hands. By day, the Legion blasted its way deep into the Jewish Quarter with its artillery. At night, the night sky over Jerusalem was streaked with tracer-fire.

One morning as the battle raged, Peter and I crawled on a roof over the sandbagged ramparts manned by the Arab Legion. Lying on my sto-mach, I was fitting the legionaries behind their sandbags into my camera sights at the same time as getting the King David Hotel and the YMCA in Israeli territory as background. "The Arabs have had it," Peter said. "It's going to be a mess." I agreed as I set my shutter. "I've got to get out of here before that," Peter went on. Again I agreed as I continued to peer into my camera sights. "I'll need money to get out of here, so I've decided to sell you my story," Peter went on to say. I said, "Yes," absentmindedly, while trying to make out the flag fluttering from the King David.

"It's going to cost you plenty," Peter went on after a pause, "because that money is going to take me where there are no Jews."

"Like the moon?"

Peter didn't laugh. "There must be someplace. How about Cape Town?"

"Hardly."

"There must be a place were I'll be safe." I could feel the desperation in his voice. I put down my camera and loooked at him.

"I pulled the Ben Jehuda job," he said flatly.

I shot bolt upright for a second before remembering I was an Israeli target even without my checkered *kouffieh,* and ducked down again. "Ben Jehuda? Is that the story you want to sell *Life,* Peter?" He nodded. "I was in Damascus yesterday to see the Mufti and tried to get the £500 he had pro-mised me for the job. When the Mufti refused to pay me, I told him I was going to sell the story to *Life.*"

"Peter," I said, "over 50 people, including children were killed when that truck loaded with explosives went up. How can you expect *Life* to buy such a story?"

Home-made mortars began to land near us. "I think we'd better get out of here," I said.

I was in Amman when its citizens discovered that war was not all rejoicing. The realization came with an air raid at dawn. It killed four bakers, and left Abdullah fearful and annoyed. Pacing his palace, he bitterly complained that the Jews were trying to "kill his father's son".

The raid caused an acute outbreak of "spy-itis". With no Jews available, the blame fell on the Palestinian refugees: 340 were picked up. Several people caught pointing were arrested and detained for questioning.

It was there the Mufti's bodyguard found me. He was short, massive, and wore an Astrakhan hat on the back of his head. His hands were square, his little finger the size of my thumb, besides which he cracked his knuckles. "Some people talk too much," he told me. "Take Peter. The things he says…" The bodyguard rolled his eyes to the accompaniment of a sharp crack. "Tell Peter that writing can be even more unhealthy than talking." He turned on his heels and stalked off, his hands still working.

Back in the Old City, incessant gunfire had numbed my thoughts. I was filthy from crawling around in the dust and had contracted dysentery. One night, after the electric power failed, I didn't know whether to feel ashamed or blame the war when I walked into the Church of the Holy Sepulcher and borrowed a lighted candle to help me find my way back to the Austrian hospice where I was lodging.

Shortly after nine on the morning of May 28, I went to the Arab Legion's advance post in the Armenian Quarter. A ceasefire was in effect, and a feeling of excitement prevailed among the men gathered around the monastery courtyard. "The Jews want to surrender," a Legion officer told me. "They've sent two rabbis over."

I found them on a bench guarded by an MP. The one on his right wore a black felt hat which distinguished him as the Ashkenazi rabbi representing the European community. He seemed lost in prayer. The Sephardic rabbi, representing the Oriental community, wore a red *tarboosh* draped in black. A ricochet had grazed his face while he was making his way to the forward Arab positions. Unmindful of his wound, he stared intently at Major el Tel who was on the phone. The Major must have been receiving his orders from Glubb Pasha in Amman.

"I will only negotiate with a member of the Israeli Army," he told the rabbis. The Ashkenazi set off for the Jewish lines with the Major's demands. Curious about the Arabs' reaction to him, I followed the rabbi outside. Several of the Arabs grinned broadly. Others watched solemnly as the rabbi majestically descended the stairs. No one showed signs of hatred.

"Here comes Rabbi Weingarten!" a legionnaire announced, heralding the arrival of the Jewish community spokesman for the Old City. I wondered why he had come when Major el Tel had expressly stated he would only negotiate with an army representative. A group of six escorted Mordecai Weingarten. One was an Arab legionnaire, the others were from the Liberation Army.

To my surprise, the legionnaire held Weingarten's right hand—a friendly gesture among Moslems. The irregular on Weingarten's left held his arm with a certain diffidence. Although it was a hot day, Rabbi Weingarten wore an overcoat, presumably to add dignity to his person.

I wondered what was happening to the Haganah representative I was really interested in. Unfortunately I could not locate the Major, so I took the chance he was back at his headquarters and crossed the Old City on foot to see what I could learn. It must have been noon when I got to the first Station of the Cross. The Major wasn't there either. I was wondering what to do next when I heard the sound of an approaching crowd. A group of irregulars was coming down the Via Dolorosa. They had an Israeli in custody. I got a close-up shot of the prisoner and his guards. The Israeli looked apprehensive. I couldn't blame him, considering the murderous mood of the Arab civilians.

Inside the Major's headquarters, the prisoner relaxed and identified himself as Tawil, the military representative sent to negotiate with the Major. The two had already met in the Armenian Quarter, where the Major had laid down his terms. On his way back to the Israeli lines, Tawil had been set upon by two Arab irregulars. Flushed with victory at having captured the first Jewish prisoner, the pair refused to believe Tawil's explanation that he had just seen Major el Tel and triumphantly marched their prisoner across the Old City, where I had come upon him. I finally found Major el Tel in the Armenian Quarter. He announced that the surrender would be signed at 4pm.

The surrender took place at Zion Gate where the Haganah had broken through on the night of May 18. The terms had originally been drawn up in Arabic, but both sides agreed upon English as a common language. Sam Suki of the United Press translated the terms into English. A copy for each side was written out in longhand by Don Burke of *Time*, using my pen. The Israeli signatories were Rabbi Mordecai Weingarten and Moshe Rushnak, the military commander of the Jewish Quarter. While the serious young officer signed, Mousa Husseini looked on condescendingly. He then signed for the Arabs, followed by Major el Tel. This formality was witnessed by Dr Pablo de Azcarate, head of the United Nations Security Council's Truce Commission. I glanced at my watch. It was exactly 4:36pm on Monday, May 28, 1948.

I saw Peter one last time shortly before we entered the small enclave still held by the Israelis. "There's a deserter from the Suffolk Regiment who's with the Jews, and I'm out to get the bugger," Peter told me. "His name's Albert Melville."

The Haganah fighters were drawn up in a loose formation on Ashkenazi Square. They wore the blank expressions of men who had been under constant fire and had slept little. Nothing about them revealed the fierce tenacity with which they had withstood the Arab Legion's all-out attacks for ten days and nights.

Peter made straight for the group of prisoners. He looked them over carefully before he exclaimed "There's the bastard!" He was eyeing a man in a Haganah wool cap.

The man in the cap looked at me anxiously.

"Sir, he said in a soft voice, "I didn't mean to desert, really I didn't. I got a bit squiffy one night in the Jewish Quarter. When I sobered up, I found I couldn't get out."

Peter grinned.

"I think he plans to kill me sir, and I didn't really mean to desert."

Peter was still grinning.

I drew Major el Tel's attention to the Englishman asking what would happen to him. The Major assured me he would be treated like all other

prisoners of war. He would be transferred during the night to an intern-
ment camp in Jordan.

The prisoners of war were marched off to the Kishleh, an ancient
Turkish prison near the Jaffa Gate. Major el Tel had decided he could not
ensure the security of the prisoners. In defiance of the curfew, civilians and
irregulars came leaping over roof tops to loot leaving fires in their wake.
The Legion for its part remained cool and disciplined. To my personal
knowledge, legionnaires saved Masha Weingarten, the Rabbi's daughter.
Surrounded by a threatening mob, they opened fire as he told her to run
for her life. Yahoshua Levy of the *Palestine Post* was being dragged into a
narrow alley by an Arab irregular intent on killing him when a legionnaire
came upon them: "He shot the irregular, just like that," Levy recalled.

According to one of the surrender clauses, civilians who elected to
remain in the Jewish Quarter were free to do so on condition they recognized the sovereignty of King Abdullah. This was never implemented. Had
any Jew decided to remain, he would have been homeless in a matter of
hours and dead by nightfall. By then I had photographed a charred body in
a doorway—the last Jew in the Quarter for the next 19 years.

The civilians, for the most part, were descendants of Orthodox families which had lived in the Jewish Quarter for centuries without ever setting
foot outside its limits. Now they had one hour to pack and be ready to leave.
The relocation point was Ashkenazi Square. From there they would be
evacuated through the Zion Gate to the Israeli-held New City of Jerusalem.

Dazed by the shelling, these poor people gathered up their belongings and trudged off to the Square. There I came upon scenes of human
misery as old as time itself. Two thousand six hundred years before it had
been the Babylonians who first drove the Jews out of Jerusalem. After them
came the Romans, the Persians, and the Crusaders. Now it was the Arabs. In
some strange way, I had entered history when I marched into Jerusalem
with the Arab Legion.

Shamelessly I stalked the crowd as families gazed at their homes for
the last time. I was struck by their expressions, which had changed from
numb emptiness to real grief. Yet no one wept. Tears were a luxury these
people didn't have time for. I noticed how differently young and old
reacted. Two girls I photographed carried three bundles between them.
They wore a look of determination as they strode forward. This was not true

of the old Ashkenazi who sat cross-legged on the ground, removed from what was going on around him. All he had saved was a neatly folded prayer shawl and a thumb-worn holy book. A woman with an infant in her arms just stood there. With unseeing eyes, she gazed straight ahead, lost in some inner thought. The day before, I learned, her husband had been killed while standing at her side. An old couple slowly made their way up the hill. The woman held a cloth bag packed with food. She had also brought with her some *matzos* in a paper bag. Her husband carried the family's clothing. They had left the house they had lived in for 50 years.

The refugees had no time for a last glance at Rothchild House, pride of the Quarter with its elegant archways and pinkish limestone façade, as they trudged on. The crunch over the dusty rubble reminded me of a familiar sound I could not identify until I closed my eyes. It was like the surf rolling in along a pebbled beach.

In the uncertain light of dusk, when colors fade to tones of gray, I photographed the last refugees. Dr de Azcarate, head of the United Nations' Truce Commission, stood next to me. "Misery always wears the same face," I said. Dr de Azcarate nodded. "I'm a Spanish Republican. It was like this at Malaga during the Civil War."

The first wave of refugees reached the Zion Gate, the borderline between Old and New Jerusalem. Once through, the refugees would be in Israeli territory. Few looked back.

I walked back to the Street of the Jews. Black smoke billowed out of windows, while bright-yellow flames licked wooden balconies. The smell of burning mingled with the stench of death. Distracted by the speed with which the entire Quarter was being engulfed, I almost missed the terrified little girl running down the street. In her terror, she bared her teeth like a trapped animal.

The hospital looked like a scene from the Crimean War. In the far corner, a ten-year-old boy listlessly held a loaf of bread. His left shoulder had been shattered by a hand grenade. Uneaten biscuits littered the folds of his blanket. His wizened face made him look like a little old man. I wondered if he would ever again be able to look at the world through the eyes of a child.

A young man lay unconscious from a head wound. He had strong, handsome features, and clasped the hand of a nurse who covered her face in grief. In the hallway, a body lay on a stretcher covered with a sheet, the left leg stuck out form beneath it. One of the doctors stopped by.

"His name was Yitzak Mizrachi," he said. "He could neither read nor write, but he was a real hero: war reveals such men. When he was brought in yesterday morning, word quickly spread that all was lost."

Outside was a burning pyre. The battle for the Jewish Quarter of Jerusalem was over.

Jewish Quarter, May 28, 1948, 4:40 pm

Exodus from the Jewish Quarter, May 28, 1948

Jewish Quarter, May 29, 1948, 4:40 pm

The Aftermath

Aware the destruction of the Jewish Quarter of Jerusalem would shock the Western world, the Arab authorities across the Middle East tried to prevent the news from leaking out. Under no circumstances was Jerusalem to be mentioned. A dutiful Cairo censor even attempted to blue-pencil every reference to the city in the Bible of a departing tourist.

I knew that my photographs—the only pictorial record of the agonies the Jewish Quarter had suffered—would inevitably wind up in the censor's wastepaper basket if I didn't smuggle them out.

I did just that for the sake of posterity, should posterity care what happened in Old Jerusalem on May 28, 1948. (This so angered the Arab Higher Committee, that it sentenced me to death. But by then I was out of the Middle East.)

The Israeli War for Independence dragged on, interrupted by truces and ceasefires, until a final armistice signed with Syria 14 months later brought the war officially to an end.

As for the fate of the main Arab participants in the war: on April 3, 1949, Abdullah acquired the West Bank when the borders between Jordan and Palestine were settled. Along with this territorial gain came 400,000 urban Arabs who were better educated and considered themselves superior to the original 500,000 Transjordanian Bedouins and the half-million refugees now living in camps.

This demographic change proved to be disastrous. On July 20, 1951, Abdullah was assassinated on his way to prayers at the Mosque of Aksa in Jerusalem. The instigators were none other than Major el Tel and Doctor Moussa Husseini in reprisals for Abdullah's treasonable behavior toward the Arab cause in the 1948 war. (The fundamentalists' explanation for Abdullah's attempts to improve relations between the Arabs and the Israelis.) He was succeeded by his son, Talal, who at the time of his father's assassination was undergoing shock treatments in a Swiss clinic and lived one floor below me at the Hotel Beau Rivage in Lausanne. Soon afterwards he gave up his throne to his 16-year-old son Hussein and retired to Turkey where he died.

July was not a favorable month for Arab royalty. On July 26, 1952 Farouk, compelled to abdicate, sailed off to a luxurious exile.

The end of the Hashemite kingdom of Iraq was far more traumatic. Faisal II (the son of Faisal I who led the Arab revolt with Lawrence) was butchered in a revolutionary military coup along with his prime minister. Iraq broke off its friendly relationship with the West as military coups replaced elections until finally the country wound up with Saddam Hussein.

The Grand Mufti sought political asylum in Pakistan. No one is quite sure what happed to Fawzi. In March 1956, King Hussein, Abdullah's grandson, dismissed Glubb Pasha in a matter of hours. According to his obituary in *The Times* of March 18, 1986, Glubb and his wife arrived in London with £5 in cash and little more in the bank. Knighted by the Queen, the British government then washed its hands of Sir John Glubb.

King Hussein, far less astute than his grandfather, in 1967 allowed himself to be dragged into the Six Day War and lost to the Israelis all of his grandfather's territorial gains in East Jerusalem and the West Bank. After some extremely deft political zigzags for his own personal salvation and the survival of his kingdom, Hussein, at the time of writing, is attempting a working relationship with the Israelis.

The
Break

Speaker at a conference in a Belgrade Machine Tool Works, 1949

Peasant family on *Novo Doba* (New Times) co-operative farm near Irig, Yugoslavia, 1949

Tito stands alone

Rebecca West, who was considered the great authority on Yugoslavia because of her monumental book *Grey Lamb, Black Falcon* (which was also nick-named "The Great Orgasm" because of her devotion to the Serbs), refused to believe that Russia had broken with Yugoslavia on June 28, 1948. Her incredulity was hardly surprising. At the time, Yugoslavia was a miniature Soviet Union. Few people believed in the possibility of a communist schism, forgetting the earlier religious wars.

One of those who did was Robert Borden Reams, the Counselor of the American Embassy in Belgrade. He not only had the perspicacity to anticipate the break, but the courage to face temporary unpopularity for reporting it to the State Department.

Six days after the split, Yugoslavia sent the United States a clear mes-sage. Its ranking officials, led by Djilas, Tito's number two, appeared at the annual Fouth of July garden party at the Embassy which they had so far shunned. Aware of the importance of this breakthrough, the Embassy staff kept the party going past the usual hours of six to eight Everybody was having a good time when the garden lights started to go out. The Ambas-sador's wife—a woman who would not permit her husband to play the piano until he got posted to an Embassy more suited to her taste—was standing on a chair putting them out.

Although I couldn't say I'd foreseen the break, it didn't surprise me. During the war, Tito had already displayed his independence by notifying Stalin, who provided advice, but not military aid: "If you cannot send us assistance, then at least do not hamper us." *Life* took it for granted I'd be able to take Tito's picture. I did not share the magazine's confidence.

Even Stalin could not see Tito he was so inaccessible. Western dip-lomats only saw him when they presented their credentials or when he gave official receptions once or twice a year. Now his aloofness had spread to the Soviets and their satellites.

I had managed to get one of the few visas Yugoslavia issued to journ-alists by attending the Danube Conference. At least I was in Belgrade, one month after the break. There I met up with my old friend and wartime partner, Stojan Pribecivic. My one hope of getting pictures of Tito was at the Fifth Party Congress which was holding its closing session that afternoon. This didn't work out. Admission was limited to party members.

Eager to hear what Tito had to say, however, Stojan and I visited old conservative friends—the kind known in Belgrade as "reactionaries" for having been capitalists. Grinning, our host greeted us with drinks and the latest twist to the song "Tito, Tito, Beloved by all the youth." The new refrain went: "Tito, Tito, beloved by all the reactionaries."

The Party Congress had been called to deal with Yugoslavia's dismissal from the Cominform. This information bureau, created in 1947 with the participation of the European communist parties, was subject to the Soviets' will. Stalin treated the Secretary General of every communist party as though his very existence depended upon his whim—even if, as in Tito's case, he was a chief of state. Stalin therefore expected that in response to his expression of displeasure, the Yugoslav Politburo would expel Tito from the party and name a successor more compliant with Soviet desires.

A brilliant tactician, Tito broke the news of the break with Russia to the Yugoslav public by first broadcasting Yugoslavia's reply—so that everybody knew how Tito felt before they heard the Cominform's denunciation. We all listened to Tito's speech. His voice came over the radio calm and unemotional, until he spoke about the Partisan war. Then it rose steadily as he relived the epic. By mocking the Yugoslav war effort, where 10 per cent of the population had perished, Stalin had offended what was most sacred in the nation.

After we had finished listening to the broadcast, Stojan was called to the telephone. We were instructed to go at once and wait in the street below. A car would come and pick us up. Tito was not mentioned, but we guessed he was sending for us.

"My camera's at the hotel," I whispered to Stojan.

"I must run back to the hotel and get my jacket," Stojan was explaining to the voice on the other end of the receiver to gain time. "Come as you are," the voice said, and hung up. I was going to see Tito without my camera and I couldn't begin to think about the consequences.

Tito received us at the White Palace where a reception was in progress. It reminded me of a post-election celebration. I had never seen Tito in better form.

I told him how terrible I felt. He laughed. "You're the only photographer I'm going to see, and you are not happy?"

"What do you think will happen to me when *Life* learns I saw you without a camera?"

"*Dobro, dobro,*" Tito said. "I'll see that you get my picture. But I can't give you all day as I did during the war. I don't have time for that."

When I tried to pin him down to a definite date, he laughed again. "Don't worry. I won't forget. You'll hear from me."

While I waited for my call, I pieced together some of the events which had led up to the break. Vladimir Ribnikar, once the influential owner of the liberal daily, *Politika*, told me. "Shortly before the break with Russia became public, I was summoned to the Central Committee. I was handed the complete correspondence between Stalin and Tito and left alone to read it. I didn't know what to expect, but when I was through reading, I suddenly felt relieved, as though the windows had been thrown open and fresh air had poured into the suffocating atmosphere I'd been living in."

This correspondence had come after years of Russian exploitation. The Soviets were against the Yugoslavs developing any industry which did not mesh with their own. They expected Tito to export all the country's raw materials to Russia. The Soviets also took over all the airfields, the most profitable air routes, and the control of air navigation. The exploitation also applied to agriculture, commerce, and industry, including the art world. Yugoslav theaters were supposed to perform only Russian plays, stock their libraries with Russian books, and fill the airwaves with Russian music.

The final straw came with a letter from Djilas requesting that the Soviets reduce the number of Russian military advisers stationed in Yugoslavia. Stalin was outraged. He couldn't believe that Djilas had written that "Soviet officers were morally inferior to officers in the British army", and Stalin denounced Djilas as "anti-Soviet". "The so-called Marxist Djilas... wanted to ignore the fundamental differences between the socialist Red Army who liberated the people of Europe and the bourgeois British army, whose duty was to oppress and not liberate people."

Stalin also admonished the Yugoslavs for daring to compare the Soviet ambassador, a responsible communist representing the government of the USSR, to a bourgeois diplomat, "an ordinary functionary of a bourgeois state..."

I soon realized that if Stalin assumed he could bring Tito to heel by ordering Yugoslavia expelled from the Cominform, he was greatly mistaken, just as the Western world was mistaken if it did not believe in the possibility of inter-communist struggle. To the non-communists in the country, Tito was the lesser evil, and they stood loyally behind him. The pro-Stalinists within the party itself were quietly rounded up by the police. They could hardly be denounced as communists, since Tito claimed to be one himself. So they were branded "Cominformists" and tossed into jails for "rehabilitation".

As Tito recalled later, "our disagreement with the leaders of the USSR started early in the war. The Russians did not want an independent movement in Yugoslavia which would be primarily concerned with the interests of its own country and its own people. They wanted a movement which would obey them blindly and serve as a mere tool of their policy…a policy dedicated to the expansion of the Soviet Union's power without regard for the interests of other countries, especially small ones. We did not like that."

I was still waiting for my call from Tito while I carried on with my coverage of the Danube Conference. I got some sense of the international reception of his speech when, at a party attended by the conference delegates, I heard Andrei Vishinsky, Stalin's grand inquisitor during the purges of the 1930s, declare to Sir Charles Peak, the British Ambassador: "Now that Yugoslavia is out of the Soviet bloc, it can no longer be considered a communist state."

"From a Russian point of view," Sir Charles replied, "I think you're perfectly right."

I got a call from Vlado Dedijer, whom I had photographed in Cairo and later met up with in Italy. He had a proposal for a future assignment he thought I might enjoy. The Yugoslavs wanted a photographic survey of the country and its people. He would hire me for the job. It was a remarkable offer, as no foreigner was allowed to travel around the country, let alone take pictures. "It won't cost you a penny if I do it as a *Life* assignment," I told Vlado. "It will be published in the magazine, and won't be regarded as government propaganda."

Vlado suggested that I come back in 1949. Bob Reams told me: "Do it, by all means." But there remained a problem. My passport needed to be renewed. This meant it would be stamped "Not valid for travel in

Yugoslavia," since Tito was still on the enemy list for shooting down an American transport flying over Yugoslav territory. "Don't worry," Reams shrugged reassuringly. (When my passport was renewed, there was no interdiction to travel in Yugoslavia.)

That August 15, 1948, however, I had only two more days before my visa ran out. I thought I was going to have to leave without seeing Tito again. Then I got a cryptic call. "Take tonight's Orient Express with Stojan. Get off in Ljubljana. You'll be met." This meant Tito was not in Belgrade, as everybody assumed.

Tito's driver met us at the Ljubljana Station. We drove to the summer resort on Lake Bled, 50 kilometers from Ljubliana. Our 10am appointment with Tito was canceled without explanation.

His secretary, Zonko Brkic, took us on a picnic. "Tito's idea," he volunteered. "*Stari* (the old man) wants you to see Lake Bohin and his favorite waterfall." We sat in a field, ate sandwiches made of thick slices of Slovene ham and butter, drank beer, admired the waterfall, and, above all, wondered whether something serious was up.

The next morning we saw Tito for half an hour. He looked haggard and was not his usual self until I took his picture before the statue of a defiant Partisan fighter. I asked him about Tigar, his German shepherd dog. "Tigar," Tito said, "is taking advantage of the summer vacation by swimming in the lake." He whistled for him, however, and Tigar came running. I took a shot of them together. When Tigar became exasperated with fleas, Tito told him, "Don't scratch in front of the American public. It's not polite." He then offered Stojan and me a drink, apologized for not giving me more of his time, and hurried off.

I suspected that the political situation had deteriorated until Zvonko explained why we had not seen Tito the day before. "He was running a high fever and only crawled out of bed this morning to give you the opportunity to take his picture as he had promised," adding, "I must ask you not to mention the fact that *Stari* is sick. He wants this to be a diplomatic illness."

Peasants on *Novo Doba* (New Times) co-operative farm near Irig, Yugoslavia, 1949

Yugoslavian peasant's son, 1949

Tito on Mitzi, his Lipizzaner horse with Tigar, his German shepherd dog, Island of Brioni, 1949

Tito's Great What-is-it?

A year later I was back in Belgrade. Yugoslavia did not have one friendly neighbor. There was no traffic across the Italian border because Tito had made a claim on Trieste. The Greek frontier was sealed, although Tito no longer helped the communists in their civil war. Relations with Austria were cool, owing to border disagreements over Carinthia. At Stalin's bidding, the Albanians, Bulgarians, Hungarians and Romanians created almost daily border incidents. With no friends in the Eastern bloc, and few as yet among the Western countries, Yugoslavia stood alone that summer of 1949.

Stalin set out to destroy Tito in his own country by accusing him of being "a lackey of capitalism". Tito coolly enraged him by refuting these "Cominformist" denunciations with the claim that since the Yugoslavs adhered strictly to Marx and Lenin, it was they—and not the Soviets—who were genuine communists.

Stalin saw in this heresy a threat. Tito was a Western man with much more in common with the Czechs, the Poles, the Hungarians, the Romanians and the Bulgarians than with the Soviets. What if "Titoism" spread? The heretics had to be destroyed.

Stalin ordered the liquidation of possible Tito sympathizers. Xoxe Coxe, Albania's number-two communist, was accused of being a "Tito agent". He was shot. Lazlo Rajk, Hungary's ex-chief of secret police, confessed to complicity with Tito. He was hanged. Traicho Kostov, a founding father of Bulgaria's communist party, was accused of being "a Tito puppet". He was also hanged. As the witch-hunt spread, 15 Czechs were executed in Prague on similar charges.

Stalin also threw the might of the Soviet Union and its satellites into an economic blockade of Yugoslavia. His timing was perfect. Yugoslavia had not yet recovered from the war. Its economy was still in a chaotic state of transition from Balkan capitalism to Soviet socialism. Its labyrinthine pre-war bureaucracy was only compounded by the strictures of Marxism. And the cumbersome five-year industrialization plan was dependent upon Soviet co-operation: close to 50 per cent of Yugoslavia's exports were to go to Cominform countries. The moment these countries broke their trade agreements, the industrialization program in Yugoslavia was left to flounder. In a bold move, Tito overhauled the government: 120,000 civil servants, all Partisan faithful, lost their jobs.

The government had second thoughts about the Soviet industrial methods which prescribed: "a mass of rituals aimed at producing incentive through a competitive spirit aimed at increasing the industrial quotas into record-breaking production percentages,"—regardless of quality. Tito settled for punching a clock and putting in a day's work.

With the idea of adapting industry to Yugoslav communism, the government came up with the concept of "self-management through workers' councils". "Every worker a shareholder," a plant director explained to me. Companies could now negotiate contracts with foreign countries without official sanction, and keep 70 per cent of the foreign currency earned. "Demand and supply," the manager explained, "is the Marxist key to production." (The problem was that qualified managers were at such a premium, they were not required to be dedicated Marxists. With salaries in no way commensurate with the job's responsibilities, a number of chief executives were jailed for embezzlement.)

There was also a childlike sense of competition between the republics. When Belgrade completed a huge film-producing complex suitable for the entire six republics, the other five expected studios of their own. Enrico Mattei, the Italian oil tycoon, recalled that when Tito consulted him over building a refinery, "I suggested the port of Rijeka in Croatia as the most suitable location."

"The trouble," Tito told him, "is that every republic will want its own refinery."

Facing a dearth of skilled labor, Tito asked the International Labor Organization in Geneva if he could send 2,000 Yugoslavs to Western countries for instruction, on the guarantee they would not advocate communism and would return home in a year. (They all returned except one, who got married and settled down in Western Europe. "That's love," Tito said philosophically.)

Stalin then denounced Tito for calling his peasants, "the strongest pillar of the Yugoslav state." (Soviet dogma pronounced that only city workers could be the foundation of the state.) Eighty per cent of the population was rural, and besides, the peasants had contributed both food and men to the liberation war. Tito's approach to the agrarian question had originally been the expropriation of land and the creation of co-operatives. Joining had not been compulsory: 70 per cent of the farmers were not interested. (In Tito's own village, only eight out of 60 peasants joined a co-op.)

At first, these peasants, who were called *privatniks*, were compelled to sell a high percentage of their crops and livestock below the state market prices. They simply hoarded their produce and consumed it themselves. (Peasants broke dozens of eggs into pails of milk and force-fed their calves, then ate the succulent veal themselves.)

The government relented, peasants were allowed to own up to ten hectares of farmland. Soon the *privatniks* were on their way to town in their narrow horse-drawn carts loaded with produce. There they sold it at three times the official price, to the indignation of the city dwellers.

City life was full of discomforts. Belgrade's population—under 250,000 before the war—shot up to 400,000. After the Liberation, apartment houses had been rationed to one room per person (with exceptions made for certain professions, such as authors, who were allocated an additional room in which to write). These measures failed to meet the need. (It was commonplace for newlyweds to live separately in their respective parents' homes while seeking lodgings of their own.) The government expanded the city across the Sava River to a sandy wasteland and named it New Belgrade.

With no skilled labor available, students from all over the country gave up their summer vacations to work on this project. Youth battalions lived in barracks and marched to the construction sites, singing as they went, flags fluttering. There they toiled until the economic blockade brought work to a halt. A desolate landscape of concrete shells stood out against the New Belgrade sky while weeds took over the area for years, before conditions improved and the construction work was completed.

There was a shortage of goods in the stores and the quality of what could be found was shoddy. Bookshops were the one exception. They were generously stocked. Trotsky's writings, along with Arthur Koestler's *Darkness at Noon*—banned in the satellite countries—could be purchased, along with the works of Dickens, Balzac, Tolstoy, Jack London, Sinclair Lewis, and Conan Doyle's *Adventures of Sherlock Holmes* (which Tito had enjoyed in his youth). Prices were reasonable and books were soon out of print. Those

489

who knew the language found part-time employment doing translations. They were not the only ones to moonlight. With government office hours from 7am to 3pm, and salaries totally inadequate, Yugoslavs had the afternoon free for a second job. Doctors treated patients at home. The legal profession, which had been in the doldrums during the Russian period, thrived once again. Actors from the state theater appeared in Yugoslav films. Movie-going was a favorite pastime. Cinemas were continuously sold out. Besides Yugoslav films, they showed French, English, and American features.

During this period of readjustment from their "Sovietization," Tito, fully aware that he personally had contributed to making Stalin a symbol of Marxist brotherhood, dissociated himself with methodical care. It took 16 months for the full blast of public criticism to be turned on Stalin. (I noticed a clearance-sale atmosphere in the department stores when Stalin's portraits were marked way down.)

My interpreter Teddy Pahor gave me an insight into the way a young Yugoslav felt about those times. Teddy, who was a Slovene, had a remarkable gift for languages. He had learned English by listening to the BBC and sounded just like an upper-class Englishman down from Oxford—which was absurd when you knew what a hand-to-mouth existence his childhood had been with his father out of work most of the time. Teddy told me he received an education his family could never have afforded before the war. Though not a member of the communist party, he was solidly pro-Tito. (Teddy felt this was the thing to do after all the government had done for him.) During our travels, he confided his hopes for the future. "My dream is that economic conditions will improve so that I can get married and live decently. I look forward to coffee being plentiful again, to when a kilo of sugar won't cost one fifth of my weekly wages, and when razor blades will be available. Can you imagine?" Teddy sighed. "It pays to smuggle razor blades, lighter flints, and clock hands into Yugoslavia."

He felt that Tito had been right to break with Stalin. "It means I have to eat black bread," Teddy said, "but I'm free to say that Walt Whitman is the greatest poet in the world."

As I traveled around the country, I was curious to know how Tito was making out under such terrible stress. I remembered an account of how he sat coolly in a terrace café under the assumed identity of engineer Babic, as he observed the German Army enter Zagreb. How was he bearing up now? I soon found out when, as usual, I was whisked off to see him without any warning.

"What do they say in America about my fight with the Cominform?" was Tito's cheerful greeting as I walked into the drawing-room of his villa on the island of Brioni on a summer afternoon.

Once an exclusive resort when it belonged to Italy, Brioni was even more exclusive now that Tito spent his summers there. I was taken to the brand-new hotel which faced a deserted pier. It was a remarkable place. It had no name, and flowers bloomed where I expected to find hall porters and the reception desk. The absence of cash registers was explained by the lack of cash customers. Tourists were not allowed on Brioni, and the only visitors were guests of Tito. My suite had two radios, one in each room. My bathroom, however, had neither mirrors nor running water. When I mimicked brushing my teeth, the maid produced two bottles of lukewarm beer. (Over the next 30 years, guests included Richard Burton, Willy Brandt, Che Guevara, Nikita Krushchev, Sophia Loren, for whom he laid a red carpet reaching into the Adriatic, Nasser, Nehru, and Elizabeth Taylor.)

Despite Tito's hearty greeting, there had been an early reminder of Russia's relentless pressure on Yugoslavia. When I had arrived at the villa, I had been detained in the hall until I had been identified by his secretary, who knew me. Only then was a door thrown open and I was ushered in to Tito.

In answer to his greeting I said, "Americans would like to know more about your fight with Stalin. You should write your memoirs." He laughed and changed the subject by asking what kind of pictures I had in mind. I said, "A formal portrait."

In shirt sleeves and without a tie, Tito decided that he was not suitably dressed for a formal portrait. While he disappeared to get changed, I reflected on the fact that being well dressed was something of a national crusade for Tito. I remembered a conversation I'd had with a former Partisan major, a woman, who now held a government position. We had been reminiscing about how bleak Belgrade was after the liberation, when Partisan women were in battledress and civilian clothes were drab. "Although foreign currency reserves were dangerously low," she told me, "Tito earmarked part of these funds for the purchase of lipstick and nylon stockings

491

from the United States. His policy was to get the women out of uniform as quickly as possible. With women looking more attractive, he worked out the men would find ways to improve their own looks.

"We were so earnest in those days," she said with a smile. "We thought only of building schools and factories. Attaching any importance to clothes struck us as frivolous—but not Tito. When I went to London in 1945 with the first Yugoslav delegation to travel abroad, I found his cabled instructions—every woman in the delegation was to visit the hairdresser and wear a skirt at the meetings."

Tito reappeared wearing the jacket to his white suit and a polka-dot tie held in place by a gold clip in the shape of a Moorish sword. I took the portrait and then inquired after his old companion.

We found Tigar stretched out on the lawn. He joined us. Several years later—old and ill—Tigar clung to life until Tito got back from a state visit abroad. "It was as if Tigar waited for the old man to get back," an aide told me. There would be other German shepherds, each one named in memory of that great dog.

"Now. Let me show you my speed boat," Tito proposed as he briskly led me to a landing pier. He hopped on board his Chris-Craft, started up the engine, and went swooping around in wide circles. When I asked him if he liked speed, he nodded in contentment. "I was once a test driver at Daimler-Benz."

Tito then took me to his billiard-room for a game of pool which he enjoyed with three cronies. General Zezelj, in charge of the bodyguards, had saved Tito during the seventh German offensive by arriving in the nick of time with reinforcements. He was an amiable colossus. Few things pleased him more than to display his massive gold cigarette case inscribed, "To General Zezelj from J.B. Tito." Dr Ivo Popovich was a surgeon, born in Pittsburgh. Tito always took him along when he traveled. When I made trips with Tito, I shared with Dr Popovich the back seat of a black Packard identical to Tito's except that ours was not bulletproof. Before we drove off, the jovial doctor would solemnly lay out gauze-wrapped surgical instruments at our feet in the event of an emergency. Branko, Tito's secretary, made up the trio, a sulky-looking man who laughed only when Tito did. They had only recently taken up billiards and made up in enthusiasm what they lacked in skill.

After lunch, I got word that Tito wanted to show me Mitzi, his eight-year-old Lipizzaner. "She's a circus horse," he said with pride as he rode up on her. I saw an opportunity to get different shots. "Do you fish?" I asked. "We'll go fishing," Tito replied, before riding off.

By the time we reached the pier, Tito had changed again and was waiting for us. We took bottles of white wine, a soda syphon, and a scrawny kid in short pants aboard the motor launch. "Who is he?" I asked Tito.

"Son," Tito replied laconically.

When he noticed that I was about to photograph the child, whose name was Misa, Tito produced a small comb from his hip pocket and smoothed down his tousled hair. I later discovered that no one outside his immediate entourage knew Tito had a younger son from his second marriage. And certainly no one dreamed that the Marshal of Yugoslavia occasionally played marbles with an eight-year-old.

Tito was an impatient fisherman. We cruised around under the protection of armed corvettes, a further reminder that it was not only fish Tito was having problems with.

It was dark when we got back to the villa. Tito led me into the dining-room. He sat at the head of the table and beckoned me to sit on his right. The other dinner guests were General Zezelj, Dr Popovic, Branko Vucinic, and his chauffeur, Lt Colonel Nikica Prlja. Tito helped himself to some pale-pink wine which he mixed with soda. Told to help myself, I was about to pour some wine from Tito's bottle when he discouraged me. "Not very strong," he said, recommending a potent-looking black wine.

We had noodles for the first course. Tito's tastes in food were simple. His favorite dishes were Slovene, the kind his mother had cooked. (Driving back to Belgrade once, Tito stopped at a roadside inn 30 kilometers from Ljubljana which prepared one of his favorite dishes—a strudel made with cheese and bacon. From then on, whenever he was driving through Ljubljana, the innkeeper was notified to have some strudel ready.)

During dinner, Tito told us about the time he was an escaped POW, and lived with the Kirghiz tribesmen while hiding out from the Russian White Guard. The chief gave Tito a horse which had not been broken in and asked him to show what he could do. In words and gestures, Tito related the wild ride—whipping through the forest, ducking branches and ripping his clothes for some ten kilometers, after which the exhausted horse slowed down. The chief then offered Tito his daughter in marriage. We had all stopped eating and were were listening intently, especially General Zezelj, who gaped in wonder while he kept repeating, *"Bogati… Bogati!"* ("Oh God…Oh God!")

"When did you learn to ride?" I asked.

"As a boy on my grandfather's farm," Tito replied. "If I took off my shoes I could stand under the horse without the top of my head touching its belly."

The second course was steak. Tito was served stew. From time to time, he fed Tigar a juicy treat. (Tito also gave Tigar chicken bones, which he munched like pretzels.)

"I wrote a lot in Siberia," Tito remarked as he poured himself some wine, musing, "I enjoy writing here."

"Do you write longhand?" I asked.

Tito nodded. Knowing how busy he was, I recommended the use of a dictating machine, something which was then a novelty. "You attach the microphone to your shirt so you can pace up and down the room while planning what you want to say next."

Tito didn't respond. I assumed he wasn't interested. (The next morning Doctor Popovic collared me, "What's the name of that machine you fasten to your shirt?" he asked. "The old man wants one.")

The conversation switched to motion pictures. "American films are fine, but some are a little foolish," Tito observed. He loved the movies and saw one practically every night. He was liberal in his tastes. When he heard that the Italian picture *Bitter Rice*, featuring Silvana Mangano's legs, had been censored, he remarked, "There's nothing there to hurt them," and suggested the film be generally released. His favorite pictures, however, were westerns and Laurel and Hardy comedies.

"Do you also like Chaplin?" I asked, wondering if he had seen *The Great Dictator*, then showing in Belgrade.

"Modern Times," Tito said, pantomiming the scene of Chaplin on the production line.

"He's made other pictures since," I answered.

"You mean *The Great Dictator*," Tito said blandly. "I liked that too."

After fresh pears and Turkish coffee, we went into the living-room to see an American picture called *Yours Forever*. "Hope it's good," Tito said.

This picture, adapted from Louis Bromfield's novel *Mrs Parkington*, was something of an embarrassment for me. At one point, a woman in ermine, after sweeping aside children singing carols in the snow, wandered over to a sideboard and helped herself to a large tumbler of liquor.

Tito, a talkative movie-goer, nudged me and whispered, "Visky."

Greer Garson then appeared on the screen looking 80. Luckily, there was soon a flashback. When Tito saw Miss Garson as she really looked, he quite literally sat up. In a following scene, Walter Pidgeon came careening down Main Street in a horse and buggy.

"Cowboys," Tito said hopefully. But this was the last horse we saw until a fox-hunting scene, 30 years later. Miss Garson was then in conversation with a distinguished gentleman with a goatee. Tito immediately identified him and nudged me, "King of England Edward Seven."

In between, we witnessed a terrible mining disaster due to callousness on the management's part. At this point, the lights were switched on to change the reel. I blushed while an embarrassed silence filled the room. Luckily, in the following reel, capitalism made a great recovery, thanks to Miss Garson. She paid off the family debts and observed, "Power is not something to dissipate. Power must be reserved for those who know how to use it." Once again, Tito sat up.

Years after the break, Khrushchev visits Tito, Belgrade, 1955

Khrushchev, Mikoyan, and Bulganin visiting the Monument to Fallen Soldiers, Belgrade, 1955

Natalie de Montesquiou, France, 1949

French Father, Mousseaux, 1949

Ambiguous
Times

New York Interlude

In February 1949, Wilson Hicks ordered me back to New York. He was unhappy with my work. He felt that "my beat was not my meat". The El Azhar University story with its gloomy fanaticism didn't fit his vision of a Moslem world according to *Kismet*.

He was also displeased that my pictures of the early Christian tomb in Jerusalem, the pictorial rights of which he had acquired for $5,000 had not turned out to be the photogenic success he had anticipated. (He had felt compelled to send another photographer to re-shoot the story improved by having an Arab stand on a nearby wall to provide human interest.)

Hicks was further aggravated by his combat photographers, whom he felt required disciplining now that the war was over. He didn't particularly care that they had brought distinction to the magazine, and made the public aware that a great picture was no less eloquent and heart-rending than words. Pictures had a way of lurking in people's memories. Who could ever forget Margaret Bourke-White's pictures of Buchenwald's living dead?

Offended by the tone of Wilson Hicks's letter, I replied that if he wanted a court martial to go ahead. If not, I'd like to propose a story on the France of Marcel Proust on my return. Although in those days a photographer had little recourse beyond the picture editor, I sent a copy of my letter to Harry Luce, the founder of Time Inc.

New York had changed greatly since my first visit there in 1938. The United States had awakened to the fact that it was the only country which emerged from the war far more powerful than it had gone in. With no devastated cities and an exuberant population, everything was bigger and better than ever. America, with its extraordinary gift for technical achievement, was exploding with ideas and vitality, and so was *Life*, under its new managing editor Edward K. Thompson. With a circulation of over seven million, *Life* exerted an influence the TV networks would only overtake with satellites. With 45 talented staff photographers, *Life* covered the world with a voracious enthusiasm. Thompson took full advantage of the advances in photography, including catching on film what the eye couldn't see, such as the trajectory of a bullet fired from a pistol. So while everybody looked towards the glowing future of the American century, I focused on the past that was rapidly disappearing.

In his reply to my letter, Harry Luce made it clear that Time didn't conduct court-martials. When I got to New York I called up his secretary. She told me that Mr Luce would be free to lunch with me that coming Monday at the Louis IV at 1pm if I were available.

Available? I showed up at the restaurant a quarter of an hour early. At lunchtime the Louis XIV was the favourite hang-out of Time's senior editors. They were all there and didn't appear particularly friendly until I was joined by Harry Luce.

When the subject of Italy came up, I reported how the great art historian Bernard Berenson had been very impressed by *Life*'s color cover story on Giotto. This delighted Harry Luce and gave me an opportunity to mention that while we worried about Italians becoming communists, they didn't run around in silk blouses with tasseled belts playing the balalaika. They wore jeans and played the guitar.

"Why didn't you do a story on Berenson?" Luce demanded.

"I was in Lebanon recovering from dysentery when *Life* asked for the story," I told him. "But Dimitri Kessel shot it." I then explained why I felt I'd be more useful to *Life* in Europe than in the States. Harry Luce said he would think about it.

After lunch I reported to Ed Thompson's office, where I was spending the week watching *Life* being edited. The phone rang. Harry Luce was inquiring about the Berenson story. It was promptly brought up, and published the following week. Luce agreed to my returning to Europe and I got the go-ahead to shoot my French story after Yugoslavia.

Wilson Hicks asked to see me, and proposed a drink after office hours at the Louis XIV. There promptly at 5pm, I ran into Howard Black who was to Time's business side what Harry Luce was to editorial. A friendly man with a passion for prize fights, he invited me to join him. Three whiskey sours later, at 6:30, Hicks showed up. Taken aback that I was enjoying myself while waiting for him, he suggested we talk. "I've decided to send you back to Europe," Hicks told me.

"I know," I said. "I've booked my return on the *New Amsterdam*.

Jean de Montesquiou with café owner Raymond Olivier, Paris, 1949

France, 1949

The Proustian France story came to me in Paris as I strolled through the Tuileries on an early autumn evening while a light drizzle made the black asphalt shiny. Unexpectedly, the fragrance of roasted chestnuts brought back memories of my schooldays in France, very much the way a *madeleine* dipped in tea awakened in Proust his *Remembrance of Things Past*. I vividly recalled standing in class, listening to our teacher impress upon us the grandeur of *la patrie* and having the day off whenever an old field marshal from the First World War was given a state funeral.

We were steadily indoctrinated with stories about France's civilizing influence as it spread culture and Gallic wit across Europe. Now, after the débacle of 1940, I wondered what remained of the traditional France I had grown up in. Aware of the great part it had played in my education I wanted to record what remained of that world.

To convert such a personal vision into a pictorial story for an American magazine I sought inspiration from Proust's masterpiece, which provides a remarkably accurate picture of French life in the previous generation. My hope was to present the present-day French generation in pictures for the readers of *Life*.

Proust had drawn his sharply-observed and thinly-disguised characters from France's social elite—a number of them from the Montesquiou family, which, thanks to a Montesquiou who had been his guide, Proust had been given the opportunity to observe at first-hand. What I needed was to attach myself to such a family.

Why not the Montesquious? I had met Count Jean, a nephew of the Montesquiou who had helped Proust. I decided to make him a proposition.

"I have a car and an expense account," I said to the Count. "Show me France."

First of all I suggested lunch. Suspecting his gastronomic tastes, I took him to Le Grand Vefour, a restaurant already into its second century as it looked out on the gardens of the Palais Royal. Watching Jean de Montesquiou's performance as he savored a trout *crêpe* and sipped a dry white Montrachet was a lyrical experience. The thick, juicy slices of

Châteaubriand with Béarnaise sauce met with his approval. The red Clos de Vougeot reminded him of the French general who ordered "eyes right" when this troops marched past that venerable vineyard. The climax to the lunch was a golden *soufflé de pommes*. "This marvel," Jean declared, "took two centuries of culture to produce." He topped the meal with coffee and an Armagnac 1886. Sighing contentedly, he agreed to show me France.

Count Maurice Henri Jean de Montesquiou Fezensac, known to his familiars as Jean, was 47 when we met. He was born at 107 Rue de la Pompe, the smartest address in Paris at the turn of the century, and one which reflected the privileged life his family enjoyed: when Jean's mother got married, Gustave Eiffel's wedding present was to beam a white light at night from his tower on to the window of the living-room where the wedding presents were displayed.

Of medium height, balding, with a tiny moustache, Jean affected bow-ties, wore a stiff-brimmed felt hat and carried a cane. He had an older brother, Fernand, who had inherited the family château. The brothers had a distant cousin, Pierre de Montesquiou, the Fifth Duke of Fezensac and titular head of the family. Though the family links were not as close as they had been in Napoleon's time, the bonds remained strong. They met at christenings, marriages, and funerals.

This family had been picked out by history in 1030, when an heiress named Montesquiou married a Fezensac. This merger of wealth and aristocracy would produce one of France's most powerful and glamorous families. The Montesquiou-Fezensacs provided military leaders for the armies of the kingdom, the Republic and the Empire, a president of the legislative assembly, a commissioner of finance, several ambassadors, a governess for Napoleon's heir, along with the dashing musketeer D'Artagnan, who was no figment of Alexander Dumas's imagination, but a Montesquiou on his mother's side.

Jean was always very much aware of his ancestry as he grew up in the family château at Longpont, 50 miles north east of Paris, in the very center of what the French had come to call "the road of foreign invasions". His education was in keeping with his social status. Jean never attended school but was tutored by the château's abbot, who guided him through *les hautes etudes*.

Too young to fight in the First World War, Jean's generation was overlooked by the Second. He spent those years at home with his Hungarian-born wife Natalie. (Countess Natalie Csaky's ancestors were the chieftains of one of the seven tribes which settled in Hungary around the first millennium.) After World War II, Natalie was ruined, her wealth wiped out by the Hungarian and Czech communists' appropriation of her estates.

Though they were greatly reduced financially, Jean and Natalie still lived spiritually in the old world they were born in. I got a glimpse of it as Jean showed me around. He first led me to the forlorn offices of *La Revue des Deux Mondes*, once France's most influential publication. He had a meeting there with a member of the French Academy who guided the *Revue*, about his writing an article about a French engraver working on a limited edition of *Don Quixote* at Les Baux near Avignon.

We paid a visit to the ballerina Janine Solane at her studio, where she was rehearsing with her company for a special performance at the National Theater of Chaillot during the Paris season. Solane choreographed her own ballets to the music of Bach and Beethoven. After the inevitable *baise main*, the pair had an earnest conversation. She was to be a major character in his forthcoming novel.

We listened to Reine Lorin, an ex-classical actress who now declaimed poems. She was rehearsing *The Tree*, by the Belgian poet Verhaeren, in what used to be the studio of the sculptor Bourdelle. (She had selected this studio, which now belonged to the City of Paris, as *The Tree* had been the sculptor's favorite poem.) Standing in front of one of Bourdelle's huge statues, the *diseuse* rehearsed for a public recitation she was to give.

Jean introduced me to his cousin, Countess Gerard de Brye—born Odette Montesquiou, the name she used when giving harp recitals—just as a performance was beginning in her salon. She played musical settings to poems by Count Robert de Montesquiou, as well as her own compositions. To Jean's delight, *thé goûter*, France's version of the British five o'clock tea, was served with *petits fours* and port wine.

When Carrère, the Parisian cabaret, offered its premises for a literary tea, Jean was one of the performers. He recited pages of dialogue from of his books *Sirocco or The Tale of the Night*.

Before leaving for his own château, Jean visited his uncle's outside Paris, The Château de Maintenon had been commissioned by Louis XIV for his mistress Madame de Maintenon, and was of the vast proportions and luxury Louis took for granted. Although some tiles on the roof had blown

away as the result of US bombing during the war, its great gallery and intimate salons were elegantly decorated with luxurious period furniture,
bibelots and large paintings on the walls. As it required the staff of a grand
hotel to run it, the present-day owners of the château, the Duke and
Duchess de Noailles, only occasionally dropped by. The Duke was Jean's
godfather and uncle. Seated in the small salon where Louis visited his mistress, with a painting of the monarch in peacock garb looking on, the de
Noailles seemed utterly out of place. There was something quietly demen-
ted about the whole visit, especially when the Duchess asked me who in the
United States she should bill for her broken roof tiles.

When the Paris season was over, Jean and Natalie retired to their
château in peaceful Mervan in north eastern France. The Château de la
Roche, more a fortress than a castle, had been built in the days of Louis
XIV by one of France's greatest military architects on a high bluff overlooking the village of La Roche Millay. The château had come to Jean
through a series of family inheritances. His grandmother, the Duchess of
Noailles, had left it to one of her daughters, the Marquise de Virieu, who in
turn passed it on to her sister, Jean's mother, who bequeathed it to her son.

When in residence, Jean confronted the difficulties of running this
white elephant with the limited revenues from the farmland and forest
which had come with the château. (He would devote a morning to fixing a
telephone wire, and the broom that swept the salons was so threadbare it
looked as though the maid was cleaning the fortress with a toothbrush.)
Such ignominious details, however, were kept from the local villagers, who
were flattered that a Montesquiou resided in their midst.

Life at the château followed a definite pattern. From 8am until noon,
draped in a large white bathrobe. Jean did his "creative writing" in the
library. Though it was early morning, the light there was dim as Jean kept
the blinds closed to prevent sun rays from fading the original Aubusson
upholstery of his Louis XVI armchairs. Then, at noon, Jean appeared for
lunch in a three-piece suit. (Careful about his digestion, he unbuttoned his
belt before the meal.) By mid-afternoon he had changed into his maroon
smoking-jacket before visiting Natalie in her boudoir where she wore a tea-
gown. Jean would then recite to her what he had written that morning.
Although they occasionally dressed for dinner, the pair lived by the sun,
frequently sitting in semi-darkness to save on the electricity bills.

Whenever Natalie ran out of Gauloises, Jean went to the village. As the local squire, he made it a practice to remain neutral over La Roche Millay's feuding factions: in those early post-war years, La Roche Millay was divided between those who feared God and those who feared "the reds". (While "red" might well have described a communist, more often than not it applied to a radical socialist, a member of the party that was neither radical nor socialist, but middle-of-the-road.) In La Roche Millay the members of the two factions almost never mixed. There had been much excitement after the Liberation, when those who feared God and had peacefully obeyed the *diktats* of the German occupation accused the members of the French Resistance of being "reds". Things had calmed down by the time I got there, to the point that when a fire broke out in Jean's château, most of the volunteer firemen were "reds". Many of the priests now came from the working class and held liberal views that shocked the sedate villagers of La Roche Millay.

By tradition, Jean had the power to punish any priest he considered a red. By tradition, too, he entertained the parish priest for dinner once a week: a special treat. If the priest was in Jean's disfavor, he would be invited on Friday and served codfish.

The main square of Lay Roche Millay faced the entrance to Jean's château and, as in all French villages, had a World War I memorial. Chickens ran loose around its base. There was also the Hôtel de la Tour, and one café. Mme Jublot, the retired tobacconist whose husband tended bees, was the village gossip. Her home was at the intersection by the Hotel de la Tour. From there she observed everything that went on as she sat at her ground-floor window hour by hour. Whenever Jean passed he stopped to chat. Everyone in the village greeted one another.

Occasionally the quiet monotony of life was rudely interrupted, as was the case when Mme Doreau, the elderly lady who ran the grocery store, dropped dead. The entire community went to the funeral. The shops were closed. Everybody wore their Sunday best. The four village agnostics hung outside the church while the service was conducted, then joined the procession. Naturally Jean and Natalie attended the funeral.

Along with his château, Jean had acquired an old retainer in his seventies. Jean Maric Pacot first came to the château in 1905 as a poultry boy when the Duchess of Noailles was the owner. He was still there in 1949.

Whenever Pacot mentioned the château he said "*mon château*". Its upkeep was his life's achievement. Pacot could no longer handle the heavy work but he was still the custodian of the château and overseer of Jean's farm. When Jean traveled down to supervise the running of the farm in the winter, he stayed in his janitor's lodge because the château was too costly to heat. On these occasions Pacot produced a bottle of wine from his cellar which he served with biscuits.

Pacot's wife was called Rose. The pair had two children born in the lodge. Their daughter had died of burns when she overturned the stove. Their son Henri was a butcher.

Every free moment of her day Rose spent at her kitchen window, her cat on her lap, watching what went on in the square. Her favorite crony was her neighbor, who stood outside the window in the street while they gossiped. While Rose was relatively cool, the neighbor was an explosive character who punctuated her statements with wild gestures. In 35 years Rose never invited her neighbor into the lodge.

The Pacot's son Henri was their pride and joy. They had invested their savings in a butcher's shop for him at Château Chinon, 15 miles from La Roche Millay. When the war broke out in 1939, Henri was drafted. Taken prisoner, he only returned to France in 1945. During the years he was a POW, his wife Yvonne single-handedly carried on the family business. On his return, when Henri discovered that a considerable number of people in town had been making money on the black market while he was a prisoner, he decided to cash in on the black market himself. In those days, Paris firemen drove to Château Chinon to collect kindling. In exchange for a lamb for their mess, the firemen carted back large hunks of meat to Paris in their trucks, undetected by the checkpoints. There, because meat was in such demand because of rationing, it sold for twice the price.

As Henri looked at it, he had helped relieve a meat shortage in Paris. However he never dared tell his father about his black market activities. With his profits, Henri acquired a second butcher's shop and hired its ex-owner as an employee. He also bought and sold cattle. By the time I met him he had seven million francs-worth of cattle.

The biggest event in the Pacots' life was the annual lunch their son gave for the Montesquious. They started talking about it months before. When the Sunday arrived, the pair were all dressed up in black and beaming with satisfaction. Henri's wife was so busy cooking and serving she was unable to join her guests at table, but Henri, far more sophisticated than his parents, casually tucked his napkin under the chin indifferent to Natalie's disapproving looks.

There was ham cooked in sherry, covered with cheese and baked. Then came the traditional Sunday chicken roasted to a golden crackle. This was followed by a formidably rich cake. Knowing Jean's addiction to sweets, Henri served a second cake with no less cream and chocolate. Seven of the eleven bottles of wine on hand were emptied. By the time the guests were ready to leave in the late afternoon, Jean had asked Henri for a leg of lamb, which he got at a discount. In his parting words, Jean reminded his hosts to be sure and visit him and the countess sometime for a cup of tea.

"It's vintage time," Jean announced. "We've been invited to the Leflaives." We stopped off for lunch at their Château de Migny in Burgundy's rolling Côte de Beaune. The Leflaives were one of the six owners of the three hectares of the Chevalier Montrachet vineyards, regarded as producing France's greatest dry white wine, which, for my edification, Jean pointed out "should be drunk on one's knee with head bared".

Joseph Louis Gustave Leflaive was 79. In his youth he had been in the submarine division of the French Navy. (With his chief engineer he had gone to Tokyo to help build up the Japanese fleet in 1892.) After the navy he had gone into business for himself manufacturing the first shells sent up to Verdun during World War I. When his business failed after the war, he returned to his vineyard, remarking philosophically, "We always return to our wine in our old age."

M. Leflaive displayed a distinctly pre-war courtesy, greeting his helpers with a "Good morning, gentlemen", while keeping a keen eye on the first crates of grapes which were brought in. "Owing to the bad weather, we will only have half of our usual output," he remarked, adding, "It will be a memorable year." M. Leflaive then took his guests over to his cellars to sample his 1947 vintage. (According to the family tradition, 12 cases of each vintage were reserved for every member of the family.)

A turn-of-the-century atmosphere prevailed over the entire Leflaive domain. M. Leflaive was so deeply religious he never touched a drop of Chartreuse after the monks who distilled it were expelled from France in 1905. (He also refused to drink the no-less delicious liqueur the French government manufactured in their stead.) Only when the monks were allowed back to France did Chartreuse reappear on his dining-table. The Leflaives' daughter Anne was no less devout than her parents. She made frequent visits to Rome for audiences with the Pope and wrote uplifting novels.

During our lunch, the conversation, for my benefit, turned to the sales of Montrachet in the United States. For the past 20 years, Bellow's, a firm of distillers, had distributed the Leflaive Montrachet wine. When the war broke out in 1939, M. Leflaive was prevented from fulfilling his American order, so he hid the wine for the duration of the German occupation and only shipped it out in 1945. When a guest remarked that this must have provided a financial windfall, M. Leflaive cut him short. "A world war," he observed, solemnly, "is not an excuse for breaking an agreement."

Customer at Lock & Company, London, 1949

Miner in North Wales, 1951

Miner with his son, North Wales, 1951

Hyde Park, London, 1949

At a London tailor, 1949

Henry, Seventh Marquess of Angelsey, in a replica of the uniform worn by his
ancestor at the Battle of Waterloo, Plas Newydd, Isle of Angelsey, 1950

A Cruise in the Aegean

In the spring of 1954, Marie Jose of Savoia, the exiled Queen of Italy, told me that she and her husband Umberto had been invited on a cruise. She sipped her highball through a straw as we sat in the elegant comfort of her Swiss villa. The Savoias, she went on to say, along with the other European royals, were to cruise the Aegean that summer. A liner had been chartered to accommodate them all. Such a cruise, on such a scale, at such a time was surely the extravaganza to end all extravaganzas.

I wondered who could be that frivolous. "Frederika," Marie Jose announced cheerfully. The news that Queen Frederika of Greece had dreamed up such a project was all the more outlandish. Greece was barely recovering from a costly civil war.

This cruise had a firmer grip on unreality than a Hollywood musical. I could just imagine all the royals on deck as a grand finale. I found the story irresistible, and felt sure *Life* would too. No one believed me. "They can't be that irresponsible," *Life*'s publisher exclaimed, summing up the general skepticism. But it didn't bother me as Marie Jose had given me the sailing date.

I had met Marie Jose through Tamaro de Marinis, the by-then 80-year-old world authority on rare books and manuscripts. (Since 1910, J. P. Morgan had relied upon him to make acquisitions for his library.) At the time the Queen was writing a history of the early ancestors of the Savoias, but unfortunately most of her research material was in Rome's public libraries, which were inaccessible to her in exile. The one person in Italy who could take out any book, for any length of time, was Mr de Nicola, the President of the Italian Republic. De Nicola was a personal friend of Mr de Marinis, and a royalist, so he gladly took out the required reference books from the library. As a matter of protocol, he could not send them personally to the Queen, so he gave them to Mr de Marinis, who asked me to take them to Marie Jose on my forthcoming trip to Switzerland. Through Mr de Marinis, the Queen had a preface for the book by the Italian philosopher Benedetto Croce. All she needed now was a publisher. I arranged for Mondadori to publish the book in Italy. Marie Jose mentioned the cruise on one of my visits in the summer of 1954.

In July, Colonel Dimitri Livides, the Grand Marshal to the court of His Majesty, the King of the Hellenes, made it official: Europe's royals were to be the guests of King Paul and Queen Frederika for a 12-day cruise in The Aegean. The liner *SS Agamemnon*, converted into a cruise ship for the occasion, would sail out of Piraeus on August 20 to pick up its royal passengers—first in Marseilles and then Naples. The passenger list would not be made public. No photographer would be allowed on board. This was to be a private *divertissement*, paid for from a fund set up by the late shipping magnate, Eugene Eugenides, "for the promotion of international tourism to Greece."

Life wanted the story. The ban on photographers didn't disturb me as I had met "Freddie" on several occasions and had come to the conclusion that she appreciated the value of publicity. I felt I could do business with the Queen of the Hellenes.

Confident, I landed in Athens a week before the start of the cruise. My attempt to endear myself to the Grand Marshall was a fiasco. My audacity in asking to ship out with the royals left him speechless. My audience with the Queen barely more successful. "Why, you're a commoner," Freddie exclaimed, dismissing my plea. She did, however, toss me a bone: I was granted permission to photograph the royals visiting historical landmarks, but under strict supervision. (I could not take pictures of them eating or swimming.) This offer was less magnanimous than it might appear. The sightseeing took place on widely scattered islands with no way for me to get from one to the other unless I chartered a boat to keep up with the *Agamemnon*. The offer, however, confirmed what I suspected: that Freddie needed publicity for her cruise to comply, at least in appearance, with the statute of promoting international tourism for Greece. But if this satisfied Freddie's sense of propriety, it didn't satisfy my needs.

I was trying to figure out my next step when *Life* cabled me. The French magazine *Paris-Match* planned to have a photographer on board the *Agamemnon*. Could I get on board, too? If not, the French photographer would cover the story.

"Hire the Frenchman," I cabled back. Convinced that *Paris-Match* was bluffing, I backed my conviction by chartering a yacht to the consternation of Paul Hurmuses, *Time* magazine's Athenian stringer. My gamble was that the Frenchman would not get on board, and that *Life*, at the very last moment, would again turn over the story to me, leaving me no time to plan anything.

The best yacht I could find in Pireaus was the *Toskana*, a sturdy schooner with an auxiliary engine, but no match for the sleek *Agamemnon*. We then plotted a course which would allow me to keep up with the fast cruise ship on an every-other-or-so-island basis. With Hurmuses's car, we could also catch up with the royal sightseers on a number of their mainland stop-overs. According to our schedule, I could join the royals at Olympia in the Pelopennese, on the islands of Santorini and Mikonos in the Cyclades, at Cape Sounion in Attica, at the Acropolis in Athens, in the ancient amphitheater at Epidaurus, and finally at Delphi, below Mount Parnassus. That done, I sat back and waited.

On August 20, the *Agamemnon* sailed for Marseilles.

The cruise ship was in Naples when I ran into King Umberto, Queen Marie Jose, and their son, Prince Victor Emmanuel, in the lobby of the Hotel Grande Bretagne. They were to join the cruise in Corfu. Prince Victor Emmanuel obligingly loaned me his father's confidential copy of the passenger list. From this classified document, I learned that five Kings, three Queens, one Imperial Highness, 63 Royal Highnesses, one Prince, two Princesses, one hereditary Count, one Count and two Countesses had accepted Freddie's invitation. They were listed by order of precedence: the King of the Hellenes came first and Prince Alexander of Yugoslavia last.

I had no idea who Alexander might be. It was comforting to note that King Umberto didn't know either. Alongside the Prince's name, the Italian monarch had written: "Paul's son?" Neither of us suspected at the time that Alexander would become Umberto's son-in-law.

In Queen Frederika's own words, the purpose of the cruise was "…to stress the solidarity of the Continent's former and present-day dynasties." Conspicuously absent from this family reunion were Freddie's English cousins. The British royal family's lack of solidarity was hardly surprising. Since Cyprus had become a political issue, British government property in Greece was frequently bombed.

A book of etiquette was issued to the royal guests. It laid down in French the rules of conduct to be observed during the cruise. Protocol was abolished at all times aboard the *Agamemnon*. (The complexity of seating arrangements was solved: all gentlemen would draw the name of a lady from a hat and escort her to table.) Informality was *de rigeur*. The gentlemen were told to wear short-sleeved white shirts and black trousers for dinner. Cummerbunds were optional. Bikinis were prohibited on the beaches. Precedence would be observed only on shore for the benefit of the native population. At such time, King Paul, Queen Frederika and their son, Prince Constantine, would lead the way.

Although there was officially no "first among his equals" some passengers did get better accommodation than others. King Paul was given the captain's quarters, Queen Frederika the first mate's. The chief engineer relinquished his cabin to the Grand Duchess of Luxembourg. Queen Juliana of the Netherlands was settled into state rooms 18 and 20. Her consort, Prince Bernhard, was located at number 16. The King and Queen of Italy rated three state rooms, as did the pretenders to the French and Spanish thrones. The ex-King of Romania and his wife shared cabin 6. Also in the one-cabin class were the ex-King of Bulgaria, their Royal Highnesses of Denmark, Norway, and Sweden, a lone Hapsburg, the inevitable clutch of Bourbon-Parmas, and the Princes and Princesses of Baden, Bavaria, Hanover, Hesse, Hohenlohe-Langenburg, Mecklenburg, Schaumburg-Lippe, Schleswig-Holstein, Thurn und Taxis, and Würtemberg.

On August 23, as the *Agamemnon* docked in Corfu, New York cabled that *Paris-Match* had failed to deliver. Early the next morning I reached Olympia, where the first Greek games were held. There was no one in sight, not even another photographer. It was 10am when five shiny buses drove up. Clusters of tourists streamed out in disheveled confusion. They were soon spread out along a sun-baked dirt road which led to the religious city. They wore that determined look tourists have in the morning before exhaustion sets in. On first sight, nothing about this group distinguished it from any other conducted tour. A closer look did reveal that they were not unknown. The fat lady with espadrilles was not just any fat lady, but Her Majesty, Queen Juliana of the Netherlands. What struck me most was how monarchy required gaudy uniforms, white plumes, a haughty attitude and clattering horses to establish the mystique of sovereignty.

I was preparing to take my first picture when two plain-clothes men accosted me. They would have dragged me away had not Queen Frederika called them off, remarking pleasantly, "So, you're taking pictures, Mr Phillips."

"Yes, ma'am. May I come aboard the *Agamemnon,* please?" The Queen didn't bother to answer.

The royal visitors were now scattered among the ruins. King Paul guided a group interested in antiquities. Queen Frederika, protected from the sun by a parasol, gallantly escorted by Prince Axel of Denmark, took pictures with her diminutive Minox. Smiling at her camera were the pretenders to the thrones of France and Spain. With the exception of Umberto and Marie Jose—the only tourists equipped with guidebooks—everybody had a camera, from a $5 box Brownie carried by the ex-King of Romania's wife, to a 16-mm movie camera with telephoto lens mounted on a revolving turret wielded by Queen Juliana's husband. "Now, let's have some cheesecake!" Prince Bernhard called out gaily as he filmed the leggy Princess Dorothea of Hesse.

Meanwhile, Queen Juliana, escorted by Air Vice-Marshal Caralambos Potamianos, listened intently to his explanation that the verb "to love" was originally Greek. The younger royals took souvenir pictures of themselves.

Cane in hand and walrus moustache bristling, King Paul's 85-year-old uncle, Prince George of Greece, picked his way along the grassy path. He cut a quaint figure in a turn-of-the-century motorist's cap. (The doyen of the cruise, Prince George ignored Freddie's sartorial edicts and wore his admiral's uniform to dinner.)

In a shady spot beneath a pine grove, an elaborate buffet was set up. I barely managed to get a shot of the picnic before the two plain-clothes men intervened on Freddie's orders.

After lunch, the Queen of the Hellenes made up for it, in her own way. To the cheerful chorus of "Oh, yes! Good idea!," "Auntie Frederika" rounded up her son, Prince Constantine, Princess Beatrix of the Netherlands, Spain's Prince of the Asturias, Italy's Prince of Naples, Henri of France, and, for good measure, ex-King Simeon II of Bulgaria (deposed at age 9). "These young people," Freddie told me, "are the future rulers of Europe. Take their picture."

Today, Constantine is an exiled king. The exiled Spanish pretender is on the throne and his Queen is Constantine's sister, Sophia. Princess Beatrix is now Queen of the Netherlands, married to a German commoner whose mother was Baroness von dem Bussche-Haddenhausen, not quite noble enough for the cruise. The Italian prince and his cousin, the Bulgarian monarch, are in business. Henri of France is a banker.

Guidebooks recommend two days at Olympia. The royal sightseers took it all in—the religious city, the temple of Zeus, the stadium, the Hippodrome, the museum, the statue of Hermes, and the buffet lunch—in four hours flat. By two o'clock, they were ready for a swim. The beach at Katakolon was inviting. I was kept out by the plain-clothes men.

The *Toskana* took 26 hours to reach the island of Santorini. Its cliffs of red earth, brown stone and black volcanic ash streaked with white rose perpendicularly from the sea to a towering white town. Santorini looked like a giant plum cake topped with heavy whipped cream floating in the Aegean. I had dressed the ship. The *Toskana* was decked out with international pennants, code flags, and my personal ensign—a bold white *LIFE* on a field of red hastily sewn together in Piraeus to welcome the *Agamemnon* when she steamed into Santorini. Three-hundred-and-fifty sloping steps led up to the town. A pack of mules was on hand.

By the time the passengers came ashore, I was part way up the zigzagging stairway waiting for the royals at a bend. King Paul led the procession. Arms on hips and grinning broadly, he rode up to me.

"Where did you get that dreadful thing?" he asked, pointing to the *Toskana.*

"It's the best I could do, sir," I replied. "Since the *Agamemnon* wasn't available."

"Weren't you afraid of getting drowned in such a tiny boat?" Queen Frederika asked.

"Why no, ma'am. But, I'd much rather sail on the *Agamemnon.*"

Prince Bernhard's mule trotted up. "Schooners are fun," he chuckled.

I was trying to keep up with their mules when Colonel Livides, the Grand Marshal, caught up with me. "Where did you get that beautiful yacht?" he asked.

Panting, I reached the 350th step. There, two plain-clothes men were waiting for me. I gasped for help. Queen Frederika granted it.

After a quick tour, the royal party started back down the steps on foot. Precedence made way for youth as they swiftly outdistanced their elders. Keeping in step with Simeon of Bulgaria, I gleaned information about life on board ship. The young set stayed up past 3am, dancing to an eight-piece band. They loved getting into costumes and once disguised themselves as sailors. Another time they all jumped into the swimming pool with their clothes on. (After that, Frederika had the pool drained every night.) Simeon was so friendly and helpful, I slipped him two rolls of film, asking him to shoot some shipboard scenes for me with his Leica—just in case I didn't get on board the *Agamemnon*.

The following evening, the *Toskana* put in at Mikonos, with its windmills equipped with sails so that they looked like primitive helicopters. Rising above the dazzling whitewashed town were terraced farms crisscrossed by low stone walls. Along the esplanade, tourists relaxed at waterfront cafés sampling fried *kalamarakia* and sipping *ouzo*. We anchored there.

When I came up on deck next morning, I found the police had roped off the esplanade to hold back the crowds awaiting the arrival of the *Agamemnon* from Delos. Two young men paced up and down the esplanade. By their age, haircuts, clothes, gestures and equipment, they were obviously from *Paris-Match*. I invited them on board for coffee. The photographer of the team was the Frenchman who was supposedly to sail on the *Agamemnon*—only to end up on my schooner.

The cruise ship lay at anchor in the bay, glistening white, inviting, and yet inaccessible. As the *Toskana* circled around her, I waved to the passengers leaning against the rail. They waved back cheerfully, but paid no attention to my pleas. I might have been a bumble-bee buzzing round a jar of honey.

The tour of Mikonos followed the usual pattern of threatened arrest and release. Before boarding the ship's launch, Queen Frederika allowed me as far as the gangway. There I posed her with King Paul so that the "*no*" of *Agamemnon* was visible in my picture.

The following morning, I photographed the royal junketeers at Poseidon's temple on Cape Sounion, where Lord Bryon once scrawled his name on a marble colonnade.

That afternoon, the royal visitors drove up the Acropolis to view the Parthenon. There they did what tourists in Greece have done since Niepce invented photography—posed between the 35-foot-high Doric columns.

The next item on the agenda was the command performance at Epidaurus. Shortly before I was to leave for the amphitheater, I had a visitor—a member of the shipping family which operated the *Agamemnon*. His visit was strictly PR. I got a glimpse of the royal cruise through a ship owner's eyes. It cost $2,800 a day to operate the *Agamemnon*, and $4.20 to feed each blue-blood. The ship's cook—a master at preparing such specialties as *dolmades, moussaka and souvlakia*—made up the daily menu, which was then submitted to King Paul's chef, who in turn presented it to Queen Frederika for final approval. The meals were hearty, yet the royal guests frequently ordered sandwiches between meals.

"The sea air is so invigorating," my visitor sighed. He volunteered that Coca-Cola was a huge favorite, but was reticent about the consumption rate of the 2,500 bottles of resinated wine, and the 3,000 bottles of beer stocked on board. My visitor now had a question: "When will *Life* publish the story on the cruise?"

"Never," I said.

"Never?" he exclaimed. "Do you mean to say *Life* isn't going to publish a story on Her Majesty's cruise?"

"That's right."

"Why…that's…impossible," he stammered.

"Nothing's impossible with *Life*," I assured him.

"Then why did you charter a yacht?" he asked, doubting my sincerity.

"That was a terrible mistake," I sighed. "But I so wanted the story to be a success."

"And why isn't it a success with all the beautiful pictures you've taken?"

"Because my boss has very set views. The way Mr Edward K. Thompson sees it, if *Life* goes on a cruise, he expects to have pictures taken on board ship. And what Mr Thompson thinks, goes."

Finally convinced, my visitor blurted out, "*Life* must publish the story. Her Majesty has promised her guests you would."

I knew then I would get on board the *Agamemnon*.

In Epidaurus, I kept out of Frederika's way. For once she didn't have to rescue me from the plain-clothes men. I wanted her to be aware of my absence. Climbing to the top of the 3,000-year-old amphitheater, where Hippolytus was to be performed, I gazed down on a block of cushioned seats roped off for the royal theatergoers. They arrived attired according to Frederika's directives. I looked around in vain for an admiral's uniform, until I realized that it was way past old Prince George's bedtime.

The royals were seated on rising tiers—a collection of regal figurines in a huge display case. All of them were related in one way or another, but it was impossible to trace the bloodlines without an *Almanach de Gotha*. I tried to see how far I could get without help, starting at random with Queen Marie Jose. She was the daughter of King Leopold of the Belgians. Her husband, King Umberto, was the brother of Queen Giovanna of Bulgaria. Giovanna's son, King Simeon, was the nephew of Princess Mafalda—a sister of Umberto—and the cousin of three Hesse brothers—not to be confused with the Hesse brothers and sisters on board the *Agamemnon*, to whom they were nonetheless related. At that point, I gave up and watched the performance.

The next morning I drove to Delphi, last port of call and my last opportunity to get aboard the *Agamemnon*. An improvised "Royal Olympic Games" was in progress at the ancient stadium. Young princes high-jumped over knotted silk scarves, gracefully held by young princesses. François of France (who was to die a few years later in the Algerian war) received the laurel crown and a kiss from the gorgeous Dorothea of Hesse.

Noticing Queen Juliana crowning the young French prince, I took a picture. I must have violated some obscure dynastic taboo because the Queen turned on me. She did not want the picture published. Later, in my haste to airmail the films to New York, the royal command slipped my mind. *Life* published the picture, which happened to be the most flattering one I had taken of the Dutch queen. My unintentional act of *lèse majesté* enraged Juliana. Her ADC wrote *Life* a letter bitterly complaining about my conduct.

After being dressed down by Queen Juliana, I was pounced upon by the two plain-clothes men before Queen Frederika intervened. "Is it true *Life* isn't going to publish any pictures of our cruise?" she asked, dismissing the cops.

"Unfortunately yes, ma'am," I said, suitably contrite.

"Why?"

"I haven't got the kind of pictures my editors want," I explained.

"And what sort of pictures do your editors expect?" Frederika demanded.

"Pictures taken on board the *Agamemnon*," I said.

"You want *dirty* pictures?" the Queen exclaimed.

527

"Dirty pictures, ma'am?" I echoed, taken aback.

"You know very well what I mean," Frederika snapped. "Young people smoking, drinking and dancing barefoot." She sounded exasperated. Her outburst suddenly alerted me to how much the Queen of the Hellenes was out of touch with the times.

"*Life* isn't interested in dirty pictures, ma'am," I said, reeking with self-righteousness.

"Well, what sort of pictures does *Life* want?" Frederika asked me impatiently.

"A group shot on board ship, ma'am."

"In that case, you may come aboard," Frederika granted.

At Itea Harbor, where the *Agamemnon* was anchored, I was the first to scramble up the ship's gangway. As the passengers came aboard, I herded them to the afterdeck with the help of a bull horn, "Queen Juliana, this way please ..."

Europe's royals were in high spirits, and much less formal than at the start of the cruise. Although many did not know one another personally when they came aboard, they either used their first names—a royal custom—or resorted to nicknames. Prince Bernhard was "PB", Crown Prince Constantine, "Tino". Prince Kraft Hohenlohe-Langenburg responded to "Stromboli" or "Plumcake". I was much more formal. I addressed them through my bull horn with "Please, sir." and "Thank you, ma'am." as they all draped themselves in several tiers around King Paul and Queen Frederika. With everybody in place and facing the camera, I snapped the group picture I had visualized from the outset.

My assignment was completed. Lightheartedly, I leapt into the launch, which took me ashore without giving a thought to Simeon and the pictures I had asked him to shoot for me. I had all I needed now and was in a hurry to get my story off.

A few weeks later, Simeon dropped by the *Life* bureau in Rome and left the rolls of unexposed film with a word of apology for not having taken any pictures for me. A real gentleman.

European royalty posing on the afterdeck of the *Agamemnon*, Itea Harbor, 1954

Algiers, 1959

Back to Algeria

In the autumn of 1959 I returned to Algeria. *L'Echo D'Alger* reported my arrival over half of its front page. "A native son returns. A *Life* photographer, he will tell the truth about the Algerian War..." My wife Anna Maria joined me and we spent the first days in Algiers. The Hotel Saint George, which I had so often passed as a child, put us up in General Eisenhower's suite. During that time, I planned my visit to Bouira, the village in Greater Kabylia where I was born, but which we had left when my father went to war, before I was old enough to remember anything about it.

I am what they call there a *pied noir*, literally a "black foot", meaning a European born in North Africa. I was a slightly unusual one, as my father was a British subject and my mother an American citizen. In 1904 they met in Munich and got married in Troy, New York. Back in Europe they decided to visit North Africa for a fortnight and eventually spent 20 years there. My father bought the farm where I was born on a Friday the 13th in 1914.

Getting to Bouira in 1959 was more difficult than in my parents' time. Finding a driver willing to make the trip there strained the talents of the concierge at the Saint George. Members of the FLN—the Arab independence movement, the Front de Libération Nationale, also known as the *fellagha*, *fellouze*, or *fells*—frequently attacked vehicles along the mountain roads and slit the throats of its European occupants. An armored car patrolling the road picked us up in the gorges of Palestro and escorted us along the deep meandering valley of the Ouad Djemaa, all the way to Bouira.

We were met by a French colonel who was waiting for us at L'Hôtel de la Colonie. The hotel, which was down the road from the family farm, had neither changed its name or its management since my parents' time.

"Frankly, my friend Ruggieri," the colonel was telling the Italian owner when we arrived, "it's about time you renamed your hotel. Times have changed you know."

I found out how true this was when we went to stay with the Marcellin family. The Marcellins' farm was ten miles from the one my family once owned and I had known them since I was in short trousers. When we got there, steel shutters barred all of the windows. All the Arabs employed on the farm had left. Some months before, while inspecting his vineyards, Marcellin had been ambushed by FLN and wounded. An atmosphere of seige prevailed.

Sunday lunch, however, was still typical of my father's time. We must have been 20 at table. The food was good and plentiful, the rosé wine heady, and the conversation explosive with the French Algerians openly displaying their fury at De Gaulle. It was the fury of fear I felt. The *colons* believed that De Gaulle, in his refusal to insist on Algerian integration into France, was threatening their way of life.

"De Gaulle be damned," snorted my neighbor. "He can say what he likes, that Arab-lover. We'll never leave this country."

"We wanted a military dictatorship, but not the one we got."

"He's too liberal," another guest chimed in, flapping his arms grotesquely in imitation of De Gaulle making a speech.

"He's popular with the Moslem population," a voice down the table said plaintively.

"And so he should be, the way he discriminates against us," someone added.

"I could give you a list as long as my arm of ignorant Arabs with good jobs," another voice grumbled.

"Aren't you supposed to have Arabs fill responsible jobs?" I asked.

"Of course, but let's not exaggerate."

"Take the amnesty for political prisoners—if you can call assassins who ought to be shot political prisoners. We don't approve of that."

"What else can you expect from an Arab-lover?"

"Why are you so down on De Gaulle?" I asked. "You paved the way for his return to power. What's he done wrong?"

"It's not so much what De Gaulle's done, as what he hasn't done, and what we suspect him of trying to do. He must come out for integration once and for all," another voice said, adding hastily, "Integration of Algerian territory into France, that is."

"What about integration with the Arabs?" I asked.

"By all means. There must be a spiritual integration."

"I have never liked that word."

"Why did you use it?" the man's son asked.

"Because we had to say something."

"But you did promise integration. You know that," the son insisted.

"He's been in Paris three months, and now listen to him," his mother complained.

This kind of talk was so widespread among French Algerians and yet it eemed to me so unrealistic, I thought I should seek a more serious point of view. I asked Roger Marcellin, who as a French senator was a recognized spokesman for the *colons,* to sum up their position. "The Algerian question has been settled once and for all with the referendum of September 1958, in which the Europeans and the Moslems who went to the polls voted for the union of Algeria and France," Marcellin told me. "Algeria is, and will always remain, French, because that is the expressed will of all its inhabitants. We can't hold referendums every week simply because a tiny group of unpatriotic Frenchmen, inspired by foreigners and paid by foreigners, wants to impose its rule here through terror and murder."

"What about the Algerian government-in-exile?" I asked.

"Unthinkable! This pseudo-government fled Algeria. They represent nothing." He was really in earnest. But what he said made little sense to me.

We were standing in the courtyard of his farm, when his head man came up to us. He had a close-cut black beard, a sign of mourning among the Kabyles. When they were through, I asked Marcellin for whom he was in mourning.

"His son," Marcellin told me. "He was executed at Aïn Bessem for being a *fell.*"

"Why, that's around the corner from you," I said. "Couldn't you intervene?"

"I had him executed."

And he continued to employ his head man as though nothing had happened. No wonder he allowed no Kabyles inside the farm at night, and relied on French troops stationed in the neighborhood.

A few days later, a little Kabyle girl, disregarding the curfew, got an early start picking jasmine. A French sentry in the dim light of dawn, mistaking her for a *fell,* killed her. He was heartbroken, but Marcellin's wife took it in her stride. The Marcellins had little sympathy for the Kabyles. These fierce mountaineers, who are said to descend from the Goths, always resisted foreign invaders of North Africa: the Romans, the Arabs, the Turks, and finally the French. After the French defeat in the Franco-German war of 1870, the Kabyles staged a revolt in 1871, spreading terror among the *colons* until it was ruthlessly put down. After the Second World War, they again rebelled against France, which led to the Algerian war being fought in 1959. (Even among the Moslems forming the rebellious FLN, the Arabs were circumspect about the Kabyles. When I met up with members of the FLN, the Arabs would say about me, "Remember, he's from Kabylia.")

With Marcellin I traveled over his acres of vineyards, wheat, and almond trees. It was the place his grandfather started with a land grant from the French government. Now, with grandchildren of his own born in Algeria, Marcellin was rich. But for him to become what he was today, Marcellin and his family had to lavish years of care and hard work on their land. Perhaps Marcellin was thinking of this when he suddenly said to me, "I would die if I ever had to leave Algeria and my farm." Then I felt sorry for him.

I visited what had once been my father's farm. The farmhouse, now the property of a Moslem Algerian, was dilapidated, and though this would have broken my father's heart, I was angry for other reasons. I was angry because Marcellin had tried to play on my emotions about the farm.

"You'll find it very run down," he had told me. Then, ignoring the fact that the farm next door, which was also owned by a Moslem, was well kept, he added, "But what can you expect from Arabs?"

I had spent the first 12 years of my life in Algeria. During all of that time I had referred to the Arabs and Kabyles alike as *ratons*, unaware it meant a small rat. It had taken me a long time to get over the French Algerians' contempt for the Arabs I had grown up with, though I say this with very mixed feelings, because after all, as an American, I had nothing to lose, and they did.

I had a chance to see how the Moslems were living when we visited the village of Bezzit, a collection of tin-roofed huts squatting on the crest of a lonely hill in the Djurdjura Mountains. Until recently there had been no road to Bezzit. Although it was only nine miles, as the crow flies, from my father's farm, the impoverished Kabyles who lived there often used to go months at a time without seeing a Frenchman or getting any help from France. Now Bezzit, like a hundred other Algerian villages, was a kind of showcase where the best aspects of France's "pacification" program were being put into practice. Cleared of the *fellaghas*, guarded by the French army and by Moslem *harki* who had volunteered to bear arms for France, Bezzit was the recipient of aid and guidance which, had France offered them earlier, might have prevented the rebellion altogether.

Bezzit was presided over by a Moslem mayor and Captain Billotet, a French SAS (Specialized Administrative Sections) officer. A fat, jovial man who in another age might have been a lusty friar, Billotet was chief engineer, plumber, planner, guardian and father confessor to the village. Billotet's greatest problem in keeping his area calm, however, had been the long-standing feud between the mayor of Bezzit and the head man of a small community nearby called Beni Fouda. The feud, which probably went back to the days of the Prophet, disrupted friendly relations between the two communities since the people of both villages were solidly behind their chieftains.

"This was very bad," the captain observed to me. "But I solved it by getting the mayor of Bezzit's daughter married off to the head man of Beni Fouda." With this stumbling block out of the way, Billotet, like SAS officers everywhere, got his villagers to build roads around the community and supervised the setting up of prefabricated schools which replaced the Kabyle schools destroyed by the FLN. Now French army volunteers acted as teachers for Moslem children, who, they admitted, were often brighter than their counterparts in France. The SAS program also ran dispensaries and arranged to fly seriously ill patients out of the hills to a base hospital by helicopter. The army encouraged village morale with native dancing parties, trucked in extra food and milk for the villages, and taught the Kabyles how to make the most of their agriculture. It also helped the more emancipated Moslem women set up classes in hygiene, sewing, and cooking among their pitifully backward sisters.

The enthusiasm of SAS officers for the villages which had promised their loyalty to France sometimes spurred them into outlandish rivalries. When I told another officer how Captain Billotet had built a small café in Bezzit, he looked pained. "Some men never know when to stop," he said, then added, "Of course we're putting up a hunting lodge."

All this seemed promising, but somebody would have to continue the kind of kind of help to the long-neglected primitive villages which the SAS officers were now administering. Such help was important not only for its effect on Algeria, but on the entire Moslem world. Throughout my trip to

Algeria I was reminded of what a Tunisian friend had said to me: "We denounced the Russian terror in Hungary like you Westerners. But I notice you Westerners do not denounce French oppression in Algeria which is just as bad. Is it because tyranny is only denounced when it is communist and forgiven when its is practiced by the West? I hope this is not the case. If it is, I am certain the next generation of Moslems will turn its back on the West and you will have lost far more than Algeria."

After three years of SAS aid, after an expenditure of millions of dollars on "loyal" Algerian villages, and after the loss of more than 100,000 lives on both sides in the war, happy dances were only possible in Algeria under the protection of French soldiers. As I watched the dances and saw the schools, I could not forget one fact. To get to and from these "pacified" villages, a man must travel with an armed escort and sometimes a squad of soldiers riding behind in a truck. The bitterness in Algeria was too deep-rooted and too old now for France to repair it by simply building up one portion of the Moslem population while still engaged in a brutal war with the other.

Flying over the Kabylia hills, I heard about the French army's difficulties from Colonel Gabriel Favreau, the commanding officer of the Foreign Legion's 5th Regiment. As I peered down onto the sprawling green forests, barren ridges and dry *oueds*, the colonel said, "lovely country for sightseeing, but lousy to fight in." I could not see a single human being, and yet the colonel assured me the *fellaghas* were watching us fly past.

"Even with bananas [helicopters] we can't catch them. By the time the first banana full of troops lands, the *fells* have gone—faded into the rocks. If we sight one on a slope, he rolls into a ball and bounces down the hill. Yesterday one of my legionnaires was about to get a *fellouze* when the *salopard* drops a bundle. Naturally my legionnaire stops to look. By the time he finds out it's a baby, the son-of-a-bitch has vanished."

The hopelessness of seeking a final military solution to the Algerian problem struck me hardest at the Foreign Legion post at Yakouren in the Northern Kabylia. One evening after dinner Colonel Favreau and I were alone in the mess when he asked me about the price of a Polaroid camera. "I want to get a couple so that as soon as we kill a *fell,* I can take his picture and have him identified at once."

"A hundred dollars or so," I told the colonel.

Family of a Kabyle worker on a French *colon's* farm, Kabylia, 1959

French marines after finding massacred Arab civilians, outside Souk el Dnine, Kabylia, 1959

"Good," he said. "I'm going to raise the rates of our regimental bordello by 10 per cent. I'll have the money for two Polaroids in no time."

At this point a sergeant broke in, "He's talking now, *mon colonel.*"

"Can he be seen?" the colonel asked.

"Seen, *mon colonel?*" The sergeant sounded puzzled.

The colonel nodded at me and casually replied, "Seen in mixed company?"

"*Oui, mon colonel,*" the sergeant replied. "The prisoner spoke of his own free will."

In the intelligence officer's tent a single electric bulb cast harsh shadows. The *fellagha* prisoner looked to have a large welt under his right eye, but he seemed cheerful enough.

This was the first live *fellagha* I had seen. It was his slyness which struck me. The passive resistance of this single Moslem suddenly became for me the passive resistance of all the Moslems I had ever known since childhood. The more he smiled while telling his story, the more I became convinced that the French would get nowhere in Algeria using force.

"He says the arsenal and the food cache are near Bou Nouman," an officer said.

The colonel glared at the prisoner. The prisoner smiled and scratched himself with his chained arms. "Why did you wait so long to tell us this?" the colonel thundered. "I'll tell you why. So your pals would have time to move the stuff."

"*Ah non, mon colonel,*" the prisoner said, "I swear to you. You'll find it full, full of everything: guns, flour, everything."

Next morning the chained *fell* prisoner was put on a light Alouette helicopter with us following behind. We were dropped off on a precarious mountain ledge near the village of Bou Nouman. A legionnaire emptied a single bag that contained all the supplies that had been found in the arsenal: a half dozen gun stocks, a hammer, a pair of pliers, and two files at the colonel's feet.

"Keep the hammer, the pliers, and the files," Colonel Favreau snapped. "Burn the rest." I admired his self-control.

Frustrated in his attempts to clean up an elusive enemy, the French professional soldier in Algeria was also painfully confused. On the one hand, most of the junior officers preferred Moslems to the French Algerian *colons,* whose mistreatment of the Moslems they held largely responsible for the war. On the other hand, these same officers found themselves killing Moslems in part to restore the kind of "order" the *colons* wanted. Beyond this, professional soldiers confronted a tragic possibility. After their defeat of 1940 in Europe, in Indo-China, and after successive withdrawals from Tunisia and Morocco, the French army felt it could not survive the shame of yet another defeat. Moreover, quitting Algeria would mean the loss of the overseas bonuses, and return to dull garrison life in France.

General Challe, the French commander in North Africa, said to me, "If we are forced to abandon Algeria, this is the end of the French army. The army will rebel." (It did so in April 1961 under the command of General Maurice Challe and three other generals. The rebellion was rapidly put down by De Gaulle).

The only place where I was not oppressed by the feeling of desperation that hung over the war-torn country was at "Kimono 10," the one spot where despair should have been strongest. Kimono 10, named in memory of the Indo-Chinese war, was a commando unit where ex-*fells* now served with the French army against their former comrades. The use of turncoats was a contemporary example of the old French adage, "It takes an Arab to catch an Arab."

The army was not too choosy about who they took into this commando unit. As one officer explained to me, "Of course we know they are murderers, but we do have standards: if he attacks a car filled with passengers, that's all right, if he slits the throats of its occupants, that's not."

Once a *fellagha* made up his mind, the transformation to French commando was rapid. An Arab could be fighting as a *fellagha* on Monday and by Wednesday be a fully-fledged commando fighting against the FLN. The formalities of changing sides were simple. The *fellagha* must come over of his own free will. He must bring at least a shotgun. "The gun was essential," Captain Duclos, Kimono 10's commander, told me. "If they turn up unarmed, I send them back for a gun."

The new men were given a uniform like French paratroopers and drew $46 a month, which was good pay for a worker in Algeria. Service was on a day-to-day basis. The former *fellaghas* were free to quit any time they want, but none of them did The FLN would make short work of any Moslem ex-commando who tried to return to civilian life.

Kimono 10 operated in a well-defined area, the home region of its Moslem commandos. More than 90 of the command's 150 men were Moslem and knew the local terrain as well as the local *fellagha* company, called a *katiba*. Fighting between the commandos and the *katiba* was not part of a large impersonal war, but a bitter struggle between men who knew and hated each other.

Anna Maria and I were invited to the wedding of Salah Charabi, a new-comer to Kimono 10. Before the civil ceremony, Anna Maria was taken to the women's quarters where she met the bride. The bride showed Anna Maria a Christian Dior dress she had planned to wear, but "word had come down" she was to wear Moslem clothes and the veil. She pointed sadly to all her European clothes and sighed. Before Anna Maria left, the bride presented her with a dozen fresh eggs and a live rabbit.

After the ceremony was over, we were drinking champagne when it was reported that a *katiba* had been spotted. All the wedding guests, except for Anna Maria and the bride, leapt into their vehicles and Kimono 10's rifle team was off. I rode in Captain Duclos's jeep, which had a metal plate across the lower half of its windshield. As the captain jockeyed his vehicle over steep ridges and down slopes, he told me that "last Sunday we got twenty-two of them." The jeeps and trucks were now scattered across the countryside and in the distance we could see a group of Moslems running. I could feel Captain Duclos's tense excitement which, to my shame, I shared. The lead group was closing in when our jeep's radio reported that a commando patrol had spotted a *fellagha* and was after him. We changed our course to join them. We bounced past a peaceful Moslem farm where a horse was treading corn in a circle. The Kabyles didn't look up. They didn't even look up when we heard a short burst of gunfire. Then we saw the commandos moving toward a farmhouse. When we got there we found the men standing around. Two of them were searching the body of a dead Moslem.

"He's a *fellouze* all right," the captain said. "Look, he's wearing bush boots, and we've prohibited their use."

The captain was right, the dead man was a *fell*. A childlike drawing found on him proved it. The green and white flag of the FLN had been drawn with colored crayon on a scrap of paper. Captain Duclos examined the *fellouze*'s shotgun. Looking down at the body, he said softly, "He didn't suffer." It was then I noticed that the soles of the bush boots had been cut

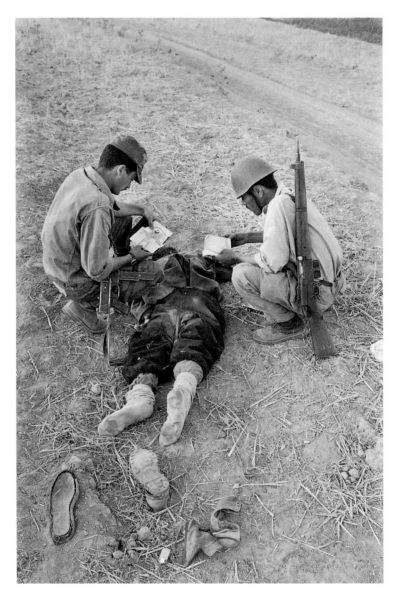

Pro-French Arab commando checking the papers of a suspect
they had just gunned down, Kabylian mountains, Algeria, 1959

off. "No other *fellouze* can use those boots now," Captain Duclos explained as we walked away, leaving the dead man unburied.

Outside the hamlet of Souk el Dnine I came upon a squad of French marines. Usually boisterous, these leathernecks were silent. "They're in there," one volunteered with a jerk of his thumb toward a narrow opening in a tight cluster of aspen trees growing amid a tangle of briar that looked like a barbed-wire barrier set up by nature.

"Don't be shocked when you find some of them partly undressed," the army doctor said to me. "We examined the bodies to see if they had been tortured."

"Tortured?"

"The *fellaghas* torture their victims when they have a grudge against them."

"And were they?" I asked.

"One had his throat slit—'the Kabyle smile', you know," a marine said. "Another got his eyes gouged out."

"Why did the *fellaghas* do it?" I asked.

"Hard to say," a captain answered. "The dead men are all Moslems, of course, but we can't identify them because their papers have been taken away. Most of them are wearing city clothes, so we don't think they're from around here. Maybe they were prisoners being taken somewhere and were killed when the *fells* heard we were conducting operations in the neighborhood. Sometimes that happens. They get rid of their prisoners and then scatter."

Better smoke one of your American cigarettes," a marine said. "Two are beginning to bloat, and with this heat the smell's pretty bad."

"If you don't go farther than where the kid's lying, it's bearable," another marine explained.

"He can't be a day over 13," a voice added.

I cleared the ditch and made my way along the narrow path edged with a curtain of briar. I pushed the curtain and stared. Ahead the path widened into a small clearing. Some 20 bodies, a few of them children, were scattered across the clearing in a trail of death. The pale blue of the clothing, combined with the utter stillness, made the scene unreal. With a mounting sense of horror, I crossed the clearing, taking pictures as I went. Without warning, the smell of death became unbearable. Blindly, I dived into the dense briar and clawed my way out. Only later when I was jotting down notes did I notice that the sleeves of my jacked were torn and my hands were bleeding.

For a month I had been a witness to violence. Although the French were strong enough to remain in Algeria indefinitely, no amount of force could break the subtle will of ten million Moslems, or put an end to *fellagha* resistance in this terrible civil war. I could only be grateful fate had spared me from taking part in it. At my mother's insistence, we moved from Algiers when she became aware what was happening to her little boy. I was the only "English", a minority of one in a school of 600 boys, French, French-Algerians, Jews, Moslems, Spaniards, Italians, Portugese and Maltese, and I found myself forever in fights. My worst moments were the history classes about Joan of Arc and Napoleon. Classmates would turn around threatening me with their clenched fist as they hissed, "You murdered our saint. You just wait until we get out of class." This invariably ended in a scuffle. On one occasion, I was tripped by one while kicked in the face by another. At this defending a British Empire I knew nothing about.

With Napoleon, all went well until Waterloo. The rest of the time, I was just like any of the other young toughs. We would rip off the nightshirt a youthful Arab wore while he tended his sheep. We tossed firecrackers into the grocery stores of the Moabites to simulate an anti-Semitic riot. I spent the money I collected selling lottery tickets for the boy scouts' charity, and even picked my mother's purse to buy a round of ice-cream from the vendor outside our school. Had I remained in Algeria, I would, in all probability, have been fighting the Arabs alongside the *colons.*

Kasbah, Algiers, 1959

E.U.R., Rome, 1960

Luchino Visconti and Romy Schneider on the set of *Boccacio '70*, Rome, 1960

The Viscontis

Success came naturally to a Visconti like breathing. In 1395, Gian Galeazzo Visconti was appointed Duke of Milan by the Holy Roman and Germanic Emperor Winceslaws. Ever since, success has been attached to this aristocratic north-Italian family. As the Viscontis were both liberal in their politics and with their money, their position in court was not always easy. They fought in turn the Papal states and the Hapsburgs to help achieve unity and sovereignty for Italy. They thought nothing of contributing the family silver to raise a regiment in Italy's ill-fated 1848 war of independence. But success has remained as faithful to the Viscontis as they have to Italy. And like Italy, they have always bounced back.

Take Luchino and his brothers, Luigi and Edoardo. The year was 1960. Count Luchino Visconti had aroused Italian cynics with his neo-realistic films, overwhelmed the pageant-loving English by the lavishness of his opera productions, and scandalized the jaded French with his stage adaptation of 'Tis A Pity She's A Whore. Already known to the European art-house circuit for his movies, Visconti was about to get a far greater audience in the United States. In 1962, he would direct Burt Lancaster in Lampedusa's best-selling novel, *The Leopard.*

Luchino's younger brother, Count Edoardo Visconti, was a success even by Milanese standards. President of Carlo Erba, the third largest pharmaceutical company in Italy, he looked forward to pulling ahead of his rivals with the completion of a mammoth plant in 1963.

Luigi, the older brother, who had become the Duke of Grazzano-Visconti after his older brother Guido was killed in the war, hoped that sometime between premiere of *The Leopard* and the factory's inauguration, he would be able to meet the demand for basset hounds which a smart international clientele was snapping up at $750 the pair.

Italians took all this for granted. Nothing a Visconti did surprised them, ever since one of their illustrious ancestors ordered the construction of Milan's Gothic Cathedral during the Renaissance. In a country overflowing with nobility, the Viscontis were more a dynasty than a family. With their medieval ancestors and their relatives among the crowned heads of

France and England, they satisfied the Italian passion for titles. Every male bore a striking resemblance to the eagle-beaked Gian Galeazzo, whom death alone in 1402 had prevented from crowning himself King of Lombardy.

The Viscontis were renaissance men both in looks and behavior. Long before Luchino directed at La Scala, his uncle casually underwrote the opera house's staggering debts. The Viscontis' combination of extravagant disregard for conventions and a lofty charm flattered the Italian desire for the grandiose, and few satisfied it more completely than the Visconti brothers' late father.

Don Giuseppe Count Visconti di Modrone and the first Duke of Grazzano-Visconti took on art, business and politics with true renaissance enthusiasm. A humanist, he financed Milan's classical Teatro Manzoni, wrote plays which he and his wife performed on their own stage, and painted family frescoes after Raphael. As a matter of course, the Duke also ran Carlo Erba, the pharmaceutical company his wife had brought him as a dowry, and even found time to launch a brand of soap, shaving lotion, and toothpaste, which he named after himself.

Don Giuseppe's greatest achievement was of utopian proportions. He converted a potato patch surrounding his *castello* into a thriving community of a thousand inhabitants. Dedicated to the arts and crafts, it became knows as Grazzano-Visconti. The Duke endowed Grazzano-Visconti with a school for artisans, a kindergarten, a theater, a cemetery, a train station, a post office, a bridge, a hotel, two restaurants, and several stores, all in Gothic-style architecture. Every building, including the station, conformed to the manner of his XIVth century *castello*. A stickler for details, he also created a smart medieval dress the locals wore on Sundays.

Don Giuseppe's sons all inherited qualities from their father: Guido was a romantic; Luigi a grand seigneur; Luchino a master showman; and Edoardo an astute industrialist.

Luigi, like his crony the late Aly Khan, had a passion for horses. A gentleman jockey, he wore the green and white Visconti colors in every major flat, hurdle, and steeplechase race from Naples to Merano between 1930 and 1942. Italy's champion during those years, he accumulated 400 trophies and 27 fractures in his pursuit of the sport.

Luchino's tastes were less athletic than aesthetic, although he, too, once owned a racing stable. Friends still recalled his bucolic parties. "The

The Visconti brothers: Luchino, Edoardo, and Luigi, at the Carthusian monastery
in Pavia where their ancestor Gian Galeazzo lies buried, 1960

stables were draped with lights and the mangers were filled with buckets of iced champagne."

Edoardo, the businessman of this branch of the family, ran Don Giuseppe's perfume business until the outbreak of World War II. "Edoardo is a born leader," Luigi said, with an older brother's grudging pride.

During the war, Guido, the eldest brother, fought against the British in the Western Desert. Even under heavy fire he refused to take cover because, "a Visconti didn't bow to the Windsors," he would say. Mortally wounded at El Alamein, Guido cried out 'Viva il re!'"

Pre-war Italy was a very different country from what remained of it on VE Day. Then, the Viscontis' future looked no brighter than Italy's, which even optimists believed to be in ruins for the next half century.

In the spring of 1945, Luigi only had a few souvenirs left: the bulk of his silver trophies had all been melted down to contribute to the war effort. Luchino's one movie, mangled by censorship, had not been released. Edoardo's pharmaceutical company was in critical condition. In those days not even the buoyant Italians expected their agricultural country to become an industrial state capable of producing the Italian miracle by 1960.

Symbolically, Edoardo regained control of the family business in Milan on Armistice Day. "I had volunteered with the British Special Forces, and was dropped behind the lines to report on German troop movements. Asked where we should make our jump, I thought of Luigi, and said, 'San Siro race-tracks in Milan.'" With the German surrender, Edoardo settled a private score. "I fired my pharmaceutical company's director," who until then had been protected by his fascist affiliations.

The situation was dramatic, he recalled. "I had 2,500 employees on the payroll, no money, no raw materials, no fuel, and no markets." Undaunted, Edoardo turned to the United States for aid. By 1949, the American Home Products owned stock in his pharmaceutical company and had two representatives on its board of directors. The American Export and Import Bank granted a loan. Edoardo was now ready to recapture old markets and seek fresh outlets.

The old factory was overhauled and the number of employees increased by 50 percent. Visconti also increased his ties with American business. He entered with the Armour Chemical Company of Chicago into a joint venture. "My pride and joy is my new chemical plant," he declared. It was three-and-a-half times the size of the old factory.

Luchino also proved to be a novelty in Italian show business. At the time Edoardo was struggling to revive the family pharmaceutical company, Luchino rescued his film *Obsession* from the censors. *Obsession,* and his second picture, *The Earth Shakes,* are now generally regarded as two of the great Italian realist films of the post-war period.

The Earth Shakes also proclaimed Visconti's contempt for public opinion, very apparent in the six operas, seven films, and 29 plays he had so far directed. In *The Earth Shakes,* his poor Sicilian fishermen spoke in their own incomprehensible dialect, making this the only Italian film requiring Italian subtitles.

Luchino aroused the censors and the bigots and, with a malice verging on sadism, he never disappointed them. On stage, at the opera house and on screen, Visconti's opening nights offered the thrills of a Latin American football match. In one picture, he showed a disastrous Italian defeat with a pimp for a hero. After *Rocco and His Brothers,* the harrowing story of a poor Southern family's struggle for survival in Northern Milan, Luchino was called a communist for drawing attention to the dismal national problem of "internal emigration".

It had required some coaxing, however, to get Luchino to find out how the poor Southerners lived before he filmed *Rocco.* "Luchino, a communist?" Suso D'Amico, his scenarist, burst out laughing. "Visconti's like the Leopard. He's aware of a new world, but he doesn't like it."

Luchino awakened passion in Italian producers. ("Imagine demanding new sets to match the new personality of the new actor playing Stanley Kowalski in a revival of *A Streetcar Named Desire!*") And abroad, he defied tradition. Told he could not go backstage with his cast on the opening night of Don Carlos at Covent Garden, he pleasantly replied, "In that case there will be no opening night."

"Outside of Shakespeare's tragedies and Chekov's *Three Sisters,* Visconti respected nothing," one assistant observed wryly. This was certainly true of *Salome* at Spoleto's Festival of Two Worlds. Visconti edited Oscar Wilde's text which he considered "too long". He reminded the actor playing John the Baptist, "You're not an apostle yet. That comes later. Just imagine you're Giuliano the Sicilian bandit and act accordingly."

"I want the public to say after the performance, 'Did you see what I saw?'" he told his Salome, the American Margaret Tynes, and he made some drastic changes in the dance of the seven veils. "She can't take her clothes off in the dance of the seven veils," Visconti grumbled. "I'll bring her on naked." Margaret Tynes, a minister's daughter, crossed herself. "Don't worry," he reassured her, "you'll have jewels here and there."

But for all of this, Edoardo the industrialist remained the greater talent scout. In 1945, he revived a beauty contest which had originated in his father's time to promote toothpaste. Out of these contests emerged Gina Lollobrigida, Silvana Mangano, Lucia Rose, Eleonora Rossi Drago, and a "young thing" the judges nearly overlooked. "Don't you realize this is a promising colt?" Edoardo protested. Thanks to his intervention, Sophia Loren became "Miss Elegance".

Luigi, for his part, discovered how nerve-wracking it was to be associated with Luchino in show business. "In those days, a play couldn't open without a permit from the authorities," he explained. "Well, we did. Luchino never worried about the producer of *La Via Del Tabacco* (*Tobacco Road*) going to jail. I did. I was the producer."

While everybody agreed that no one was better suited than Luchino to direct *The Leopard,* they were appalled by the endless possibilities for luxury Lampedusa's novel afforded. "In that book he described every room of the Leopard's huge Sicilian palazzo down to the last detail. And that's how it's going to be in the movie," Suso D'Amico predicted.

For one wild moment, Luigi hoped that one of his pets would play the Leopard's dog. But Luchino's scruples for accuracy prevented his casting a basset hound in the part of a Neapolitan mastiff. Luigi's fondness for dogs had been a family trait since the notorious Barnabo Visconti bred a pack of 5,000 in 1359. "Barnabo fed the keeper to the hounds if they grew lean," the third Duke of Grazzano-Visconti gloated, although he himself was most considerate of his own kennel keeper.

The third Duke and his number-one basset hound—"Keperland Artist"—were a familiar sight in Grazzano-Visconti where Luigi lived for most of the year. There was something comical about the pair sauntering down Via Luigi Visconti: the basset with his drooping eyelids and the doleful expression of a British peer after a binge; the Duke, the image of someone about to have a ball. Whenever the Lord of Grazzano-Visconti stopped to chat with the town folk, a look of incredible boredom came over the basset.

Keperland Artist assumed the same pose when he appeared with his owner at dog shows. Among the flurry of prancing borzois, the basset and his master seemed relaxed. But the minute they came before the judges, their twin competitive spirits were evident, and by the time they had trotted through their paces, Keperland Artist had picked up a new set of laurels for the Duke of Grazzano-Visconti's kennels.

Luigi was so successful as a breeder that he flew to England for additional basset hounds for stud. One of these trips coincided with Luchino's court case in Milan to answer charges that scenes in *Rocco And His Brothers* were "immoral". Luigi, the monarchist, simply sighed, "When I think that Luchino was once a very close friend of Prince Umberto. Saw him all the time…" Edoardo, a conservative, said "Luchino's Tolstoyan." Luchino, however, was more of a palazzo pink—a critic of privileges from a strongly entrenched privileged position.

Luchino lived in a sumptuous Roman villa. The large rooms were filled with antique furniture and art collections. They were, however, only dimly visible in the semi-darkness Luchino affected on and off stage. In this atmosphere, more Medici than Marx, Luchino Visconti held court. "He can't live without a court," his scenarist explained. Cloistered in the villa, with his entourage on tap, Visconti was happy.

He also enjoyed making other people's lives difficult. He insisted on keeping the lighting at a minimum, even while he was being photographed.

I had been photographing Sophia Loren and her husband Carlo Ponti. My story was complete when Loren agreed to pose with Luchino. He agreed on condition it was after dinner, as he had an engagement he refused to break. "Say, 10:30."

"I don't know if that's possible," I told him. "Everybody knows Sophia retires early."

"Too bad."

Convinced she would say no to such an ungodly hour, I regretfully left word that Visconti was unavailable before 10:30pm.

At 9:30 that night, I was notified that Sophia and her husband would be at Luchino's home at 10:30. I called him to say the appointment was on. He made an ironic comment about them being after-dinner guests.

Luigi Visconti with "Keperland Artist", his prize basset hound, at the Bellagio International Dog Show, 1960

Edoardo Visconti and his son Brandy hunting, Lerici, 1960

Edoardo Visconti with his son Brandy after hunting, Lerici, 1960

I was the first to arrive, and discovered that the unbreakable dinner date was with a pretty young man. When Sophia and Ponti showed up, I suggested Luchino's elegant and well-lit studio for the picture. He refused and compelled me to work beneath a hideous 100-watt bulb. If it hadn't been for the fact that Sophia Loren had made such an effort to await his pleasure, I would have walked out.

While I took pictures, Luchino told Sophia Loren that *The Duchess of Malfi* was the perfect play for her to appear in. (And a great play for him to direct.) He only interrupted himself to point to the puny lightbulb and remark, "What else can you expect from a photographer?"

To Luigi's horror, Luchino attended the 1959 Moscow Film Festival as a member of the jury. But in Russia, too, the renaissance man held court. A press photographer daily presented a red carnation to "the most beloved director". The artist Illya Glasounov sketched Visconti's portrait. (It eventually joined all the other Visconti portraits hanging in Luchino's workroom.) In the end, though, the Moscow visit only convinced more people that Visconti was a communist. His reactions to Russia had a strong Milanese flavor. "Take the leading film directors," he said in amazement. "They don't expect to earn more money than the mediocre ones."

Whenever the Visconti brothers met, it was hard to tell the artist from the businessman.

"*Rocco*'s doing well in America," Luchino said lightly.

"Do you get a percentage?" Edoardo asked.

"No."

"Pity. I'm all for a percentage, even a modest one per cent."

"True enough, but they couldn't offer that with what they paid me."

"I see.".

"But I'll get a percentage on *The Leopard*".

"Fine."

By comparison with Luchino or the new wave of Milanese millionaires, Edoardo lived in a modest villa, rather than an ornate palazzo, but in all other respects he was a typical North Italian tycoon. He owned a yacht and a Ferrari, both Milanese status symbols. The energy he displayed in business carried right through his weekends. From spring to autumn, Edoardo sailed, and from autumn to spring he hunted. Friday evenings he streaked down the *autostrada* at 130 miles an hour, overtaking cars by the dozen. At such times, he told me, "A bad driver dents his car; a good driver gets killed." He hunted with the same recklessness as he drove his Ferrari. Up at 4am to go duck shooting on his 2,500-acre game preserve, he would fidget in his blind, shoot at a snipe he admitted was far too far away, laugh at his own impatience, and strike off, knee-deep in mud, to search for game that wouldn't come to him.

In summer, Edoardo prowled around his villa overlooking the Mediterranean. He discussed with his gardener the prospects for the year's olives and next year's wine. "I suppose I could live off this land if the communists took over," he reflected dubiously—he never really believed they would. It was only when sailing his Bermudan sloop that he calmed down as the wind rose. "How peaceful," he sighed. At that moment a larger and faster yacht overtook him. Edoardo raced back to port in the vain hope of catching the swifter craft. He must get another yacht.

While Luigi was tracking down pedigree basset hounds in Scotland, and Luchino had interrupted work on his next picture to face hearings on his last one, Edoardo completed the acquisition of his new boat. Now, all he needed was to wait impatiently for Spring. As for the old Bermudan sloop—"The kids will enjoy it."

Luchino Visconti, Romy Schneider and Alain Delon, Rome, 1960

Enzo Ferrari, Monza, 1961

Pork boutique, Milan, 1962

Michelangelo Antonioni and Monica Vitti in Ravenna, 1963

Cecil Beaton, Salisbury, Wiltshire, 1978

About photojournalism

Looking back over half a century, I can bring into focus much that once appeared indistinct and only vaguely threatening. Many of the conflicts in the world today have their origins in the past 50 years, and the nature of my work has meant that I have witnessed some of them at close hand. Several times I have entered history. Two thousand years after the Caesars marched into Rome, I drove through the same triumphal arch with an American army. Later, following in the footsteps of the Babylonians, Romans, Persians and the Crusaders, I entered Jerusalem with an Arab army. I have watched the British Empire founder, and the Soviets grab the leftovers of the Hapsburg Empire in an attempt to dominate the world through Marxism. I was also present when Tito rebelled against Stalin and the first crack appeared in the monolithic structure of communism.

Today, however, it is no longer possible for me to be a member of Churchill's British delegation to the Tehran Conference one week, and the American mission to Saudi Arabia the next. Times have changed. In 1938, when I crossed the Austrian border at about the same time as Hitler's invading army, I was the only photographer on hand to document the disappearance of a thousand-year-old nation. Eighteen years later, when the American actress Grace Kelly married Prince Rainier in Monaco, 1,800 representatives of the press—mostly photographers—were there to record the event. The wedding was also televised and watched by the whole of Europe. The moment Grace Kelly become a princess, even before the photographers had trooped out of the church, the story was moribund. From that day on, photojournalism would take a back seat.

Until *Life* came on the scene in 1936, pictorial reporting had been pursued on a fairly modest scale. Photographers in London, where I first worked, were looked down upon by the writing press (a published picture the same size as an article brought in ten times less). The notable exception at that time was Germany, where illustrated magazines were investigating the possibilities presented by the Leica, the miniature camera which was about to revolutionise photographic reporting. But after Hitler came to power in 1933, the magazines gradually disappeared, and it would require the vision and financial resources of Henry R. Luce, along with a readership spread across the American continent, for *Life* to advance photo-journalism, as it came to be known.

Life was almost three when war broke out in Europe and became the only story to cover. The magazine sent reporters to all the belligerent countries. For us this meant unheard-of freedom. Despite the fact that pictures had to be passed by the official censor, the editors in New York no longer had direct control over their photographers and they had to rely on our judgement. We made the most of the opportunity. The war created a new breed of independent-minded photographers whose work not only brought glory to *Life*, but went a long way towards influencing the way people look at pictures. The bumbling "press photog" had become a romantic character and we made sure to live up to that image. We were flamboyant and irreverent and we made America dream. To this day Robert Capa, who death finally caught up with in Indo-China, remains the popular idea of the war photographer, the nonchalant daredevil who gazes out at the world through half-quizzical, half-amused eyes, while a cigarette dangles from his lips.

"Photojournalism" as a term entered the language the same year war broke out. As I remember it, the first time the words photographer and reporter were linked together in print was in December 1939. I had just completed a story on Canada going to war. As usual I had supplied the *Life* writer Hubert Kay with copious captions and research along with my pictures. As I was the magazine's "Photographer of the Week", Kay wrote a box about me.

"I've coined a term for you," he said. "I've called you a 'reporter-photographer.'" Kay, the writer, had naturally put the words ahead of the pictures, but with use the term became "photo-reporter" and, eventually, photo-journalist.

When I got my start with *Life*, everything was new and I had to make up the job as I went along. Unlike my six colleagues who worked in the States, where *Life* photographers were greatly appreciated, I spent most of my time in hostile environments. I had followed the war in Europe across three continents, and when the war was over, like other colleagues who had worked alongside the Allied troops, was no longer an innocent youth of the light-hearted Thirties. The war had taken its toll. All of us had recurring nightmares. Mine was that I was awaiting execution. The dream was so real it always took me most of the next day to shake off its terrible spell.

Now our assignment was the post-war world. Some photographers chose Asia, others, like myself, remained in Europe—a confused continent slowly becoming aware that it was no longer the centre of world power, which had passed to the Americans and the Soviets, whose armies were sprawled across its countries. In Europe, the exhilaration of liberation had given way to sullen resentment.

My assignment, ironically, was the Eastern Europe I knew from before the war. What struck me most was that, in spite of almost total devastation, these countries emerged with the very same mentality that had plunged the world into two great wars. The horror of the Nazi occupation had in no way dimmed the prejudices that shaped each country's national character. They had learned little, and kept looking back to the past rather than face the present. When I worked there, I received the same criticism I had received in 1938: if my pictures showed either compassion or condemnation I was accused of manipulation. People were slow to realise that anti-Semitism in eastern Europe had outlived the Jews.

In the years that followed, and in accordance with the law of diminishing returns, photojournalism reached the apex of fame at the time of its decline. *Life*, which had done so much to promote pictorial journalism, folded in 1972. (It was never the same after being resurrected as a monthly.) Then color photography, which had rarely been used, became a major fixture of the magazines and produced a new crop of color-minded photographers. Camera technology was perfected to the point where the miniatures used by professionals today are as complex as a computer. These combined factors were to produce a generation of reporters who, in their outlook, and in their appearance, were very different from the ones of my generation. In my time we were expected to dress for the occasion: black tie for most ceremonies, white tie for weddings, and a grey top hat for the Derby. Today's photojournalists look like big game hunters stalking their quarry with their powerful tele-lenses and loose-fitting bush jackets with large pockets.

But for all their dashing manner and sophisticated equipment, the opportunities for them to cover international stories are much more limited today. I was made aware of how differently things were done when I was talking to John Loengard, one of *Life*'s more recent picture editors. I had mentioned that the magazine sent me to South America in 1939. While in Buenos Aires I was assigned to fly to Tierra del Fuego and get pictures of Cape Horn. I was in Patagonia for eight weeks, traveling aboard antiquated airplanes, buses, coastal steamers and a 30-foot sailboat with an auxiliary engine. I had stayed in hovels where I burned paperbacks to keep warm, and had slept in the southernmost habitation on the American continent, sharing a room with a pet llama. My odyssey ended 20 miles from the Horn, when the Spanish skipper of the chartered sailboat told me in the midst of a storm, "Hombre, I have seven children and the ambition to have at least eight. We're turning back."

"Today," Loengard said, "we'd assign the story on Monday and have you on the Tuesday flight to Buenos Aires. By the time you got there we'd have made arrangements to fly you to Patagonia and get helicopter shots of Cape Horn. On Friday you'd be back in New York."

These changes began in 1950, when *Life* expanded its staff in order to station a photographer in every European capital. I had enjoyed such freedom I couldn't conform to the discipline essential for expanding news-gathering organizations such as *Life*. For years, photographers like me had relied upon our own knowledge of the type of story the magazine was interested in: we worked out the theme of the story, made the necessary contacts, photographed it, captioned it, and found the quickest way to get it back to New York. We were genuine photojournalists—a term much abused by photographers who thereafter would work with a writer respons-ible for planning the story, setting it up and doing the captions, while all they had to do was shoot the pictures lined up. I knew I could never work that way. Although I was only 36, I belonged to a past generation.

In the Spring of 1950 I resigned from the staff of *Life*. Ed Thompson, my managing editor, accepted my resignation, as he, too, recognised that I was too independent for what had become such a large corporation. We came to an agreement over the phone: I could go off and shoot anything I liked, but I would give *Life* first choice of running the pictures. For this I would be paid half the amount I had been earning, to be readjusted according to what was published. This worked well, and enabled me to do the kind of story I could never have covered if I'd stayed on the staff. The phone arrangement lasted for the next seven years.

At the same time that the approach to photojournalism was undergoing changes, so was the public's appreciation of both photography and photographers. When I was a ten-year-old boy at school, our teacher asked what plans his pupils had for their future. They named the army, the navy, the airforce or the fire department. I said, "photographer", which led the teacher to remark. "Phillips doesn't aim high in life, but at least he knows what he wants to be."

Today I am more than 80 years old, and photography is considered a bright young art. Critics have taken to writing about it with the same high seriousness that they do about painting, sculpture, literature or music. We have arrived. As for me, I remain a photographer and go on taking pictures.

New York, August, 1996

JOHN PHILLIPS

Poet and Pilot Antoine de Saint-Exupéry

Essays by John Phillips and Charles-Henri Favrod.

With a letter by Antoine de Saint-Exupéry.

Best known today as the author of the children's classic *The Little Prince,* Saint-Exupéry was also acclaimed in his time as a novelist, poet, pioneer of airmail flights in the 1920s, and pilot during World War II. On the 31st of July, 1944, at the age of 44 he took off from Sardinia on a reconnaissance mission over Southern France. He never returned.

This book documents some of the last weeks of Saint-Exupéry's life in photographs taken by John Phillips. Photographed at an air base on Sardinia during May 1944, the images are printed here for the first time. The pictures are accompanied by a facsimile of a letter written by Saint-Exupéry during the night of May 29, 1944. Also included is a brief biographical essay by Charles-Henri Favrod, former director of the photomuseum *Musée de l'Elysée* in Lausanne, Switzerland, and a memoir by John Phillips.

A moving tribute to a man who was that rarest of combinations, a genuine man of action and a fine writer.

Clothbound, 9 x 12 in., 80 pgs, 180 duotone reproductions. ISBN 1-881616-23-1